JOY OF
THE WORM

THINKING LITERATURE
A series edited by Nan Z. Da and Anahid Nersessian

Joy of the Worm

SUICIDE AND PLEASURE IN EARLY
MODERN ENGLISH LITERATURE

Drew Daniel

The University of Chicago Press
Chicago and London

The University of Chicago Press, Chicago 60637
The University of Chicago Press, Ltd., London
© 2022 by The University of Chicago
Published 2022
Printed in the United States of America

31 30 29 28 27 26 25 24 23 22   1 2 3 4 5

ISBN-13: 978-0-226-81649-4 (cloth)
ISBN-13: 978-0-226-81650-0 (paper)
ISBN-13: 978-0-226-81651-7 (e-book)
DOI: https://doi.org/10.7208/chicago/9780226816517.001.0001

Library of Congress Cataloging-in-Publication Data

Names: Daniel, Drew, 1971– author.
Title: Joy of the worm : suicide and pleasure in early modern
    English literature / Drew Daniel.
Other titles: Thinking literature.
Description: Chicago : University of Chicago Press, 2022. |
    Series: Thinking literature | Includes bibliographical references
    and index.
Identifiers: LCCN 2021041556 | ISBN 9780226816494 (cloth) |
    ISBN 9780226816500 (paperback) | ISBN 9780226816517
    (ebook)
Subjects: LCSH: English literature—Early modern, 1500–1700—
    History and criticism. | Suicide in literature.
Classification: LCC PR408.S845 D36 2022 | DDC 820.9/3548—
    dc23/eng/20211101
LC record available at https://lccn.loc.gov/2021041556

The University of Chicago Press gratefully acknowledges the
generous support of Johns Hopkins University toward the
publication of this book.

DEDICATED TO THE MEMORY OF
MARGARET LOUISE FARRELL
1920–1978

Contents

Renaissance Self-Finishing

Razors pain you;
Rivers are damp;
Acids stain you;
And drugs cause cramp.
Guns aren't lawful;
Nooses give;
Gas smells awful;
You might as well live.

DOROTHY PARKER, "Resumé"

Humorously deflating an ethical absolute into a practical matter, Dorothy Parker's poem works through the suicidal impulse in order to empty it out. Making light of plight, this tetrameter trifle proceeds via a productive sophistry: the question "Should you kill yourself?" is bypassed in favor of "How should you kill yourself?" There is no particular means that avoids pain, damp, stains, smells, or illegality, and the drudgery of such considerations drains the scenario of its punctual force. In encouraging the person on the ledge to inhabit their body at the moment of self-killing rather than their suicidal mind, Parker foregrounds the sensory openness of that body, its vulnerability to pain and privation. Coaxed by degrees across two quatrains, the would-be suicide is walked back toward an imaginary place that inverts these fraught end points: if not absolutely painless, dry, sweet-smelling, or law-abiding, then at least more nearly so. But the focus isn't really upon the mortal body but upon the equipment required for the body's disposal. Means upstage ends. Suddenly, the tools of suicide loom larger than the suffering body they deliver to death, and we trip on a pileup of razors and acids and guns and ropes. Suicide sounds like too much trouble.

Parker's morbid bonbon of a poem exemplifies a broader dynamic that will interest me in this book: the means by which literature can work through the possibility of voluntary death, both inhabiting and containing suicidal ideation, alternately ramping affects up and dialing them down, running out the clock until a feeling cools off. "Comedy" names the generic zone of affective transformation and energetic exchange in which mockery and rehabilitation trade places. On site, damage and repair can be hard to distinguish. Parker's "Resumé" expands upon the questions of intent already coyly posed by the title of the book in which it appears: *Enough Rope*.[1]

Is Parker mocking those who lack sincerity in their fatal resolve, or working overtime to distract her own self-destructive will? In either case, is she addressing a friend, herself, the reader, or all three? What are the terms of survival held out by the slender hope that one "might as well" carry on? Like survival itself, comedy doesn't (always, only) feel good. Here, comedy lets us forgive ourselves for our continuing failure to die.

While Parker's poem glances at political surrounds in the invocation of the law and its obverse, another register is a complete no-show: religion. Attuned to a mind and body at war, Parker doesn't seem to worry about the consequences of suicide for the soul, or the transcendental possibilities of divine punishment or forgiveness that might follow from the suicidal decision. A tempting term to describe such a suspension of posthumous concern would be "secular": Parker's poem, true to its historical location in modernity, cruises suicide as a possible choice in a material world of suffering bodies.[2] Bracketing for now the complexity with which both "modernity" and "secularity" can be troubled, rolled forward or back at will, such a suspension was not quite available in the period and context that concerns this book: post-Reformation early modern England. For Hamlet, the question of suicide is strongly overdetermined by the existence of "an Everlasting" who *has* "fixed / His canon 'gainst self-slaughter" (1.2.131–32).[3] Dominant theological frames across confessions presented such deaths as heinous sins against God, committed at the instigation of the devil. Even when Christian sanction lifted, to exempt a select category of admirable martyrs or virtuous pagans from broad and categorical abhorrence, for early modern people voluntary death was always a serious matter.

Except when it wasn't.

For a case in point, consider the following story. Awaiting death, a man writes a book. Confined to the Tower of London and certain of his coming execution, in 1534 Sir Thomas More writes *A Dialogue of Comfort against Tribulation*, a fictional dialogue between the young Vincent and his wise uncle Anthony, set against the backdrop of Hungary clenched in anticipation of imminent invasion by "the Turk."[4] However driven by tacit complaint against Henry VIII, More keeps homily foremost. Through the Socratic sock puppetry of intergenerational dialogue, More asks himself and his readers how we ought to experience tribulation: as a spiritual resource, an index of divine trial, a joyous path to our own salvation? Given the grim circumstances in which it was crafted, it is perhaps unsurprising that More's text relays a longing for death. Given the predominant contemporary theories of where such urges came from, it is perhaps equally unsurprising that More understands the urge to kill the self as an instrument of satanic temptation.

But what one might *not* expect is the generic form that his discussion takes. Namely, the situation of self-killing becomes the windup for a grotesque joke. Spurred on by the devil, a familiarly shrewish wife desires that her husband kill her so that *he* will go to hell. She nags and wheedles him into the act, pestering him relentlessly while he is chopping wood, and then placing her own neck upon a block and demanding that he end her life:

> "By the mass, whoreson husband, I would thou wouldest; here lieth mine head, lo!" And wherewith down she laid her head upon the same timber log. "If thou smite it not off, I beshrew thine whoreson's heart." With that, likewise as the devil stood at her elbow, so stood (as I heard say) his good angel at his, and gave him ghostly courage, and bade him be bold and do it. And so the good man up with his chip-axe, and at a chop chopped off her head indeed. There were standing other folk by, which had a good sport to hear her chide, but little they looked for this chance till it was done ere they could let it. They said they heard her tongue babble in her head, and call "Whoreson, whoreson" twice after that the head was from her body.[5]

This gruesomely misogynist story illuminates a surrounding and still-ongoing patriarchal poetics that it has been the task of feminist history to reconstruct and analyze: everyday fantasies of femicide are part of a spectrum of gendered discipline that linked sermons and conduct manuals with scold's bridles and Scottish branks in the early modern period, as they link casual sexism and workplace microaggressions with "incel" massacres and domestic abuse today.[6] Though it clashes against his enshrined critical reputation as a doting father who gave his male and female children identical humanist educations in Greek and Latin, the cartoonish violence of More's misogynist tale comes as no surprise to those familiar with the lurid cruelties recounted in the ballad sources for Shakespeare's *Taming of the Shrew*.[7] Here, misogyny reworks More's own immediate situation; condensing the logic of fantasy, one might suggest that More is the shrew, Henry VIII is the husband, and the book he is writing is the tongue that will not be silent even after death.

Contemporary readers might well find this story unpleasant and therefore resist the discovery of humor within it. Such reflexes draw an ethical cordon around the representation of harm and damage, one already anticipated in Aristotle's definition of "the laughable" in the *Poetics* as "a sort of error and ugliness that is not painful and destructive, just as, evidently, a laughable mask is something ugly and distorted without pain."[8] Pain matters. When the generic rules of the road are observed, comedy is not supposed to depict suffering past a certain threshold. But the Aristotelian injunction not to derive comic pleasure from harm is less like a Mosaic tablet carved in stone and more like a "NO SWIMMING" sign perched beside a cool blue pool on a hot day. Five seconds on Reddit will show you that people laugh at harm and damage all the time. Sometimes, as in More's joke about decapitation written as he awaited his day on the block, or in Parker's funny poem about suicide written in between her multiple attempts, the people doing the laughing have serious reasons for refusing to take serious things seriously.

But sometimes they don't. Proscribing some reactions and encouraging others, everyday life in "emotional communities" requires ongoing labors of comportment, the ongoing stage-managing of seriousness and its licensed holidays.[9] Injunctions about laughter and its customary restraint work toward an intelligible moral end, and typically assume a tacit self-understanding: we do not want to be known as the kind of people who would take the wrong sort of pleasure from a story of suffering, pain, and death. But the task of reading More's cruelly comedic story requires that we enter the habits of mind that not only generated and circulated such stories but also assumed they would give pleasure to their audience. To use a contemporary expression, we have to *sit with* these stories, and assess them for what they reveal about the elasticity of norms.

In this story, a subject ensures her own death voluntarily, and solicits another person to assist her in the practical business of ending her life. She makes sure that she dies en route toward a seemingly more important goal: the damnation of her husband. We are not in the presence of depression or a pathological mood disorder, nor is the topic presented as tragic or lamentable at the level of tone. Far from a path to damnation, this death is presented ironically, as "good sport," a merry jest and good riddance to a scold. *We are not, that is, in the presence of what modern people would understand as "suicide," but we are in the presence of self-killing.*

Between Self-Killing and Suicide

The distinction between "self-killing" and "suicide" names both a difference in connotation and a specific historical rupture. Early modern people used an array of terms to describe voluntary death. When a substantive noun was called for, a composite, variously spelled "self-murther" or "self-murder," was popular, but they did not use the word "suicide," because the word had not been invented yet.[10] It enters the language only in 1643, when Sir Thomas Browne, in the midst of revisions to his prose meditation *Religio Medici*, adjusts the phrase "the end of Cato" to read "the end and Suicide of Cato."[11] In due time, the present book will assess the force and valence of Browne's lightning flash of neologism, measuring the dis-

tance the word has traveled from the moment it was minted to its connotations today. I am not asserting in a narrowly nominalist manner that the
term's creation signaled all by itself a decisive and instantaneous conceptual change. Rather, it was the fate of Browne's term to come to designate
an action that modernity has significantly overwritten in its own image.

Mindful of these moving targets, I distinguish "self-killing" from "suicide" in order to highlight what we think we already know about "suicide,"
so that a conceptual gap can reopen. For modern readers, "suicide" summons up a paradoxical climate, at once drably familiar and highly charged.
This climate is defined by public health prevention protocols, psychiatric
observation, unequally distributed SSRI prescriptions, demographically
stratified incidence rates, and seemingly endless spirals of loss. Like any
"complex behavior," suicide occasions disciplinary conflict between rival
ways of knowing, as competing frames jostle to define a shared object of
concern.[12] Despite their differences, both Freudian psychoanalysis and
subsequent psychological treatment paradigms frame suicide in terms of
clinical understandings of bipolar disorder, post-traumatic stress disorder,
or major depression; suicide is a "patient outcome" to be avoided, through
either therapeutic treatment or pharmaceutical intervention.[13] It is best
understood at the level of the individual. By contrast, Durkheimian sociology encourages a totalizing view of suicide, as a demographic phenomenon of implied "social forces" acting upon and within variegated populations in scientifically predictable ways that can be analyzed through the
parsing of statistical data. It is best understood at the level of the group.
Together, these rival fields—both of which, at different altitudes, evaluate motivation—have generated the hybrid modern field of "suicidology,"
a prevention-oriented domain of knowledge that attempts to bridge the
discursive chasm between these theoretical perspectives within a broad
"ideation-to-action framework."[14]

Suicide is both universally accessible to mortal beings and yet deeply
inflected by the fundamentally political fact that unequal access to resources and social power tends to track with variable rates of attempted
and completed suicide. Accordingly, we live in the era in which the overlapping plights of the indebted,[15] the farmer,[16] the veteran,[17] the opioid
addict,[18] the unemployed,[19] the trans person,[20] the person of color,[21] the
young person[22]—in all of the attendant complexity that intersectional
analysis rightly insists upon—find their objective correlative in variably
rising and falling waves of death. These observable variations would seem
to confirm Durkheim's essential point that "for each social group there is a
specific tendency to suicide explained neither by the organic-psychic constitution of individuals nor the nature of the physical environment. Con-
sequently, by elimination, it must necessarily depend upon social causes

and be in itself a collective phenomenon."[23] As a practical example of how to address such "social causes" at the policy level, current economic research demonstrates that in communities that increase the minimum wage, suicide rates decline.[24] Alarmed at declining life expectancy within the United States relative to other developed countries, even unabashedly pro-capitalist economists such as Anne Case and Angus Deaton are calling for ambitious structural change to health care, educational opportunities, and employment in order to stem the rising tides of such "deaths of despair."[25]

Sharpening the implications of treating suicide as a collective phenomenon into a Foucauldian critique of psychology's individualist bias, in *Suicide: Foucault, History, and Truth* (2010) Ian Marsh argues that "suicide" binds kinds of persons to types of acts within an overarching regime of medical power-knowledge whose core tenets can be loosely paraphrased as follows:

1. A completed suicide is the violent, tragic act of a mentally ill person.
2. Everyone at risk of committing suicide should be counseled away from this outcome.
3. Suicidal behavior is prima facie evidence of someone in psychological crisis.
4. Accordingly, suicide is best explained by psychiatrists, psychologists, and medical professionals.[26]

At first glance, these broad generalizations might seem self-explanatory, even obviously and intuitively right to many readers. Presented with borderline situations and edge phenomena that do not conform to them (a terminally ill patient requesting end-of-life assistance, a soldier rushing into battle, an activist protesting injustice, a person taking part in extreme sports, a person hoping their family's finances are stabilized by a life-insurance payment in the wake of their death), our response would likely be, "Oh, but I don't mean *that* when I say suicide." Such intuitive distinctions are borne out by the linguistic history of the words that cultures use to designate an action; linguist David Daube points out that "the description of suicide as a kind of killing antedates its description as a kind of dying."[27] There has been a broad but decisive shift from an ethical focus upon the self-killer as agent to a medical focus upon the departed as victim. This change tells us something: the distinction between "suicide" as preventable tragedy and "self-killing" as chosen act is not simply a matter of historical nicety about the coinage of 1643 but indexes ongoing conceptual impasses in how we imagine and argue about life, ethics, value, and autonomy.

At times in this book, as I read the cultural artifacts of the sixteenth and seventeenth centuries, I will draw upon and engage insights and claims from contemporary writers in psychology, psychoanalysis, sociology, bioethics, and suicidology. In advocating for the distinction between "self-killing" and "suicide," I seek, in sympathy with Marsh, to push back against "the assumption of psychopathology in those who wish, or attempt, to end their own lives."[28] Simply put, "self-killing" includes a wider array of forms of voluntary death than "suicide," because it is not saddled with overfamiliar connotations of pathology and mood disorder. Early modern literature teems with such an array of forms because it was written before those connotations took hold.

Like Marsh, I too am interested in "how individuals are constituted as subjects in relations to the truths of suicide," but the individuals I am discussing are characters within plays and poems and romances, and narrators within prose.[29] I am interested in genre's power as aesthetic frame (or, in Rosalie Colie's terminology, "set on the world") as it locates individuals within socially extended power relations that precede them and steer our affective reactions to scenes of harm, slaloming between sorrow and laughter.[30] To risk some overbroad assertions of my own, genre is a technology that manages difference and repetition as it depicts and reinforces or playfully subverts ongoing processes of social stratification.[31] Genre's technology mediates the dialectical conflict between group and individual within all literary representation as such. A less inflamed way to say this is that we scan individual characters and their actions against an inescapably prior, tacit background of expectations regarding socially legible types and narrative outcomes.[32] Genre is one name for that background.

Genre Trouble

Omnipresent yet slippery, genre is what nobody really believes in but everyone relies upon. Whether one is writing literary criticism or simply grazing the pull-down menu on Netflix, we expect genre's thin but sturdy tether to bind together an implausibly wide array of qualities within a work: the kinds of action within a plot, the way a story will end, the kinds of characters who will appear as primary, the kind of language that they will use, and the emotional tone a work solicits. Taking its origin from the very concept of originality, "genre," in its derivation from the Latin word "genus," provocatively conflates birth, origin, race, sort, and kind.[33] That last word is primary in early modernity, for its protobiological connotations relay Aristotelian naturalist habits of mind, homely metaphors of animal husbandry, and shifting logics of racialization. Describing the relational networks of early modern genre systems in *The Resources of Kind,*

Rosalie Colie notes the basis of early modern genre theories in "a body of almost unexpressed assumptions, many of them versions of classical theory or practice, which took for granted certain basic rules of expression."[34] What are those rules?

It is hard to spell out the implications of Aristotle's inescapably significant yet notoriously incomplete lecture notes without generating an inert, unappealing straw person in the process.[35] More a gappy cluster of suggestions than a stern rulebook of prescription, the *Poetics* is, for better and for worse, not a unified theory of art, but its core terms and structural antitheses usefully reveal the gearbox of social stratification that churns within aesthetic categories.[36] A revealing case in point is Aristotle's contrast between those who are *spoudaios* (noble, good, serious) and those who are *phaulos* (base, common, unserious) within dramatic art and poetry; this conflation of social location in a hierarchy with ethical norms of evaluation and emotional temperaments or tacit "attitudes" casts a long and suggestive shadow. Further reinforcing these habits of sorting, the medieval and early modern recirculation of the Virgilian *rota* tethered grand, middle, and low styles of speech to correspondingly high, middle, and low social positions: the heroes of epic speak one way, and the shepherds of pastoral another.[37] Such assumptions fit some authors, works, and characters better than others, and subsequent artists across mediums were to do increasingly wild backflips off these stiff pronouncements. But the expectation of normative alignment between kinds of stories, kinds of agents, and emotional stances proposed by Aristotle, and reified by his subsequent translators and readers and interpreters, stuck for a reason.

Centuries of artistic practice and everyday habits of decorum presume self-killing's essential seriousness, which follows obviously and intuitively from its irreversible lethality when completed. These absolute stakes secure the place of voluntary death as a suitable, even definitive, subject for tragic representation and the attendant catharsis that it was the purpose of tragedy to elicit, the right sort of object for "the mimesis of a memorable act possessed of *megethos* or amplitude."[38] From Ajax to Antigone to Jocasta to Phaedra and beyond, self-killing ticks the boxes of tragic definition: it is an action of a certain magnitude undertaken by powerful agents who typically speak in a dignified manner and suffer in a way that prompts the purgation of fear and pity in readers and audience members, who are expected to take the unfolding spectacle of such deaths seriously. The overlap of a generic mode and an attitude toward that mode was ratified by language; in medieval and early modern English, "seriousness" and "sadness" were literally synonymous.[39]

Comedy, at least in the overtly schematized definitions extracted from Aristotle's *Poetics* by medieval and early modern commentary, entails a symmetrically contrasting but complementary scaffolding: a humorous tone, a set of suitably risible agents of the middling sort, an accordingly low manner of speaking.[40] These elements join and prime an audience for merriment and mockery, to laugh at what is ugly and ridiculous in the spectacle before them. In the early modern period such priming work also included nervous promises not to overstep "mirth with modesty" into legally actionable slander or violations of propriety; Nicholas Udall's prologue to his play *Ralph Roister Doister* (ca. 1553) promises fun, but also reassures its hearers that it is a work: "Wherein all scurrility we utterly refuse, / Avoiding such mirth wherein is abuse."[41] Genre is a matter of knowing one's place. When, in act 5 of *A Midsummer Night's Dream*, the aristocrats snicker at the rude mechanicals' staging of *Pyramus and Thisbe*, their reaction confirms the intuitions that structure the class matrix of early modern genre theory: "hard-handed men" (5.1.1909) tend to be laughingstocks.[42] That said, we should avoid reifying early modern generic distinctions as overly strong or categorical. If the titular examples of Xystus Betuleius's *Susanna: Comedia Tragica* (1538) or Nicholas Grimald's *Christus Redivivus, comedia tragica, sacra et nova* (1543) are any indication, the cheerful fusion of generic categories that we might at present regard as oxymoronic was in fact quite permissible in the period, and habits of hardening distinction between them emerged only gradually.[43]

Stories solicit stances toward actions, opening out the array of possible relations that we can take to one another; sequences of cause and effect calibrate punishment and reward, as literature encourages us to identify with some agents and to disidentify with others, to regard some actions as heroic and others as shameful. Hotwiring together mirth and abuse, More's text imagines self-killing as *both* a demonic temptation *and* a source of comedic fun. So far, the intellectual history of self-killing has emphasized prevalent attitudes of horror at such deaths, and the divine register of satanic temptations as their principal etiological explanation. As a case in point, consider Doctor John Dee's diary entry from 1577: "3. Nov. William Rogers of Mortlake, about 7 of the clock in the morning, cut his own throat by the fiend his instigation."[44]

Dee was not alone in thinking this way. The most strikingly documented case of this phenomenon is that of seventeenth-century woodturner Nehemiah Wallington, a Londoner whose notebooks record numerous suicidal crises and suicide attempts; driven by religious despair and the fear of damnation, Wallington transcribes a tempter's voice commanding him to "destroy thyselfe now."[45] Pamphlet literature of the period repeatedly represented cases of self-murder as the tragic result of demonic or satanic suggestion. The anonymous author of the salacious pamphlet *The Bloudy Booke, or the Tragicall and desperate end of Sir John Fites [Fitz]* (1605), on the verge of narrating his titular criminal's final self-destruction, pauses to imagine the disgraced knight troubled with "the threatninges of Sathan, who visibly (it may be) appeared vnto him, menacing him with eternal damnation for his fourmer wickednesse."⁴⁶ The assumption of self-killing's demonic provenance was widespread, and surely contributed to the reflexive attitudes of scorn, horror, and disgust that such deaths occasioned during the period. But these examples of religious abhorrence are not the whole story.

The intellectual history of early modern attitudes toward voluntary death has largely avoided a reckoning with what this book will show is in fact a pronounced contrary aesthetic tendency: *surges of positive affect, humor, and pleasure found within textual representations of self-harm, self-sacrifice, and violent death.* If courtrooms and churches and diaries were spaces in which the severe punishments and moral repudiation took place, then plays and poems and romances and prose meditations offered adjacent but distinct spaces, where heads can roll to the sound of laughter.

This emphasis upon positive affect prompted by a negative occasion puts me distinctly at odds with previous scholarly accounts. Many intellectual histories of suicide exist, notably Alexander Murray's ongoing multivolume series of monographs on *Suicide in the Middle Ages*, Georges Minois's *History of Suicide: Voluntary Death in Western Culture*, Marzio Barbagli's *Farewell to the World: A History of Suicide*, and the extended archive assembled by Margaret Pabst Battin for the transhistorical and global anthology *The Ethics of Suicide: Historical Sources.*⁴⁷ The classic intellectual-historical account of early modern English attitudes to voluntary death remains Michael MacDonald and Terence Murphy's coauthored *Sleepless Souls: Suicide in Early Modern England* (1990).⁴⁸ Shrinking centuries down to three pithy sentences, MacDonald and Murphy offer a usefully compact fast-forward through the just-so story of changing Western attitudes toward suicide:

> Ancient philosophies that condoned and in some cases celebrated suicide gave way in the Middle Ages to theological condemnations and folkloric abhorrence. The Reformation intensified religious hostility to self-murder in England and some other European countries. Finally, in the eighteenth century, Enlightenment philosophy and the secularization of the world view of European elites prompted writers to depict suicide as the consequences of mental illness or rational choice, and these concepts still dominate discussions of self-destruction today.⁴⁹

Contracting from this summary of the West-in-general to the specific shifts within England captured in their source documents, MacDonald and Murphy detect an observable curve, first sloping upward and then gradually downward, in the intensity of a broadly held attitude of "severity." This shifting affective barometer implies a kind of unified cultural stance that, upon closer examination, frays along dividing lines of social class:

> The thesis that we argue below can be stated briefly. During the early modern period attitudes and responses to suicide first hardened and then grew more tolerant and sympathetic. The intensification of hostility to self-killing in the sixteenth and early seventeenth centuries was the result of the Tudor revolutions in government and religion—the rise of the modern state and the Protestant reformation. The decline in severity to suicide after 1660 had more complex causes. They included local hostility to the forfeiture of self-murderers' goods, the abolition of the prerogative courts during the English revolution, the governing elites intensifying reverence for private property, the reaction against religious enthusiasm, the rise of the new science, Enlightenment philosophy, the increase in literacy among the middling classes, the vast expansion of the periodical press, and the gradual absorption of empirical epistemology into the mentality of the middle and upper classes.[50]

There is, then, a secularization hypothesis within an institutional and legal history that drives the book's case studies. MacDonald and Murphy track a slow, general withdrawal from consideration of supernatural interference when inquests and courts examined the causal factors in individual cases of voluntary death.[51] Participants in inquests and court cases hoped to distinguish the category of felo-de-se (a contraction of *felonia de seipso*, a phrase rich with biopolitical ironies that defines life as a form of property that agents have consciously and deliberately stolen from themselves) from the far smaller number of cases in which a subject did not understand the consequences of their own actions, which were ruled non compos mentis.[52] Part of a series edited by Keith Thomas, *Sleepless Souls* arguably shows the influence of Thomas's classic thesis regarding "the decline of magic" as it tracks a shift in *mentalité* from 1500 to 1800. Broadly stated and supported with extensive evidence from court records and letters and print media, their thesis is not, I think, generally false (it is hard to debate a causal claim that distributes causality across nine different factors). I am indebted to its groundwork, and I do not intend to disregard its utility as an account of what court records show.

More recent historical work has sharpened some of the details. Discussing city records between 1601 and the 1640s, historian Paul Seaver notes that there were four distinct categories of verdict possible for coroners in cases of unusual deaths: misadventure, homicide, self-killing, and "acts of God."[53] The requirement of forfeiture of possessions to the government in cases ruled felo-de-se remained on the books in England until 1870.[54] Looking at the records of the vicar general, Seaver notes thirty-one cases in which apparent suicides were licensed for Christian burial: "In the course of the next four decades a series of vicars general in the name of the bishops of London granted thirty-one licenses for the Christian burial of suicides, but these petitions never challenged or extenuated either the fact of self-murder or the moral opprobrium attached to the act."[55] Location inflected method; perhaps due to the larger number of apothecaries, people in London were more likely to kill themselves with poison, while Kentish citizens tended toward drowning.[56] Interestingly, only two of the thirty-one cases mentioned temptation by the devil.[57] Still, the prevalent trajectory of the intellectual history of self-killing as a transition from supernatural explanation to the dawn of psychopathology holds fast in the field at large, and is neatly signaled in the title of a relatively recent anthology of essays—in which Seaver's own work appears—on the topic: *From Sin to Insanity: Suicide in Early Modern Europe* (2004).[58] Case closed?

The textual moments that detain me in the present book supplement this story with a counterarchive of recalcitrant objects, unruly scenes, and discordant but exemplary cases that seem to me to complicate and partially resist the teleological tendency of such narratives and the secularization hypotheses they rely upon. There are early cases of celebration in the midst of the "age of severity," and there are late examples of horrified censure in the midst of cresting tolerance. In the texts that interest me, I see neither a straightforward "age of severity" nor the lenience and toleration to come, but a third term that is mostly missing from MacDonald and Murphy's account and others in its wake, and indeed from most discussions of the subject: levity. Of course, as anyone who has been the object of homophobic or racist jokes can attest, one can be both an object of levity and an object of censure or horror at the same time. In some of the cases examined in this book, that precise combination is present. But in many other examples that I will consider, the reader will encounter aesthetic modes that are underdiscussed in early modernity, unruly forms of self-sacrificial camp, suicidal slapstick, morbid parody, and the darkest shades of "black comedy" alongside the expressions of vehement severity or reluctant compassion that standard histories have primed us to expect.[59] Taken collectively, these examples complicate the secularizing passage from horror to tolerance, and suggest that the "age of severity" was also an age of levity.

By contrast with the legal archives that understandably tend to dominate the historical literature, *Joy of the Worm* is unabashedly a work of literary criticism, grounded in readings of particular works by particular

authors, in which the affordances of literature surpass the decisive bina-
ries of coroner's verdicts. These readings open out a peacock's fan of unexpected and striking stances toward self-killing. I do not intend to catalog all possible stances on the topic in the period, because that broader
survey work has been done. Among literary studies on the subject, I am indebted to early studies of the representation of suicide by S. E. Sprott and
Roland Wymer, and, more recently, to Eric Langley's *Narcissism and Suicide in Shakespeare and His Contemporaries* (2009) and Marlena Tronicke's
Shakespeare's Suicides: Dead Bodies That Matter (2018).[60] Precisely because
both broad surveys and author-specific surveys of the subject of voluntary
death in early modern literature and Shakespeare exist, I am better able
to focus upon the particular tonal and generic effect of joy-within-death
that aligns my particular objects, without feeling the need to include every
character, scene, speech, or incident potentially relevant to the fairly ubiquitous human scenario of voluntary death. Accordingly, some examples
(Spenser's Cave of Despair in *The Faerie Queene*, Shakespeare's *The Rape
of Lucrece*, Milton's Samson) that one might justifiably expect are absent.
They are undeniably cases of self-killing in early modern English literature, but they do not meet an additional but perhaps unexpected requirement: they do not spark joy.[61]

Joy of the Worm

It is the wager of this book that More's tale, and the assemblage of texts to
which it will here be joined, can collectively illuminate a perverse and pervasive aesthetic mode within early modern English literature: representations of self-killing that imagine the scene or prospect of voluntary death
as an occasion for humor, mirth, laughter, ecstatic pleasure, even joy and
celebration. In honor of the "clown" who brings Cleopatra the basket of
figs and fatal serpents in *Antony and Cleopatra*, I call this literary dynamic
of pleasure in self-destruction "joy of the worm." Let me say at once that
my examples do not imply a communally shared and singular attitude toward death as a desirable outcome by each author whose work I am interpreting in this book. In some cases, positive affects at the prospect of death
help to ease one's passage out of life; in other cases, humorous mockery,
parody, and comedic responses within scenes of self-killing function therapeutically to critique the urge to die, encouraging readers and audiences
to reconsider the force of passion. Censure can yield to rescue, but there
are no guarantees of survival. Some texts offer us handholds out of the
pit; some egg us on toward self-destruction. Neither entirely antisocial nor
resolutely prosocial, "joy of the worm" changes form and switches sides as
it wriggles into tight corners.

Though it may seem heterodox or recondite, this recurring textual phenomenon illuminates ongoing and categorical chasms between art and ethics, and jostles the fragile links that bind mortal individuals to their communal surround. The seemingly minor aesthetic mode named by "joy of the worm" opens a broader set of questions about the relationship of generic frames and codes of decorum to power, inequality, and the uneven distribution of agency. When laughter surfaces, who is laughing, and at whom? Sidestepping the now overfamiliar subversion/containment dyad that would dutifully muster aesthetic forms into service as either conservative reification or radical contestation, I hope "joy of the worm" might prompt reconsideration of how literature participates in ongoing processes of social stratification that it also corrodes.

Specifically, the dignity of self-possession implicit in the classical and scriptural archives of self-killing discussed in this book stands at a particularly revealing remove from the captivity and indignity imposed on enslaved people. When I say that genres modulate our relation to voluntary action by encouraging identification with some agents and disidentification with others, against a backdrop of ideas about social groups, I do not indicate simply a generality already flagged by the difference between *spoudaios* and *phaulos* in Aristotle's *Poetics*, or the Virgilian *rota*'s chilling and warming effects upon different audiences.[62] What I mean specifically is that the self-possession implicit in self-killing is structurally based on the repudiation of enslavement. Self-killing presumes an agency antithetical to enslavement's ideological script.

This antithesis is not some existential fact, for, as scholars of slavery have extensively documented, countless enslaved people killed themselves.[63] But this seeming antithesis between enslavement and suicide was a highly influential, historically produced rhetorical framework that worked to occlude such actions, recasting them as exceptional, rare, or, more directly, as proof of a characterological distinction between the nobility of the suicided and the "slavish" accommodation of those who endured enslavement.

Though I will be reading its recirculation in early modern literature, the source of this framework is classical. In *Arbitrary Rule: Slavery, Tyranny, and the Power of Life and Death* (2013), Mary Nyquist analyzes this dynamic in classical texts as a case of "war slavery doctrine," a particularly pervasive, and deeply perverse, ideological framing of slavery as if it were governed by warrior codes of honor, in which antagonists in war mutually agree that the consequence of loss on the battlefield will be the forfeiture of their lives to the victor.[64] Because military prisoners were potentially subject to immediate execution, this dynamic redefines the lives of enslaved people as the free gifts of their enslavers, who are imagined as having claimed those lives in battle and graciously spared their captives from immediate death.[65] As Nyquist demonstrates, this doctrine simplified and polarized the historical complexities of actual Greek and Roman sociomilitary practices, but circulates widely across historical, legal, and rhetorical discourse in authors as diverse as Aristotle, Livy, and Cicero.[66]

A frequently retold story from Seneca exemplifies the curious blend of explicit idealization and implicit shaming operative in this discourse:

> History relates the story of the famous Spartan, a mere boy who, when he was taken prisoner, kept shouting in his native Doric, "I shall not be a slave!" He was as good as his word. The first time he was ordered to perform a slave's task, some humiliating household job (his actual orders were to fetch a disgusting chamber pot), he dashed his head against a wall and cracked his skull open. Freedom is as near as that—is anyone really still a slave? Would you not rather your son died like that than lived by reason of spinelessness to an advanced age?[67]

This deeply consequential tale, which is relayed by Montaigne and became near proverbial in early modernity as "the story of the Lacedaemonian boy," performs a key function by resignifying survival within slavery as a conscious and voluntary acceptance rather than a situation of extreme, ongoing, and violent coercion.[68] As inverse corollary to the "scenes of subjection" that make up the majority of enslavement's violent archives, the story of the Lacedaemonian boy frequently features in accounts of classical slavery; for my purposes, it tells us something equally important about the specific ethical allure of self-killing within a social order that relies upon a spectrum of coerced labor.[69]

The refusal to immediately kill oneself rather than live as an enslaved person rezones the living body into the ontological support for a characterological claim of degeneracy. It is significant to me that in the story, the command to fetch a chamber pot is the decisive punctum that occasions the display of suicidal virtue: the story does a kind of ideological work of scatologizing the body of enslaved people, locating them at a kind of revealing proximity to a debased and intimate object. At once treasonous to their former people and compliant to their new master, the slave functions as antithetical foil to the slaveholding Roman citizen or free Greek, who is thereby reified as distinct in "kind" from the slaves they hold. Cicero's slogan in the *Philippics* epitomizes this view: "Nihil est detestabilius dedecore, nihil foedius servitute" (Nothing is more detestable than disgrace, nothing more shameful than slavery).[70]

In the light of this contrast, the suicide of elite Greeks and patrician Roman citizens becomes charged with a dignity whose inverse condition is the ongoing debasement of the living slave.[71] In a truly perverse transvaluation of subject positions, in clinging to mere survival within conditions of wretchedness and dispossession, the slave demonstrates not fortitude but, allegedly, a constitutive and characterological weakness: their life of labor convicts them of lacking the strength and self-control that "honorable" suicide supposedly displays. War slavery doctrine thus reifies the Aristotelian naturalizations of slavery articulated in a Greek context within the *Politics* and readapted and reinflected in Roman culture.[72] This operation conveniently brackets the rather blatant misfit between the Stoic doxa of voluntary death as *eulogos exagoge* (sensible removal) and the political chessboard of constraint, if not outright imperial command, in which such elite acts of philosophically inspired "freedom" actually occurred.[73] Nyquist's own interests in *Arbitrary Rule* lie elsewhere, in the seventeenth-century rhetoric of tyranny and anti-tyrannicism, but her account assists me in drawing out a key formulation of suicide's valorization in the classical period that echoes across its recirculation in early modernity.

Framed as antithesis to enslavement, self-killing presumes agency. For an agent to act, they must have a goal, the capacity to work toward it, a sense that it is desirable, and the power and capacity to attempt the act. But, as Kathleen Stewart reminds us, "Agency can be strange, twisted, caught up in things, passive, or exhausted. Not the way we like to think about it. Not usually a simple projection toward a future."[74] We can halfheartedly want our own death. Longing to die but lacking the will to follow through on that longing names a lived condition of such exhausted agency. Consider the stifled oaths and grim jokes of servants and slaves in Roman comedies who make passing small talk about self-annihilation as they move from task to task. Beaten out of the house by her enslaver, in the first scene of Plautus's *Aulularia* (*The Pot of Gold*) the servant Staphyla cries out: "Utinam me divi adaxint ad suspendium potius quidem quam hoc pacto apud te serviam" (O that the gods would drive me to hang myself rather indeed than that I should be a slave in your house on these terms).[75] She delivers this gut-wrenching "laugh line" in the first scene and keeps working as the comic play whirls around her. Slaves in Roman comedy are not afforded the climactic tragic arc of Ajax; their work is needed. Like the delicacies they pile upon a banquet table but do not eat, the grandeur of tragic *megethos* is denied them. By contrast, when in Shakespeare's *Antony and Cleopatra* the servants Iras and Charmian join Cleopatra in death, their entrance into tragic grandeur is framed not as a manumission from slavery but as an ultimate expression of loyalty to a mistress, the high-water mark of a thoroughgoing subjection.

In these cases, violence proves agency firsthand, because the punctual temporality and irreversibility of a violent action looks like a sharpened, high-contrast epitome of all action. As Brian Cummings points out, "Suicide above all, in the recognition of the mortal self, brings an intense concentration on the agency of the person."[76] Violent action confers identity; one shows that one is the kind of person who can act, at least once, at the last. Describing fantasies of "redemptive violence," Stewart flags the stickiness of their appeal: "To say that a thing like redemptive violence is a myth is not to say that it's like a bad dream you can wake up from or an idea you can talk people out of. It's more like a strand in the netting that holds things together."[77] Caught within the "netting" of the social, the slave is, by definition, captive within power's matrix; reinforcing ongoing debasement, war slavery doctrine shores up the grandeur of self-killing's citizens by blaming the victim.

The sleight of hand by which suicide is made rhetorically equivalent to "freedom" not only appears in the works explicitly set in the classical period but also gradually pervades early modern discourse around the subject. If the rejection of enslavement marks the negative choice of what agents thought they were choosing *not to be* in killing themselves (or imagining killing themselves), that does not yet explain what it was that they *were* choosing to be. Thus, "joy of the worm" also requires a positive dimension, the affective surplus of intensity, excitement, and charge that the act of death is imagined to channel and release as compensatory reward and ecstatic counterfantasy.

Jumping into the Fire

Throughout many of the scenes and extended speeches about voluntary death to which I will be attending in this book, death is imagined not in Christian terms, as a soul departing a body en route to ultimate judgment, but instead in Empedoclean terms, as an elemental merger with the universe, a transition backward to a prior state of the component materials of life. Death is thus not "annihilation" but "return," and there is a kind of homesick longing for origins that sits uneasily, to say the least, within the Christian eschatological frameworks that were the theological norm, regardless of confession, for the majority of the authors in this volume. The Empedoclean framework licenses a materialist attitude toward death as recombination rather than rupture or trauma, in effect rethinking the valence of death itself.

What was that framework? Adapting Pythagorean doctrines of the tetrad that are at once mathematical and mystical, Empedocles was the first philosopher to identify earth, air, fire, and water as the four distinct kinds of material from which the universe itself is composed. Though his work or works of philosophical poetry are largely lost and now survive only through the quotations of other authors and the occasional intact papyrus, a corpus of discrete fragments has been constructed into an evocative, if deeply incomplete, composite of its own.[78] In fragment 12/6, Empedocles identifies four ῥιζώματα ("rhizomata" or "roots") from which the earth and all of its components are constructed, symbolically invoking each with a distinct god or goddess: "First, hear of the four roots of all things, / gleaming Zeus and life-bringing Hera and Aidoneus / and Nestis, who moistens with tears the spring of mortals."[79] Regardless of how we evaluate the role of deities within this fragment, one must not mistake Empedocles's doctrine for the simple insistence that earth, air, fire, and water are "all there is." Going beyond those four "roots of all things" (he does not use the word "element"), Empedocles also posits two additional forces: love (*philia*) and strife (*neikos*), forces that, respectively, bond together the roots into temporary forms or work to dissolve those bonds and destroy those forms.[80] Weaving these four roots and two forces into a unified ontological history of the universe, Empedocles bequeathed to the Western philosophical tradition both an account of the material composition of all matter and a vibrantly poetic account of the affective consequences of that material-compositional doctrine. The assembled fragments imply an ethical drama of progressive reincarnation across forms in which ascension to "divinity" is held out as a theoretical ideal placed in permanent tension with a dark vision of the ultimate fate of total dissolution shared in common by all distinct, local forms.

On the intellectual-historical level, the dramatic story of Empedocles's own leap into the flames of Mount Etna, recirculated by Diogenes Laertius and others, tended to fold materialist ontological doctrine and self-destructive action onto each other. In his third-century-CE *Lives of Eminent Philosophers*, Diogenes Laertius sketches an influential, if parodic, portrait of the homosexual vegetarian philosopher resplendent in purple robes, gold belt, metal sandals, and laurel wreath, surrounded by boy attendants, declaring his own godhead in a gravely serious, pompous voice.[81] At a remove of hearsay, Diogenes Laertius's text coolly transmits the Sicilian mystic's fiery plunge:

> Hippobotus... asserts that, when he got up, he set out on his way to Etna; then, when he had reached it, he plunged into the fiery craters and disappeared, his intention being to confirm the report that he had become a god. Afterwards the truth was known, because one of his slippers was thrown up in the flames; it had been his custom to wear slippers of bronze.[82]

Sacred mystery snags upon the rocks of wardrobe malfunction. For the admirers and detractors who relayed this postcard from the edge, whether they did so as a comedy of pretensions to godhead or a tragedy of intellectual commitment, the exemplary force of Empedocles's last act was compounded by its site-specific connotations.

Etna was a busy intersection between classical and Christian imaginaries. Overlaying two distinct workshops of material and spiritual transformation onto each other, it is said to cover Vulcan's forge (referenced by Hamlet when he speculates that "my imaginations are as foul as Vulcan's stithy" [3.2.80]), but it was also one of the imagined earthly locations of Purgatory.[83] In his *Divine Institutes*, Lactantius attacks Empedocles for his swan dive into Etna as a risible example of philosophical overreach and "ostentation"; this cool estimation of fiery death returns in early modernity when Milton consigns Empedocles to the "paradise of fools" in *Paradise Lost*.[84] Voluntary death might here be sent up as a bad form of self-seriousness, but also as an eminently consistent outcome of the philosophy Empedocles died proclaiming.

In the medieval and early modern period, this assumed connection between materialism and self-killing would have been redoubled in the false but widely believed tradition, apparently initiated by St. Jerome, that Lucretius took his own life in a fit of love melancholy.[85] The links between the two philosopher-poets at the level of shared language and adjacent materialisms are attested openly in Lucretius's own text and confirmed in subsequent scholarship: Empedocles initiated the genre of philosophical didactic to which Lucretius's *De rerum natura* belongs, and in which Empedocles's "rhizomata" become Lucretius's "radices" or "stirpe"; Lucretius hails Empedocles as an admirable precursor to Epicurean doctrine.[86] But their author functions were bound together more tightly still by the allegation of self-killing, for both stories tacitly imply that belief in combinatorial ontology can have fatal consequences, and this link between thought and action seemed compounded by the doubtful deaths of early modern Lucretian disciples and translators such as Michele Marullo and Thomas Creech.

The Empedoclean doctrine transvalues death by locating it within inevitable cycles of change whose bedrock assurance in the indestructible persistence of the "rhizomata" across those cycles lends a tacit support to fantasies of a material endurance beyond personhood. Reversing temporality through a kind of magical inversion, death becomes not a forbidding entry into an unknown but a regressive source of comfort: one rebecomes what one always already was. As Thomas Joiner and other suicidologists attest, while every case is different, this fantasy of death-as-return or death-as-materialist-merger surfaces frequently within suicidal ideation; it is one of the "peculiarly positive" visions of death that those at risk of self-harm rehearse to themselves to smooth their path toward lethal action.[87]

Whether they abide simply at the level of ideation or act as a "volitional moderator" that increases the likelihood that persons who long to die will actually carry out their plans,[88] elemental poetics are shown in the works under analysis in this book to accomplish two things: Firstly, elemental poetics ward off or diminish the terror of death as a material process. Fantasies of resolving into the elements work as counterweights to, or the long-term conclusion of, threatening processes of putrefaction. The airy and fiery and liquid poetics of Empedoclean combinatorial ontology massage away the threat of the material bodily transformation of death as abject and disgusting by replacing it with images that counter that psychic threat, as when Hamlet wishes that his "flesh would melt / Thaw, and resolve itself into a dew" (1.2.129–130). Secondly, elemental poetics ward off or diminish the terror of hell. The elemental fire of Empedoclean ontology acts as a cover or screen for a Christian understanding of sinful death (which would be the case for "the violent against themselves," specifically) as one that could only lead to fiery eternal punishment. Marlowe's Faustus relays the force of this fantasy clearly when he cries out, "O soul, be changed into little water-drops, / And fall into the ocean, ne'er be found. / My God, my God, Look not so fierce on me!" (scene 14, lines 79–81)[89] The heat of the father's judgment prompts the fantasy of reabsorption into an elemental ocean of being in which one might lose one's body and evade punishment.

Applying a psychoanalytic framework to this disavowal of theology in favor of a classical doctrine, we can see a gendered transposition in which the Christian framework of death as a passage through the castrating agon of paternal judgment is upstaged by a fusional fantasy of death as a return to the mother.[90] The Empedoclean elemental commonplace does all sorts of different work in different contexts—its ubiquity means it can mean anything, because it is, quite literally, a theory about all things—but on the topic of self-killing, this schema is important not simply because of its direct link with Empedocles's own demise but also because it functions as a soothing counter-eschatology.

If the elemental poetics of self-killing repeatedly imagine the surrender of life as a redemptive merger with the elemental materials that also constitute nonorganic matter, does that indicate that such representations are best understood in a psychoanalytic register as expressions of the death drive? From a certain vantage point, Freud's metapsychological architecture of libido and death drive as absolutely antithetical psychic forces suggests an Empedoclean analogy:

> After long hesitancies and vacillations we have decided to assume the existence of only two basic instincts, Eros and the destructive instinct. The aim of the first of these basic instincts is to establish even greater unities

and to preserve them thus—in short, to bind together; the aim of the second is, on the contrary, to undo connections and so to destroy things. In the case of the destructive instinct, we may suppose that its final aim is to lead what is living into an inorganic state. For this reason we call it the death instinct.[91]

As described here, Freud's imagined antithesis sounds rather like the rival forces of love and strife at work within the Empedoclean schema, in which love forms material bonds and strife dissolves and destroys them.

But it must also be said that the critical invocation of the "death drive" prompts nods of assent from some corners and titters of derision from others. There are substantial conceptual obstacles facing its articulation, and lingering disputes (participants include, across fields and critical camps, Louis Althusser, Jean Laplanche, Jonathan Lear, and, more recently, Philippe Van Haute, Tomas Geyskens, and Todd McGowan, among others).[92] For my purposes, the most generative account is provided in Adrian Johnston's observation in his monograph *Time Driven: Metapsychology and the Splitting of the Drive* (2005), that "the death drive is impossible to isolate from the alloys it forms in conjunction with other drives."[93] Johnston's invocation of "alloys" finds support in a late remark in the *New Introductory Lectures on Psycho-Analysis*, from 1933, in which Freud joins a metallurgical metaphor to a mathematical one when referring to a ratio of libido and death drive within any given expression of drive: "Every instinctual impulse that we can examine consists of... fusions or alloys of the two classes of instinct. These fusions, of course, would be in the most varied ratios."[94]

Replacing a binary with a broad array of expressive fusions, Johnston clarifies and partially revises drive theory, but he does not attempt to "synthesize" libido and death drive, as if they were "really" one drive; rather, in the broader argument of the book he claims that at the core of all drives, however they are mixed or alloyed, an internal structure of scission leads ineluctably to self-defeat: "The death drive is a self-defeating mechanism, and, if it represents all drives, then Freudian theory implies that drives are, by definition, designed to sabotage themselves."[95]

Johnston's argument takes place at such a high altitude of theoretical generality that it may not be clear what possible explanatory force it could have with respect to my analysis of the representations of self-killing in early modern literature. But the registration of the drives as a fusional manifold between sexuality and a longing for death-as-inorganic-return identifies the dynamic that I hope to track and trace in all its local variety and difference across the archive of my examples. When we spectate upon the death of another, that dynamic—joy in the midst of death—might just look like "sadism" or an off-loading of primary aggression, finding its occasion to gloat in a kind of hypertrophied schadenfreude; when such joy is experienced at the prospect of one's own death, it might well look like the farthest shore of "masochism," perhaps bearing out Anne Sexton's remark in a letter about self-destructive fantasies that "suicide is a form of masturbation."[96]

I am not interested in a narrowly diagnostic assertion that such joy indexes a particular perversion or marks a clinically legible type of identity; indeed, such a claim is precisely not what I am up to in this book. Instead, building from Johnston's revision of Freud, I see "joy of the worm" as an expression of a basic metapsychological possibility available to all persons, in which libido and death drive variously mingle and register their expressive force in fantasies, in language, and in action. Sparking off unexpected charges of mirth and laughter in the midst of aggressive scenarios of destruction and damage, "joy of the worm" offers another name for the alloys of libido and death drive, the varied ratios of pleasure and harm, that I find within literary representations.

What does the drive's wiring toward self-sabotage mean for the understanding of self-killing, an action that, when completed, decisively defeats the self? Ironically, if a drive toward death is understood as structured in order to be self-defeating with respect to its own interior aims, then voluntary death itself must be at some level impossible for the psyche to conceptualize fully—and this confirms precisely Freud's intuition, expressed in "Thoughts for the Times on War and Death," that "at bottom no one believes in his own death."[97] Given the impossibility of death at the level of both firsthand experience and unconscious belief, if we accept the terms of Freud's assertion, then suicidality must only ever be a kind of psychic bluff, a stratagem by which aggression is released upon a version of the ego, or displaced aggression intended for others is stored and expressed in a symbolic gesture lined with an interior of protective disbelief.[98] That is, psychoanalysis can help us describe the self-splitting, self-hatred, narcissistic fantasies, and libidinal longings that swarm within suicidal ideation when they are present, but it also confronts us with a model of the self that both longs for and yet at some level cannot grasp the very deaths that sometimes result from conscious action. This suits some scenarios of self-killing quite tightly, and others not at all. Psychoanalysis does not have a unified theory of suicide as such, and that is not evidence of a fatal flaw but, in fact, an entirely unsurprising outcome of the fact that an action that is open to all does not have an essence.[99] Sociological theories divide their causal accounts along taxonomies of motivation in order to address the same basic starting point: self-killing's fundamental expressive plurality.[100]

To return to the larger intellectual-historical picture: despite these provisional limits on the utility of any grand unified theory, I think Johnston's understanding of the death drive as self-defeating—disavowing the very extinction it also longs for—illuminates the particular palliative function of Empedoclean (and Lucretian and Epicurean) ontologies of material merger as imaginative alternatives to, or barricades against, Christian eschatology for the early modern people who recirculated them within works of art. In imagining personal death not as a termination but as a reentrance into circulation within combinatorial ontology—a return, as it were, to the lap of Venus Genetrix—the prospect of death as the annihilation of personhood is sublated: the elemental substrates of our being cannot be harmed, cannot die, and can only recirculate endlessly as rhizomata undergo the workings of love and strife. Instead of firming up visions of posthumous personhood by promising personal resurrection in the body, this elemental fantasy suggests that, for some, ancient materialism modeled a different sort of metaphysical consolation.[101] In the parlance of suicidologists, these fantasies (or examples of "mental imagery") operate as "volitional moderators" that move sufferers from thought toward action.[102]

From Shakespeare's Cleopatra imagining herself in death as "air and fire" to Middleton's Timon merging with the "salt flood" of the ocean to Addison's Cato hailing "the varieties of untried being" within an endlessly recombinant "Crush of Worlds," the early modern representations of ancient suicides examined in this book cast a lyrical glow upon violent acts through an elemental poetics of materialist merger. In still other chapters, exemplary figures from classical history and culture (Empedocles and Lucretius but also Seneca and Cato) resurface as ideals of living and dying, spurs to critical thought, or counterexamples and worst-case scenarios whose ends prompt authorial speculation about the relationship between actions and the philosophies that perhaps produce them.

It is time to bring the array of theoretical dimensions, backdrops, and contexts indicated in this introduction together: "joy of the worm" is an affective phenomenon of unexpected positivity in the midst of scenes of self-harm, self-sacrifice, and voluntary death. For the early modern authors, readers, and audience members in its grip, "joy of the worm" defines a stance of transhistorical cross identification with exemplary agents that registers the fusional alloys of sexuality and death drive as they bypass (or rework) standing Christian theological injunctions against voluntary death. In many but not all instances under discussion, "joy of the worm" connotes *both* a socially stratifying generic work, rooted in war slavery doctrine, that texts enact when they valorize self-possession and agency against the abjected other of the enslaved person, *and* the Empedoclean fantasies of self-dissolution as a positive materialist merger with the elemental components of the universe that texts make portable for their recipients. Parasitic upon the norms of seriousness it also violates, maneuvering some agents toward death and others away from it, claiming possession of a self in order to dissolve it, snaking across the historical passage from self-killing to suicide, "joy of the worm" displays the sharp teeth and fatal pliancy of genre.

Tone Warning

Drawing precedent from the work of Saidiya Hartman's *Scenes of Subjection* and, within early modern studies, Paul Kottman's *A Politics of the Scene*, this book takes "the scene" as its primary unit of measure in sounding an archive of harm and damage.[103] Which is to say that this is not a set of readings of entire works but a set of close readings of particular scenes or passages in which self-killing pressurizes genre; at a higher level of organization, this focus upon the relatively smaller scale of the scene also explains why, after this extended introduction, this book has many shorter chapters and an interlude rather than a smaller number of more extensive readings. In some cases, the moments I examine are catastrophic or definitive; in other cases, the thought of self-killing passes across a text, but does not occasion climactic action or clinch authorial decision. This variability is intentional, and part of an attempt to balance attention to self-killing as irreversibly fatal action with the ideational everyday of self-killing as arguable notion, unrealized threat, or consolatory fantasy.

Self-killing is both an irreversible action and a passing object of thought. For those in the blast range of loss, it is utterly serious. But, as Parker's poem and More's merry tale show us, it can always be the object of thoughts and representations that are not. Attending to the history of how early modern artworks explored the space between action and thought entails attending to a range of objects that exceed ethical thresholds of kindness and restraint, and seem to gleefully trample upon human life. This amounts not so much to a *content warning*, since the reader knew when she picked up this book that it was about self-killing, but, instead, to a *tone warning*, and one that is offered sincerely: *the objects I will discuss adopt tones toward violent death and suffering that are ludicrous, flippant, and occasionally cruel.*

Tone has been usefully defined by Sianne Ngai as the "affective relay between a subject and an object."[104] The attunement across intersubjective boundaries that tone enacts is necessarily variable across differences of category and scale: we can speak of the tone of a phrase, a scene, or an interaction, but also of the tone that is characteristic of a character, or a person, or an author, or a social milieu.[105] Tone abides both between persons and in the experiences of reception and encounter that readers and audiences cocreate as they engage or shrink back from tone's linking work as "the dialectic between objective and subjective feeling that our aesthetic encounters inevitably produce."[106] At no small risk of strain, this book asks "tone" to do load-bearing work in indicating the affective linkage and attunements across such broad ontological levels. When I say that, for example, the severed head in More's story is an example of "joy of the worm," I'm assuming that More intended for us to feel something, and that that something was pleasure; which is not the same as saying that the head might not also generate a sharp burst of horror, disgust, or shock at the moment of violence at its center. In the case of "joy of the worm," "tone" names the relay of a positive affect where it seemingly does not belong.

"Positive affect" sounds vague, but then, for some readers, so does "affect." Do I just mean emotion? Literary humanists drawing inspiration from the field of affect theory tend toward liturgical throat clearing about the distinction between "affect" and "emotion" in the opening chapters of their books, yet frequently ignore this distinction once the wheels are in motion. In part, this is because fundamentally biological claims about, say, the temporal lag between a cognitively registered brain state and a culturally legible emotional display presumes an empirical apparatus that could verify the presence or absence of that lag, and that apparatus is not of primary interest to most humanists.[107] Closer to my own period, in the texts I am discussing, there is a variable attention paid to the psychophysiology of humoral illness and its diagnosis and treatment; it is fundamental to some texts and more or less absent from others. In part this is because self-killing is an action that is open to all comers, even if early modern persons naturally expected melancholics to be more at risk of self-harm and self-destruction. In early modern culture, there was no singular affect that always necessarily produces or accompanies self-killing, nor was there a singular affect that always necessarily accompanied responses to it. As Eugenie Brinkema puts it in *The Forms of the Affects* (2014): "There is no reason to assume that affects are identical aesthetically, politically, ethically, experientially, and formally; but only reading specific affects as having and being bound up with specific forms gives us the vocabulary for articulating those many differences."[108] Punting from generality, "joy of the worm" names a specifically positive cluster of affective responses to self-killing within the genre system of early modernity.

That said, self-killing is a special case when assessing the transmission of affect. The standard alibi when we want to write about a subject, and especially a painful and violent topic, is to claim that our first and foremost goals are compassion and understanding. This valorizes the critic as ethical agent, replacing ignorance with insight, cruelty with clarity. Fraught with risk, suicide sets the stage for pious displays of what Heather Love has termed "the ethical charisma of the critic."[109] But suicide radiates certain distortion effects that trouble this familiar hermeneutic scene by seeming to pit the interests of understanding and compassion against each other. Chiefly, to articulate forcefully why someone would want to kill themselves is to potentially increase the risk that someone else will kill themselves. Whether or not one intends to "romanticize," within the hypervigilant prevention protocols of the present moment, to talk about suicide *at all* is to risk increasing the lethality of the subject for people who are constituted as already vulnerable. To see these protocols at work, simply google the word "suicide": you will immediately be told that "you are not alone; confidential help is available for free" and provided with the phone number for the nearest National Suicide Prevention Lifeline.[110] Talking someone off a ledge becomes the paradigm for public speech about suicide; the other is framed as at risk, in need of manipulation away from their own projected desires and tendencies. This is more than a little paternalizing, and it reifies the control of what sociologist Terry Williams, in *Teenage Suicide Notes: An Ethnography of Self-Harm* (2017), has described as a "chemocratic" administered world.[111] That world presumes the pathologization of suicide and parasuicidal behavior already critiqued by Marsh; by widening the gap between "suicide" and "self-killing" within this book, I hope to dislodge its hold upon the subject.

I want to prevent suicides; I do not (always) want to prevent self-killing. When my stepfather was dying of an incurable terminal illness, I helped him negotiate the complex legal procedures within the state of California that permit people to acquire medication that they can use to end their own lives. This required a series of psychological interviews designed to determine that he was not suffering from a mood disorder, creating the strange, and, to us, more than a little bleakly humorous, requirement that he demonstrate that he had less than six months to live but was somehow not in any way "depressed" about that fact. Having passed these examinations, he was granted access to the medication, which he ultimately elected not to use; the knowledge that he had access to this route out of life made his own death process significantly less frightening and traumatic. In advocating for a distinction between "suicide" and "self-killing," and in being, under certain conditions, for self-killing and against suicide, I rely upon a conceptual distinction to navigate such changing landscapes of risk.

The Chapters That Make Up This Book

In the chapters that follow, I will focus tightly upon particular scenes in early modern texts in which voluntary death is at stake either as fantasy or as completed action, in order to probe how different authors imagined alternatives to censure. In each case, "joy" modulates: sometimes, as in the More story, it is a kind of spectatorial joy at a pronounced distance from the subject of self-killing. In other cases, that "joy" is one that we are encouraged to emotionally invest in and see in a de-pathologized register as the farthest reach of an exemplary practice of freedom, duly mindful of its antithetical dependence on enslavement as grounding condition. My analysis does not seek to relay "joy of the worm" but, more modestly, to anatomize it.

As the book reaches from the mid-sixteenth century to the early eighteenth century, it is my hope that these distinct examples can do double duty, offering revealing testimony of the thorny individuality of particular authors while also complicating the overall picture of early modern England's repertoires of sympathy and aversion. As this happens, the book itself becomes increasingly sorrowful in its own exemplary materials as the cultural window of opportunity in which "joy of the worm" was made manifest first opens and then gradually closes. The reader will notice a gradual phase shift away from comedic representations of "joy of the worm" as the pleasures it makes possible lose their tone of levity and take on the mantle of sobriety and sublimity.

Here are very brief summaries of each chapter. Chapter 1 contrasts the dialogue between Pyrocles and Philoclea in book 4 of Sir Philip Sidney's *Old Arcadia* with the anguished, seemingly final speech of Hebe in John Lyly's *Gallathea*, as examples of "failed seriousness." In each case, characters in crisis reach toward a tragic outcome that the surrounding text forecloses, short-circuiting suicidality through a strategic form of early modern camp. Chapter 2 considers the tangled timing and unexpected slapstick of Antony's botched suicide attempt and Cleopatra's negotiations with a clown as means through which William Shakespeare's *Antony and Cleopatra* upends the normative representation of the *Romana mors* ideal established within *Julius Caesar*. In a final comparative chapter on Shakespearean drama through the contemporary lens of "RIP trolling," I examine Hamlet's behavior at Ophelia's funeral in *Hamlet* and Timon's mocking offer of a hanging tree to the citizens of Athens in *Timon of Athens* as paired examples of "suicide trolls" taking deliberate pleasure in the breaking of decorum.[112] Rethinking the alleged exemplarity of Hamlet, the chapter concludes with a methodological discussion of the limits of transhistorical comparison and an argument for what I term "good enough presentism."

Moving from the complexities of generic space within drama as cultural practice to a broader array of textual modes, in its second half the book shifts to exemplary works of seventeenth-century prose. Chapter 4 considers the conflict between witty paradox and sober theological treatise within John Donne's *Biathanatos*, and the role that generic tension plays in stage-managing Donne's heterodox entertainment of Christ's death as a case of self-killing. The book then pauses for an interlude upon the passage in Sir Thomas Browne's *Religio Medici* in which he invents the word "suicide," in the context of philosophical reflection upon a nonpathological "hope for death" that might sustain and nourish life. Sidestepping assertions about Browne's place in the historical emergence of liberalism and toleration, this interlude reconsiders Browne's coinage of the word "suicide" as part of a historical process that downgrades the exemplary force of Stoic catastrophe in favor of an unenacted ideational everyday.

Chapter 5 uses the contemporary protocols of suicide prevention to examine the tense negotiation between Adam and Eve in book 10 of John Milton's *Paradise Lost* as they consider the possibility of voluntary extinction within the generic space of an epic poem bounded by Greek tragedy and Hebrew scripture. Even as Milton's Eve reworks the Virgilian representation of Dido, Adam's recognition of something "sublime" in Eve's proposal to preempt the human race opens onto contemporary debates in queer theory surrounding reproductive futurity and negativity, the "antinatalist" position, and fantasies of human extinction within environmental ethics. In the book's sixth and final chapter, the climactic scene of self-killing in Joseph Addison's *Cato, a Tragedy* is considered as both a cumulative restatement of the traditions of suicidal representation under analysis and a decisive historical marker of a shift in aesthetic values. Stiffly ceremonial in its celebration of self-possession as a kind of hypostatized patriotism unto death that makes it a key touchstone for the ongoing takeover of Stoic ideals by conservative masculinity and libertarian propaganda, Addison's work signals the vanishing of the playful mockery of the urge to die that animates so many of the works that precede it.

The book concludes with an epilogue that synthetically restates the cumulative impact of this sequence of close readings along the passage from "self-killing" to "suicide" as it constellates a significant cluster of key works of early modern English literature across genres. Gear-shifting toward the contemporary moment, I also consider the problem of vicarious habituation attendant upon the circulation of representations of self-killing in musical subcultures and in the Shakespearean classroom.

I want my analysis to do something to the subject I'm describing. Tracking what came before and after Browne's coinage of the word "suicide" in the writings of Sidney, Lyly, Shakespeare, Middleton, Donne, Milton, and Addison might also further the separation of "self-killing" from "suicide" that that coinage made possible. Working to de-pathologize voluntary death without overcompensating into valorization, "joy of the worm" deflates tragic seriousness in favor of a broader affective palette of possible responses to loss, and downsizes the minimum threshold of self-possession and agency these acts require. Understanding genre as a technology that converts risk and harm into pleasure, "joy of the worm" can help sharpen our understanding of the intricate generic affordances of the past. Going beyond that, I hope that it might help us rethink the ongoing scenes of self-destruction in which we remain enmeshed at present.

Failed Seriousness in the *Old Arcadia* and *Gallathea*

CHAPTER ONE

Sacrifice enters cultural play... as a trick, as a hoax.

ARTHUR LITTLE JR., "Altars of Alterity"

Time after Time

A friend tells me a story: She was playing in a cover band in a bar and they had just finished a popular ballad when a drunk and distraught woman in the audience loudly demanded that they play it again. Heckling back and forth—the woman demanding, the band refusing—escalated until the woman produced a knife, which she held against her wrist, saying that she would kill herself right there if the band did not play the song again. Showing that she meant it, she made small cuts into the skin that began to bleed, and as other audience members nearby tried to reason with her, the band dutifully proceeded to play the same three-minute pop song, over and over and over. Eventually, people in the bar talked the woman out of her crisis, and, upon the tenth iteration, she finally put the knife away. The song in question was Cyndi Lauper's "Time after Time."

Though suicide isn't funny, this story almost is. In part there's the joke-like structure of a long windup followed by the punchline reveal that the song at the kernel of this emotional crisis of mandatory repetition is, itself, a song about repetition. Specifically, the song's lyrical promise—"If you're lost, you can look and you will find me / Time after time"—repetitiously offers unconditional love, a stable and therapeutic "holding environment," a seemingly boundless willingness to assume on-demand care work.[1] The banality of the pop song and pop singer as parent/partner substitute overwrites an odd identificatory parallel between wailing Cyndi and knife-wielding customer (each, whether donor or recipient of care, stuck in an emotional loop). The passage from violent surprise to peaceful resolution makes this story, though it is true, seem artful.

Endings matter, and the survival of the woman lets this be more of a joke than it is, because it models the urge to die and the threat to kill the self as an everyday feeling rising to a decisive crisis that can be worked through, collectively, to a comic resolution. In this story, art saves a life, repetition becomes difference, and the knife is put away.[2] There's something deflationary about it, but only in the wake of the fatal threat at its core, and yet it can circulate as funny—the friend who was present relayed it as such to me, and we laughed as she told the story—precisely because no one dies. Harm has been limited, and threats have been lifted, and so it feels, somewhat, permissible to laugh at the comedic reveal of the song title, which is, in its own way, deflationary too. That song? Really? Part of why laughter at this story doesn't feel entirely nasty is that we as readers are invited to reflect on our own emotional investment in pop songs, our own moments of playing a piece of music over and over and over. Whether we like pop music or opera or harsh noise, we have all been the child in Freud's "Beyond the Pleasure Principle" (1920), demanding the repetition of the same bedtime story, over and over, to the letter, with no deviation.[3]

Why tell this story at the start of a chapter about the representation of the urge to die in Sir Philip Sidney and John Lyly? This is a story about genre, and about the way that genre modulates our relation to self-destructive urges, letting us gain purchase upon what is serious by refusing, entirely, to take something serious seriously. We are permitted to adopt other stances toward what is serious when a generic frame primes us to regard it as less than serious, less than life-threatening. How does art bring self-destruction toward the comedic threshold, and why might it do so?

There are obvious reasons why one might align Sidney's pastoral prose romance *The Countess of Pembroke's Arcadia* (i.e., the *Old Arcadia*) (1578–80) and Lyly's pastoral tragicomedy *Gallathea* (1588): both works exemplify a certain high-summer cultural moment in the history and evolution of Elizabethan literary style.[4] Both works helped define their authors as tastemakers and men of influence, however variably closer and farther away these men were from the sun of favor at Elizabeth's court. Both works draw upon and revise the pastoral traditions of classical literature, both works place a pair of protagonists in cross-gendered disguise and explore the queer romantic possibilities that result, and they both have quasi-miraculous deus ex machina conclusions that liberate their protagonists from tightly plotted, seemingly inescapable constraints with a lightning speed that feels both invigorating and abrupt.

So far, so familiar. Overfamiliar, even. But in this chapter, though I respond to and build upon the surrounding web of connections and correlations between Sidney's prose romance and Lyly's drama, I intend to concentrate, admittedly in a myopic manner, upon two specific scenes in which characters express a curiously subsidiary affect within the broad range of scenarios of self-killing with which this book deals: the desire to be sacrificed for others. Specifically, both Pyrocles in book 4 of Sidney's romance and Hebe in the middle of Lyly's play seem to arrest the forward motion of their respective texts in order to dwell, at extraordinary length, upon the valedictory process of leaving the world. Both, albeit in entirely separate contexts, are brought to a pitch of emotional intensity in which they come to welcome their own deaths.

They do not do so because of despair. That is, neither Pyrocles nor Hebe is in the grip of a depressive mood disorder as contemporary diagnostic protocols understand it. Rather, they long to die so that others may live and survive beyond them. Outlined broadly like that, each case is locatable within the Durkheimian explanatory matrix of "suicidal altruism."[5] That said, their sacrificial frame permits an ethical relation to voluntary death that also echoes key components of Christian faith and acts of martyrdom that express devotion to that faith, even as the pastoral and quasi-pagan settings of both works also place these characters at a protective remove from any overly strong resemblance to confessional specifics. Their imagined sacrifices are meant to be received as deliberate public acts of personal valor rather than as private spasms of sinful despair. To reiterate the distinction made in my introduction, they are cases of self-killing rather than suicide.

In an early modern variant of what Elizabeth Freeman has termed "temporal drag," this shared framing of an earlier historical moment permits citational play, at once drawing energy from the precursor it sublates and ironizing its codes.[6] But instead of modeling a generational delay or developmental lag (as in Freeman's case, which focuses upon the performance of outmoded styles of lesbian self-presentation), in these works a temporally and culturally "otherwise" frame of culturally prior pseudo-antiquity allows a textually localized but intensive exploration of a feeling arguably central to the theological present in which these works were written: sacrificial longing. However modulated by Reformation differences between confessions, the urge to admire Christ's sacrifice and to emotionally invest in and inhabit that state of willing submission to suffering through meditative practices of *imitatio Christi*—practices that Ross Lerner has memorably termed "interminable consideration"—rendered the affective repertoire of sacrifice both omnipresent and arguable across a broad spectrum of available forms of early modern Christianity.[7] Burlesquing the urge to die while giving it voice, book 4 of Sidney's *Old Arcadia* and Hebe's scene in Lyly's *Gallathea* seem to solicit admiration for the ethical premise of self-sacrifice precisely in order to overturn and cancel its expression. In response to these vocal longings for death, both Sidney's Pyrocles and Lyly's Hebe run aground upon narrative outcomes that are more humiliating than heroic.

Pyrocles longs to die to demonstrate his remorse and to protect someone else from the shameful and potentially fatal consequences of his own actions. Screwing himself up into a pitch of heroic determination, he attempts suicide but picks the wrong object (literally—his chosen implement is too blunt) and a long argument ensues, in which he is persuaded to trade in his fantasy of self-destruction for survival. Hebe is offered as a sacrifice to a sea monster on behalf of her community and, in the midst of reconciling herself to her fate, comes to long for the monster to devour her so that she can die nobly on behalf of that community. Her offer is rejected when the monster does not deign to appear. These two figures stand in strong opposition to each other: one longs for death and tries to achieve it; the other is more or less forced into a position of being exposed to death and bemoans that fact until, in what she thinks are her final moments, she comes to embrace it.

What unites the scenes of Pyrocles and Hebe despite their manifest differences, and their central distinction with respect to the will to die? Rather than functioning as dramatic climaxes of violent release, they are both scenes of failure and frustration, in which the longing to die is stifled. The knife, having been brandished, must be put away. If the pathos of Pyrocles's vexation and Hebe's lonely exposure to monstrosity solicits our pity, that counterforce of comedic possibility encourages us to take pleasure in the very disparity between each figure's subjective investment in being sacrificed and the surrounding work's own apparent stance toward that investment.

In other words, Pyrocles's blunted suicide attempt and Hebe's fatal aria of sacrifice anticipate that phenomenon of passionate excruciation, stylistic excess, and "failed seriousness" that twentieth-century aesthetics once knew as "camp."

Wither Camp

Does anyone really care about the allegedly critical power of "camp," let alone need a definition of this now drearily ubiquitous critical term, at this late historical moment in its putrefaction? As filmmaker Bruce LaBruce notes in his hybrid lecture/performance "Notes on Camp/Anti-Camp" (2012), the term, once redolent of insider subcultural knowledge circa its midcentury articulations by Isherwood and Sontag, has been transformed into "the ideological white noise of the new millennium" as it has fractured outward into an array of forms that LaBruce gleefully taxonomizes as Classic Gay Camp (Bette Davis), Bad Gay Camp (Liberace), Good Straight Camp (Robert Altman), Bad Straight Camp (Damien Hirst), High Camp (Oscar Wilde), Low Camp (burlesque), Reactionary Camp (heavy metal), Liberal Camp (Dr. Ruth), Conservative Camp (Donald Trump), and so on.[8] In the wake of the disastrous banality of the 2019 Met Gala, whose "Camp: Notes on Fashion" theme prompted inert gestures from the usual cast of billionaires and celebrities, camp now seems ice-cold, ready for permanent storage.[9]

Like "duende" or "rococo," the term "camp" connotes a charged aesthetic cluster of objects and qualities, a restricted repertoire of affects and effects, without yielding to precise articulation. Camp's glittery peaks conceal deep epistemological crevasses, but it has always had a curiously constitutive relationship to early modernity. One of its first forays into print, in Christopher Isherwood's *The World in the Evening* (1953), featured a mini-disquisition that found the sensibility afoot centuries before its christening: "High Camp is the whole emotional basis for ballet, for example, and of course of baroque art.... High Camp always has an underlying seriousness. You can't camp about something you don't take seriously. You're not making fun of it, you're making fun out of it. You're expressing what's basically serious to you in terms of fun and artifice and elegance. Baroque art is basically camp about religion."[10] "Basically" is doing a lot of work here. One may well snicker at the tacitly Protestant bias that produces such judgments, but devotees of Crashaw and Bernini might also be willing to grant the larger point. Though Sontag would dismiss Isherwood's framing as flimsy and jejune, Sontag too features some early modern precursors in "Notes on 'Camp.'"

Snugly tucked into a parenthetical aside, Lyly makes a curiously apt early modern stowaway within Sontag's foundational, if not definitive, account of the books, films, furniture, clothes, buildings, attitudes, and human beings that constellate that "unmistakably modern" sensibility.[11] Having alleged that camp takes root in the eighteenth century, amid the folly gardens and artificial ruins of the Gothic, Sontag hedges her bets with a casual backward glance toward the early modern period, and it is there, in a torrent of name-dropping, that we discover this lonely representative of the English literary Renaissance: "A pocket history might, of course, begin farther back—with the mannerist artists like Pontormo, Rosso, and Caravaggio, or the extraordinarily theatrical painting of Georges de La Tour, or euphuism (Lyly, etc.) in literature."[12] How are we to assess Sontag's judgment that Lyly's writings might constitute a crucial early modern contribution to camp sensibility? To force a pocket history to empty its pockets, when exactly did that happen? Is camp something we find in the past or do to the past?

Here one might wish to distinguish between "weak" and "strong" versions of such a claim. The "weak" version would go like this: Lyly's art, or, for that matter, Sir Philip Sidney's art, is camp for us in the present, because of the pleasurable strain involved in measuring the distance between our own aesthetic moment and the elaborate rhetorical effects of artificiality we find when we read *Euphues* or the *Old Arcadia*. However seriously Lyly or Sidney may have taken themselves, we cannot quite take them so seriously, and so we can only read across this barrier, when we read them at all. Sontag flags a threshold of surplus intensity as the defining criterion: "Camp is art that proposes itself seriously, but cannot be taken altogether seriously because it is 'too much.'"[13] Caught in the glare of that "too much-ness," camp is what we do to highly stylized authors from the past, the price of their survival into the present.

The "strong" version would claim that Lyly and Sidney were, in their own historical moment, consciously attempting to produce camp effects. This, of course, only begs the question of what early modern camp could be in the first place. Skittish at spoiling the fun with a serious, hence non-camp, precision, Sontag glancingly defines camp as "the sensibility of failed seriousness, of the theatricalization of experience.... a consistently aesthetic experience of the world. It incarnates a victory of 'style' over 'content,' 'aesthetics' over 'morality,' [and] irony over tragedy."[14] Given the strong flavor of nineteenth-century aestheticism attendant upon most if not all of these imagined victories of X over Y, the alleged discovery of such an agenda in an early modern author or artwork prompts justifiable fears of a passé sort of presentism, the victory of one more recent past over another, older past. Indeed, it is hard to imagine any early modern artist consciously taking themselves to be attacking "morality" itself, Sidney least of all, and if that is truly definitive of camp, then the strong claim looks doomed from the start.

But if we regard the theatricalization of experience (note 36), the affirmation of irony over tragedy (note 38), and an aroma of "seriousness that fails" (note 23) as keynotes for the strong claim about camp, then in this chapter I would like to consider, and, yes, consider seriously, the possibility that Sidney's prose romance *Old Arcadia* and Lyly's play *Gallathea* (1585/1592) constitute examples of just such a sensibility, and prove its circulation in early modern English literature. I hope to reconsider these works to flag the ethical problems generated by the forms of solidarity at work in camp's pleasurable response to sacrificial "excruciation." Specifically, I'm interested in how *Old Arcadia* and *Gallathea* draw camp pleasure from a seemingly inhospitable and recalcitrant emotion: the longing to sacrifice oneself for the sake of others.

An Idle Toy

For a work of pastoral romance that Sidney passes off as an idle toy written one page at a time for the amusement of his sister and her female coterie at Wilton, *The Countess of Pembroke's Arcadia*, now known as the

Old Arcadia in contradistinction to its later revision, pulses with turbulent affects that sometimes spill over into acts of startling violence. Spik-
ing out of the stately progression of aureate sentences and rhetorical set
pieces at odd angles, Sidney's characters erupt with passionate complaint,
as the orderly choreography of singing contests and courtly conversation
are upended by riots, summary amputations, executions, sexual assaults,
and rapes.[15]

This volatility is not a surprise, given the range of emotions that the romance as a form can sustain, and in part it reflects a shared kinship with
the precedent set by epic. Taking both its title and its prosimetrum for-
mat from Jacopo Sannazaro's *Arcadia* (1504), a copy of which Sidney may
have purchased in Venice during his travels abroad, Sidney's work borrows plot elements and components from a broad array of sources beyond
Sannazaro.[16] From Dido's death in the *Aeneid* to the self-destructive passions of Theagenes and Charikleia in Heliodorus of Emesa's *Aethiopica*
to Orlando's madness and despair in Ariosto's *Orlando furioso* to Rinaldo
persuading Armida not to kill herself in Tasso's *Gerusalemme liberata*, the
epic and chivalric romances that provided the DNA for Sidney's romance
already abound with scenes of mental disturbance, threats and attempts
at self-killing, and actual deaths.

But the extremity of these actions and passions tilts against what seems
to have been the understood spirit in which the *Old Arcadia* was read as a
manual of courtly utterance, written by the man Spenser called "the precedent of all chivalry," and Dorothy Stanley, not to be outdone, termed "the
politest Author of his Age."[17] Indeed, Heylyn's *Cosmographie* indicated
the prevalent climate of the work's posthumous reception when he hailed
the *Arcadia* as "A Book, which besides its excellent language, rare con-
trivances, and delectable stories, hath in it all the strains of Poesie, com-
prehendeth the universal Art of speaking; and to them who can discern,
and will observe, affordeth notable rules for demeanour, both private and
publick."[18] If there is much within the *Old Arcadia*'s plot, and in particular within the rigors of book 5's climactic trial scene, to support the idea
that the work exists to model "notable rules for demeanour" by modeling
the consequences of their violation, Sidney's wayward authorial tone, and
the polyphonic complexity of the eclogues that repeatedly interrupt, comment upon, and distract from that plot's advancement, suggest that there
is significantly more to this work than a lavish exercise in courtly modes
of speech.

Self-killing moves from fantasy scenario to active threat amid the passionate turbulence of book 4, and I intend to read the scene describing
Pyrocles's attempt to take his own life and his subsequent debate about
the ethics of self-killing with Philoclea within that book in some detail.

But before I do that, I must briefly rehearse, insofar as that is possible, the circumstances that have led to this crisis, fully granting that the summary of a romance plotline is likely to induce a certain ludicrous camp effect of its own: fearing a cryptic prophecy that forecasts ruin to his marriage, family, and kingdom, Duke Basilius relocates his duchess, Gynecia, and his daughters, Pamela and Philoclea, to the pastoral hermitage in the Arcadian countryside. Having fallen in love with a painting of Philoclea and resolving to meet her, young prince Pyrocles disguises himself as the Amazon Cleophila; his noble friend Musidorus disguises himself as the shepherd Dorus. Together they ingratiate themselves into the ducal family while pursuing the daughters, but complications ensue: both Basilius, falling for the disguise, and his consort, Gynecia, seeing through it, become enamored of Cleophila/Pyrocles. Pamela and Dorus fall in love, as do Philoclea and Cleophila/Pyrocles. After a cascade of tricks, distractions, and misadventures that fling the romance's various blocking fathers, snooping servants, and clingy would-be lovers off the trail, each of the pairs of young lovers are finally alone with each other.

It is at this point that the *Old Arcadia*, notoriously, seems to spin off its generic axis, as, in separate but clearly interrelated incidents, both Pyrocles and Musidorus sexually assault the young women. Having either promised marriage or explicitly pledged not to threaten the chastity of their female companions, each of the noble young protagonists breaks faith and oversteps their word: Pyrocles rapes Philoclea, and Musidorus attempts to rape Pamela but is interrupted by a riotous crowd of Phagonian rebels.[19] Meanwhile, Basilius, fresh from a bed trick in which Cleophila is swapped out for his own wife, downs a magic potion that induces his (apparent) death. Thrown into turmoil by the discovery of the corpse, the advisor Philanax declares a state of emergency. At this high point of dramatic tension, the lovers Pyrocles and Philoclea are caught in flagrante delicto by their erstwhile gamekeeper Dametas and are imprisoned together. Having been caught together while unmarried, both Pyrocles and Philoclea can potentially be sentenced to death; even should Philoclea be spared, her honor seems at risk of being irreparably compromised. It is this crisis that precipitates the entrance into the text of self-killing as an earnestly proposed solution to an insoluble problem.

Or, seemingly in earnest, for, as Andrew Weiner points out in *Sir Philip Sidney and the Poetics of Protestantism* (1978), "The presentation of Pyrocles' attempt to kill himself approaches farce."[20] Indeed, the precise tone of how Sidney handles this grim subject seems to short-circuit Marx's famous slogan: instead of a sequential historical passage ("first as tragedy, then as farce"), we are thrust into farce about tragedy.

Style is notoriously open to interpretation: Is it a short list of favorite subjects, plot points, and habitual elements, or a diffuse but pervasive tone of voice? As Jeff Dolven has indicated in *Senses of Style: Poetry before Interpretation* (2018), the concept's elasticity means that style can shrink down to a cluster of riffs and tics (easily parodied), or inflate outward into a totalizing vision of life.[21] If a writer's style suffuses their work and seeps from it because of an inbuilt temperamental setting, then why would we expect that that author's style would suddenly shift simply because they are writing a scene that happens to be about self-killing? Like the modern hush in the voice when speaking the word "cancer," we expect in the present moment a certain kind of funereal sobriety, or an appalled catch in the throat, when the topic is self-killing. Instead, Sidney's text zigzags oddly between distinct modes of address: in the *Old Arcadia* the conflict between the warm front of passionate outbursts and the cold front of sententious oratory generates lightning zaps of self-consciously "witty" rhetorical elaboration that are both dazzling and superfluous.

Sidney's tendency to mix modes manifests itself in Pyrocles's initial declaration of fatal intent, which starts in a tone of sobriety and sincerity, only to jolt us with the punning impertinence of an extravagant closing flourish of admiration at the fitness of death as a "firsthand" experience:

> "Be it so," said the valiant Pyrocles, "never life for better cause, nor to be better end, was bestowed; for the death be to follow this fact (which no death of mine shall ever make me repent), who is to die so justly as myself? And if I must die, who can be so fit executioners as mine own hands which, as they were accessaries to the fact, so in killing me they shall suffer their own punishment?"[22]

Is Pyrocles serious? If the epithet "the valiant Pyrocles" serves as a placeholder of his structural position in the romance plot, the willingness to be sacrificed so that others might live makes good upon such expectations, giving us an idealized agent about to embark upon a final gesture at absolute cost to himself so that someone else can be protected from harm. But what are we to make of Pyrocles's narcissistic pleasure in noticing the thought that his own hands, which are about to commit self-murder, will themselves be punished with death by virtue of that act?

"Narcissism" can founder upon the historical question of definition. In *Narcissism and Suicide in Shakespeare and His Contemporaries* (2009), Eric Langley has introduced a powerful and productive analysis of a certain kind of Ovidian narcissistic apparatus at work in early modern representations of self-killing, while avoiding any overt engagement with Freud.[23] Here we could speculate that the rhetorical pleasure in the performance of wit constitutes a displacement in Pyrocles of his own guilt: it was his hands that committed the sexual assault that exposed Philoclea to the threat of death, and so in killing himself with his own hands he destroys the guilty party. In "Mourning and Melancholia" Freud suggests that a perverse fold is required in order for the ego to gain the strength to act violently against its own interests:

> The ego can kill itself only if, owing to the return of the object-cathexis, it can treat itself as an object—if it is able to direct against itself the hostility which relates to an object and which represents the ego's original reaction to objects in the external world.... In the two opposed situations of being most intensely in love, and of suicide, the ego is overwhelmed by the object, though in totally different ways.[24]

The definitive character of these remarks has been somewhat overstated.[25] Freud is speculating, and is not claiming that this is the sole and only explanation of all cases of suicide as such. To connect the dots between a clinical diagnostic framework and the alien terrain of early modern aesthetics, Pyrocles's rhetorical sundering of the self into constituent parts literalizes Freud's self-splitting. In judging the hands that acted, Pyrocles both acknowledges and disavows culpability, and in planning suicide precisely as a devotional token of being "intensely in love," Pyrocles occupies both of Freud's "opposed situations," the heat of his passion melting an alloy of contrary drives.

But neither Langley nor Freud are quite adequate to the sheer flippancy of Sidney's achievement here at the level of tone: the weird joy of self-satisfaction that thrums within this witty verbal display at the prospect of self-killing. This perverse affective fold of extreme self-regard in the midst of apparent self-hatred registers the constitutive work of genre as it modulates a tragic action with comedic potentiality. Pyrocles's apostrophe upon his own hand might also be an announcement of Sidney's own classical learning, chiming as it does with the Athenian funeral practice of amputating the right hand of people who took their own lives.[26] This passing conceit of joy in punishing the hand that kills the self may be a glance historically backward at that Greek custom, or it may not.[27]

Whatever its source, this distracting riff upon the pleasing fitness of means by which to achieve irreversibly fatal ends keeps recurring, and becomes, in all senses, clunky when Pyrocles happens again upon a bar from the cell window that he had wrenched loose earlier while attempting escape. Rediscovering the bar, Pyrocles prays to it: "O bar, blessed in that thou hast done service to the chamber of the paragon of life, since thou couldst not help me to make a perfecter escape, yet serve my turn, I pray thee, that I may escape from myself."[28] With this flourish of demi-zeugma,

Pyrocles uses the self-sameness of the word "escape" to paper over the distinct moral differences between the proposed scenarios of flight and suicide as means to redress the imminent threats of sexual shame and execution, and arrests himself in the midst of his plan to die with gratuitous extra servings of wit. Wit need not negate the seriousness of a situation; in a discussion of Ajax's punning jokes upon the resemblance between his name and the cry "alas," Blair Hoxby notes that "Lessing, for one, argued from historical examples that deep pain could find vent in wit."[29] But the foregone conclusion of Ajax's death offers a center of gravity notably lacking in Sidney's text, which cruises flippancy. Tone matters here. Is this sort of wordplay the nervous padding of Pyrocles putting off an unpleasant task, or a sign that Sidney is losing tonal control of his own scene?

Hedging his bets, Pyrocles moves from the nonsentient bar to the transcendent divinity, following his preliminary prayer to the bar with a higher address to the ultimate authority figure. Because it lays out the essential arguments that will return and modulate throughout the debate to come, and because it is the deliciously extended windup to a materialist punchline of defeat, I take the risk of reproducing at length Pyrocles's prayer to Jupiter and its immediate consequence in full:

> "O great maker and great ruler of this world," said he, "to thee do I sacrifice this blood of mine; and suffer, O Jove, the errors of my youth to pass away therein. And let not the soul by thee made, and ever bending unto thee, be now rejected of thee. Neither be offended that I do abandon this body, to the government of which thou hast placed me, without thy leave, since how can I know but that thy unsearchable mind is I should do so, since thou hast taken from me all means longer to abide in it? And since the difference stands but in a short time of dying, thou that hast framed my heart inclined to do good, how can I in this small space of mine benefit so much all the human kind as in preserving thy perfectest workmanship, their chiefest honour? O justice itself, howsoever thou determinest of me, let this excellent innocency not be oppressed. Let my life pay her loss. O Jove, give me some sign that I may die with this comfort." And pausing a little, as if he hoped for some token, "And whensoever, to the eternal darkness of the earth, she doth follow me, let our spirits possess one place, and let them be more happy in that uniting."
>
> With that word, striking the bar upon his heart side with all the force he had, and falling withal upon, to give it the througher passage, the bar in truth was too blunt to do the effect; although it pierced his skin and bruised his ribs very sore, so that his breath was almost past him. But the noise of his fall drave away sleep from the quiet senses of the dear Philoclea, whose sweet soul had an early salutation of the deadly spectacle unto her.[30]

We have the structure of a joke: a long windup followed by the comedy of a certain failure to launch. Imagined as both the means of "violent refuge" and "final dispatch," the bar is also more than a little grimly comedic in its material recalcitrance, exemplifying the space of comedy as one in which, to quote Sianne Ngai and Lauren Berlant, "objects violate physics, or, worse, insist on its laws against all obstacles."[31] Like the creaky door hinge in a Jacques Tati film, the obstreperous bar toggles from background to foreground, becoming "vibrant matter."[32] At the risk of lowering the tone myself: as a scene of failed penetration, the sexual comedy of the bar's blunt but fruitless efforts leers forth into view. Refusing to be instrumentalized as a heroic sword, the bar pushes back.

Let me be blunt. Sidney's blunt bar conjoins two distinct but equally blunt observations, one from suicidology and the other from genre theory. Suicidologists such as Thomas Joiner have argued that what distinguishes those at risk of voluntary death from those who actually die is, quite simply, the acquisition of "the ability to enact lethal self-injury."[33] You might want to die, but if you don't have easy access to a way to kill yourself, you are likely to live. In providing an object for the job but ensuring that it will fail, Sidney's authorial agency shows up as the material preemption of Pyrocles's characterological agency: Pyrocles has not been given "the right tool for the job." This withholding is precisely in keeping with a broad observation, no less blunt, from genre theory: Terentian five-act comedies do not kill main characters.[34] Genre as a relational system of constraints upon narrative outcomes tends, in its broad outlines, to confirm that tragic plots end in accelerating sequences of deaths, while comic plots end in forgiveness, reconciliation, marriage, and (mostly) survival. As Stephen Neale puts it, "The existence of genres means that the spectator, precisely, will always know that everything will be 'made right in the end,' that everything will cohere, that any threat or any danger in the narrative process will always be contained."[35] Though Neale's context is Hollywood rather than Arcadia, these blunt observations suit the occasion of Sidney's blunt bar. The bar is genre's safety railing, effectively "childproofing" Sidney's romance from lethal self-injury.

But we are not done with the bar. What follows is one of the more curious scenes in early modern literature, as Pyrocles and Philoclea bat arguments for and against the right to end one's life back and forth as if at a university debating club, while one conversational partner spasmodically attempts to turn theory into practice by taking stabs at himself with this blunt object. Lurching between violent action and prolix discussion (in his commonplace book, Milton notes this passage as "disputed with exquisite reasoning"; Langley aptly describes the scene as "exhaustive and impressively informed"), the resulting colloquy wants it both ways: the sheer extent of its argumentative layout suggests a leisurely symposium, but Pyrocles's repeated attempts on his own life raise the stakes beyond rhetorical victory.[36] The emblematic rigging of the debate—Pyrocles has blunt objects and blunter arguments—cannot quite ensure that Philoclea will succeed in driving her own point home.

Eventually, action upstages argument. The debate risks dragging on at torturous length until, finally unpersuaded, when Pyrocles attempts to kill himself yet again, Philoclea physically intervenes:

> With that, he would have used the bar, meaning if that failed to leave his brains upon the wall, when Philoclea, now brought to that she most feared, kneeled down unto him, and embracing so his legs that without hurting her (which for nothing he would have done) he could not rid himself from her, she did, with all the conuring words which the authority of love may lay, beseech him he would not now so cruelly abandon her.[37]

The embrace of the legs is an immediately legible gesture based in classical literary representations of supplication. As Leah Whittington has indicated in *Renaissance Suppliants: Poetry, Antiquity, Reconciliation* (2016), such a signal of abasement transvalues subject positions and reworks extreme asymmetry: "The suppliant's lowliness can sometimes be a source of extraordinary power."[38] Clasping his knees emphasizes their disparity while simultaneously enforcing a physical closeness of touch that might jar Pyrocles out of his self-absorption. Going further, Philoclea intervenes by threatening to mutilate herself and then take her own life in order to deliberately undo the preservative work that Pyrocles imagines his self-destruction might achieve. In destroying his investment in his own death as a Durkheimian "altruistic" gift that would preserve her integrity and beauty, she preemptively cancels his act. Ironically, the only way out of self-destructive fantasy is to heighten its imagined exemplarity through the threat of an unstoppable mimesis.

Sidney imagines a freedom to kill the self that would not be in conflict with freestanding divine imperatives but would somehow derive pardon from the sheer supererogatory force of chivalry, a chivalry now disastrously compromised by Pyrocles's own actions. At the level of conscious argument, both sides are engaged in a critique of the passions on behalf of reasoned judgment. Yet, as a dramatic incident, we see that displays of affect, of being "carried away" by passion, are simply more effective as determinants of action than rational argument. Passion works, and works precisely as a way to work through certain affects—not to succumb to them, but to leave them behind. To use the language of Katrin Pahl, to be caught up by an affect is to be "transported" from one affect to another.[39] The transports offered by "joy of the worm" are not always innocent. The term can connote the transport out of the world or back into the material components of the world promised by self-killing; it can also connote the *raptus*, or transfer of a virgin, implicit in the legal categories used to categorize rape. But what Pahl intends by the term is a demonstration of the manifold of "emotionality" within which we move across and between particular affects, both positive and negative; Sidney's romance, with its endlessly extensible parataxis, meandering shifts of genre and emotional intensity across its prosimetrum form, seems to me to deploy the limit case of self-killing to explore and enact such affective transports as it flirts with tragedy's fatal extremes.

Sidney is not simply shoving his romance toward tragedy in general, but toward one tragedy in particular: the story of Lucretia. Made famous by Livy's *History of Rome*, infamous by Augustine's vexed commentary in *City of God*, and rendered subsequently ubiquitous across medieval and early modern culture, Lucretia's exemplary suffering and its violent political aftermath had been in pervasive circulation for centuries.[40] Drawing upon this precedent, Pyrocles's instinctive proposal of self-killing as a response to rape makes a certain grimly intuitive sort of "sense." When Sidney presented his readers with a narrative sequence in which rape is followed by an onrush toward retributive self-murder, he was showing his sister and her circle, and his later readers, the way that a classical readymade could be relied upon to solve a pressing problem: the expected "cleanup" operation in the wake of sexual violence.

Critics of Sidney have noticed the family resemblance, with Debora Shuger terming the incident "a parody of Lucretia."[41] Perversely, like Bottom hoping to play all the roles in *Pyramus and Thisbe*, as ravisher casting himself in the role of suicide, Pyrocles aspires to occupy *both* the position of Sextus Tarquinius and that of Lucretia. In doing so, Pyrocles short-circuits the moral ricochet of the original Lucretia story in order to secure investment in the pathos of his remorse. Shifting to the language of the present, feminist philosopher Kate Manne has memorably termed emphasis upon, and emotional investment in, the feelings of a male abuser "himpathy."[42] Though the term "empathy" had yet to enter English when Sidney's text was written, we can see a kind of bid for "himpathy" *avant la lettre* here in Pyrocles's showy and self-aggrandizing bid to turn himself into a masculine Lucretia.

But we are not in a tragedy, and that makes a difference insofar as it constitutively cordons off from narrative possibility the self-murder of a principal protagonist, however questionable his deeds. Generic cues limit plot outcomes, soothing readerly anxiety with the assurance of rescue (to see this at work in a romance in which the gendered positions are otherwise, one could compare Philoclea's rescue of Pyrocles from self-destructive passion with Rinaldo's rescue of Armida from her own suicidal crisis in canto 20 of Tasso's *La gerusalemme liberata*). Describing the mediating role of genre within the *Old Arcadia*, Elizabeth Dipple reads Sidney's prose romance as implicitly structured around the underlying template of a five-act Terentian comedy.[43] The assumption of such a framework guarantees the hymeneal closure of survival into forgiveness and marriage on the other side of the trial scene, boosting confidence that attempts at voluntary death will safely remain attempts. Secure in the knowledge that a book 5 is yet to come, we are thus permitted to take stances toward Pyrocles's self-destructive turbulence of bemused, critical spectatorship instead of deathwatch alarm.

Adopting such a standpoint, we can care about the outcome of the sufferings of persons that we are also invited—to use the terminology of comedy theorist Elder Olson—*not to feel concern for*.[44] Quite simply, there is something about Pyrocles's self-seriousness that is hard to take seriously. Inviting the reader to take that stance toward him has a deflationary effect, offering a comedic rejoinder to the hold of absolute fantasies. Such sangfroid is of a piece with the comical manner that Sidney adopts across the *Old Arcadia* when depicting injury and bodily harm generally. Consider Sidney's tone of bloody burlesque when the Phagonian rebels are dispatched:

> But the first he overtook as he ran away, carrying his head as far before him as those manner of runnings are wont to do, with one blow strake it so clean off that, it falling betwixt the hands, and the body falling upon it, it made a show as though the fellow had great haste to gather up his head again. Another, the speed he made to run for the best game bare him full butt against a tree, so that tumbling back with a bruised face and a dreadful expectation, Musidorus was straight upon him, and parting with his sword one of his legs from him, left him to make a roaring lamentation that his mortar-treading was marred for ever.[45]

The vigorous Monty Python–esque slapstick of these gruesome deaths shows up for the reader as ludicrous physical comedy, but it conveys a direct classist message: this is what we do to rebels. Sidney's way of folding the "serious" into the "unserious" mediates political antagonism through the generic filter of romance conventions; these amputations are the corollary of, rather than a deviation from, the elaborate rhetorical set pieces of aristocratic gallants playing shepherd. The very decorum and elegance of the long oratorical speeches find their punctum in the eruptions of class-stabilizing violence that remind readers that ambient aristocratic ideals sit

cheek by jowl with the abjection of the rude, low, and expendable under-
class who are kept out of view until narrative expediency requires them.

However embarrassing for critics and readers in search of morally im-
proving instruction from this text, such classist cartoons are surely meant
to contribute to the *Old Arcadia*'s status as the lighthearted toy of occasional entertainment at Wilton that Sidney claimed it was.[46] The stylization of these deaths constitutes part of the moral machinery of romance:
the due punishment for rebellion is not only mutilation but buffoonery in
the midst of mutilation. While Sidney hopes to critique the "childish vehe-
mency" of passion, his own critique occasionally tips over into that very affective position.[47] What is the extent of authorial control over tone here? If
Pyrocles is not in control of his argument or his affect, is Sidney? The allegation of camp effects can trigger an uncomfortable, and perhaps unveri-
fiable, set of questions regarding authorial control, intentionality, and the
causal relations between what authors set out to do and how their works
show up for readers in time.

However much the five books of the *Old Arcadia* were, as Fulke Greville put it in his dedication to Sidney's works, "scribbled rather as pam-
phlets for entertainment" than intended as works of serious moral philosophy, the received vision of the *Old Arcadia* is that it is both a draft that
Sidney substantially revised and, even in that state, a significant document of early modern aesthetics.[48] This is in part because of the syncretic
confidence with which disparate elements from romance, pastoral, and
comedy are engaged, revisited, and blended together. The result is both
broadly inclusive in its sources and polychronic in its temporal dislocation, situating its occasionally tart engagements with contemporary politics and Elizabeth's court in an "otherwhere" at a suitably distant historical and geographic remove.

In presenting a Sidney as a poet of "uncertainty" and flux, and in flagging moments of excess and tonal failure or disjunction, I part ways with
the mainstreams of politically and religiously oriented Sidney criticism,
which tend to treat him as a highly learned master rhetorician, cooling his
heels at Wilton after bruising interactions at court and the Sidney family's always troubled financial situation forced him to lick his wounds, but
also implicitly settling scores and passing judgments through the allegorical sock puppetry of his "scribbled" entertainment. The guiding assumption of serious criticism has been that Sidney's ambition and learning produce a uniquely self-conscious sequence of public literary performances
in which he advocates for Protestant geopolitical interests, chides hesitant
Elizabethan policy, and, in the case of *The Defence of Poesy*, tartly evalu-
ates the current state of vernacular English poetics. As a commanding
and justly influential study of Sidney, Blair Worden's *The Sound of Virtue:*

Philip Sidney's "Arcadia" and Elizabethan Politics (1997), with its dense and knotty evocation of the text's complexly modulated relationship to republicanism and resistance theory, might be taken as a case in point of this broader critical consensus regarding the essential seriousness of Sidney's endeavors. While such criticism has produced thoughtful considerations of the relation of Sidney to his contexts and precursors, it must be said that such relentless high-mindedness and public-facing concerns do not entirely square with the turbulent, farcical, and occasionally jarring texture of the work itself. Though his subject is the Sidney of the *Defence* rather than that of the *Old Arcadia*, my own reading is perhaps closer in spirit to Robert Stillman's scalar recognition in *Philip Sidney and the Poetics of Renaissance Cosmopolitanism* (2008) of the "systematic downsizing" that the literary performs upon the political and ethical conflicts staged within it.[49]

If Weiner detects a faint aura of "farce" in the debate between Pyrocles and Philoclea and the curious incident of the bar in the night, I would suggest, with apologies to Sontag, that we apprehend Sidney's simultaneous overlay of intense stylization and personal excruciation as an example of what I would term "sacrificial camp." That is, Pyrocles's earnest desire to sacrifice his own life for another is a bid for seriousness, but insofar as the bar refuses to do its work, we are confronted with a striking example of Sontag's core formula for camp: "a seriousness that fails."

Hebe's Claim

Scenes of "failed seriousness" in the midst of self-sacrificial passion are not unique to Sidney. In the second half of this chapter, we pass from Pyrocles's highly wrought but ultimately unsuccessful harangue to the arresting valedictory aria of Hebe, which grinds the plot of Lyly's *Gallathea* to a halt before its fatal outcome is unexpectedly circumvented by divine comedic reprieve. The outlines of the plot in question are as follows: due to an ancient outrage against Neptune, a city on the Humber estuary must propitiate the angry sea god every five years with the sacrifice of the fairest and chastest virgin to a monster sent by the divinity, or face destruction. Two doting fathers, Tityrus and Melebeus, each convinced in the superiority of their respective child, encourage their two daughters, Gallathea and Phyllida, to escape conscription by dressing as boys and fleeing to the forest, where they meet and fall in love with each other. Adding further amorous complication, Cupid intrudes into the forest, violating the sacred hunting ground of Diana and her court of nymphs, and inspiring the nymphs, too, to fall in love with the disguised girls. An array of displaced millers' sons, mariners, alchemists, and astronomers are overlaid, and the mixture is stirred vigorously by the comedic forces of desire and mutual misprision. In an astonishing climax that adapts Ovid's tale of Iphis and Ianthe from book 9 of the *Metamorphoses*, the disguised female couple are permitted to marry as one of the girls (though we do not know which) is magically transformed into a boy.

Unsurprisingly, critical attention has been lavished upon the impudence of this conclusion, and it has launched powerful readings of the dynamic performativity of onstage transvestite disguise, the "homonormativity" of "nature's bias," and the open question of where and how to talk to about queer erotic possibility and/or its heteronormative cancellation in the Renaissance (of note here are readings by Laurie Shannon, Douglas Bruster, Valerie Traub, Phyllis Rackin, and Sarah Carter).[50] Equally unsurprisingly, many readers have noted the complex circuits of patronage, flattery, and critique at work in the play's feinting gestures toward Queen Elizabeth's personal predicament in the wake of the failed seriousness of her last plausible consideration of marriage. The play functions as part of an ongoing argument about Lyly's tumultuous career as a court artist (a process that began with R. Warwick Bond's biography and early studies by John Dover Wilson and G. K. Hunter, and has carried on with subsequent adjustments from Philippa Berry, Ellen Caldwell, Kent Cartwright, and Leah Scragg).[51]

Most recently, Andy Kesson has forcefully overturned generations of critical doxa around Lyly, advocating for a renewed interest in Lyly's work, in particular with regard to the richness and complexity of female dramatic representation that it affords. In contrast to the minor and garish figure that studs orals lists but is rarely the subject of prolonged critical scrutiny aside from hat-tipping gestures toward his impact on the evolution of English prose style, Kesson's Lyly is less "Euphuistic," less courtly, more ambitious, and more mercurial. Tilting against the minor reputation, Kesson waxes not so much reparative as evangelical: "Lyly reorganized the prose sentence, found a new voice for subversive irony, and showed his contemporaries how to rewrite the rules for dramatic composition."[52] While I may at times rehearse the painful disparagements that have been brought against Lyly's art, and against the effect and impact of his style in particular, I hope to lend support to Kesson's attempt to assert the subversive energies at work within Lyly's texts.

A wallflower at the critical dance, the figure of Hebe has languished in relative obscurity. In speaking of "Hebe's claim," I borrow luster from Judith Butler's account of Antigone's "promiscuous obedience" as a disruptive gesture that pits heroic self-killing against the imperatives of state violence, and I do so as a form of camp travesty: like Antigone, Hebe longs to die for a cause, but she has the bad luck to be a minor character in a tragicomic play.[53] Given that we are talking about a company of child actors in which everyone on stage is technically a minor, this last word must be handled carefully. But even in that context, Hebe makes an unexpected and expansionist bid for the center of what Alex Woloch has taught us to call "character-space."[54]

At the imagined catastrophe of the play, in act 5, when it is time to yield up the required fair virgin, Hebe is brought forward as a possible replacement for the vanished Gallathea and Phyllida, a last-minute understudy for tragic centrality. "Passionate" and "naïve," Hebe would seem tailor-made for camp's strategic blend of identification and detachment;[55] and she launches with eloquence and energy into an elaborate, indeed show-stopping, speech of farewell, only to suffer the unkindest fate of all: rejection at the altar. Insufficiently fair, the sea monster refuses to eat her and she is led offstage in disgrace by carping attendants, her moment over. It is Hebe's fate, within and without the play, that interests me. As sacrificial citizen, scapegoat, comic butt, pathetic victim, and potential object of camp pleasure, Hebe solicits interpretation, protection, defense, redress—but what are we to make of Hebe's desire to die? What are we to make of Lyly's desire to "camp" the will to self-sacrifice at the center of this play? And how might that open out our understanding of how "self-killing" extends toward a terrain that takes us beyond the mood-disorder paradigm of "suicide"?

Lyly takes a perverse delight in freighting his frothy comedy with tragic heaviness its slender frame can barely support, while also slyly undercutting our faith in the justice of the sacrificial demand.[56] Since in the frame narrative Tityrus both establishes a transgression (Neptune was offended) and relocates its cause overseas in a bygone past (it was the visiting Danes, not the local citizenry of the Humber area, who in fact committed the outrage), the justness of the divine cause is destabilized and called into question; we sense that the god must be honored but that those who die in order to do so will shed "guiltless blood."

Questions of guilt and perversity are raised explicitly, but also rerouted, in act 4, by the village Augur, who confronts the town with the stark choice it faces if the god is slighted: yield up a victim or die. Beneath the glassy surface of its author's rhetoric, the Augur's speech churns with victim-blaming sophistry: "If you think it against nature to sacrifice your children, think it also against sense to destroy your country. If you imagine Neptune pitiless to desire such a prey, *confess yourselves perverse* to deserve such punishment" (4.1.4–5; italics mine). The pendant suspension of Lyly's syntax here requires care in its decoupling: an exemplary dialectical machine, such parallelism sublates the very distinctions it also indicates, leveraging the experience of sonic similarity into an implicit argument for the fitness of its tendentious equations and sleights of hand. Here the formal neatness of the Augur's singsong assertion that "if the pitiless desire prey, the perverse deserve punishment" almost, but not quite, covers over its own violent reification of predation-as-justice. Following from the preceding contrast between "nature" and "sense," the Augur's declaration rehearses the historical temporality of blame (humans offended Neptune, humans are to blame) in order to ground the ongoing circularity of ritual time, a looping return to the scene of the crime that sacrificial gestures can acknowledge but never conclusively redress. Since we know from Tityrus's opening speech that it is all the fault of the Danes anyway, the Augur's rhetoric reopens the question it tries to resolve.

The Augur speaks in order to silence the claim of pity, and the threat it poses to communal self-preservation. In a Girardian reading of the framing narrative, Jacqueline Vanhoutte notes that:

> the English community with which Gallathea is concerned closely resembles the primitive pastoral communities studied by Girard in *Violence and the Sacred*. According to Girard, sacrifice forms the basis of such communities because it harnesses the internal violence of individual members and re-directs it into a "proper channel." … The sacred provides a mechanism by which the "impure" violence of the community is transmuted, and catharsized, into the "pure" violence of sacrifice. The divine thus becomes an external projection of internal, communal violence.[57]

But the Augur's speech can be read against the grain of this Girardian explanation. The Augur's prolix repetitions work to massage away the sacrilegious option that his speech acknowledges but seeks to banish: the possibility that the community might refuse the sacrifice and thus risk, or even embrace, collective destruction. To do so would be perverse, because it would betray the community's mandate to preserve itself, its collective conatus. The spectator caught in the throes of pity must thereby confess herself perverse, and be brought to see her own attachment to the sacrificial object as a form of political bad faith with the future of her own community. This would be tragic-business-as-usual, were it not for the comedic outcome that breaks the guilt-sacrifice-expiation circuit and reveals the arbitrary injustice at its core. In the toss-up between Gallathea and Phyllida as potential offerings to the monster, what matters is not which of the two will be offered, but the simple fact that one of them will be. Indeed, this is the very logic that returns in their sexual transformation. The exemplary virtues of the sacrificial victim ("the fairest and chastest virgin") are insistently hyperbolic and singular. The rhythm of regular feedings reveals a cyclic machine at work, but the cynical substitutability of agents functions rather like the casting machinery for a company of rapidly aging-out boy actors: each one is the fairest, until the next one is.

This tottering mechanism grinds spectacularly to a halt in act 5, scene 2, when an all-too-willing substitute for the departed Gallathea and Phyllida is brought forward. Reminding the audience of the sacrificial occasion, Lyly primes the pump of audience expectation with an ominous prelude:

AUGUR: Bring forth the virgin, the fatal virgin, the fairest virgin, if you mean
    to appease Neptune and preserve your country.
ERICTHINIS: Here she cometh, accompanied only with men, because it is a
    sight unseemly, as all virgins say, to see the misfortune of a maiden, and
    terrible to behold the fierceness of Agar, that monster.

[*Enter Hebe with others to the sacrifice.*] (5.2.1–6)

What follows is a set piece of extended speech, a torrent of pathos and language that works overtime to achieve the aura of seriousness, elevated style, and emotional intensity suitable to an occasion that, in its broad outlines, connotes the putative generic essence of tragedy long promised but so far deferred: the sad spectacle of a virtuous character suffering unjustly a sacrificial fate she does not deserve. From Sophocles's Antigone and Euripides's Iphigenia, in Greek tragedy, to Jephthah's daughter "bewailing her virginity," in Judges 11:39 (and recreated in the drama of George Buchanan), the figure of the doomed, solitary woman accepting her fate instantaneously telegraphs a familiar tragic plotline of mounting dread building to climactic sacrificial violence.

Embracing the occasion, Hebe launches into a rhetorical tour de force:

Miserable and accursed Hebe, that being neither fair nor fortunate, thou
shouldst be thought most happy and beautiful. Curse thy birth, thy life, thy
death, being born to live in danger, and, having liv'd, to die by deceit. Art
thou the sacrifice to appease Neptune and satisfy the custom, the bloody
custom, ordained for the safety of thy country? Ay Hebe, poor Hebe, men
will have it so, whose powers dally with our purpose. The Egyptians never
cut their dates from the tree because they are so fresh and green. It is
thought wickedness to pull roses from the stalks in the garden of Palestine,
for that they have so lively a red; and whoso cutteth the incense tree in Arabia,
before it fall, committeth sacrilege. Shall it be only lawful amongst us
in the prime of youth and pride of beauty to destroy both youth and beauty,
and what was honored in fruits and flowers as a virtue to violate in a virgin
as a vice? But, alas, destiny alloweth no dispute. (5.2.6–24)

Though we would do well to heed Kesson's skeptical objections to the term "Euphuism" as a critical fabrication unknown to early moderns, it is hard not to hear this passage as the lulling sound of "Euphuism" as a syntactic tic, a trick of pendant suspension and equipoise that dazzles as it numbs.[58] Portable to any occasion and subject matter, Euphuism's emphasis upon display and indifference to local occasion models a certain kind of courtly formality that is, itself, antithetical to the strong passions purportedly here being expressed; such control exemplifies M. C. Bradbrook's remark that in Lyly we see "an impossibly elegant world, which in its simplified outline and heightened speech makes no attempt at naturalism."[59] The distance between the occasion and the feeling might be just as, if not more, substantive in the production of a camp effect as Hebe's infelicitous failure to arouse. Reflections upon the gardening habits of Egypt and Palestine can hardly be a top priority for someone who is tied to a tree and about to be eaten, but in Lyly's exquisitely stylized world they are altogether apt. Here we are hearing the Euphuism machine go to work on a received idea: the pathetic death of the beautiful virgin at the hands of a sea monster.

Hebe's status as suitably beautiful victim is open to doubt. Indeed, her step into the sacrificial limelight might be read as a bid for what Lauren Berlant, describing an altogether distinct historical, racial, and political context in American culture, terms "Diva Citizenship": "when a person stages a dramatic coup in a public sphere in which she does not have privilege. Flashing up and startling the public, she puts the dominant story into suspended animation."[60] Hebe interrupts the symmetry of the Gallathea-Phyllida romance, gate-crashing into the space reserved for the "fairest virgin in the village." And yet, as Hebe herself acknowledges in her reference to "deceit," she is *not* the fairest virgin in the village. Does this thereby make her ugly, and would that ugliness in turn make her somehow worthy of being the object of mockery and ridicule, if not the violence and death mandated by the plot? Is she unattractive, or is she simply, relative to the seemingly shareable yet absolute status imputed to both Gallathea and Phyllida, "not the fairest"? If the sheer misogyny of these unsatisfying options risks spoiling the prospects of camp fun before it starts, the issue cannot be avoided: it is central to Lyly's high-contrast effects of hyperbolic, aureate extremity that his goddesses, nymphs, and prettiest girls in the village find their foils in the awkward, the ugly, the monstrous.[61]

Though we are tipped off by Hebe herself midspeech, this status as "ugly" is seemingly confirmed in the wake of the sea monster's failure to arrive and consume her, when Neptune cruelly passes judgment: "To be young and fair shall be accounted shame and punishment, insomuch as it shall be thought as dishonorable to be honest as fortunate to be deformed" (5.3.17–20). Within the dramatic frame that Lyly ultimately fashions, Neptune is the blowhard, whose promises of blood vengeance go unrealized in the Diana-Venus peace treaty that concludes the play. But whether or not his language of deformity triggered snorts of laughter at Hebe's fate, it may be rooted in the core text of early modern genre theory, Aristotle's *Poetics*, not yet translated into English at this point, but known via its Arabic and Latin and Italian translations, and in the commentaries of Madius, Robortello, Scaliger, Castelvetro, Joubert, and others.[62] Ugliness and deformity, within certain bounded limits, are central qualities of the comic genre. Let us return to the epochal passage in which Aristotle defines comedy as "a representation of people who are rather inferior; not, however with respect to every [kind of] vice, but the laughable is [only] a part of what is ugly. For the laughable is a sort of error and ugliness that is not painful and destructive, just as, evidently, a laughable mask is something ugly and distorted without pain."[63] When, in the wake of the failure of the sacrifice, we overhear that Hebe is described as "deformed," we may object that this overstates the case considerably, but it would have been a kind of essential marker of the generic requirements established by Aristotle for comedic characters. It retroactively reifies her as the proper object of mockery. In presuming a status she does not deserve, Hebe's "ugliness" (real or imagined) is thereby converted into a personal failing that reinforces her flawed, hence unfit, status as sacrificial victim.

Hebe's overdetermined status as less-than-she-appears is arguably rooted in the complex webs of beauty and pride around which one of the classical sources for Lyly's drama turns: the legend of Andromeda as relayed by Ovid. Andromeda's presentation to the sea monster was punishment for her mother Cassiopeia's boast that her daughter's beauty exceeded that of the Nereids. In the Ovidian retelling, the boastfulness of the mother is balanced against the daughter's reticence and virginal modesty, here described as Perseus interrogates the shy virgin: "As he continued to urge her, she, lest she should seem to be concealing some fault of her own, told him her name and her country, and what sinful boasting her mother had made of her own beauty."[64] Measured against the modesty of the Ovidian original, Hebe's recognition that she has been offered in "deceit" sets in motion the wheels of mockery that will come to engulf her pathetic speech of submission.

But we are not done with the mythological complexity that Lyly is here rehearsing, for Hebe, in relaying her own name, further tangles the prospects of audience sympathy. "Hebe" denotes the goddess of youth and the daughter of Zeus and Hera; in marking her youthfulness, the pathos of her seemingly imminent death is amplified.[65] G. K. Hunter suggests a passing allusion to Hebe's supersession by Ganymede as Zeus's cupbearer: just as the mythological Hebe was found "insufficient" for a sacred office by the gods because she inadvertently exposed herself while serving nectar, so too that mark of insufficiency is carried over here.[66] Yet Anne Lancashire, in her earlier edition of the play, draws our attention to the fact that, in Latin, the word "hebes" denotes "dull, stupid, dim, faint, and sluggish."[67] Faced with these available but uncertain implications, what sort of pejorative thrust did Lyly intend with this name? Despite and in the very teeth of her eloquent capacity to construct Euphuistic rhetoric, her investment in a tragic seriousness to which she is not entitled shows her up as clueless, obtuse.

Unaware of the distorted genre space in which she is enmeshed, Hebe relentlessly goes on. In doing so, the sheer extent of her arresting speech achieves a pathos that sharply exceeds the terms of engagement that Lyly's play has so far set for itself, even as the increasingly hammered fact of her own name works to ramp up the likelihood that her complaints are the windup for a comedic punchline:

> Die, Hebe, Hebe, die, woeful Hebe and only accursed Hebe. Farewell the sweet delights of life, and welcome now the bitter pangs of death. Farewell you chaste virgins, whose thoughts are divine, whose faces fair, whose fortunes are agreeable to your affections. Enjoy and long enjoy the pleasure of your curled locks, the amiableness of your wished looks, the sweetness of your tuned voices, the content of your inward thoughts, the pomp of your outward shows. Only Hebe biddeth farewell to all the joys that she conceived and you hope for, that she possessed and you shall. (5.2.25-35)

With the notable exception of Kesson, previous critics, when they have discussed Hebe at all, have taken her, as it were, straight. Hunter praises the "exquisite refinement of the emotions" and notes "the evocation of the tenderness of virginal feelings."[68] As if at a wine tasting, Hunter observes that "what would have been cloying without the spice of danger, what would have been rather heartless without these hints of flowery tenderness, becomes by the combination of the two a more affecting and effective image."[69] One might well want to consider the ethics involved in turning the prospect of rape and death into a mere "spice of danger" (as it turns out, the camp reading is arguably just as misogynist); for now I simply want to contest Hunter's reading on tonal, rather than ethical, grounds.

Hebe's dilation is provocative, a willful claiming of space that stands out against the backdrop of a play in which child actors keep the tempo brisk through tightly interlaced volleys of witty stichomythia. Hebe's "enjoy and long enjoy" exemplifies her passive-aggressive stance more broadly across the scene: as a masochistic embrace of her fate, it obviously contrasts the imagined life of pleasure that awaits the surviving members of the community with the imminent pain and death that will secure that life, and yet the languor of her "enjoy and long enjoy" also stretches out the showstopping moment in which that sacrifice is announced with a flex of diva citizenship. It registers the unbearable force of self-destructive desire at work in this context of compulsory social pressure. It also offers us the cue, as if we needed one, that this speech is failing. As Cicero warns in his exposition on the turn toward the emotions, it is hard to sustain peaks of pathos, because "nothing dries faster than tears."[70]

On a surface level, these benevolent farewells from one about to die a virgin recall Antigone's cry that she dies "without marriage, without bridal, having no share in wedlock or in the rearing of children," and lay claim to the ethical force of an exemplary submission on behalf of community.[71] But they are spiced with an eagerness that risks toppling over into something else, a performance that, in its excess, registers an affective charge of intolerable pleasure in the prospect of subjective annihilation, which we can hear in the imperative cry: "Die, Hebe, Hebe, die, woeful Hebe and only accursed Hebe." What was tender and admirable when immediately and succinctly expressed by Gallathea, the "proper" object of this violent threat, becomes comedic, estranged, and grating in its repetitious extension from the wrong girl, the "ugly" girl, whose desire erupts here and claims our attention. One thinks of Saint-Évremond's 1675 text "My Opinion of a Play Where the Heroine Does Nothing but Lament Herself."[72] And this excess of wretchedness and wretched excess redouble each other until the putative "ugliness" and the fact of rhetorical amplification become circuitous confirmations of each other.

Eventually, the long arc of Hebe's ramping pathos reaches a climactic peak. In that peak one is tempted to identify the operation of the death drive throbbing beneath the sheltering twin covers of an ambient Christian *contemptus mundi* tradition and an emergent early modern neo-Stoicism of suffering and acceptance:

> Farewell, vain life, wretched life, whose sorrows are long, whose end doubtful, whose miseries certain, whose hopes innumerable, whose fears intolerable. Come, death, and welcome, death, whom nature cannot resist, because necessity ruleth, nor defer, because destiny hasteth. Come, Agar, thou unsatiable monster of maiden's blood and devourer of beauties' bowels, glut thyself till thou surfeit, and let my life end thine. Tear these tender joints with thy greedy jaws, these yellow locks with thy black feet, this fair face with thy foul teeth. Why abates thou thy wonted swiftness? I am fair, I am a virgin, I am ready. Come, Agar, thou horrible monster, and farewell world, thou viler monster. (5.2. 45–57)

In this flashing juxtaposition of "yellow locks" and "black feet" within an imagined scenario of sacrifice/rape, Lyly's language draws energy from, and reinforces, an emergent discourse of race thinking that structures white women as objects of violence by evoking the threat of the black male rapist that here momentarily subtends the monstrosity of the Agar; this flickering racialization of an unseen threat works to heighten its affective intensity, but it is also something of a trick on Lyly's part at Hebe's expense. If, in the words of Arthur Little Jr. that form this chapter's epigraph, "sacrifice enters cultural play very much as a trick, as a hoax," here the "trick" is not simply the substitution of Hebe for other village girls, but the sleight of hand by which Hebe is made ridiculous for articulating a racialized cluster of desires and fears that the text both solicits and encourages us to disavow.[73]

In the cascade from jaws tearing joints to feet stomping hair, in the delirious epithet of "beauties' bowels," we topple from sublime horror to ridiculous breaches in decorum, an excess that plunges from pathos to bathos. To just come out and say it, I hear this speech as simultaneously passionately sincere in its subject position of utterance and as ludicrous and laughable upon arrival in its generic context. It is certainly possible that a key component of what renders it laughable, what grants permission for the listener to hear this speech against the grain of its situation, is precisely that, in its final arcing phrase, what we hear is not fear or aversion but the imperative of demand: "I am fair, I am a virgin, I am ready. Come!" While some might hear only inadvertent innuendo in this statement, to my ears this sounds like desire, desire in the midst of self-destruction. This is, in other words, "joy of the worm," for here we are confronted by a particularly molten example of what Adrian Johnston has termed the "alloys" of libido and death drive.[74] As readers or audience members, what are we to do with this desire? And how to control the pleasurable scandal of its failure to generate the expected response?

If Hebe's star turn as sacrificial victim is a bid to achieve tragic seriousness through the willful embrace of her own death, then in witnessing the deflationary anticlimax of a sea monster that refuses to arrive on cue, we are witnessing "a seriousness that fails," and thus, Hebe, like Pyrocles before her, passes through the valley of the shadow of death and into the territory of early modern camp.

Hebe attempts to claim for herself tragic generic contours within an artwork that is cannily and intentionally serving up those contours for an audience presumed to share a certain sophisticated familiarity with classical tragedy and Ovidian myth, a certain sensibility that, in a comic mode, avows "irony over tragedy." By this reading, Lyly, and Sidney before him, are practitioners of the most fragile of Sontag's exempla: deliberate camp, a fraught and hybrid space whose primary examples in "Notes on 'Camp'" come from film.[75] While Sontag praises performances in which a cannily camp-savvy male director coaxes the requisite passionate naivete out of an actress (her example is Fellini directing Anita Ekberg in *La dolce vita*), most works of deliberate camp arrive stillborn, because they cannot escape the circular constraint of the very knowingness that occasions their own construction. They are mere self-parody, and lack the lightness of touch in the midst of excess that camp requires.[76]

With Hebe, Lyly has constructed an unselfconscious and naive girl caught at the nexus of death and desire and, most deliciously of all, unaware of the generic frame that encloses her failed seriousness in the ongoing project of comedy's successful nonseriousness. But here we encounter a strong potential obstacle to my reading: the violent extremity of Hebe's situation. If we flinch at her image of the jaws tearing into the flesh, then her pronounced terror sours the fun. Some critics do, indeed, insist upon this, and hence do not hear the speech as laughable at all.[77] Indeed, taken straight, Hebe occupies a position with respect to her social surround that philosopher Jill Stauffer terms "ethical loneliness": her solitary trauma is denied recognition and, in that denial, redoubled.[78] Furthermore, the norms advocated by at least some authors in early modern genre theory about proper objects of laughter might have encouraged sympathy toward Hebe's case; as Marvin Herrick relays in *Comic Theory in the Sixteenth Century*, Madius, in his *De ridiculis* (1550), notes "three classes of people that should not be laughed at: the poverty-stricken, the wicked, and the virtuous. Paupers, unless they are insolent, deserve pity rather than ridicule; the wicked merit hate; *ridicule of the virtuous is contrary to good taste*."[79] In judging the world itself the "viler monster," an actor looks out at the court as it laughs at a girl about to be killed for the sake of the community and passes lonely judgment upon them. Hebe's claim upon our sympathies can face-plant into camp, but, contrariwise, it can also force its way toward an ethical referendum on the limits of camp.

What if camp as the delectation of "failed seriousness" constitutes a prophylactic limit to our sympathetic investments, insofar as it requires, to take up Derrida's account of irony, the negative certitude of a decisive judgment of failure in order for its pleasure of recuperation to proceed?[80] Far from offering a redemptive means by which to love artworks, or characters within them, that have passed beyond the frame and become "too much," embarrassing, dated, or passé, camp might also be a stumbling block to a more cogent set of responses. In particular, the cross identification implicit in a time-honored gay male practice of adoration-cum-mockery of suffering female figures (in opera, popular music, and film) stands open to reconsideration here as a gendered form of solidarity always haunted by the prepositional question of whether camp's devotees are laughing at or siding with its characters.[81] If Hebe as "ugly girl" and "failed sacrificial victim" precipitated a certain kind of laughter in the audience in 1588— and I think, but cannot prove, that it did—what would it mean to want to do justice to the full complexity of Lyly's text at the present moment? Would doing justice mean reinscribing camp's ludic imperatives, or surrendering them to the pileup of passé pleasures?

If this is a moment of genuine terror at the prospect of rape and death, then it becomes, or ought to become, harder to insist that it is also a moment of comedy at a potential rape victim's expense. As Aristotelian genre theory had made clear, comedic plot scenarios had to stop just short of genuine injury or damage. We may realize full well that we are witnessing a comic play, but Hebe does not know that. Early modern literature did not, of course, shy away from depicting rape as humorous, as the light comedy of Hellenore's multiple "ravishments" in book 3 of Spenser's *Faerie Queene* makes all too clear.[82] Across the archive, genre tends to condition and frame the extent to which we extend or suspend sympathy, and in the process contours response. Giving us not tragedy but "tragedy" as comic springboard, like Pyrocles's hapless flailing with a blunt instrument, Lyly's camp staging encourages us to laugh at Hebe's excruciation while still feeling her pathos.

Suppose They Give a Human Sacrifice and No One Comes?

Having begun this chapter in the warm glow of a bar band looping Cyndi Lauper's "Time after Time," we must now relocate to a chilly forest outside Paris, where a huddled group of acolytes assembles to celebrate mystic rites. In 1937, as polarization and panic set in among the political radicals of Paris, Georges Bataille founded a secret society.[83] This group was actually a group within a group, an assemblage of adepts nested within the larger assemblage of the College of Sociology, whose institutional ambition belied its status as a series of talks in a bookstore. Behind closed doors, inspired by the dream vision of a headless body rushing toward him, Bataille founded the mystical sodality of Acéphale, and extended invitations to a small circle of initiates to join him by swearing an oath of absolute allegiance unto death. Given the strong injunctions against describing their actions to outsiders both during its active period and in the wake of its dissolution, Acéphale has been subject to rumor and misrepresentation, most of which hinge upon a widely spread rumor that the group was abandoned when Bataille asked its members to sacrifice him in the woods.

It would be easy to foist a "wild psychoanalysis" interpretation onto these ambitions: in the wake of the death of Bataille's lover Laure, Bataille

enters a grief-stricken longing to join her in death. Immersed in the theorization of sacrifice as a binding force of social energies, Bataille appropri-
ates the theories of the College of Sociology to provide a mystical cover for
his own suicidal ideation. What is refused throughout this archive, above
all by Bataille himself, is an underlying specter which is occulted even
from the occult. That specter is comedy:

> If there is anyone among us who thinks that what has been agreed between
> us will not be real, that there will be ways out of it, that any slackness will
> only be suppressed in our writings and not in our actions, then it is time for
> him to withdraw; he must realise that what exists between us is inflexible
> and that it is something that will make an impact; *it might become a tragedy,*
> *but it will not in any circumstances end in comedy.*[84]

Like Dostoyevsky's command to his brother not to think of a white bear, so
too with Bataille's hapless codicil: nothing prompts comedy quite like humorlessness. Yet if Bataille feared comedy, his deeper affective goal was a
familiar emotion that will concern me throughout this book: joy. Enumerating the propositions of Acéphale, Bataille leaps into all caps: "The fundamental principle of the organization is JOY IN THE FACE OF DEATH,"
a phrase that returns in the letter of invitation to the adept Louis Couturier
dated May 17, 1939: "The tree we meet at is an ancient oak that has been
struck by lightning. The Sulphur we use calls to mind volcanoes. Lightning and volcanoes are connected for us with 'joy in the face of death.'"[85]

While it would be tendentious in the extreme to attempt to align the
acute particulars of Bataille's emotional and political situation with either
Sidney's Pyrocles or Lyly's Hebe, it would be dishonest if I did not admit that I do perceive a resonance and that is why I have conjoined them
here. The high-altitude extremity of Bataille's justifications for his death—
justifications that, it must be said, do not convince those closest to him—
resembles the sententious but unpersuasive oratory of Sidney's hero and
the passionate rejection of surrounding political injustice in which Hebe
was momentarily caught up. We have in the feverish climb to the fatal
event and its whimper of implosion a similar narrative arc: a long and passionate windup to a disappointing anticlimax. Bataille's fevered invocation of the logic of sacrifice as a powerfully magical sacred act of violence
rebounds, produces a distinct letdown, a cooling of affective investment, a
humdrum surrender to the contingencies of everyday survival. The group
was disbanded because no one felt like taking part in the very act that was
supposed to verify their collective passion. Failed seriousness prevails.
Whether we are back in our bar where a Cyndi Lauper song is playing
or reading early modern literature in our study, what all these incidents

share is that they are stories about a proximity to death that does not result in actual death. These are stories about approximations, close calls, near misses.

They contribute to an archive of parasuicidal feeling, and attending to such stories—in other words, taking failed seriousness seriously—can allow us to compensate for a standing bias within discussions of self-killing, which are frequently lopsided by their emphasis upon what suicidologists once called "completed suicide." While the numbers are, by their nature, not entirely reliable, the number of attempted suicides outnumbers completed suicides by a considerable margin: the American Foundation for Suicide Prevention asserts that for every completed suicide in the United States there are twenty-five attempts.[86] If 44,000 people kill themselves in the United States each year, then the number who attempt is upward of 1,100,000.[87] The number of those who suffer from suicidal ideation or intrusive thoughts about self-harm is larger still, and is estimated at 9.3 million.[88] Though their particular ratios were different, what evidence there is suggests that the phenomenon of ample instances of ideation, a smaller number of attempts, and a much smaller number of completed self-killings that characterizes the modern era was also true in early modern England: as Michael MacDonald and Terence Murphy describe in *Sleepless Souls: Suicide in Early Modern England*, the case histories of the physician Richard Napier offer a ratio of 11 completed suicides, 57 attempted suicides, and 99 patients who discussed the desire to die openly.[89]

Which is to say that the discursive field governed by the desire to kill the self greatly exceeds the relatively smaller subset of the population who carry this desire out. How do we talk about talking about self-killing? As Edwidge Danticat puts it, "Death always wants to hog the stage."[90] What if the scene-stealing, definitive importance of completed self-killing means that far more common experiences—suffering intrusive thoughts about one's own death, longing to die, trying and failing to die—are being considered only in their relation to frustrated, virtual outcomes?

These questions prompt a further question, a question that is not camp at all, but that seems to me to speak to the core issue prompted by these scenes from the *Old Arcadia* and *Gallathea*, situated as they are at the vexed intersection of the aesthetic and the ethical: as critics and readers, how ought we to comport ourselves in relation to artworks that powerfully recirculate the desire to die? This is a matter of intersubjective comportment, but it's also about our thresholds for vicarious habituation and exposure to other people's affects. Whether we are in the classroom or playing in a cover band in a bar or wandering in the fog of our own solitary ideation: How far do we let the desire to die articulate itself before we intervene?

When the longing to die becomes a rhetorical performance of a plan to act, part of responding is precisely evaluating its seriousness, determining whether or not this is a passing mood, a tentative threat, or a serious feeling. If it is the last of these, such a determination occasions a mixture of acknowledgment and resistance: we must both take such announcements seriously—in the sense that, at the level of action, we want to prevent such actions—and also reject or withhold assent to their possibility. Whether we are begging someone on our knees or singing the same pop song ten times, the labor of persuasion that taking suicide seriously asks of us can be burdensome, demanding; it calls for skills of improvisation and accommodation for the demands of someone else, even as we try to hold fast to our refusal of their core demand.

Against the backdrop of this phenomenological description of the encounter with the demand to die, why bring up the camp paradigm of "failed seriousness" at all? The risks of trivializing a serious subject, of seeming to disregard or flatten genuine human suffering on behalf of an outmoded aesthetic category looms rather large as an occupational hazard of such a response. To offer a last-ditch justification for the power of camp as a means of frame breaking—itself a betrayal of camp's spirit—I offer this: *camp's refusal to take self-killing seriously might be a way to brace ourselves against the affective undertow that pulls us toward self-killing in the first place.*

Alternately energizing and deflating bids for pathos, "joy of the worm" shifts valence as it moves up and down distinct scalar levels. From the perspective of would-be self-sacrificial agents, "joy of the worm" surfaces in the witty playfulness of Pyrocles's narcissistic investment in his own speech acts of threatened self-harm, and in the erotic charge that Hebe ramps toward as she imagines her own imminent death. From a contrary direction, "joy of the worm" surfaces in the authorial pleasure of deliberate sabotage that Sidney and Lyly take as they invite us to resist the claims that Pyrocles and Hebe make upon our sympathetic investment. Perceiving voluntary death as a stylized act, perceiving it as a worn-out cultural gesture, perceiving it as, precisely, a stock trope capable of generating camp effects might itself be a way of refusing to take self-killing seriously so as to protect one's readers, one's audience members, one's friends, oneself from the bad form of seriousness at the core of the urge to die. In defiance of its own seeming critical exhaustion, camp offers a technology of survival.

CHAPTER TWO

Slapstick and *Synapothanumenon* in *Antony and Cleopatra*

It is not worth the bother of killing yourself,
since you always kill yourself too late.

EMIL CIORAN, *The Trouble with Being Born*

Let's Keep Going!

I want to begin at the ending. But not, yet, the ending of *Antony and Cleopatra*. Rather, let's start at the ending of *Thelma and Louise*, Ridley Scott's 1991 paean to suicide and /as the couple form.[1] The film's extramarital adventures conclude in a denouement so notorious that "spoiler warnings" seem spurious, but—spoiler—when the festive comedy of road-movie wanderings leads to drawn weapons and orders to surrender from scandalized tokens of the patriarchy, Geena Davis's Thelma Dickinson and Susan Sarandon's Louise Sawyer look deeply into each other's eyes, kiss, and go for it, driving off a cliff and into history. They die together. Or do they? We do not hear or see the crash, as the film, in a canny *Aufhebung* of the classic cliffhanger ending, fades to white before the moment of impact, massaging finitude with a choral swell. Is this happy or sad? A lesbian *Liebestod* or a fast, fatal friendship? Beautiful or pathological? A tragicomic all of the above?

Regardless of the world's oppressive need to know, Thelma and Louise have surely achieved what looks to us today like a familiar romantic ideal: neither outlasts the other, both are in perfect synchronization, without the asymmetrical mourning duties that arise from what Michael Cobb has termed "the inevitable fatality of the couple."[2] If suicide pacts are tragic, then why does this conclusion feel so ecstatically joyous, and where did this ideal commence?

The Greeks had a word for it: *synapothanumenon*, the "order or agreement of those who will die together." This word enters English, briefly, when it appears in Thomas North's translation of *Plutarch's Lives*, in his account of the changing tone of the Alexandrian revels that Antony and Cleopatra keep together as they affirm their own mutual bonds in the face of encroaching geopolitical disaster and defeat. It shows up as a new dispensation among the lover's intimate circle of associates as the decisive military failure at Actium transvalues their ongoing potlatch of sovereign expenditure into a reciprocally binding obligation to die:

> For these things there was kept great feasting, banqueting, and dancing in Alexandria many days together. Indeed, they did break their first order they had set down, which they called *Amimetobion* (as much to say, no life comparable), and did set up another, which they called *Synapothanume-non* (signifying the order and agreement of those that will die together), the which exceeding sumptuousness and cost was not inferior to the first. For their friends made themselves to be enrolled in this order of those that would die together, and so made great feasts one to another; for every man, when it came to his turn, feasted their whole company and fraternity.[3]

Antony and Cleopatra's coinage, if that is what it was, itself relays and plays upon a prior term that was ready to hand from Greek drama: *synapothne-skontes* (men dying together), a title of now-lost comic plays by both Diph-ilus and, later, Alexis.[4] In particular, Diphilus's now-lost play offered a model for Plautus's *Commorientes* and for a scene in Terence's *Adelphoi* (Brothers).[5] A chic literary reference to Greek originals, the reworking of these titles and phrases is a status-confirming gesture in keeping with Antony and Cleopatra's place at the apex of their respective Roman and Macedonian/Ptolemaic elites.[6] But if it is of a piece with prevalent tastes and habits of the ruling class of the period, it also does a specific emotional work, finding in literary precursors a frame through which to aggressively transvalue an impending political tragedy into a comedic confraternity. This morbid nickname might make the inevitable look voluntary, even fun. In North's Plutarch, Antony and Cleopatra are affirming a commit-ment in circulation within their intermixed households and battalions of maids and soldiers. *Synapothanumenon* is not simply a union of two lov-ers longing to die in synchronization, as in Baucis and Philemon's humble request of the gods in Golding's translation of Ovid: "Let bothe of us tog-ither leave our lives."[7] Rather, *synapothanumenon* names a lateral and plu-ral affiliation that goes beyond the couple form, and entails the urge to die nobly and in concert across wider chains of command, love, and service.

Yet it is an ideal that arrives already in the satirical shadow of its prior presentation as a fit subject for comic plays. There's something unwork-able about the very attractiveness of this ideal that made it, and makes it still, a juicy satirical target: whether shrunk to the amorous pair of the pres-ent or expanded to the notional household/faction assemblages of its an-cient original contexts, coparticipants in suicide pacts rarely actually die together precisely on cue and in sync. It is one thing to pledge to die to-gether while feasting and carousing, another to take up sword and serpent and keep one's promise. But if the shadow cast by a fatal pledge can generate tragic dread and suspense, it can also prime the pump for comedic rejoinder and bathetic descent from the ideal. There are no guarantees of compliance with other people, who might always be overstating their ardor. Closer to home, it's harder than it looks to kill yourself, let alone to kill yourself in sync with someone else. As Brian Cummings notes in *Mortal Thoughts* (2013): "Suicide in Shakespeare, odd though it is to say it, does not happen alone."[8] The tricky part of dying doesn't end with one's own demise. Even if you decide to die and find the help you need to make it happen to your satisfaction, you can never quite stabilize the open question of posthumous reception: What genre am I killing myself within? Does anything guarantee that my tragic death will not be the object of comic laughter?

I want to argue that this asymmetrical force field, defined by the passionate, doomed temporal ideal of *synapothanumenon* and its comedic prefiguration as *synapothneskontes* subtends Shakespeare's tactic of slapstick excrucation in the vexed scenes of self-killing strewn across his drama. While the present chapter will also examine *Julius Caesar* early on and *King Lear* at its close, this tactic comes to a particularly exemplary point in *Antony and Cleopatra*. Going further, I think that that very excrucation can tell us something about genre's capacity to extenuate and evaluate the actions imitated within it. Stretching the time of death out, delaying and interrupting the decisive act, ruining its somber pathos with intrusive gags, upstaging it with servants and clowns who steal the limelight and spoil the mood, the ideal of "dying together" is subjected to an athletic obstacle course of cross-generic assault. In the process, we see Shakespeare experimenting with how to stage suicide, frustrating the singularity of will with intrusive back talk, showy one-upmanship, and sudden improvisatory tenderness, fraying the decisive character of action on the rough edge of contingency. He does so in order to critique the ideal of both *synapothanumenon* specifically and *Romana mors* generally, showing these cultural forms up as citational, self-belated, and always subject to flat tires en route to the fatal cliff. Wrong-footed by the dramatic phenomenology of suicidal slapstick, the amorous tragic pair gets cross multiplied by the queer comedic interference of the social surround in all its unruly multiplicity, cracking open the self within self-killing at its penultimate point of departure.

Turn Away Thy Face

We can't talk about snub noses if we don't already know what a nose is. Before I can argue that there is a slapstick dimension to the scenes of self-killing in *Antony and Cleopatra*, my tonal allegation requires some familiarity with the prior cultural ideal of *Romana mors* that Antony and Cleopatra's

To F R. W. *Esquier.*

Simile de Aiace se-
ipsum interficiente
(super cuius tumu-
lum virtus plorans
pro falso iudicio)
apparet ante, folio
tricesimo. Nam
cùm Achillis arma
per Agamemnonis
iudicium, Vlyssi ad-
indicabantur, Aiax
illius iniuriæ impa-
tiens, & postea in-
sanus, se-ipsum in-
terficitbat, sic in-
quiens vt Ouid. ha-
bet 13. Metamorph.
Hectora qui solus, qui
ferrum, ignémque, Io-
uémque,
Sustinui toties, vnam
non sustinet iram:
Inuictúsq; virû vicit
dolor, arripit ensem:
Et meus hic certè est,
an & hunc sibi posset
Vlysses?
Hoc ait, vtétudm est in
me mihi, quíq; cruore
Sæpè Phrygum maduit,
dominimunc cæde ma-
debit.
Ne quisquam Aiacem
posset superare, nisi
Aiax,
Dixit, & in pectus,
&c.

W H E N B R V T V S knewe, A V G V S T V S parte preuail'de,
 And sawe his frendes, lie bleedinge on the grounde,
Suche deadlie griefe, his noble harte assail'de,
That with his sworde, hee did him selfe confounde:
 But first, his frendes perswaded him to flee,
 Whoe aunswer'd thus, my flighte with handes shalbee.

And bending then to blade, his bared breste,
Hee did pronounce, theise wordes with courage great:
Oh Prowes vaine, I longe did loue thee beste,
But nowe, I see, thou doest on fortune waite.
 Wherefore with paine, I nowe doe prooue it true,
 That fortunes force, maie valiant hartes subdue.

Fides.

Figure 1. Brutus falling on a sword. From Geffrey Whitney, *A choice of emblems, and other deuises, for the moste parte gathered out of sundrie writers, Englished and moralized...* (Leyden: [Plantyn], 1586) (STC 25437.8/leaf I3 verso/p. 70). Photograph used by permission of the Folger Shakespeare Library.

infelicitous acts at once approximate, parody, and fall off from on their way to execution. Happily, Shakespeare provides a handy precedent for comparison in *The Tragedy of Julius Caesar*, likely written eight years previously, in 1599. Though the play as a whole is hardly free of its own comic and even slapstick dimensions (witness the death of Cinna, which can be played as the blackest of black comedies), the suicides of Cassius and Brutus provide a usefully "straight" comparative yardstick against which to measure the deviations that will dog Antony and Cleopatra's botched, digressive, and cluttered scenes of self-killing. In *Ambitiosa Mors: Suicide and Self in Roman Thought and Literature*, Timothy Hill describes the literary inheritance that, then and now, vividly aligned self-killing with Romanness as such: "For anyone with a more than passing acquaintance with Latin literature the phrase "a Roman death" [*Romana mors*] readily evokes certain well-defined and familiar images—the defeated general falling on his sword, the senator holding his wrists out for incision by his Greek physician—ubiquitous in Late Republican and Early Imperial writings."[9] Such scenes frankly depict the dependence of the would-be self-murderer on assistants, professionals, and seconds who will ensure that the process of self-killing is completed, but they do so in order to valorize the courage and fortitude of the act. Such deaths were made familiar in the early modern period across a multitude of media, from the emblem-book iconography of Brutus as noble pagan falling upon his sword shown to young children on the cusp of literacy, to the depictions of Seneca and his wife's deaths in the *Nuremberg Chronicle* for the upscale consumer of printed books, to the frequent scenes of politically mandated deaths depicted in tragic drama.[10] In the cases of Brutus and Cassius in Shakespeare's *Julius Caesar*, these deaths centrifugally draw out the distinct characters of the two friends even as they turn upon the sticky vicissitudes of the same insistent dilemma: finding a willing accomplice.

Cassius is the first to kill himself, and he does so in a kind of frenzy of on- and offstage action that can be difficult to stage effectively: the herald Titinius runs offstage, is supposedly seen being captured, and the relay of this news to Cassius convinces him that his own hour is at hand. He orders his prisoner, Pindarus, to kill him, symbolically dying before the moment of death in a final act of self-veiling, before Pindarus runs Cassius through with his own sword:

CASSIUS: Come hither, sirrah,
In Parthia did I take thee prisoner,
And then I swore thee, saving of thy life,
That whatsoever I bid thee do
Thou shouldst attempt it. Come now, keep thine oath;

Now be a freeman, and with this good sword
That ran through Caesar's bowels, search this bosom.
Stand not to answer. Here, take thou the hilts
And when my face is covered, as 'tis now,
Guide thou the sword.

[*Pindarus does so*]

Caesar, thou art revenged,
Even with the sword that killed thee. [*He dies.*] (5.3.36–46)[11]

Cassius of the "lean and hungry look," who sees through the affairs of men, remains manipulative in his final act of death, even as he solicits the covering of the face that can do such acts of transparent seeing and mindreading. We can choose to read the decision of manumission at his death as a beautiful final gesture of generosity, a fitting emblem for the moment when a soul will be "set free" from its body, but Cassius's realpolitik drives him to cast a household slave as his last conspirator. He has found someone who has a completely reliable motive for carrying out Cassius's order: not fidelity to his loving master, but the prize of freedom that awaits on the other side.

Dramatically, this transaction of present obedience for posthumous freedom stands in sharp contrast to Brutus's struggle to find a partner in his assisted suicide.[12] Brutus's first choice turns out to be a dud. Volumnius refuses point-blank:

BRUTUS: Thou see'st the world, Volumnius, how it goes;
Our enemies have beat us to the pit.
It is more worthy to leap in ourselves
Than tarry till they push us. Good Volumnius,
Thou know'st that we two went to school together.
Even for the love of old, I prithee
Hold thou my sword hilt whilst I run on it.

VOLUMNIUS: That's not an office for a friend, my lord. (5.5.22–29)

Friendship is a stumbling block: out of his very loyalty, Volumnius cannot bear to kill Brutus. The remembrance that "we two went to school together," instead of functioning as a means of coercion, snaps Volumnius out of the vexation of the present and into a passing reverie about the "love of old." Perhaps the implicit equality of that schoolmate relationship breaks the vertical hold of military chains of command, or perhaps Volumnius simply lacks the stomach for the deed.

Regardless, Brutus must shop around among the soldiers in the camp to find someone who is worthy of the high office of taking his life. Luckily he finds Strato, whom he preemptively flatters in order to assuage his fears of further disobedience:

BRUTUS: I prithee, Strato, stay thou by thy lord.
Thou art a fellow of good respect;
Thy life hath had some smatch of honor in it.
Hold then my sword, and turn away thy face,
While I do run upon it. Wilt thou, Strato?

STRATO: Give me your hand first. Fare you well, my lord.

BRUTUS: Farewell, good Strato. [*He runs on his sword.*]
Caesar, now be still.
I killed not thee with half so good a will. [*Dies.*]

This veiling of the act of death shows us the final limit point of the deeper friendship that Strato demonstrates and that Volumnius demurred from granting to Brutus: after a flickering, tactile moment of contact between hands in a Roman handshake of fraternity, the face must be covered in order for Brutus to deliver the killing blow to himself. There is a distracting sort of casuistry to the preference for running rather than being stabbed while holding still, as it passes agency (and with it, guilt) back onto Brutus, but the veiling may be more significant. This transaction can come off as a kind of confirmation-in-reverse of the core insight of the familiar Levinasian drama of responsibility: "The approach to the face is the most basic form of responsibility.... To expose myself to the vulnerability of the face is to put my ontological right to existence in question. In ethics, the other's right to exist has primacy over my own, a primacy epitomized in the ethical edict: you shall not kill, you shall not jeopardize the life of the other."[13] Even though this is a Roman pagan context and thus not under the sway of the biblical injunction "Thou shalt not kill," Brutus's commandment to turn away the face seems to bear out and confirm Levinas regardless, for Brutus seems here to sense that the turning away of the face will damp down or silence the pull of infinite responsibility that would emanate from his own face if it could still be seen at the final moment.[14]

What do we make of the "good will" with which Brutus says that he kills himself? As contemporary readers and audience members enmeshed in the cultural landscape of mood disorders, suicide-prevention hotlines, and mantras about the necessity of self-care, we are likely to run up against a strong force of our own cultural limits to understanding. Unless one is in a discussion of euthanasia for terminal patients, more often than not at present we want to believe that suicide is an index of some or all of the following: a deeply irrational pathology, a treatable mood disorder rooted in brain chemistry, a collapse of meaning and significance at the level of social bonds, a rupture in the network of family and friends that might intervene and rescue the suicidal person.[15] It is very difficult for many of us in the present to think our way outside this framework, to de-pathologize such feelings and to imagine a state of mind in which self-harm could be enacted with happiness and joy. Even as we try to think this through as "relief at the prospect of the end of pain," we already project the idea that what this person really wants is not their own nonexistence, but the cessation of some other evil circumstance.

In this resistance, in this attachment to "chemocratic" and pathologizing narratives, we are more like early modern people than we realize.[16] If they lacked our specific language of chemical imbalances and mood disorders, they too had a psychophysiology of humoral imbalance in which to locate self-destructive affect, at least in some cases and situations, within a matrix of medical meaning subject to regulation through diet, bloodletting, laxatives, and fasting. In early modernity, a Greek medical framework that regarded health as balance and illness as imbalance was in dialectical tension with a Christian framework that regarded suicidal feeling as sinful despair or seduction at the hands of demonic temptation.[17] In trying to understand Roman acts of self-killing that precede this later dialectic, we are asked to reorient our ethics and fundamentally rethink what our commitments and requirements for a life worth living really are. For the patricians of Shakespeare's Roman plays, there are modes of being that violate one's identity, one's self-standing, one's capacity to be and remain "oneself," states that are worse than death, and chief among them are the states of subjection, military defeat, and subsequent enslavement.[18]

As indicated in the introduction to this book, Mary Nyquist, in *Arbitrary Rule: Slavery, Tyranny, and the Power of Life and Death*, terms this ideological backdrop "war slavery doctrine."[19] This doctrine frames the life of the slave as the free but always retractable gift of a conqueror to a conquered prisoner who stands under a commuted sentence of death. As exemplified in Seneca's "tale of the Lacedaemonian boy," survival within slavery was frequently represented as if it constituted a conscious and voluntary choice rather than violent coercion. Accordingly, suicide was valorized as the act that decisively elevates a subject beyond the reach of would-be enslavers.[20] In the light of this contrast, the suicide of a patrician male Roman citizen becomes charged with an aura of self-possession as ethical dignity whose inverse condition is the ongoing debasement of the slave.[21]

Within the framing of war slavery doctrine, it is better to die than to be exhibited in triumph by others, and one can joyously affirm one's superior virtue by choosing death over survival under such conditions. As Maurice Charney puts it: "The foremost defining element for the Roman character in Shakespeare's plays is the willingness to commit suicide rather than to live ignobly or suffer death by another hand."[22] For the Romans of Shakespeare's plays, the decision to die is the very hallmark of freedom: if one can freely choose death without a display of passionate fear or sadness, then one has truly mastered one's passions. This perspective is defended by Strato when he boasts to his interlocutor Messala that in death Brutus is "Free from the bondage you are in, Messala. / The conquerors can but make a fire of him, / For Brutus only overcame himself, / And no man else hath honor by his death" (5.5.54–57). Brutus has no conqueror, and dies unbeaten, unbroken: "Brutus only overcame himself." In framing this action in this way, Strato also offloads any residual guilt he might have felt as the direct and instrumental agent of Brutus's death. Strato held the sword, but his participation, having been secured beforehand, seems after the fact to melt away, to dissolve from view, leaving only Brutus. The veil now covers the hand that held the sword.

If I have tarried in my account of the suicides of Cassius and Brutus, it is in order to draw out the overdetermined nexus of masculine and patrician valor, self-consistency, and force attendant upon the early modern presentation of *Romana mors* in Shakespeare's drama, and its obverse in the rhetorically supercharged state of survival in enslavement. The complicated web of negotiations, seductions, and bargaining with nearby slaves, school friends, and male accomplices characteristic of patrician male Roman self-killing is not there presented as risible or foolish, and it clearly demonstrates the plurality of suicide as a social form in which one dies with others on behalf of a self that requires and solicits support from bystanders, thus complicating the notion of Stoic values as inward and indifferent or hostile to others. These are scenes of tenderness and fraught emotion in circulation between desperate men at the end of their tether, and while their moods modulate and shift, there is nothing particularly comic about them. Simply put, this is a tragic play. Accordingly, these are tense, frightening, and pitiable scenes of self-destruction that largely achieve the austere seriousness to which they aspire.

Shall I Strike Now?

In vivid contrast to the Roman plays that precede it, *Antony and Cleopatra* constitutes a critical transvaluation of the heroic enterprise *tout court*. If Brutus functions as the paragon of patrician masculinity, Antony is, as the saying goes, a horse of a different color. Besmirched by rumor, fre-

quently drunk, and sometimes in drag, Antony's patrician Roman man-
hood cannot hold fast, but continually melts and "discandies" into a categorical swirl of its ostensible opposites (woman, beast, foreigner, slave).
Amplifying the fact of his uxorious subjection to Cleopatra with his pronounced and concomitant disinterest in the masculine imperatives of Romanness, Shakespeare's Antony suffers from a bad conscience about what
Sir Philip Sidney would have called, in the Christian register of sin, "an in-
fected will" or what, from an opposite intellectual corner, Deleuze would
define as "the conscience that multiplies its pain, which has found a technique for manufacturing pain by turning active force back against itself:
the squalid workshop."[23] There is an oft-noted disjunction between the
coolly manipulative, triumphant Antony of *Julius Caesar* and the ravaged
figure at the center of the later work; grasping toward a psychobiographical
explanation, some critics have further noted that Shakespeare was forty-
three when he wrote the play, the same age as Antony within it.[24] For the
Antony of this play, no less than in the disastrous battles at sea that precipitate his doom, the grand final gesture of self-killing becomes one more enterprise in the "squalid workshop" of self-fashioning as self-finishing that
doesn't quite come off as planned.

Sometimes, mimesis is harder than it looks, and the "imitation of action" winds up just looking like an imitation. All too often, it is precisely the
ersatz thrust of "imitation" that haunts the scenes of self-killing in *Antony
and Cleopatra*: as the grand action of a certain magnitude that magnetizes
tragic plots as their catastrophic apex, self-killing is deadly serious and yet,
in this play, always also somewhat phony. Before it is an accomplished fact
in *Antony and Cleopatra*, suicide is a rumor born by messengers to test Antony's reaction. This spuriously tragic news sets in motion Antony's own
desire to join her in death, for Antony perceives his own survival past the
(imagined) death of Cleopatra as a torturous downgrade in nobility: "Since
Cleopatra died / I have lived in such dishonor that the gods / Detest my
baseness" (4.14.55–57). Antony thus experiences the condition of "tragic
overliving" discussed by Emily Wilson in *Mocked with Death: Tragic Overliving from Sophocles to Milton* (2004):

> Tragedies of overliving show characters who claim that the end of their
> story should already have come…. These characters express a self-
> consciousness that undermines the unity of the self and of dramatic char-
> acter. They become opaque both to themselves and to the reader or au-
> dience. On one level, the discontinuity between past and present actions
> produces a sense of confusion or despair in the character, which must be
> shared by the audience or reader. But the representation of characters who
> evade orderly narrative structures and definition may increase the illusion

of realism. Characters who question their own stories break the dramatic frame; we are led to find them puzzling in the way that people in real life are puzzling.[25]

Against the battering contingencies of happenstance, the *synapothanumenon* ideal promises to offer a kind of generic frame for the arc of a life, but it also imposes a sense of temporal urgency; Antony must pass out of his own life as if through a kind of closing window of access to the ideal, and the longer the interim drags on, the more aware he becomes of the slippage of decorum. But in experiencing "overliving" as, specifically, a detestable sort of "baseness," we see the structural impact of war slavery doctrine as Nyquist defines it: for a patrician to survive past the point of an ideal self-determined death is to compromise their nobility, to undergo a slide downward along the vertical index of social hierarchy toward the bottom rung of servility. Antony finds his own survival tainted insofar as it resembles the mere survival rhetorically projected onto the abjected figure of the slave. Shakespeare's corpus abounds with such rhetorical flourishes that build energy from the invocation of the "slave" as abjected other (one could compare Antony's remark with Hamlet's "O what a rogue and peasant slave am I" (2.2.469) line in this regard).

Accordingly, Antony conscripts Eros to the duty of killing him in an exchange that, at least at first, resembles the stage business of Cassius and Brutus in *Julius Caesar*: the slippery human-resource task of securing assistance in pulling off a fatal deed. Under the aegis of *synapothanumenon*, the problem works differently: here, it's not that one cannot punctually kill oneself because good help is so hard to find these days, but rather because pushy underlings are all too eager to join in on the action, and hog the limelight as they do so. Unlike the standoffish Volumnius or the docile Pindarus and Strato, Eros has other ideas. Here self-killing occasions a darkly humorous trick, as Eros punningly both enacts and violates Antony's command in a joke-like overlay of literal obedience gone wrong.

EROS: Farewell, great chief. Shall I strike now?

ANTONY: Now, Eros.

EROS: [*kills himself*] Why, there then! Thus do I escape the sorrow
Of Antony's death. (4.14.95–97)

If, given the intense sincerity of Eros's devotion to his master, it risks bad taste to call this slapstick, consider its precise combination of fast timing, a physical action/reaction circuit, a punning gag upon a literal command, and an incongruous, surprise outcome. As Castelvetro warns in his commentary on the *Poetics*: "Men are moved to laughter when they hear someone's words, however laudable in themselves, given an unexpected turn."[26] Turning the command awry, the scene escapes sorrow all too well, as it proves, in performance, quite capable of triggering nervous laughter, and worse, from audience members struck by the black comedy of Eros's hyperconformity.

The valence of that conformity is up for grabs. The greatness of the "great chief" is both announced and undercut in the disjunction between the obsequious speech and the impertinent action. If this suicidal switchback is surprising—and in performance it has the instantaneous facticity of a car accident and the sleek reveal of a well-delivered punchline—it is also familiar. The dramatic dynamic of the unexpectedly volatile minor character who wittily steals the scene from under the nose of their lofty social superior cites the ancient dramatic tradition of *alazon* and parasite familiar from Greek comedy.[27] As Janet Adelman has pointed out, this dynamic circulates broadly as dialogue sparks across differences of power, caste, and class in the play, and the interactions with Enobarbus also savor of this tradition. Adelman notes: "The long scene in which Antony rages in Hercules' vein and Enobarbus consistently undercuts him (act 3, scene 13) is fundamentally comic in structure [and] follows the classical pattern of *miles gloriosus* and servant."[28] Shakespeare here tests the capacities of this comic pattern to bear the weight of fatality, and in the process slapstick becomes a dramatic affordance through which to examine how the face-to-face Levinasian encounter can modulate, deform itself, and surprise its coparticipants with the full shape space of open actions.

As a military commander who "can't get no respect" even as he issues a seemingly irreversible order, Antony must improvise. Taking things into his own hands but, as Adelman puts it, "bungling" the execution in a manner consistent with the play's ongoing thematics of faltering leadership, Antony attempts to imitate Eros and fails. It's a spiral of bad mimesis: Antony is, himself, imitating Eros's imitation of Cleopatra's imitation of self-killing. Self-killing is at once a historical fact charged with the pressure of the spectator's retrospective certainty (we know it will eventually happen and that it will eventually succeed) and yet also something of a sham, undone from within by its overfamiliarity as belated trope and its practical difficulty as present task. Antony knows, and we all know with him, what it is supposed to look like, but in the flow of events on stage, it proves surprisingly, humiliatingly, hard to do.

Hedged about by the shadowy gap between shameful prior attempts and heroic prior successes, Shakespeare's suicidal slapstick stages self-killing as never more of a put-on than when it is also all too real. The play's repetitive tic of foregrounding proxies as objects of violence (from whipped ambassadors to stricken errand boys to poisoned maids) has occasioned much critical discussion in responses to the play.[29] Part of this is a scalar logic by which to measure decrepitude from below. Queens and generals demonstrate their falling off from expected protocols of decorum in their volatile lashing out at symbolic targets, and the contagion of shame and despair that passes self-destructive energy from master to underling registers the consequence of that decline as affect blurs outward and downward through increasingly shaky chains of command.

Self-killing is at once a genuinely irreversible act that extinguishes singular lives and an affirmation of the extended network of relational bonds that curiously reinforces social adhesion (the fidelity of lovers, the obedience of servants) even as it "slits the thin-spun lives" that make up that network.[30] The play manifests the contagious nature of self-killing—dubbed in contemporary suicidology "vicarious habituation"—as a kind of intersubjective pedagogy, an art of losing that one hopes to master, but which always stands in the shadow of failure and impotence.[31] Antony learns this first hand, and the jokes keep coming:

> Come then, and Eros
> Thy master dies thy scholar. To do thus
> I learned of thee.
>
> [*He falls on his sword.*]
>
> How, not dead? Not dead? (4.14.101–104)

The pathos of greatness in eclipse is here inverted into the bathos of a conclusion that can't, quite, punctually conclude: far from a noble hero's death, Antony's attempt at voluntary death has all the bustle of someone running to make it to a closing subway car door, and stubbing their toe halfway there. In the gap between Antony's distinctly grandiose stab at modesty and its infelicitous outcome, there slips the banana peel of comedy. Having magnanimously demoted himself to the status of a scholar, Antony goofs. The hapless query "Not dead?" is a line that can be delivered with outrage or despair, and it can be accompanied by gouts of stage blood sufficiently grotesque as to preempt laughter. But... it can, and frequently does, trigger laughter from an audience blindsided by the "heavenly mingle" of the violently unexpected and the inevitable.[32] Of course Antony is a failure; that is the tragic point of the play.

Limping onward, half-alive, the staggering Antony both recalls and lampoons the vividly familiar emblems of self-sacrificial valor that were essential to the ongoing yet tacit romance of early modern culture with *Romana mors*. Seneca's text "On the Proper Time to Slip the Cable" hailed the ideal Stoic self-execution as a matter of conscious self-control and the due observance of decorum; by contrast, Antony's actions look hasty, improvised, and slipshod.[33] The gory materiality of Antony's work in progress puts him at an absolute dramaturgical remove from the play's most enduringly strange scene, Enobarbus's apparent death from an attack of shame and despair, in act 4, scene 9.[34] Though there is some medical precedent for imagining death from heartbreak in period medical literature such as Jacques Ferrand's *A Treatise on Lovesickness* (1610), against the backdrop of the surrounding play's copious scenes of self-killing Enobarbus's death is striking for the pronounced absence of any apparent physical explanation. Coming when called, this death models in its punctual convenience a kind of absolute self-mastery strikingly at odds with Antony's slipups and technical hitches. Whereas Enobarbus dies from a kind of surplus of sincerity that trumps action, Antony moves from sorrow to mounting vexation as the possibility of punctual action recedes. Ironically, precisely because of its haphazard execution, Antony's self-killing is brought closer to the messy contingency of many of the actual Roman deaths of historical record. Far from precisely controlled affairs, the deaths of both Cato and Seneca involved grotesque and gratuitous agony as the practical process of ensuring their own deaths was in each case staggered across numerous humiliating medical and familial obstructions, unforeseen delays and hasty detours en route to their final exits. This slippage between theory and practice is resolutely suppressed in the numerous and typologically Christlike early modern visual depictions of Seneca's death as a stern, punctual, and solemn affair.[35] Shakespeare's Antony, in the very sloppiness of his failure to live up to the ideal of the cult of *Romana mors*, discloses encrypted historical truths of embarrassment, improvisation, and suffering that challenge that ideal.

After the High Roman Fashion

Once his comically extended dying process finally grinds to a halt, Antony's concluded death induces a temporal "knot extrinsicate": not the knot of a body and soul reciprocally tethered, but the knotted temporality of a pledge to die together that has become tangled and literally preposterous, as Cleopatra now lags behind her own intended successor. Cleopatra's situation confirms Emil Cioran's Wildean maxim, used as the epigraph for this chapter, that "it is not worth the bother of killing yourself, since you always kill yourself too late."[36] Caught within "a paroxysm of chronology," as Eric Langley puts it, cause and effect become confounded.[37] The verification of Antony's death as a completed suicide triggers a telling passage from speculation to action as Cleopatra resolves to close the gap that separates her from him, but in so doing also notes the belated and mimetic dimension that, as it were, dogs her loyal gestures:

> All's but naught.
> Patience is sottish; and impatience does become
> A dog that's mad. Then is it sin
> To rush into the secret house of death
> Ere death dare come to us? How do you, women?
> What, what, good cheer! Why, how now, Charmian?
> My noble girls! Ah, women, women! Look,
> Our lamp is spent, it's out. Good sirs, take heart.
> We'll bury him; and then, what's brave, what's noble,
> Let's do't after the high Roman fashion
> And make death proud to take us. (4.15. 83–93)

Beneath the call for cheer, mixed emotions bubble upward as doubts intrude. There are curious, fleeting Christian resonances in the misgivings about sin that haunt these speculations; they are of a piece with similar reflections that Brutus briefly engages in before wholeheartedly embracing the suicidal ethos of *Romana mors* in *Julius Caesar*. Rigging the deck to preempt his audience's potential misgivings, Shakespeare occasionally ventriloquizes anachronistic bursts of proto- or demi-Christianity into valorized pagan characters (a dynamic that, as we shall see, returns in redoubled form in Addison's *Cato*).

Here such brief considerations of possible sinfulness precede a decision to die that ultimately embraces a studied, citational artificiality: to kill oneself in a "high Roman fashion." If the reach toward highness is of a piece with a woman who deliciously mocks her rival for Antony's love as "dwarfish," the gesture toward self-killing as itself a matter of "fashion" reveals the high stakes of self-finishing. Within the context of Shakespearean tragedies as a chronologically clustered group, this gesture, too, is itself already conventional, for observations along these lines ricochet across Shakespeare's tragic plays set in historically later periods, from Macbeth's steely refusal—"Why should I play the Roman fool and die / On mine own sword" (5.8.1–2)—to Horatio's hotheaded vow that "I am more an antique Roman than a Dane" (5.2.325). The Romanness of the action was proverbial, a given.

But was it equally open to all comers? As a foreign queen whose body is insistently racialized from the opening speech describing her "tawny front," Cleopatra's bid for entry into the category of Roman greatness is heavily overdetermined by her status as alternately alluring and repellent outsider to Roman norms.[38] Since Adelman's *The Common Liar* (1973), it has now become an accepted truism of the critical tradition that the play is powered by the antinomy of Rome and Egypt; awareness of this polarity can sometimes calcify into a goes-with-everything binary that always appears when summoned. Ten years after Adelman's intervention, Barbara Vincent notably aligned Antony and Rome with tragedy and Cleopatra and Egypt with comedy in her article "Shakespeare's 'Antony and Cleopatra' and the Rise of Comedy."[39] More recently, premodern critical-race studies have cross multiplied the terms of this binary by rightly insisting upon the knotty specificity of how Cleopatra's blackness and gender cocreate the threat she poses for Roman interlocutors as a vector for racialized desire and disgust; in *Things of Darkness: Economies of Race and Gender in Early Modern England* (1995), Kim Hall notes that "Cleopatra's darkness makes her the embodiment of an absolute correspondence between fears of racial and gender difference and the threat they pose to imperialism."[40] Surveying the critical traditions that rhapsodize upon this death as an elevating passage into Romanness, in his analysis in *Shakespeare Jungle Fever: National-Imperial Re-Visions of Race, Rape, and Sacrifice* (2000), Arthur Little Jr. has brought attention to the cultural process by which a black woman becomes racialized as white through virtuous self-sacrifice, revealing the category of whiteness itself as open to a curiously posthumous mode of fungibility.[41] If race is best understood as, in the words of Geraldine Heng, a "system for the articulation and management of human differences," then Cleopatra's insistent refusal of the attempts of others to manage the meanings of her racialized and gendered differences ripples across the scenes of the play; as she claims access to the "high Roman fashion" for herself, she works to counter this ongoing force of management even in the midst of the constraining endgame of surrounding geopolitical circumstance.[42]

Send in the Clown

How long does it take to decide to die? Cleopatra's death begins with the movements of the geopolitical chessboard that make her exhibition in triumph increasingly likely, and it has no clear ending point, projecting as it does forward in time as Cleopatra imagines herself being reproduced upon the stages of the early modern future, in a later, more humiliating triumphal exhibition. This temporal smearing seems antithetical to the time dependence of comedy in general and slapstick in particular. Slapstick calls for a heightened awareness of sudden changes of state, the physical tracking of operations and mechanisms, the rapid-fire transformations at a brisk tempo characteristic of witty stichomythia. Yet, I want to argue, a kind of temporal slapstick intrudes even here, amid the smear of an ending that can't quite end, but keeps, awkwardly, extending itself, as a routine mechanically encrusts upon living dialogue.

[*A noise within*]

CLEOPATRA: Wherefore's this noise?

[*Enter a Guardsman*]

GUARDSMAN: Here is a rural fellow
That will not be denied your highness presence:
He brings you figs. (5.2.231–34)

The guard's pronouncement connotes both social class and the concomitant unary trait that would accompany it: rudeness, experienced as a jarring noise that ratifies the guard's judgment before we have even met the rural fellow in question.[43]

In Shakespeare's tragedies, the stage direction of "noise within" often presages the contingent blast of the unfamiliar and the uncouth as it slops onto secluded royalty: both Laertes's boisterous entrance and Ophelia's reentrance in act 4, scene 2, of *Hamlet* are prefaced by a "noise within." In the case of *Antony and Cleopatra*, this rude blast of obtrusive sound announces the generic cross breeze of comedy across the arc of the play's decisive progression into tragedy. And it gives me the slender license to directly invoke slapstick, a term that enters English in the 1890s as a designation for a literal "slap-stick" used to make a comic noise of impact to coincide with the glancing blows of pantomimed conflict in comedy routines, the rough-and-tumble smacks and whacks surely heard when, say, Matthew Merrygreek wails on Ralph Roister Doister, or Cleopatra manhandles a messenger.[44] While Elizabethan stagecraft made do with thundersheets and squibs, the coming of the slapstick sonically announced what was already familiar within the public theater: that the disruptive noise of comedy was a key material index of its powers to shock, disturb and delight.

CLEOPATRA: Let him come in.

[*Exit Guardsman.*]

What poor an instrument
May do a noble deed! he brings me liberty. (5.2.235–237)

Cleopatra's poor instrument denotes both the alleged "figs," here elevated and transvalued into the metaphysico-political abstraction of "liberty" itself, and the down-at-heel flunky who bears them. This antithesis flags the elevated end toward which Cleopatra is working: a *Romana mors* that will forever place her out of the reach of the Imperial state whose values she both one-ups and confirms in her choice of this exit at this time.[45] In a familiar irony, Isaiah Berlin's celebrated distinction between the positive freedom to do things and the negative freedom from constraints is about to sink its fangs into flesh; here "liberty" turns out to be not the freedom to roam beyond sovereignty, but the freedom to make a sovereign decision to place one's body beyond the reach of the state.[46] Yet the bearer of this tragic doom is notably off-message, as the Folio makes apparent:

[*Enter Guardsman and Clown*]

GUARDSMAN: This is the man.

CLEOPATRA: Avoid, and leave him. [*Exit Guardsman*]
Hast thou the pretty worm of Nilus there,
That kills and pains not?

CLOWN: Truly, I have him: but I would not be the party
that should desire you to touch him, for his biting
is immortal; those that do die of it do seldom or
never recover. (5.2.240–46)

Cleopatra is the first person to praise the worm, and here prettiness connotes both the beauty of its iridescent markings and the nicety of fatal painlessness, ensuring passage toward nonexistence without suffering with an imagined precision that would be, itself, "pretty," perhaps lending corollary beauty to the corpse it creates. Describing that corpse, North's translation of Plutarch notes that "some say also, that they found two litle pretie bytings in her arme, scant to be discerned."[47] The Clown is obedient in confirming the answer to the question, yet oversteps into a flirtatious language of desire and touch. Taking Cleopatra's needlessly languorous epithet as his cue, he begins to pun and joke. Though painless, the worm's "biting is immortal," and yet this permanent outcome gets undercut with a groan-worthy gag: "those that do die of it seldom or never recover."

There's something in the basket, something deadly but contained, and the outburst of this deliberate laugh line can stand in for the fearful release that it forestalls. In performance this snappy rejoinder can land with pathos-shattering comic force, or it can register as a sinister "off" note that heightens our fear and dread (which the RSC production in 1992 drew out by having the Soothsayer bring the figs and take over the Clown's dialogue; some productions give him a red nose, others have him ominously whisper).[48] The leap from pun to outright joke is taut with the obverse affects that roil beneath the brittle surface of banter. Self-killing is haunted by both the fear of pain and the fear of failure, and both anxieties are in circulation here within Cleopatra's guesses and the Clown's glancing answers. But that very tension makes his rudely gamesome manner a deep relief to the audience.

What to make of the tart reply that "those that do die of it seldom or never recover"? Literal idiocy or coy sarcasm? The fact that the Clown's cryptic remark can suggest folly or sagacity with equal support indexes a fraught moment in the construction of tone, as the scene hops unstably between available options. Faced with the remark upon the page, we are alert to the playtext as verbal pattern that can toggle back and forth between meanings, but in the rush of performance the scene registers as a kind of dramaturgical tourniquet as Shakespeare ties off tragic momentum via comedic detour.

Acceding—but under duress?—to the logic of flirtation and wordplay now in effect between her and this menial delivery man, Cleopatra prompts another outpouring in order to make sure that this plan is going to work:

CLEOPATRA: Remember'st thou any that have died on't?

CLOWN: Very many, men and women too. I heard of one of them no longer than yesterday: a very honest woman, but something given to lie; as a woman should not do, but in the way of honesty— how she died of the biting of it, what pain she felt. Truly, she makes a very good report o' the worm; but he that will believe all that they say, shall never be saved by half that they do: but this is most falliable, the worm's an odd worm. (5.2.247-54)

Here the Clown becomes at once funnier and more frightening. The witty paronomasia upon "lie"-ing and honesty makes light comedic fare of sexuality's own clownish intrusions into language where it is not intended and always found. But as the Clown digressively proceeds, this figure of the impossible woman who speaks the honest truth of her own successful death breaks with the wished-for fantasy that suicide is painless.[49] The "very good" report speaks of biting, speaks of pain, at once orgasmic in its connotations of the pleasures that the worm-as-penis can give, but ultimately harrowing. Language coils upon itself, tangles and redoubles, as the sound of sententious proverbial wisdom produces misshapen and "most falliable" pronouncements. The Clown becomes, himself, an "odd worm," at once bearing death and tripping it up en route. He overstays himself.

If the Clown functions as padding, it may be to deafen certain offstage screams, for this conversation about the practical particulars of poison stands in a telling relationship of bad faith with the supporting archives from which Shakespeare drew material for his play. Those materials show us a very different Cleopatra: one who would never need to ask strangers for secondhand dosage information.[50] In North's Plutarch, the discussion of Antony and Cleopatra's festive *synapothanumenon* is followed immediately by an extensive, and chilling, description of Cleopatra's poison research on unwilling human subjects:

> Cleopatra in the meantime was very careful in gathering all sorts of poisons together, to destroy men. Now to make proof of those poisons which made men die with least pain, she tried it upon condemned men in prison. For when she saw the poisons that were sudden and vehement, and brought speedy death with grievous torments, and in the contrary manner, that such as were more mild and gentle, had not that quick speed and force to make one die suddenly: she afterwards went about to prove the stinging of snakes and adders, and made some to be applied unto men in her sight, some in one sort and some in the other. So when she had daily made divers and sundry proofs, she found none of them all so fit, as the biting of an aspic, the which causeth only a heaviness of the head, without swooning or complaining, and bringeth a great desire also to sleep, with a little sweat in the face, and so by little and little taketh away the sense and vital powers, no living creature perceiving that the patients feel any pain.[51]

North's Plutarch gives us a Cleopatra who is a kind of Alexandrian variant of Josef Mengele, coldly experimenting on an imprisoned and captive population of unwilling test subjects, a revelation that surfaces only in a muffled form in Octavius's posthumous explanation that "her physician tells me / She hath pursued conclusions infinite / Of easy ways to die" (5.2.353–55). Shakespeare offers a defensive distortion that overwrites the source text with a less disturbing and more sympathetic compensatory fiction. In the place of direct disclosures, Shakespeare gives us in the interaction with the Clown a comedic and digressive volley of puns, complete with tartly sexual banter. Eventually, the banter is supposed to stop.

And yet, maddeningly, it won't:

CLEOPATRA: Get thee hence; farewell.

CLOWN: I wish you all joy of the worm.

[*Setting down his basket*]

CLEOPATRA: Farewell. (5.2.255–57)

How to break this off? In a productive reading of *Romeo and Juliet*, Paul Kottman has taught us to hear the Hegelian overtones in back-and-forth cycles, a kind of reciprocal standoff between master and bondsman, which Kottman compares with circular exchanges between amorous teenagers on the telephone in which neither wishes to be the one to end the call.[52] But here the stickiness of discourse is acutely one-sided. Cleopatra tries to rid herself of the Clown, but the Clown just won't take the hint, and as this dynamic proceeds over time, we sense the Clown as a figure caught in what Walter Benjamin termed the "einziger Zug" or unary trait of comedic character.[53] Such stasis in the face of an opponent force is key to the effect of generic entanglement as this tragedy temporarily buckles with the audience's increasing comic pleasure as it tracks Cleopatra's mounting vexation.

The cue of "farewell" just isn't working, and the comic routine, torturously, grinds on, getting funnier because the Clown's jokes aren't wanted; we sense Cleopatra's interior state not through expressive soliloquy but through the clipped and disinterested attempts to politely extract herself from dialogue as such:

CLOWN: You must think this, look you, that the worm will do his kind.

CLEOPATRA: Ay, ay; farewell.

CLOWN: Look you, the worm is not to be trusted but in the keeping of wise people;
for, indeed, there is no goodness in the worm.

CLEOPATRA: Take thou no care; it shall be heeded. (5.2.258–63)

As this fool's errand drags on, the question here is not "Can the subaltern speak?" but rather "Will the subaltern ever shut up?"[54] The Clown's intrusion doubles down on the noise problem that started before he was onstage. As David Hershinow has argued, from its classical sources in Alexander and Diogenes to Hamlet and the gravediggers, Shakespeare's class-crossing dialogue frequently stages the drama of parrhesia ("truth telling" or "risky speech") as a complex site of contestation.[55] As Cynic foolery bounces between metaphysical wordplay and stark obscenity, Shakespeare "mingles kings and clowns" in order to produce snappy, prolix volleys of dialogue that are fraught with the political question of how best to advise the sovereign.

But this scene is about more than advice. If there's a familiarity to the pattern of a powerful prince beset by prating inferiors, there's a uniquely grim particularity to this scene, too: in the clinical phrase of suicidologist Thomas Joiner, Cleopatra is "acquiring the means to enact lethal self-injury."[56] The threat of imminent death puts the temporality of dialogic exchange itself under pressure. It ups the stakes implicit in earning the longed-for laugh. Time is what Cleopatra is eager to lose for good, and yet time is what the Clown insistently takes up, and in taking, gives back to her.

The worm is the snake that brings death. As a gently exasperated Emma Phipson puts it in her compendium *The Animal-Lore of Shakespeare's Time*, "The names snake, serpent, adder and worm were used indiscriminately, and little attempt was made to identify the various species."[57] The particular utility of this indiscrimination is that the worm can name both the serpent whose sting brings death and the maggot that consumes the dead corpse produced by that serpent, closing serpentine cause and vermicular effect into a closed loop or Ouroboros hoop. Sonically, the "o" in "joy" and "worm" sound the "oh" groan to come as an orgasmic cry, an "oh" that does double duty.

CLOWN: Very good. Give it nothing, I pray you, for it is not worth the feeding.

CLEOPATRA: Will it eat me?

CLOWN: You must not think I am so simple but I know the devil himself will not eat a woman: I know that a woman is a dish for the gods, if the devil dress her not. But, truly, these same whoreson devils do the gods great harm in their women; for in every ten that they make, the devils mar five.

CLEOPATRA: Well, get thee gone; farewell.

CLOWN: Yes, forsooth: I wish you joy o' the worm. (5.2.264–73)

What does it mean to wish someone "joy of the worm"? To plunge directly into bawdy, there's a coarse sense in which he is hoping she has a nice orgasm. The phrase says, "get fucked," in a roundabout way, with the serpentine rudeness of the "kōmos" lurking in the basket behind the figs of transparent euphemism. Is this a sincere desire that she feel joy, sexual or otherwise, or a risqué mockery of a female ruler whose sexual appetites were the object of ongoing rumor campaigns and opposition propaganda from her Roman foes? That Cleopatra is the object of such speculation is not simply a matter of the historical relay of the facts of her biography, but draws force from ongoing misogyny, and specifically the misogynoir of racist tropes associating black women with hypersexuality.[58] Beginning with an appalled Roman onlooker describing the transformation of Antony into a "fan to cool a gypsy's lust," Shakespeare's play both depicts and reinscribes prurient fantasies regarding the black female body, and draws some of its much-celebrated erotic power from offering access to that body to audiences and readers.

Going beyond the dirty joke in progress to the murderous threat of the real, this wish relays a sunny sort of glee in enabling death. If I say, "good luck killing yourself," do I wish you well? Is that goodwill, ill will, or an ironic acknowledgment that the communal bonds that govern intersubjective exchange are about to run out of chances? Can we wholeheartedly wish death-as-joy upon someone who seeks it? This is where the comedic force of suicidal slapstick disjoins from the Levinasian ethical encounter with the infinite responsibility we bear toward the other, tearing a hole in that infinity.

Or does it? Might the capacity to engage in self-killing with humor and joy be a minimal mode of sociability that keeps a shared belonging going up to and even within such final intersubjective cutoff points? Speaking as someone who has had to actually assist a family member in the final stages of a terminal illness in acquiring the means through which they might achieve their own death, I can attest that ensuring that a certain death is a good death—a death that someone seeks wholeheartedly—can itself be the ultimate expression of loving concern and ethical recognition. Bracketing such perhaps impertinent personal experience, it is far from obvious that the Clown's remark is meant in an aggressive or hostile manner.

But that can be hard to see. From within the pathological frameworks of present suicidology, it would seem to be no longer possible to wish someone good luck in this endeavor, because success here would constitute a definitive failure in human flourishing. For the first readers and audience members of *Antony and Cleopatra*, historical imagination permitted a holiday from the pressure of the deontic injunction "Thou shalt not kill," casting back to a time before the coming of the law, and modeling an alternate space of fatal freedom where death brings joy.[59] At the level of the play's morphological imaginary, "joy of the worm" means success from the serpent, but insofar as the serpent delivers you to death, you become a source of pleasurable feeding for the maggots destined to grow and breed in your decomposing corpse, the worms that will literalize the dead metaphor of snake-as-worm at the heart of the image. While in some sense a rude violation of decorum in its prolonged intrusion into the Queen's final assault upon eternity, the Clown's coarse joke is also of a piece with the hot, moist ferment of the play's language, which swelters and teems with imagery of serpentine slime that repurposes death as raw material for ever more life, roiling the moist carrion process of decomposition with emergent sexual generation.

At a remove from the Clown's dilatory lifelines disguised as dick jokes, what might "joy of the worm" permit Cleopatra to experience? What if such "joy" is both a cheap phallic pun and something altogether more? Death offers the dawning poetic prospect of an ecstatic merger with an infinite pagan material universe that will alter and reabsorb the constituent elements of her body, rarefied now and perfected as she prepares to ascend from circumstance to something else: "I am fire and air; my other elements / I give to baser life" (5.2.286–87).

Cleopatra's joyous embrace of material change here functions as a kind of preemptive alternative to Levinas's sour yet striking assertion that "Paganism is a radical powerlessness to get out of the world."[60] Acknowledging death as a process of separation but greeting the prospect with pleasure, Cleopatra rhetorically readjusts leave-taking into purification that does not need to see itself as "leaving" the world, because it is not alienated from the world as such. Departing from life, she deliberately takes her pleasure here in death's capacity to rejoin her with the raw materials from which all contingent forms have emerged and will continue to emerge. This is change rather than loss, and departure as gift. These lines register an elemental Empedoclean framework that ultimately diminishes the material threat of death by insisting upon the resilient presence of the four elemental "roots" of earth, air, fire, and water beneath the rippling surface of change.[61] Joy of the worm might be the energetics of transfer, the sense of pleasurable reentry into what is always already ongoing: the continuous plenum of bodies and flows.

On a more immanent political level, there are immediate concerns generated by the terrestrial chessboard in which Cleopatra's still-living body remains enmeshed while she lives: capture, imprisonment, exhibition, humiliation, and shame. By dying, she hopes to outflank a coercive opponent keen to appropriate her royal image to limn his own imperial triumph to come. Taken in that context, "joy of the worm" might well be the onrush of positive affect at the imagined thought of completing self-killing and flouting Octavius and thus securing for herself a triumphant means of self-deliverance, even at the heavy price of his threatened reprisals against her children. This is of a piece with her prior assertion that "My desolation does begin to make / A better life" (5.2.1–2), a claim that Mary Beth Rose has glossed as "suicidal victory."[62] But if the play occasionally grants such possibility, it is not Cleopatra's alone, as *Antony and Cleopatra* insistently pluralizes this seemingly most private of acts, making good upon the lateral spread of the *synapothanumenon* ideal by granting this "better life" to Charmian and Iras and Eros too.

The play commences with insistence upon the "mutual pair" of Antony and Cleopatra, and of their excessive and inviolate pair-bonding as a dissociation from others that forcibly weakens the claim of external kinds of belonging. Against that context of the couple form's exclusions, in the play's final scenes of leave-taking the lateral linkages of Cleopatra, Iras, and Charmian with each other achieve a powerful effect of pathos, and remind us of the open-ended plurality of the *synapothanumenon* ideal: the order of those who will die together has now become a form through which to resist the threat of civil and political disorder posed by Octavius's victory. Both recalling and correcting the misprisions whereby Eros and Antony could be said to have died "together," here Cleopatra and her women achieve a tighter, yet still never quite simultaneous, suicidal sequence. Cleopatra kisses Iras and Charmian, and Iras immediately falls dead to the floor.

Iras's death having come before her mistress prompts the decisive intrusion of comedy into the scene, with Cleopatra reverting to a performative display of her competition with other women:

> This proves me base:
> If she first meet the curled Antony,
> He'll make demand of her, and spend that kiss
> Which is my heaven to have. Come, thou
> mortal wretch,
>
> [*To an asp, which she applies to her breast*]
>
> With thy sharp teeth this knot intrinsicate
> Of life at once untie: poor venomous fool
> Be angry, and dispatch. O, couldst thou speak,
> That I might hear thee call great Caesar ass
> Unpolicied! (5.2.299–307)

The proving of "baseness" again registers the pulse of war slavery doctrine as a referendum upon a greatness that here beckons on the other side of life. Cleopatra's "jealous act" is not a sincere expression of hostility with

Iras, but it does register the temporal pressure exerted by the *synapothanu-menon* ideal and the jostling for priority among its plurality of members, as the couple form competes with, but also resembles, the homosocial bonds of the royal chamber. Imagining the "knot intrinsicate" that joins the soul and body as a fungible tangle that can loosen and straighten itself into eternal order, Cleopatra poetically transposes the coiled form of a serpent with the image of a rope or thread tied in knots. Prefigured in Dante's *Paradiso*, in canto 31 ("La tua magnificenza in me custodi / si che l'anima mia, che fatt'hai sana, / piacente a te dal corpo si disnodi" [Preserve the great things you have done in me, so that my soul, which you have made whole, may be still pleasing to you when its knot is untied]), this image of body-and-soul assemblage as a knot will return in Donne's reuse of the phrase for "the subtle knot that makes us man," where the word subtly recalls the description of the serpent in Genesis 3:1 ("now the serpent was more subtil than any beast of the field")[63] To speculate upon the sonic impact of the homophony within the line, audiences might hear the "knot intrinsicate" as "not intrisincate," activating the possibility that what is tied together can always be untied. The knot is subtle, serpentine, and temporary.

If much of my reading has registered the pressure of comedy upon the play and tried to activate the latent dimension of slapstick available at key moments within it, I must admit that these possibilities are seemingly warded off by the entry of a compressed lyrical language that takes over in the final exchanges of valediction between the members of Cleopatra's household, as "joy of the worm" modulates from mirth to a kind of ecstatic farewell:

CHARMIAN: O eastern star!

CLEOPATRA: Peace, peace!
Dost thou not see my baby at my breast,
That sucks the nurse asleep?

CHARMIAN: O, break! O, break!

CLEOPATRA: As sweet as balm, as soft as air, as gentle,—
O Antony!—Nay, I will take thee too.

[*Applying another asp to her arm*]

What should I stay—

[*Dies*]

CHARMIAN: In this vile world? So, fare thee well.
Now boast thee, death, in thy possession lies
A lass unparallel'd. Downy windows, close;
And golden Phoebus never be beheld
Of eyes again so royal! Your crown's awry;
I'll mend it, and then play. (5.2.308–18)

There is heartbreak here, but also the mandate of "play." In having one character complete the dying utterance of another, we register a Shakespearean trick already deployed in the capacity of Hal to complete Hotspur's last words for him in *Henry IV, Part 1*, adding a curious sort of acoustic confirmation of an affective attunement between characters. The strength of language as intersubjective thread is tested and becomes, in the moment of transition, stronger than death. As moving and entrancing as this lyrical language undoubtedly is, in performance one registers the extent to which action and language are at cross purposes. The punctuation of Cleopatra's invocation by the fact of Iras's death registers and yet fails to stop the ongoing incantation of self-killing as elemental purification. The shared recirculation of this language of elemental dissolution indexes the poetic trance that binds Charmian to her mistress in the midst of this ongoing murder-suicide.

As Charmian reenacts what she has seen her mistress do already, the play distributes self-killing across and between selves. To die "after the high Roman fashion" cannot be done alone. It names a collective work of meaning-making that requires the ongoing supplementary labor of guards and servants who relay, express, and follow through upon the desires and aims of their masters. Hierarchies of command and obedience reach across thresholds of life and death, ending with the posthumous care work of adjusting a symbol of sovereignty at precisely the point when sovereignty itself wobbles and goes "awry."

Reading against the grain, one could regard this scene not as a tender demonstration of interpersonal loyalty but as the high-water mark of ideological interpellation. We are being shown that "this is what servants are like" and "this is what soldiers are like," in a manner not entirely dissimilar to Barthes's celebrated example of a "mythological" image: the cover of an issue of *Paris Match* from 1955 depicting a youthful black soldier snapping into a crisp salute that, in Barthes's famous reading, signifies "that France is a great Empire, that all her sons, without any colour discrimination, faithfully serve under her flag, and that there is no better answer to the detractors of an alleged colonialism than the zeal shown by this Negro in serving his so-called oppressors."[64] The *Paris Match* cover leverages the facticity of photography's ostensible honesty to preempt ongoing critiques of neocolonialism via a seductive, naive image of inclusion in patriotism.

In a roughly similar manner (however crude it seems to say so), the play's careful rehearsal of postures and images of servile devotion solidifies the hold of regal authority over others. These acts of valedictory tenderness transmute obedience into pathos so that we within the audience can admire and invest in the muffled thrill of subjection unto death, perhaps finding in our own sobs as we watch this scene a tender tightening of the chains that bind us to our children, our partners, our work colleagues, our bosses, our leaders, our nation.[65] It is this force that Sir Francis Bacon signals in "Of Death," added to the *Essays* in 1612: "We read, after Otho the emperor had slain himself, pity (which is the tenderest of affections) provoked many to die out of mere compassion to their sovereign, and as the truest sort of followers."[66] Similarly, we are invited to see Iras's and Charmian's actions not as means to forestall humiliation, subjugation, or retaliatory abuse for their role in frustrating Octavius's political will, but as indexes of loyalty, identification, and participation in a morally idealized service position of care work in excelsis. They, too, are "the truest sort of followers."

Joy of the worm is the comic delivery of tragedy, the serpentine folds in which genre is made to redouble upon itself as wave upon wave of transient lives crash before us. Inverting the sententiousness of memento mori and the cadences of finitude that would press us to always remember that in the midst of life we are in death, the joy of the worm implicit in the Clown's suicidal slapstick is the reminder that in the midst of death we are in life. Crowns can always slip off. Until the moment that we finally die, we are encroached upon, jostled and interrupted and hailed and challenged, by others. We are surrounded by others who will outlive us, and our bodies become food for others: literal food for the worms, and figurative food for the thoughts of those who stand and watch and remember. There is no guarantee that they will grant seriousness to our circumstances, and much to suggest that they will not. (Suicidal slapstick might be thus distinguished from suicidal stand-up, which is what the gravediggers in *Hamlet* are engaged in: a glib stream of jokes about suicide as a topos, a dreadful crime, and a sin, but also the object of derision and communal opprobrium, fantasy, mourning, and speculation). Suicidal slapstick is an insistence upon the fact of theatrical mediation as a reminder not of the pathos of the private self's incorrigible inaccessibility—the undiscovered country within—but of the underexplored country already around us, the "kō-mos" of the rowdy, rude populace who stand and watch every spectacle, and who just might be laughing as they do so.

Conclusion: Why I Do Trifle Thus

Confronted with the tragic prospect of characters killing themselves, we are, or are meant to be, in a heightened state of alert and concern, enmeshed in a cathartic process through which pity and fear are released, purged, purified. Seen through the filter of tragedy, the act of self-killing hails us as mortal human beings, encouraging us to gasp upon the precipice at the spectacle of an imitation of an irreversible, pitiable, and violent action. When remodulated by the additional filter of slapstick, the affective work of catharsis would seem to be troubled and disrupted by a welter of contrary valences (we might see in self-killing not terror or pity or nobility or sacrifice but instead snag upon the intrusion of impurity or failure or contingency or silliness or cliché, or we might flow across and among these various relations).

In a manner perhaps in keeping with Elder Olson's generic definition of comedy as a "relaxation of concern," when self-killing borders upon or spills over into slapstick we are thereby encouraged to stand down from our concern for the agent, and instead alerted to our freedom to occupy other stances.[67] That said, we do not simply hover in a steady state of relaxation toward these characters. Part of the pleasure of the Shakespearean text is that, like the mixed emotions that Cleopatra speculates that Antony might be experiencing in her absence, it offers its readers neither pure joy nor pure sadness but their "heavenly mingle" (1.5.62). It is hardly news to assert that this is a play that realizes its own vulnerability to comic treatment.[68] Cleopatra herself prognosticates that someday "the quick comedians / Extemporally will stage us, and present / Our Alexandrian revels" (5.2.215–17).[69] But such possibility is arguably built into her own larger-than-life self-presentation, a repertoire of canny exaggeration and hyperbole that aligns Cleopatra with fooling from the get-go: in the play's first scene we are served notice that "I'll seem the fool I am not" (1.1.43). The folly matters, but the "not" does too.

Within the fertile multiplicity of the play's "heavenly mingle," it is telling that when faced with the prospect of self-killing, Shakespeare repeatedly want us to laugh. Such detours into slapstick declare that even the subject of voluntary death remains up for grabs, potentially risible, potentially open to our capacity to experience joy. Such an encouragement to laugh at death itself might be a therapeutic technology for the release of the hold of sad passions upon those in the audience who might themselves be at risk. Alternately, it might index a callous communal refusal to invest in the suffering of others, or a refusal to invest when that suffering is the consequence of having crossed over into pathology, sin, or error. Caught out by the Clown's salutation of the "joy of the worm" as it ricochets beyond Cleopatra to include our own pleasure in contemplating her predicament, we register our own joy in the midst of the pain and death of others, and our own nervous vexation at witnessing, and being implicated in, the recirculation of self-harm.

There is at present a ready-to-hand prepositional test for the ethics of laughter in the distinction between "laughing at" and "laughing with" the objects or persons who occasion our laughter; neuroscientific work on the "laughter perception network" suggests that such distinctions in valence and directionality can be mapped via fMRI at the neuronal level.[70] We are encouraged to read "laughing at" as cruelty and "laughing with" as empathy. This oversimplification has recently been updated and stratified along the vertical axis of "punching up" and "punching down" into a referendum upon the subject positions of both parties in hierarchies of advantage and authority. In allowing the potential for suicidal slapstick (or suicidal camp) to become actual in our own aesthetic response to the Clown's prompts, are we laughing at suicidal people simply for being suicidal, or are we laughing with suicidal people who, in the midst of their predicament, are reminded of capacities for humor that persist despite their personal crisis? The deictic regulation of "up," "down," "with," and "at" works to spatialize and orient the affective chaos of spectatorial response. If cashed out in an overprecise manner it produces speculative monsters: Do we laugh down at them from the superior plane of our own implied health toward their symptomatic submersion in mental illness? Do we laugh up at the nobility of someone else's bid for tragic greatness in order to ground them through a leveling judgment? Do we laugh to deny them the dignity of a generic framework that we thereby grant ourselves the power to withhold?

In a basic sense, there is something conservative in the instinct to laugh at the urge to die. This instinct survives today in the anxious parental question: "If all your friends were jumping off a cliff, would you do it too?" For some of us, the answer is yes. Once, in college, a friend and I took LSD. At the peak of our trip, we held hands and jumped off a bridge together into the river below. It felt natural, the conclusion to a happy day together throwing a Frisbee in the park. The drop into the cold water was the consequence of sunshine, and no harm came to us. But the question's shaming force as a rhetorical question that prompts the answer "of course not" is meant to scold young people out of an overinvestment: the wrong sort of intensity pouring into the wrong sort of bonds with the wrong sort of object. Queerness lurks in the figure of the person or people who would, precisely, jump off the cliff for a "friend" (cue *Thelma and Louise*). The secure modern subject must not attach themselves too fiercely to the wrong object. Tacit norms of self-preservation require an ideological bolster precisely because those norms are shaky.

The more one looks for slapstick scenes of self-killing in Shakespeare, the more examples proliferate. I would like to consider, as an extension of this archive, the "Dover cliff scene" in *King Lear*.[71] In the fourth act, the blinded Gloucester bids farewell to his unrecognized companion Edgar, who has told his father that he stands at the extreme edge of the cliff face, rendered vertiginous through a celebrated run of verbal pictorialism that stops short: "It's so high, I'll look no more, / Lest my brain turn and the deficient sight / Topple down headlong" (4.6.24–26).[72] Seeming not to notice his son's speaking voice nor the sidelong pun upon his own blindness in that speaker's winking evocation of "deficient sight," Gloucester bids farewell to life and throws himself off the cliff to what he anticipates will be his immediate death.

Except it doesn't work. Instead of a fatal impact, Gloucester bellyflops face down onto a disappointingly close obstruction: the stage of the playhouse. About to accelerate the body count of a tragic plot, Gloucester's grand designs come a cropper on the fact of flooring. A well-timed swoon and revival (implied by Edgar's "yet he revives" [4.6.49]) is the only way that Shakespeare resolves the inherent and deep awkwardness of this moment, which in performance can batten upon the dangerous generic precipice of comedy, and sometimes hurtles right down into it.[73] From the perspective of scholars in disability studies such as Rosemarie Garland-Thomson who have unpacked the tense phenomenological intersubjectivity of "staring" as a power dynamic between disabled bodies and onlooking "normates," we in the audience are placed in a not-uncreepy relation of complicity with Edgar's deception.[74] We silently observe a blind man try to kill himself, knowing or at least suspecting that he will fail. In performance, the sound of impact is often covered with a cry, a sigh, or a gasp. The audience holds its breath, fighting the array of feelings and relations generated by this moment of crisis. For at least some in the audience, that array of feelings includes a kind of snickering, adolescent schadenfreude at a botched and morbid "pratfall."[75]

Regardless of how much the right sort of blocking and lighting effects and, in film, cutaways to reaction shots can pad the flop, the playtext already knows that the scene courts comedy, specifically a comedic downsizing of the absolutes invoked by self-killing.[76] In a line that is identical in both *The History of King Lear* (Quarto) and *The Tragedy of King Lear* (Folio), Edgar gives this away in his telling aside to the audience: "Why I do trifle thus with his despair / Is done to cure it" (4.6.34–35). Here, Shakespeare offers a strikingly direct articulation of the therapeutic logic that underwrites the presentation of self-killing as a less than serious matter that I have been stalking throughout this chapter. "Trifling" offers a means by which to contest the hold of ideation, to break our relation to the fantasy of our own death. We might be rescued from our deep investment in the apparatus of tragedy by some well-intentioned misdirection, even in the form of a strategic blast of cruelty as face hits floor head-on.

Falls are fast but therapy takes time. When addressed at first after his botched attempt, Gloucester remains resolute, more annoyed than repentant: "Away, and let me die" (4.6.10). Faced with a difficult patient, Edgar courts a flippant sort of blasphemy by countering that "Thy life's a miracle" (4.6.57), knowing full well that he has rigged the miracle in question. Role reversal means that the son gives life to the father, but sometimes that gift of life takes the form of a con or a trick. Drawing upon improvisatory skills sharpened through his Poor Tom imposture, Edgar seeks to offset Gloucester's saturnine heaviness with a further "trifling" evocation of the falling body as "gossamer, feathers, air" (4.6.51). Gloucester is encouraged to imagine that he has had a close call with a demonic antagonist, but there's a camp theatricality to the descriptions of this "fiend," complete with "horns whelked and waved like the enridgéd sea" (4.6.73), that lightens the mood. Beyond these linguistic tricks, it is the feeling of moving and walking and talking—the feeling of being alive—that seems to me to push Gloucester across his own longing for death and out the other side. A few lines later Gloucester's distance from his own former affect is marked when he pledges: "Henceforth I'll bear / Affliction til it do cry out itself / 'Enough, enough' and die" (4.6.77-79). Gloucester has come to see that his own sorrow has rises and falls, a periodicity of mood changes that implies the possibility of a life at least sometimes worth living. Thus, the "trifling" work of self-killing as slapstick can teach us, on the cliff face or in the theater, how to laugh at death, and why.

In defense of suicidal slapstick, by way of conclusion I want to add one more Shakespeare if not one last Shakespeare, a Shakespeare that comes from the rich film history that informs what we think of when we think of slapstick: the silent-film tradition. In the Harold Lloyd film *From Hand to Mouth* (1919), we are told that "there are as many Wills as there are croaks in a bullfrog." Before ultimately arriving at the Will who will be the protagonist of the film's narrative proper (itself a comic tale about a will), we are shown in a quick catalog of gags a number of different men who share the name Will. On the heels of meeting Mr. Will Snobbie, whose "head would make a fine hat rack," we encounter a telling variant on this familiar name.[77] A title card introduces "Mr. Will Shake," and then asks, "Will it will or will it won't?" The camera cuts to a black man shaking dice, praying, blowing on them, taking a throw onto the ground, and rolling a snake eyes.[78] We can neither pardon nor bracket the bardolatrous racism wired into the assumed incongruity of this humorous-because-black substitute for his illustrious-because-white original. Much important critical work has been done in thinking through Shakespeare's contributions to mutually imbricated logics of heritage culture and white supremacy, but given the ambient climate of "pathological aversiveness to thinking about race under the guise of protecting historical difference" that still characterizes our field, more remains to be done if scholars of Shakespeare are to be anything other than custodians of racist prestige.[79]

Let us roll the dice, and venture that in the midst of this scene of "predatory inclusion" in the archive of presumed Shakespearean whiteness, this demi-Shakespearean figure of "Will Shake" might still do some useful critical work at present in summoning the spirit of Shakespearean suicidal slapstick as an ethically generous experience of vulnerability.[80] Will Shake stands in as the melancholy angel of slapstick as he plays with, and plays off, the precarious circumstances in which generic identities of all kinds are staked on risk, and tumble into confusion: if the willing hand that stakes the future on a roll of the dice registers the rub of contingency that gives comedies their playful swerves of surprise and snap, the final coming to rest in the snake eyes of defeat acknowledges the realities of loss and death of which tragedy is made. But on neither side of this divide, suspended in midair like the car of Thelma and Louise, do we find the way the Will shakes in the space before decision, in the tumbling state of "or" that asks, "Will it will or will it won't?," and keeps on playing. Lives end, and plays end, and chapters end too. Julius Caesar dies and Brutus dies and Cassius dies and Lear dies and Cordelia dies and Antony dies and Eros dies and Enobarbus dies and Cleopatra dies and Iras dies and Charmian dies. But before those ultimate outcomes, in the midst of play, Shakespeare seems to me to inhabit the contingent space of alternatives, spoiling the ideal of *synapothanumenon* with the spin of possibility, and the clownish noise of slapstick.

CHAPTER THREE

Trolling Decorum in *Hamlet* and *Timon of Athens*

Anger is an energy.

JOHNNY ROTTEN

In the chapters that have preceded this one, I have concentrated upon acts and attempted acts of self-killing that are motivated by what we might loosely but accurately call positive and prosocial affects: the urge to sacrifice the self for others, in the case of Pyrocles and Hebe, and to somehow join the self to another person or persons, in the case of *synapothanumenon* within *Antony and Cleopatra*. In the two tragic plays that concern me in this chapter, "joy of the worm" circulates against the strongly contrary headwinds of hatred and despair. Accordingly, joy darkens and liquefies, turning antisocial as it modulates into a sadistic kind of pleasure in the enactment of cruelty, or surfacing in private reveries that imagine death as a liquid escape from the obligations of embodied life.

Pairing *Hamlet* and *Timon of Athens* risks lopsidedness: one is a hypercanonical object of interpretation in the Western literary tradition, the other an unfinished collaborative play written with Thomas Middleton, which was never performed in the period, and which is still widely regarded as an unpleasant failure. If *Hamlet* is overrated and inescapable, *Timon of Athens* remains, relative to the Shakespearean tragedies as a group, a decidedly minor work. But from the perspective of their affective tenor and discordant effects, they belong together. To use the damning phrase of Andy Kesson, Hamlet and Timon fall squarely within Shakespeare's "grumpy man aesthetic," exhibiting a tendency toward rageful masculinity that Kesson contrasts with the more frequently comic and female dramatic worlds of John Lyly.[1] Noticing a shared predilection for imagery of venereal rot and infection, Freud regarded Timon as a further development of the "hysteric" repudiation of generative human sexuality crystallized in Hamlet's misogyny.[2] Caught in sustained feedback loops of self-laceration and long-winded bursts of outwardly directed aggression, Timon and Hamlet combine the maniacal and the tedious. Across their obviously distinct narrative situations, historical periods, and social milieu, they are joined in their pleasures. Once each man is primed by provocative circumstance or passing occasion to go on the attack, they take to deliberately hurting other people with a similarly cruel relish.

In other words, Hamlet and Timon belong together because they are trolls. A ubiquitous pejorative commonplace, "troll" denotes both an antagonistic online persona and the practices and stances ("trolling") that express that persona, which can range from low-intensity verbal insincerity, deception, and sarcastic provocation to various forms of harassment and mediated abuse whose upper thresholds of violence are still being explored and expanded as of this writing.[3] "Troll" surfaces as a descriptor by the late 1990s in online environments, spreading and intensifying as overfamiliarity with its entry-level variants prompts increasingly escalated displays of its signature maneuvers.[4] Where schadenfreude consists in a passive enjoyment in the misfortunes of others, trolling presumes deliberate cruelty.[5] While the limits and purchase of any analogy are debatable, I will in time unpack the specific force of this comparison.[6] Like early modern affective identities such as "the malcontent" or "the melancholic," "the troll" helpfully indicates a certain culturally legible alignment of feeling, doing, and being.

Though they do not resort to anonymous posts in mediated online environments, Hamlet and Timon seem to me to deserve this highly presentist term because they repeatedly and deliberately take a particularly focused form of sadistic pleasure in verbal assaults that target and exploit other people's seriousness. By the end of this chapter, we will circle back to the reservoir of positive affects that occasionally surface in these plays in scenes that articulate suicidal ideation or enacted self-harm as an antisocial escape from human life. But for the majority of this chapter, I will be looking at the specific form of "joy of the worm" that Hamlet and Timon derive from "trolling" those around them, focusing upon two exemplary moments in which they take a cruel pleasure in mocking others on the topic of suicide. That they are able to troll others at all is an index of their mastery of and reliance upon surrounding speaking conditions of decorum, and it is trolling's dependency on decorum as grounding condition that frames my analysis.

In contrast to the high stakes of suicide or the low comedy of trolling, it is hard to imagine a less charged topic than decorum. A handwave toward indefinable thresholds of "appropriateness," the term assumes a numbingly broad tacit dimension of norms and practices, the background churn in which we carry on with our lives. Typically, decorum only becomes an

acute matter of concern when a given action or speech clashes against protocols and wobbles its yielding framework of inbuilt expectations. Gertrude's crack that "the lady doth protest too much, methinks" (3.2.224) offers up one such moment; when one of Timon's guests purrs at a banquet
that it consists of "all covered dishes" (3.7.45), we encounter another. Both
are moments in which proportions go awry or snap into place, and in so doing they track the fragile edges of propriety. The hypothesized social "we"
is imagined to flinch at decorum's violation, and glide past its observance.
Not nothing, decorum requires time and energy. In practice, decorum's
flexible interpretation means that it can take and hold many shapes: a protective padding around social interaction, a reservoir in which tenderness
wells up, or a sharp hook on which to snag the exception.

Cicero declared that "the universal rule, in oratory as in life, is to consider propriety."[7] Like decorum itself, Cicero's declaration is easy to invoke but hard to cash out. For classical literary theorists and early modern
authors, "decorum of character" names the proper authorial regulation of
speech at the level of particular agents, the ideological work that personal
styles of speech and action do to shore up the legibility of kinds of personhood for readers and audience members, both at the level of individual temperamental self-consistency and against the backdrop of the broad
social categories in which we locate individuals. As such, the analysis of
"decorum" has much to offer the way we read now in the wake of intersectional analysis, scanning texts for the coextensive operations and cross
multiplications of race, gender, and class (consider Patricia Akhimie's activation of the relation of conduct to representational logics of racialization in *Shakespeare and the Cultivation of Difference* [2018] for a case in
point).[8] It is easy to summarize the outcome of decorum's regulation and
conjure a gallery of rigid types and known quantities: Farmers tell jokes
and sing songs. Dukes declaim grandly. Caesar should sound like Caesar.
The fool must sound, and therefore be, foolish. The troll trolls.

I have said that this is a book about the elasticity of norms, and in decorum's leeway we see this elasticity in operation; standing expectations
about decorum of character set the humoral thermostat of particular persons so that cholerics rant and melancholics brood, and they rig diction
to the "appropriate" occupational and educational levels (shepherdesses
should not sound like princesses, and vice versa). Precisely because of the
standing tensions provided by decorum's pretended fixity, early modern
plots draw power from the delicious spectacle of relentless cross-class and
cross-gender and cross-confession masquerade. Deploying gender travesty, tavern slumming, "turning Turk," or other feigned religious con-
versions, early modern plays stage decorum as a dialectic of norms and

exceptions across typological boundaries, allowing early modern authors and audiences to put selfhood's fungibility to the test.

Early modern understandings of decorum are not principally about a desire for ornament, but about regulating the way that language acknowledges status and in the process locates selves; summarizing Fracastoro, Rosemond Tuve notes that "as a robe of gold does not dignify a peasant, … so heroic dignity given to a light subject is unseemly. Juno must not *tug* at Aeneas; it is a carter's word and connotes the pulling of oxen and horses, or boys tugging each other by the ear."[9] Rather than a requisite list of aureate language, decorum sanctioned the capacity of authorial tone to rise and fall with a due sense of the social locales that distinct literary occasions called for: "When Puttenham boggles at a translator's calling Aeneas a *fugitive*, seeing in this 'a notable indignity offered to that princely person,' his *grounds* are impeccable: first, that the connotations of words are important and powerful and, second, that it is 'not to the Authours intent,' *he meant not to make him a fugitive*."[10] Without drawing the critical conclusions that a power analysis might supply to thicken the account of this representational system's lived effects upon those framed within it, Tuve is refreshingly up-front about the way that decorum performs an ideological work of attaching modes of speech to social positions within hierarchical constellations. Decorum's real work is the sorting of persons, and, by extension, the prompting of our anticipated attitudes toward them.

In other words, decorum and genre cocreate literature's purchase upon the real. Judgments upon what is "plausible" or "implausible" are coordinated against its constraints, but these constraints encode assumptions about the tethering of speech to rank. Whether at the intermission or in the classroom or hitting pause mid Netflix stream, one grows accustomed to the objection: "But no real _____ talks that way." There is, then, a thin but pervasive conservatism to the conventionality with which social typologies of character produce assent as they reify the operation of hierarchies transmitted through representation.[11] But the experience of reconsidering what decorum affords within representations also raises the alluring possibility that sufficiently strong forces of innovative characterization might have category-reforming force, effectively rezoning where we think shepherdesses and clowns might go and what they might do and how they will sound when they get there. If we apprehend decorum precisely in the intrusive moments when its protocols give way or are violated, then the inversion of decorum offers a revealingly open spectrum: the rude, the inappropriate, the flagrant, but also the improvised, unexpected, or jarringly new. Trolling names a cruel pleasure taken in the simultaneous exploitation and violation of decorum. Let us watch that cruelty in action.

Hamlet as Troll

There are many Hamlets packed within this "poem unlimited": melancholy Hamlet, fashionable Hamlet, scholarly Hamlet, fat Hamlet, and histrionic Hamlet, but also Hamlet the pirate, Hamlet the poet, Hamlet the pedant, and so on. Given such capacity, it is not necessarily a strong demand to add Hamlet the troll to this ever-expanding critical list. Hamlet's notable pleasure in cruelty ranges across a variable spectrum of intensity based upon the correspondingly variable strength of the ethical claim that others can make upon his good will. Here are four examples: Hamlet's slow roasting of the courtier Osric's verbal pretentions via superlative verbal display and forced alignment of contraries as "tis very cold" becomes "it is very sultry and hot" across eighty odd lines in 5.2.76–158; his mockery of Polonius's age as physically disgusting in the imagery of "eyes purging thick amber" and "weak hams" (2.2.195); the public obscenity of his "Do you think I meant country matters?" (3.2.104) query to Ophelia in front of the entire court; his private declaration to Gertrude that "You are the Queen, your husband's brother's wife / And would it were not so, you are my mother" (3.4.15–16). The brute gut punch of that last remark breaks decorum's thresholds entirely, and earns Gertrude's immediate rejoinder "Nay, then I'll set those to you that can speak" (3.4.17). There is more where this came from.

The variable willingness of Hamlet's targets to stand for this kind of behavior indexes their relative status differentials within overlapping hierarchies. To state the obvious: Hamlet is an educated male aristocrat, and his capacity for cruel pleasure is rooted in the social affordances that follow from that. In the walnut shell of half a chapter, I do not have space to list every possible example of Hamlet-as-breaker-of-decorum, but this quartet of cruel interactions already suggests the pattern's pervasiveness, predictability, and basis in prerogatives. In what follows, I shall conduct a more strategic raid upon Elsinore's resources, starting with Polonius's arch engagement with genre as a relational system of differences, progressing to Hamlet's attack on histrionic theatricality in the "What's Hecuba to him, or he to Hecuba?" speech as a test case for decorum's holding force, and then arriving at my primary example: Hamlet's "RIP trolling" of Laertes at Ophelia's funeral.

Trolling requires decorum, and decorum surfaces in Elsinore through the habitual clockwork of social forms. Trumpets sound when the king toasts, and hats are put on or taken off in the presence of royal persons. When art enters this space, it does so decorously, promising playing that will be seemly and observant of courtly tastes and due propriety. But genre's categorical mandates court chaos; Polonius activates this potential when he hails the visiting players as "The best actors in the world, either for tragedy, comedy, history, pastoral, pastoral-comical, historical-pastoral, tragical-historical, tragical-comical-historical-pastoral, scene individable, or poem unlimited. Seneca cannot be too heavy, nor Plautus too light. For the law of writ and the liberty, these are the only men" (2.2.325–29). Polonius's ridiculous list, quoted here in the longer version that appears in the Folio, and which hints at the wild proliferation of generic forms proposed by Scaliger, unleashes a turbulent and unruly profusion of subcategories and possible moves within genre's shape space, and then backtracks to the twin parental pillars of Senecan tragedy and Plautine comedy as stabilizing precursors. At some level, we are primed by the play's language to antici-pate that Elsinore will be a space of such perverse mixtures, ruled over as it is by an "uncle-father and aunt-mother" (2.2.314), whose union occasioned "mirth in Funeral and... dirge in marriage" (1.2.12). Polonius's smarmy hy-perbole about the quality and capacity of the players serves a purpose be-yond the scene-specific maintenance of Hamlet's mood; it juts out in a gesture at the surrounding playtext's own machinery. As both anguished reflection upon historically evacuated conditions of action and a slow-motion implosion of revenge-tragedy's forms, *Hamlet* draws power from the conventional norms it cites even as it stages an assault upon generic conventions and the tonal regulations of decorum that express them.[12]

Theater splits Hamlet down the middle. As object of theory, theater brings out Hamlet's stodgy and pedantic side as he lectures on best prac-tices to the professionals he is hosting. As embodied practice, theater exac-erbates Hamlet's manic side by cranking up the socially permissible range of affective display toward the histrionic.[13] As this split widens and then closes over, the spectacle of Hamlet's responses to the promise of theater gives Shakespeare an occasion to reveal dramatic practice as a technology for exhibiting and triggering affective responses. Theater channels energy through the character-regulating constraints of genre's templates and de-corum's norms.

Shakespeare takes pains to demonstrate Hamlet's familiarity with these norms. Before the players have even walked onstage Hamlet is already enumerating the King, Adventurous Knight, Lover, Humorous Man, and Lady in the hierarchical sequence of a list of dramatis personae (2.2.285–90). Hamlet's humoral temperament gear-shifts notably toward the san-guine as he waxes chummy with the players throughout lines 2.2.359–70; saying "welcome, good friends" (2.2.360), hailing them as guests, but also cracking jokes about the boy players finally hitting puberty and aging out of female roles. When the pleasantries of welcome conclude, Hamlet takes pains above all to represent himself as a discriminating connoisseur of the regulation of decorum within theatrical performance, favoring "honest method, as wholesome as sweet, by very much more handsome than fine" (2.2.381) over "matter in the phrase that might indict the author of affection" (2.2.381). As is customary given their near synonymy in the period, here "affection" and "affectation" seem each equally plausible, their difference faintly marking dissembling's hidden ethical crevasse. Gone in this scene is the Hamlet of "wild and whirling words" (1.5.132), and in its stead we have the very model of academic discernment regarding the pleasures and dangers of theatrical practice, prompting Kathy Eden's apt description of Hamlet the drama critic as essentially "an Aristotelian in the tradition of Sidney."[14] Hardly avant-garde in outlook or tastes, Hamlet himself is a fussy-sounding advocate of custom and propriety, calling above all for "smoothness," "temperance," and "discretion."

Hamlet's comments about and to the players have been mined by critics for centuries for possible insights into Shakespeare's own opinions about genre, internecine conflicts between rival theater companies, and acting technique.[15] Beyond the London context, Shakespeare was also familiar with surrounding and sometimes bitter academic arguments taking place at Oxford regarding the function and valence of tragedy; as Russ Leo describes in *Tragedy as Philosophy in the Reformation World* (2019), "The account of tragedy in *Hamlet* draws directly from... arguments between John Rainolds, William Gager and Alberico Gentili" regarding theater's threatening capacity to move audiences, and notes that for Rainolds in particular, "The spectacular and histrionic aspects of theater are not merely sinful, they are also confusing, corruptible and convincing."[16] A salutary corrective to cartoons about anti-theatricalism, Leo's account reveals the depth of Aristotelian scholarship within some of the most staunch opponents of theater, the complex engagement with the mixture of terminologies and positions within the *Poetics*, and the rapidly expanding forests of commentary that surrounded it. Pulling focus, I want to pass from a broad, culture-wide argument about the capacity of art to move people in general to a character-specific issue: Hamlet's solitary crisis occasioned by the "passionate speech" about Priam's slaughter.

Brooding in private, the threat posed by histrionic actors becomes personal:

> Now I am alone.
> Oh, what a rogue and peasant slave am I!
> Is it not monstrous that this player here,
> But in a fiction, in a dream of passion,
> Could force his soul so to his own conceit
> That from her working all his visage wanned,
> Tears in his eyes, distraction in his aspect,

A broken voice, and his whole function suiting
With forms to his conceit? And all for nothing—
For Hecuba!
What's Hecuba to him or he to Hecuba
That he should weep for her? What would he do
Had he the motive and the cue for passion
That I have? He would drown the stage with tears
And cleave the general ear with horrid speech,
Make mad the guilty and appall the free,
Confound the ignorant, and amaze indeed
The very faculties of eyes and ears. (2.2.470–87)

A hot mess of disgust and envy, Hamlet finds himself astonished at the "monstrosity" of playing. Stung with jealousy, by the end of his own arc of thought he has moved beyond self-laceration and becomes, in fantasy, both a more forceful actor and a superior occasion for amazement.

I will briefly trace these psychological pirouettes: it is "monstrous" that the actor has sufficient control over his own body that he can weep for a literary character, the ancient maternal figure of Hecuba. In the wake of generations of psychoanalytic criticism attuned to the elaboration of Hamlet's misogynist hostility, it is perhaps irresistibly easy to peel away the onion layers surrounding this symptomatic response so that the speech can be shown to not be about "theater" at all: the actor's capacity to be moved is really a screen for Hecuba's prior, deeper capacity to be moved; Hecuba's imaginary "instant burst of clamour" (2.2.453) at the death of Pyrrhus is a sound that Hamlet wishes that Gertrude had made for the death of Old Hamlet. Gertrude's insufficient mourning of Old Hamlet makes this secondhand description of a woman moved to screams and cries by grief at the death of a husband especially galling as a means of catalyzing Hamlet's hostility toward his own mother's remarriage, sanctioning hatred by counterexample as a replacement for what is truly disturbing and "monstrous" here: *not emotion but the absence of emotion*. The logic is torturous: looking through the actor toward his own mother and then through his mother turning back toward himself, it seems that witnessing the actor being moved reminds Hamlet that he remains moved that Gertrude was not moved, or not moved *enough*. Anger at histrionicism overwrites sorrow at emotion withheld.

This in turn prompts a sadistic fantasy for Hamlet ("I should ha' fatted all the region kites / With this slave's offal" [2.2.514–15]) that transfers the abjected figure of the "slave" from a flourish of metaphoric self-recrimination to a compensatory debasement of his enemy. Hamlet here loops back to the player's speech in which Pyrrhus was "horridly tricked /

with blood of fathers, mothers, daughters, sons" (2.2.395–96), an image that suits both Claudius's murderous action and Hamlet's own longed-for retribution to come. Hamlet temporarily imagines being Pyrrhus and killing Claudius in the same way that Pyrrhus killed Priam. Pyrrhus is a problem for Hamlet for multiple reasons. Covered in blood and "coagulate gore," Pyrrhus's visual appearance "as a painted tyrant" (2.2.418) indicates why the aesthetic assessment of acting technique and the familial nexus of crime and revenge are wired together.

"Tyrant" is a switch point. The tyrant is a highly charged pejorative name for murderous, arbitrary rulers (such as Claudius), whose deeds are unjust and whose deposition was sanctioned by various forms of early modern resistance theory, albeit in each case hedged around within Reformation monarchies by anxious framings and partisan adjustments (Beza, Buchanan, and the author of *Vindiciae, contra Tyrranos* for the Protestants; ultramontanists for the Catholics).[17] In Hobbes's curt phrase, "They that are discontented under Monarchy call it Tyranny."[18] But "tyrant" is also the kind of dramatic role rendered notorious via the medieval Herod plays such as the Digby "Killing of the Children" as a launchpad for the sort of overdone performance that offends Hamlet's aesthetic sensibility. The tyrant is the very role that Hamlet has in mind when he enjoins the player not to follow the example of the intemperate actor who "out-Herods Herod" (3.2.14). "Tyrant" thus brings a combustible mixture of political, familial, and aesthetic materials together in Hamlet's mind.

Caught up in a storm of affect that pushes him to trample upon his own alleged aesthetic preferences for a theater of modesty and sweetness, in fixating upon theatricality while feeling powerless, Hamlet becomes, himself, histrionic and overdone, chanting "bloody, bawdy villain / Remorseless, treacherous, lecherous, kindless villain" (2.2.515–16). At the level of prosody, the dippy dactyl duo of "treacherous, lecherous" is, I think, a sonic tell that we are meant to hear this language as artificial, especially on the heels of the antiquated alliteration of "bloody, bawdy." In performance, its delivery tips easily toward foaming-at-the-mouth fury, a height of passionate excess that prompts subsequent collapse into shamed self-recognition. Hamlet snaps out of his momentary murderous daydream and remembers that he has not, as yet, fatted any kites with the remains of his victims (a fantasy of tyrannical cruelty).[19]

If I have indulged a familiar mode of symptomatic reading that would work to "see through" the text's manifest interest in histrionicism as a defensive distortion of a deeper core of maternal fantasy and primary aggression, it must be said that this speech *really is* about art all the same. Comparing himself to the mimetic imitations of "great" action offered up by tragic actors, Hamlet realizes that he is a kind of flubbed actor; he has a "cue for passion" but veers decidedly off course from the revenger role in which he has been cast by his father. Revenge as such contradicts Hamlet's love of sweetness and modesty: the motto of the revenge tradition established by its urtext, Seneca's *Thyestes*, is "Scelera non ulcisceris, nisi vincus" (Injuries are not revenged except where they are exceeded), which was rendered in Thomas Newton's Elizabethan translation as "Thou never dost enough revenge the wronge / Except thou passe."[20] The command to take up revenge *is* the instruction toward excess, and with it, the necessary destruction of "modesty" and "sweetness." Old plays shame the present with the force of their example. Hamlet's historically situated sense of generic auto-belatedness is that he fails to live up to the codes proposed by the heroes and heroines of ancient Greek tragedy. In private he collapses in disgust at his incapacity to align himself with the unworkably distant yet emotionally powerful patterns modeled by the *megethos* of the agents within the Greek tragic art that precedes him; this disgust in turn fuels his spite and envy at the self-regulating techne of a "player" who can control passionate responses and make them powerfully felt by others.

Obscure Funerals, Maimed Rites

Hamlet's obsessive mixture of envy and disgust at the histrionic display of emotion prompts his outburst against Laertes when he stumbles onto Ophelia's funeral, and it is to that awkward occasion that I now turn. The funeral is itself already a space in which mourning's decorum is being tested by vexed, fractious outbursts and the distinct aroma of a cover-up issued by "great command" (5.1.217). The event is cast into question before it has begun, when the Gravedigger ("Clown" in the Folio) begins the play's fifth act asking, "Is she to be buried in Christian burial that willfully seeks her own salvation?" (5.1.1.). The question prompts the "suicidal stand-up" routine of the gravediggers, whose cheeky glee—singing songs and telling jokes while digging graves—models "joy of the worm" at its earthiest, but stiffens Hamlet into the priggish disdain of an aristocratic straight man.

Ophelia's death is compromised by its murky causality and all-too-suggestive circumstances; in flagging her "*as* one incapable of her distress" (4.7.174), Gertrude's posthumous narration (to which I shall return) seeks to dissolve Ophelia's agency into a matter of "non compos mentis" inadvertency.[21] Following from this marginal status at the border zone of permissibility, the ceremony forcibly overrides standing protocols that would refuse the burial of self-murderers on hallowed ground. When Laertes begrudges the inadequacy of the ceremony and the priest pushes back by indicating the "doubtful" circumstances of her death, implying Ophelia's possible damnation, Laertes overcompensates: "I tell thee, churlish priest / A ministering angel shall my sister be / When thou liest howling" (5.1.229–31).

Stung by the sense that the funeral is both too much ostentation for the priest's comfort and utterly insufficient to the scale of personal loss, the resulting push-pull prompts Laertes to a striking display of physical and rhetorical intensity. He leaps into the grave, proposes a quasi-amorous final embrace, and utters a passionate speech that reaches toward an Ovidian register of the gigantic:

> Hold off the earth awhile,
> Till I have caught her once more in my arms.
>
> [*Leaps in the grave*]
>
> Now pile your dust upon the quick and the dead
> Till of this flat a mountain you have made
> T'o'ertop old Pelion or the skyish head
> Of blue Olympus. (5.1.240–43)

Taken literally, Laertes is asking to be buried alive inside Ophelia's grave; he is announcing a kind of sibling affiliation unto death that we associate with tragic closure in general and with the bond of Antigone and Polyneices in particular. That said, in its intimacy this embrace also slides toward the activation of the tacitly incestuous sibling bond that Ernest Jones analyzed in 1910 in the original paper that he would rework as *Hamlet and Oedipus* (1949).[22]

Laertes is not just asking to be buried with Ophelia. Going further, he is asking for so much earth to be piled upon him that the grave's depth becomes a new mountain peak, and one associated with the labors of the giants who attempted to pile mountains onto mountains in order to make war upon the Olympian gods. Shakespeare would know the story as recounted in Golding's translation of book 1 of Ovid's *Metamorphoses*.[23] "To pile Ossa on Pelion" was, supposedly, a proverbial expression of fruitless, doomed labor in the period. This is a literate and educated utterance, dignified in its grandiose reference points and delivered in the high tragic manner as it binds earth and sky together. But, of course, Laertes is not speaking literally and does not expect to be taken literally; his extreme of feeling is attuned to the irreversibility of death and the seriousness of funereal occasion, and, in context, he performs, and becomes, in that performance, actor-like.

It is a performance that prompts immediate fury:

HAMLET: What is he whose grief
Bears such an emphasis, whose phrase of sorrow
Conjures the wandering stars and makes them stand
Like wonder-wounded hearers? This is I
Hamlet the Dane. (5.1.243–47)

In theatrical performance, the queer shock of this rude intrusion overrides our capacity to track the relation of question ("What is he?") to the phrase that follows it ("This is I, Hamlet the Dane"); it is a sequence that seems, at the level of syntax and sound rather than meaning, to force "Hamlet" to be that question's answer even as context suggests that this is a query about Laertes. Hamlet overrides and overwrites Laertes's grief as way of both squelching and replacing his rival. True to his pedantry and poetic aspirations, Hamlet's interest in the "phrase of sorrow" pounces on affect's form and finds it excessive, while the image of "wonder-wounded hearers" keeps mobile across the playtext the relentless morphological imaginary of wounded, abused, and poisoned ears, metaphorically recirculating Claudius's murder by way of its association with histrionic acting. It is a histrionic objection to histrionicism, and it cues the troll in Hamlet.

What is so galling about the tragic pathos of Laertes's "phrase of sorrow"? Why does this combination of action—jumping into a grave—and speech—citing Ovid—precipitate Hamlet's violent mimetic response? In a strange way, one might say that Hamlet is drawing out a subtextual implication within Laertes's own imagery. The deliberate marring of a highly formalized social ritual is also encoded into the priming location of Pelion that Laertes invokes. Pelion is not only the mountain that provided the raw material from which giants once tried to fruitlessly climb upward to the heavens. As the site of the disastrous intrusion of the uninvited Eris bearing the apple of discord into the celebration of the marriage of Peleus to Thetis, this mountain was itself the site of a notoriously disrupted ceremony.[24] Making reference to a spoiled wedding as he spoils a funeral, Hamlet mocks the grieving brother with a deliberately distasteful display of quantitative affect-measurement: "I loved Ophelia. Forty thousand brothers / Could not with all their quantity of love / Make up the sum" (5.1.258–60) George MacDonald speaks for many with the observation that "perhaps this is the speech in all of the play of which it is most difficult to get into a sympathetic comprehension."[25] But that very extremity of deliberate unpleasantness and gratuitous cruelty makes it, for my purposes, particularly interesting as an index of Hamlet the troll's assault on decorum. Here, of all places in the play, decorum's resilience is tested with particular severity.

Hamlet's behavior at Ophelia's funeral violates the sorrowful tone of funerals by pressing past grief into bombast, excess, willfully overdone expressions of emotion. Going beyond thresholds of tastefulness as he enters the terrain of the "bad actor," Hamlet's hyper-self-awareness of grief as conventional behavior attacks those gathered to mourn. In the process, he upstages the deceased in a willfully shocking and attention-seeking manner. Hamlet calls attention to Hamlet as he calls attention to Laertes's manner of grief as an overly theatrical performance that he imagines was designed to call attention to itself. Bad mimesis runs wild:

> HAMLET: Swounds, show me what thou'lt do.
> Woo't weep? Woo't fight? Woo't fast? Woo't tear thyself?
> Woo't drink up eisel, eat a crocodile?
> I'll do't. Dost thou come here to whine,
> To outface me with leaping in her grave?
> Be buried quick with her?—and so will I.
> And if thou prate of mountains let them throw
> Millions of acres on us, till our ground
> Singeing his pate against the burning zone,
> Make Ossa like a wart! Nay, an thou'lt mouth,
> I'll rant as well as thou. (5.1.252–64)

Hamlet turns what should be a solemn ritual into a scenery-chewing extravaganza of overstated ranting, the sort of thing Jonson had in mind with his jab at Marlowe's theater as "scenicall strutting and furious vociferation."[26] Where Bottom in *A Midsummer Night's Dream* imagines the tyrant role as "a part to tear a cat in" (1.2.17), Hamlet here substitutes eating a crocodile. The grief contest is an exercise in extremity, a launchpad for over-the-top, ludicrous theatricality. The schoolyard logic (he started it) is acknowledged in retrospect when, in a scene added in the Folio but missing from Q2, Hamlet offers a "nopology" by granting the resemblance of their shared losses only to follow that with a lingering grudge: "But sure the bravery of his grief did put me / Into a towering passion" (F5.2.79–80). Hamlet knows he has gone too far.

Hamlet as RIP Troll

Having said that Hamlet is a troll, it is time to specify precisely what kind. Specifically, I would like to compare Hamlet's mockery of Laertes's grief in the funeral scene with a particularly vicious subsidiary form of trolling known as "RIP trolling."[27] As its name lets on, RIP trolling refers to the organized online humiliation of the parents and friends of someone who died in tragic circumstances.[28] Attacking those grieving a death from suicide has been particularly popular, even birthing associated memes generated through the mockery of inaccuracies of spelling and grammar in posthumous social media posts paying tribute to the dead.[29] In a "raid," trolls find a Facebook page in which grieving parents and friends gather online to mourn someone (a child is especially popular) who has recently died by suicide and bombard the page with memes making fun of the dead person, ridiculing the mourning process and, in particular, the clichéd or inarticulate sentiments that get passed around in the wake of death. As one of the darkest possible expressions of "joy of the worm" recounted in this book, RIP trolling offers a particularly callous example of the "group form" of online sociality.[30]

The fact that people can and do make jokes about suicide doesn't prove that suicide isn't a serious subject. It may be that precisely *because* suicide is a serious subject, it becomes imbued with a certain allure as a juicy target for abuse from those eager to display the strength of their sangfroid, the depth of their commitment to trolling's shtick. In targeting with humor precisely the subjects that others hold dear, one is demonstrating something about one's distance from consensus. In her monograph *Kill All Normies: Online Culture Wars from 4Chan and Tumblr to Trump and the Alt-Right* (2017), Angela Nagle describes the curious blend of relations to suicide and self-harm within online forums such as 4chan:

> The forum's preoccupation with suicide… often takes the form of painful expressions of anonymous users' desire to commit suicide themselves, and at the same time it mocks suicide victims and those who express sympathy with the victims. Forum users come to the most arguably unsympathetic place imaginable to tell others of their suicidal fantasies anonymously, where they will probably be half-jokingly told to do it. They thus reject the mainstream media's suicide spectacles and instead remake it as their own dark spectacle, in which pity is replaced by cruelty. And yet, because both the act of suicide and the displays of insensitivity toward suicide victims are perceived as forms of transgression, both found a home within this strangely coherent online world.[31]

In such environments, joking about suicide is not a way of making some particularly revealing claim about suicide per se so much as it is an opportunity to reveal the integrity of one's "role faith" in trolling harder. Whether the subject is the Holocaust, slavery, religion, rape, sexual abuse, or various identities or allegiances, the portable lesson of ethnographic analyses such as Whitney Phillips's *This Is Why We Can't Have Nice Things: Mapping the Relationship between Online Trolling and Mainstream Culture* (2016) is that the turnover of targets is relatively swift, as tactics and personnel shift and media attention waxes and wanes.[32] "Why so serious?" asks the Joker, played by Heath Ledger and, later, Joaquin Phoenix, and repurposed ad nauseam online as a meme-level signifier of free-form antipathy.[33] Like the troll logic it both predicted and, in its later iterations, mirrored back, the Joker's trickster assault on the seriousness of others is intended to attract attention while preempting response.

To see trolling as worthy of horror or critique is to remain within the sphere of seriousness, and thus to self-define as a worthy target for assault: from the troll perspective, it is seriousness itself that must be destroyed, and anyone who takes assaults on seriousness seriously is therefore prima facie worthy of abuse. Attempts to nail down a consistent set of ideological commitments shared by trolls will fail, not simply because of the ad hoc nature of "raids" and the inevitable "user churn" of any particular forum's roster of participants, but because ideological commitments themselves presume a seriousness that trolling as such disavows; in a sense, the ideology of the troll is affect. That ideology was memorably phrased in a single stupid word: "lulz," a deliberately misspelled variant upon "lol," the typed acronym for "laughing out loud." What "kicks" was to beatniks, "lulz" are to trolls: a slang phrase for pleasure doomed to become passé. Elevating "lulz" to a self-certifying raison d'être, in troll parlance "lulz" becomes a Key to All Mythologies, or "the only reason to do anything."[34] Freud's metapsychology of libidinal energy would more or less agree.

Of course, there is no reason to take trolls at their word. Just as Hamlet can troll his underlings and courtiers because he is their princely superior, it is no accident that whiteness and maleness constitute the demographic baseline and psychic home turf from which many trolls and online provocateurs typically launch "edgy" humor outward, their very edges defined by a "political correctness" that they see as hedging in their freedom to be racist, sexist, ableist, transphobic, and so on. Precisely because racism and patriarchy offer considerable padding and ego defense in the form of a tacit universalism that has historically prioritized them as a group, white male trolls can affect a radical "innocence" with respect to the standing force of the hierarchies they inherit and capitalize upon. The litany of pseudodisclaimers that hedge around the display of troll-like behavior is grimly familiar as veils for this positionality: just being honest, just asking a question, just playing the devil's advocate for a minute, sorry if I offend you but I have a dark sense of humor, and so forth. Thus, white male cis trolls can see the BIPOC, queer, trans, disabled, religious, or politically committed people they offend as attached to and invested in local, identitarian projects without grasping their own social location as a location at all. Emily Dickinson's lyric question now titters from the troll cave of the comment section: "I'm nobody, who are you?"

This circular and self-serving nest of assumptions and stances constellates its opponents in its own image: hence the modern coinage of
"concern trolling." To be "concerned" as a way of leveraging power in
an ambiguous or borderline situation is to gain the upper hand over the
less concerned, and to valorize one's own position as more caring, more
thoughtful, and, tacitly, probably right about the matter in question. Nietzsche's old argument about the will to power obscured beneath the will to
truth becomes repurposed: the will to concern is a way of gaining the high
ground from which to wring one's hands and worry over others. The frame
of "concern trolling" thus remakes the serious person into a kind of troll,
but a troll without humor, a troll of militant humorlessness (if it is unverifi-
able, it might still be worth asking: How much of "the ethical turn" within
the literary-critical humanities is in fact a leveraging of precisely such
"concern troll" power?) If, in the words of Samuel Butler, "to the serious
all things are serious," then this implies its contrary: the person for whom
nothing can be serious.[35] In the case of RIP trolls, there is a kind of deliberate moral act of self-emptying, a willful claiming of cruelty as authenticity, the final removal of the compunctions of restraint that are imagined
to constitute others as inauthentic, false, "normie." In the absence of any
filter upon speech and instincts, they affect a manner that is, like Hamlet,
"indifferent honest" (3.1.121), but performatively so, and to a fault.

I seem to have rather wandered off Elsinore's grounds. But the Hamlet of the "antic disposition" and grotesque misogyny and the modern online persona of the white male "edgelord" are more than kin and less than
kind. As tendentious as this comparison might seem to some (am I concern trolling?), Hamlet's behavior at Ophelia's funeral strikes me as a kind
of early modern prefiguration of RIP trolling. First, let's get the obvious
distance and differences out of the way. His identity is known, he's not
a stranger, and this is a face-to-face interaction: "This is I, / Hamlet the
Dane" (5.1.246–47). Nonetheless, I think Hamlet's deliberate destruction
of seriousness in favor of an aggressively humorous mockery of the grieving process of others in the wake of suicide constitutes an example of RIP
trolling *avant la lettre*.

Bracketing the obvious anachronism of the comparison and the constitutive absence of the mediation of the internet, we nonetheless have the
legible emotional structure of RIP trolling: an affective display of gleeful
and sadistic scorn designed to horrify and antagonize grieving people that
works to undo ritual solemnity through the deliberate violation of decorum by humiliating mourners on chiefly stylistic grounds. Nagle's "dark
spectacle, in which pity has been replaced by cruelty," suits Hamlet's treatment of Laertes all too well. Hamlet sees histrionicism in Laertes and
decides to attack that grief rather than grieving openly for Ophelia him-

self. Indeed, the lateral turn toward Laertes looks rather like a displacement of Ophelia at her own funeral. Sticking to trolling's script lets Hamlet change the subject.

Context matters. It is not difficult to see why the example of Ophelia's "maimed rites" (5.1.242) might prove especially galling to Hamlet: his own father's rites were, in a sense, "maimed" by Gertrude's haste in remarriage. Hamlet believes that Polonius and Claudius were essentially guilty of instrumentalizing Ophelia by turning her into a pawn of their corrupt, murderous, "incestuous" court when they used her to spy upon him. In attacking other people's grief for Ophelia, Hamlet is denouncing Claudius's cynical deployment of her in the scheme to guess the secret of his antic disposition. Caught up in retroactive self-justification, Hamlet's cruelty to Ophelia was supposedly justified by the claim that she betrayed both him and herself in putting the interests of Claudius's faction above their own love for each other. The decorum of courtly subservience and the established patterns of art have been tilting askew since the play's first act; as James Marino forcefully notes, "A daughter helping her father deceive her lover rather than the other way around is a shocking perversion of theatrical convention."[36] On the other side of her "doubtful" demise due to a mental distraction that he bears no little responsibility for precipitating, Hamlet is off-loading his guilt by claiming that, in having set her against him, Claudius and Polonius—and not him—are really to blame for her madness and her death.

Though it is speculative, and, I hope it's clear, not an excuse of any kind, we could say that Hamlet might also be using his own manic, excessive, "indifferent honest," and therefore cruel persona as the "mad," "antic" RIP troll to cover up for his own genuine grief. This deliberate strategy keeps genuine outbursts of feeling at a remove through the kind of histrionic display that we already know he associates with theater at its most degraded and dangerous. By plunging tragic circumstance into cold water through a deliberately overdone performance that mocks Laertes's grief as theatrical, and therefore artificial, inflated, and false, Hamlet presses Shakespeare's generic experiment home: continuing a diminution of tragic mechanisms already underway with the downsizing of *The Murder of Gonzago* into *The Mousetrap*, here too the theater becomes the place through which Shakespeare attacks theater itself.[37] This self-destructive experiment is rooted in a founding awareness of the conventions that it mars and violates through their distorted and phantasmatic returns within the play. Theories of tragic *megethos* and catharsis get folded into actions, and actions test theories, assault theories, or ironically push off from them. Genre is not just a distant academic question (What did Aristotle actually say, and how can we be sure?), nor a matter of what entertainment one wants (What kind of play shall we stage? What do I want to feel and what do I want others to feel?). Genre is also a thickly lived medium through which emotional life gets managed: in the eyes of the RIP trolls, and the troll that Hamlet becomes, a funeral is a kind of play with rules about who says what and exactly how deeply you are or are not supposed to be moved. Hamlet ruins this funeral as a way of attacking its scripted nature, showing it up as inadequate to the intensity of its emotional occasion precisely in its overreach toward an intensity that looks too much like art.

If, in the encounter with the actor moved by Hecuba, Hamlet was feeling himself to be somehow diminished by tragedy's primordial energy and moral example, in his attack on Laertes's leap into the grave Hamlet is forcing the seriousness of Ophelia's death to push through art into something beyond. To speculate upon the motivations of this RIP troll, perhaps in his violent actions Hamlet is saying that Ophelia's real death is more serious, more real, more ungrievably huge, than the patterns of art can bear, and so Ovidian giganticism will not serve. Perhaps, Hamlet is launching an attack on bad seriousness rather than an attack on seriousness itself. But the weapon Hamlet wields in doing so is a cruel sort of competitive comedic spirit, to ensure that the tragic occasion of funeral fails, to force tragedy's resources to show themselves up as incomplete, partial, and inadequate. "Acting out" while telling someone else to "tone it down," in the funeral scene the exposed wires of Hamlet's pedantry and Hamlet's histrionicism touch and short-circuit. Turning "joy of the worm" into a poisonous weapon of mockery, Hamlet trolls tragedy's susceptibility to histrionicism by arrogating the cruelly pedantic voice of decorum itself.

Timon as Troll

In the second half of this chapter, we shift from Elsinore's killing floor to the banquet halls of Athens and the nonplace beyond its gates where Timon makes his last stand. If there are many Hamlets, the critical consensus seems to be that there are exactly two Timons, and their nonalignment is a problem. "The problem of the two Timons" was named into existence by Amanda Bailey, but it arguably surfaces in different framings and phrasings in a range of notable critical responses to the play, from critics such as G. Wilson Knight and William Empson, and, more recently, from Julia Lupton, James Kuzner, Eike Kronshage, and others.[38] The phrase indicates the challenge faced by the play's puzzled readers and audience members as they try to synthesize or link the philanthropic Timon of the play's first half—a generous-to-a-fault patrician playboy who exhausts his resources on his surrounding coterie of dependents, flatterers, and false friends—and the misanthropic Timon of the second half: a ranting crank who strips himself of his clothing, disavows his humanity, and becomes a vegan would-be hermit on the outskirts of civilization.

Between these two halves lies the play's celebrated central catastrophe: the banquet scene. Rendered insolvent as his debts mount and his requests for loans are spurned by his former friends, Timon invites his betrayers to a Last Supper. Having soaked up their erstwhile hosts's hospitality and blithely ignored his requests for a bailout, the invited guests arrive and make small talk, whispering daggers of doubt about Timon's poverty as they make eyes at the serving dishes set before them, and endure their hosts increasingly manic and bitter farewell toast. Then, with the cry "Uncover, dogs, and lap!" (3.7.80), they are served a meal of stones and water, pummeled first with invective and then simply pummeled. The stage direction is blunt: *He beats them.* Having made a clean break, Timon strips off his clothes, curses his former city, and departs for the woods.

This act of trolling—cruelly pleasurable, dependent on the credulity of others, reliant upon codes of decorum, a precursor to physical assault—is not what truly interests me, and is not what I will focus upon in my reading of the play. Rather, I want to examine the strange demi-sociality that emerges on the other side of Timon's rejection of humanity when, once he departs from Athens and subtracts himself from political economy only to discover gold beneath the ground, he is overrun with visitors trying to solicit gold, cheer him up, or reintegrate him into human community, offering bitter confirmation of the Lockean insight still to come that "property established civilized conditions among men."[39] Holding a hoard, Timon reenters social circulation as a potential creditor, patron, friend, and citizen. Even on the edge of the civil, from the point of this discovery Timon thus inhabits not a genuine "outside" but perhaps what Phil Neel has termed a "hinterland," a social space "at the edge of the wage-relation."[40] The tense scenes of unwanted interaction that follow the discovery of Timon's windfall repeatedly feint and thrust across the border of social possibility, prompting the question of who is really trolling whom. Scripting all possible interactions into further evidence of its "exceptless rashness" (4.3.487), misanthropy's capacious but inflexible generality constitutes its own brittle form of decorum. Eventually, Timon gives up and dies.

Before that point, trolling his would-be visitors, Timon teases and baits them even as his insults gradually ramp up in aggression and violence from quasi-flirtatious gibes to open fantasies of massacre. As Timon's interlocutors endure and sometimes take pains to flatter him even in the midst of this abuse, and pointedly never refuse his sneering offers of gold

as they do so, these rigged encounters relentlessly produce a similar outcome: the confirmation of misanthropy as a deliberate leveling down of
difference as such. In producing this sour outcome, Timon demonstrates
a misanthropic variant of what Jonathan Lear terms "neurtue," or neurotic
virtue.[41] The inverse of an Aristotelian virtue, which is consciously understood, responds to reality appropriately, and produces happiness, neurtue
is a neurotic capacity to improvise so that a structuring unconscious fantasy finds ratification in every significant human encounter, repetitiously
distorting reality in order to produce the desired form of unhappiness.[42]
Smooth, impenetrable, and relentless, Timon's neurtue constitutes both
the keynote of Timon as character, his "unary trait," and a significant formal challenge for Middleton and Shakespeare's drama. Yet, paradoxically,
the very rigidity of Timon's misanthropic worldview becomes a stiff diving
board that functions as a surprisingly useful tool for the leaps and feints of
both Timon and his interlocutors, circulating comedic energy around the
dark core of his angry hatred. Ratifying yet also revising Bergson's assertion that comedic laughter mocks puritanical inflexibility on behalf of social integration, the neurtue of Timon's misanthropic stiffness sets trolling in motion.[43]

Timon's sparring with the Cynic philosopher Apemantus exemplifies
this *perpetuum mobile* of invective:

APEMANTUS: Thou art the cap of all fools alive.

TIMON: Would thou wert clean enough to spit on.

APEMANTUS: A plague on thee! Thou art too bad to curse.

TIMON: All villains that do stand by thee are pure. (4.3.350–53).

And so on. One senses that this energetic exchange could go on indefi-
nitely, and that these insults could trade speakers without any particular
difference as they "play the dozens" with each other.[44] But there is a notable difference in their underlying stances toward each other. Apemantus keeps returning to the bare conditions of Timon's survival, performing a kind of surreptitious care work beneath the surface of raillery: asking
him where he sleeps, trying to get him to eat a medlar (a pear whose suggestive name gives rise to bitter quibbles), and, throughout, challenging
Timon to break character and stop the volley of insults, which eventually descends from complete sentences into a schoolyard trading of curt
monosyllables:

APEMANTUS: Beast!

TIMON: Slave!

APEMANTUS: Toad!

TIMON: Rogue, rogue, rogue!
I am sick of this false world, and will love naught
But even the mere necessities upon't.
Then, Timon, presently prepare thy grave.
Lie where the light foam of the sea may beat
Thy gravestone daily. Make thine epitaph,
That death in me at others lives may laugh. (4.3.364–73)

Self-destruction is the only way to unanswerably ensure that you can finish the volley. Timon leaps to death as a way of silencing Apemantus's claim upon him and, by extension, the claim of humanity that even its furthest outliers such as Cynical philosophers nonetheless represent.[45] The foam of the sea, an agent of silencing and mortal conclusion that also connotes a standard memento mori poetics of the solitary life as a fragile bubble, comes to sound in this passage as if it were itself laughing on Timon's behalf at those who will survive him: "joy of the worm" adopts a posthumous mode of virtual superiority toward organic life. Life is a joke and death is the last laugh.

Ruined from the start by a seemingly constitutive hypocrisy (hating a category to which one belongs), there is something theatrical and aspirational about the performativity that dogs the presentation of the misanthropic agenda.[46] Misanthropes like Timon seem to need the very stooges and targets they also disavow, just as trolls need "normies" in order to measure the force of their sangfroid. Throughout his parleys with visitors, Timon struggles to remain on message and "in character," huffing and puffing to sustain the vituperative tone that "Misanthropos" requires, while occasionally losing ground and focus.

Understanding that tone means tracking Timon's oscillations between a blustering hatred that is directed outward into murderous fantasy and an undertow that is directed inward as suicidal ideation, an oscillation we see in the exchange above with Apemantus. Karl Menninger, author of *Man against Himself* (1938) and one of the early psychoanalytic theorists of self-harm, finds three components in suicide, each with distinct affective inflections: feelings of revenge and hatred produce a wish to kill, feelings of hopelessness produce a wish to die, and feelings of guilt produce a wish to be killed.[47] The urge to kill remains proximate to an urge to die, a longing that it both enervates and keeps at bay; ultimately, these two will fuse as Timon turns antisocial aggressivity inward. Fusing multiple components into self-massacre, Timon's misanthropy sublates guilt by dislocating it from a personal condition into a general, outward-facing judgment upon humanity-as-species. It is mankind who is guilty and who thus deserves to be killed, a general commitment that in turn allows Timon to kill himself in the place of humanity as a whole, inverting the Christian logic of penal substitution as in a dark mirror. *"Self-massacre" lets the death of the self stand in for and in some sense compensate for the unenacted extermination of humanity as a group.*

Timon as Death Persuader

To the bitter end, Timon remains caught in the web of sociality he also despises. That end finally arises when, after Timon's extended but ultimately refused encounter with Flavius as the "one good man" who might counter misanthropic generality, Flavius brings Timon's final visitors to his hermitage for a fruitless last-ditch session of urgent requests and icy harangues. Fraught with panic at the prospect of Alcibiades's imminent assault on the city and perhaps hoping for a financial gift that might fund the city's defenses, the Senators hope to lure Timon home to Athens only to be, predictably, rebuffed in a wave of valedictory invective. Never one to give a sucker an even break, Timon bids the assembled flock of Athenians farewell only to further tease them with suggestions that he might relent, return, or (perhaps financially) support their cause.

Timon keeps a certain degree zero of interaction in place despite his murderous fantasies of massacre. Sounding false notes of patriotic fervor, Timon asks to be commended to his "loving countrymen" (5.2.78); either the Senators cannot hear the acid sarcasm in the word "loving," or choose to disregard it because of their hope that they too might gather up some gold. Sensing that he can wring one more humiliation out of this exchange, Timon pushes the gag further:

> TIMON: Commend me to them,
> And tell them that to ease them of their griefs,
> Their fears of hostile strokes, their aches, losses,
> Their pangs of love, with other incident throes
> That nature's fragile vessel doth sustain
> In life's uncertain voyage, I will some kindness do them.
> I'll teach them to prevent wild Alcibiades' wrath.
>
> FIRST SENATOR [*aside*]: I like this well, he will return again. (5.2.82–89)

Expanding beyond its political occasion to take on a range of causes for melancholy vexation, Timon's introductory catalog of evils recalls Hamlet's "slings and arrows of outrageous fortune" and "whips and scorns of time," and seems to imply without revealing the suicidal consequence to come. In its paired and symmetrical evocation of "nature's fragile vessel" embarked upon "life's uncertain voyage," Timon's language briefly achieves a stark lyricism that is retroactively revealed to have been a kind of aesthetic padding before the bitter punch line to come, which lands with all the greater force because of the winding up of the credulous Senators that precedes it:

> I have a tree which grows here in my close
> That mine own use invites me to cut down,
> And shortly must I fell it. Tell my friends,
> Tell Athens, in the sequence of degree
> From high to low throughout, that whoso please
> To stop affliction, let him take his haste,
> Come hither ere my tree hath felt the axe,
> And hang himself. (5.2.90–97)

Here "joy of the worm" discharges in a cruelly precise comedic crack about mass suicide. Timon leads his auditors along the switchbacks of dependent clauses up a ramp of increasing expectation in order to drive them off a cliff: just at the point when, perhaps, the hardened heart has finally softened and human kindness and generosity is about to issue forth, the bottom falls out and the troll gives a wolfish grin. Generosity is shown up as a ruse, for Timon's gift is either bitterly sarcastic or lethally sincere. The tree bears a fruit of death, and it is a death that Timon seems to hope will become universal if each citizen "from high to low throughout" would only take the necessary step.

Is this an expression of anger or of sadistic pleasure? Timon's suggestion of a tree as a handy means to die bears a telling similarity to a celebrated passage from Seneca's *De ira*:

> If the soul is sick and because of its own imperfections unhappy, a man may end its sorrows and at the same time himself. To him to whom chance has given a king that aims his shafts at the breasts of his friends, to him who has a master that gorges fathers with the flesh of their children, I would say: "Madman, why do you moan? Why do you wait for some enemy to avenge you by the destruction of your nation, or for a mighty king from afar to fly to your rescue? In whatever direction you may turn your

eyes, there lies the means to end your woes. See you that precipice? Down that is the way to liberty. See you that sea, that river, that well? There sits liberty—at the bottom. See you that tree, stunted, blighted, and barren? [*Vides illam arborem brevem, retorridam, infelicem?*] Yet from its branches hangs liberty [*Pendet indet libertatem*]."⁴⁸

The resonances of this passage with Timon's farewell to the Senators are numerous, and obvious. Seneca's phrase "why do you wait for some enemy to avenge you by the destruction of your nation" rather exactly telegraphs the relationship of the Alcibiades plotline to Timon's own vengeful fantasies about the imminent fall of Athens. Going beyond this schematic resemblance, Seneca's instrumental deployment of the natural world suggestively unites the locale of Timon's hermetic retreat with the remedy that he recommends to his fellow citizens and ultimately selects for himself: self-killing.

Within the terms of Seneca's own argument, the recognition that the means of self-killing surround us is meant to produce a feeling of calm from the pressurizing hold of negative affects, a breezy sense that life is easily set aside that recalls the throwaway bravado of Hamlet's declaration that "I do not set my life at a pin's fee" (1.4.65). But it stands at odds with the bitter valence of Timon's sneering offer to the Senators and to the citizens they represent. While the ideas are Stoic, their delivery suggests a murderous fantasy of generalized massacre rather than an urge to inspire individual liberty. Timon weaponizes a chestnut of Stoic thought against its purported ends of calm and rationality, and in so doing traverses the Senecan source, arriving at a position closer to that of Hegesias of Cyrene, the supposed author, according to Cicero's *Tusculan Disputations*, of a lost work titled *Death by Starvation*.⁴⁹ Nicknamed "Peisithanatos" (the death persuader), Hegesias's arguments for voluntary death were apparently so successful at convincing people that death was always preferable to life that he was ordered by Ptolemy II not to preach in Alexandria lest he encourage citizens to take their own lives.⁵⁰ Suicidal pessimism troubles the logic of survival on which political community depends.

Confronted with the advocacy of mass suicide, one is tempted to ask the sort of question beloved of therapists and police officers and concern trolls: Is Timon serious? Not so much poorly executed as deliberately rendered unfunny in order to provoke, the aggressive disclosure of the hanging tree as Timon's genial remedy for his countrymen's misfortune is meant to further humiliate his guests. It shows them up as venal, the credulous butts of his cunning "come hither" gesture. The same image will become a broad gag in Massinger's tragicomedy *The Bond-Man, an*

Antient Storie (1624); when the rebellious slaves of Syracuse learn that their masters are returning victorious from a battle with Carthaginians, the slave Gracullo panics and cries out: "Every man / Seeke a convenient Tree, and hang himself."[51] But Timon's speech is both darker and more ambiguous.

There is something gratuitous about the offer of the hanging tree; surely, in the hermetic retreat that Timon has created, a world from which the citizens of Athens have already been subtracted and silenced, he has already achieved the goal implicit in the hanging tree's solicitation of mass death: no people. But this "gratuitousness," its status as a deliberately unfunny and tasteless gesture of sarcastic quasi-humor allows Timon to voice a fantasy that he would otherwise be at pains to disavow: merger with Athens. That is, the offer functions not only as an aggressive threat but as a consoling fantasy. The hanging tree is a collaborative scenario that imagines, however briefly, a merger of Timon with Athens in a collective suicide pact whose material basis would make them come to him, and in their abandonment of the city in favor of nature, become like him: *beneath the sheltering cover of a final kiss-off, Timon is offering himself a final fantasy of community.*

One might well object that in offering this solution as a self-consciously excessive gag Timon guarantees its refusal. Timon is refreshing his sense of injury, perhaps in order to steel his resolve before killing himself. He needs to confirm that his judgments of the city are correct, and to cauterize the wounded bond that his now considerable sequence of visits represents. If trolling works to offend and vex, then perhaps the flood of visitors will cease and Timon will finally be free to die. We are watching the painful work of decathexis up close. But beneath the manifest level of its brusque delivery (*I am making an offer I know the city will refuse in order to wound myself and escape its claim upon me*) there lies perhaps at a deeper level still an underlying fantasy about merger with the natural world and merger with others (*Let us all die together beneath the same tree*).

If Timon is not serious, he is not not serious, either. His lies are lies that tell a symptomatic truth: the suicidal death he advocates for others he intends for himself. We sense the imminent pressure of his own death in the presentation of the tree as a limited-time offer. Timon's declaration that "shortly must I fell it" hints at his own fatal resolve, giving the tree a fragility that belies its deadly purpose. In a sense, killing yourself *is* a way to kill everyone else; recall Luis Buñuel's favorite remark of Octavio Paz that "a chained man need only shut his eyes to make the world explode."[52] Going further in this direction, consider A. E. Housman's poem "I Counsel You Beware" for a Shropshire variant on the same sentiment:

> Good creatures, do you love your lives
> And have you ears for sense?
> Here is a knife like other knives
> That cost me eighteen pence.
>
> I need but stick it in my heart
> And down will come the sky
> And earth's foundations will depart
> And all you folk will die.[53]

Aaron Kunin phrases this as a condition of satisfaction that haunts the character form of the misanthrope as an endlessly repeatable type: "For the misanthropic gesture to be truly objective, the world itself has to withdraw."[54] Timon's offer becomes a kind of misanthropic articulation of the categorical imperative: *I want to die and in so willing I also will that everyone should want to die.* It's an unhinged variant of the position that Spinoza will take in the *Ethics*: "People under the guidance of reason seek nothing for themselves that they would not desire for the rest of humanity."[55] In Timon's case, at least as Spinoza would understand it, reason has been abandoned and "another nature" has taken over; but the universalizing architecture that will become the Kantian "categorical imperative" is implicitly here in Timon's murderous general mandate.

The Salt Flood

Taking flight from the dissimulation and treachery he projects onto his final cadre of visitors, Timon's suicidal death becomes the means by which to realize a point of transit out of the shattered social surround and into the ultimate misanthropic community, the ocean of planetary being, which pulses beneath his final utterance in the play:

> Come not to me again, but say to Athens
> Timon hath made his everlasting mansion
> Upon the beached verge of the salt flood,
> Who once a day with his embossed froth
> The turbulent surge shall cover; thither come
> And let my gravestone be your oracle.
> Lips, let sour words go by, and language end:
> What is amiss, plague and infection mend;
> Graves only be men's works and death their gain.
> Sun, hide thy beams, Timon hath done his reign. (5.2.99–108)

Here the snarl of trolling fades, and something of the grandeur we expect from the valedictory movements of Shakespearean tragedy takes over. This lyrical speech exemplifies the contradictory dynamic of misanthropic communication as a speech that wants to be covered over by turbulence, whose pedagogy upon the pointlessness of human effort has itself a curious persistence, and even a kind of pride in the everlasting stability of its mansion. Plague and infection "mend" by joining together, into death-bound communities, courtesans such as Timandra and Phrynia and their clients, a local example of a tendency of organic life toward the material conditions of the inorganic to which even misanthropes succumb. The fact of death thus vitiates the founding misanthropic gesture of leaving the city by demonstrating that, whether within or without the protection of its walls, all roads lead to the grave.

Faced with this absolute, the Senators shrug and depart with a telling declaration: "His discontents are unreservedly / Coupled to nature" (5.2.109–10). At a literal level, this means that his affects are fixed; he will not budge, and accordingly they should expect nothing. But in the image of Timon's misanthropic hatred being "coupled" with nature, the senatorial kiss-off constitutes a public recognition of the politics of misanthropic allegiance to the inhuman. Perhaps Timon's last message constitutes not so much a successful moment of trolling as a uniquely successful moment of misanthropic pedagogy. In his advice to the Senators about how to avoid Alcibiades, Timon imagines a suicidal assemblage of body, noose, and tree, a conjunction of somatic and environmental materials that repeats itself in the benediction of Timon's mansion: the beachfront grave can be read as an earthwork, a melancholic multimedia assemblage whose gallery-wall plaque would read "pebbles, corpse, and salt."[56] Like Robert Smithson's *Spiral Jetty*, Timon's mansion is an earthwork dialectically embraced by the surge, turbulence, and "deathly, inhuman" threat of the ocean, evoked by Steve Mentz's "new thalassology" in *At the Bottom of Shakespeare's Ocean* (2009).[57] Finally forcing misanthropy and community into conjunction through death, this misanthropic coupling takes place on the other side of the city, in the singularly rapacious embrace of the suicidal body by its elemental material surroundings: to die in such a manner is to couple with nature.

Perhaps Timon here attains the fantasy that Romain Rolland's 1927 letter to Sigmund Freud articulated as "the oceanic feeling" of entering eternity through fusion with the transpersonal, which Freud coolly assesses in *Civilization and Its Discontents*.[58] It is notable that in Rolland's original letter, in a section paraphrased but not cited directly by Freud, there is a telling moment of quasi-suicidal longing expressed through the deliberate disavowal of survival as an ideal: "I add that this 'oceanic' feeling has nothing to do with my personal aspirations. Personally, I aspire to eternal rest; survival has no attraction for me [*Personnellement, j'aspire au repos éternel; la survie ne m'attire aucunement*]."⁵⁹ In Freud's text, this faint suggestion is drawn out via recourse to comparison with the suicidal crises staged in drama: "If I have understood my friend rightly, he means the same thing by it as the consolation offered by an original and somewhat eccentric dramatist to his hero who is facing a self-inflicted death. 'We cannot fall out of this world.' That is to say, it is a feeling of an indissoluble bond, of being one with the external world as a whole."⁶⁰ The neatly counterintuitive oddity of Freud's phrasing in this passage—that he should describe a metaphoric scenario of dissolution as precisely the affirmation of an "indissoluble bond"—might mark his own none-too-subtle resistance to sharing in the feeling that he is describing. Before Freud's restraint in repudiating the feeling within Rolland's letter to him, Middleton and Shakespeare's text already anticipates this consolatory vision of watery union in death. Entering the oceanic plenum of being by erasing his own survival, Timon inserts the body of the misanthrope into a thingly catalog of material actants, agents, and flows. The "nothing" of death gives him the "all things" of a world that patiently and seamlessly closes over his temporary personhood.

This affirmation of the world in the midst of the negation of human life touches upon one of the deeper paradoxes within "joy of the worm" as it binds lived feeling to fatal action. The joyful negation of personal survival at the level of the individual human body draws upon an elemental poetics of liquid circulation, rewriting death as material return, not to an inert biblical dust but to a primordial watery flux. Having traversed negativity in both plays, I want to circle back to Elsinore in search of the rare but significant places in which representations of self-killing become positive in the timeless and transpersonal manner indicated by Timon's fantasy; in the place of Timon's littoral language of ocean depths and surging shores, characters in *Hamlet* opt for narrow brooks and trembling drops of dew when they imagine death as pleasurable dissolution.

This poetics of suicidal liquidity shines out memorably in Hamlet's first private outburst of suicidal ideation in act 1, scene 2. A genuine soliloquy with respect to its speech situation—unlike its showier cousin, the "to be or not to be" speech—Hamlet's speech positions him as stranded across a kind of intellectual-historical chasm between classical and Christian imaginaries: "O that this too too sallied flesh would melt, / Thaw, and resolve itself into a dew, / Or that the Everlasting had not fixed his canon / Gainst self-slaughter" (1.2.129–32). Caught between desire and doctrine, Hamlet cites Empedoclean combinatorial ontology and then bemoans its supersession by Christian discourse. Suggesting both the condensation of vapor into morning dew and the melting of winter ice, the image of death as a kind of dissolution of the body back into a constitutive element that can then recombine anew formally crystallizes in Hamlet's tremulous image of his body as a droplet poised to fall. It is a kind of materialist daydream of death as transformation that precedes its Christian counterpoint, the eternal fixity of a deontic embargo against self-destruction. Hamlet deploys elemental ontology as an imaginary alternative to the theological surround, and takes momentary comfort from a thought experiment in its terms; the dawn of dew evaporates in the rising sun of Christian deity, its momentary consolation burning off in the presence of a superior force.

Early editor of Shakespeare Joseph Hunter heard a sonic aftershock of Claudius's "great cannon" (1.2.126) in Hamlet's anxiety at the prospect of an Everlasting fixing a "canon" against his desired scenario;[61] one could lean into this homophonic link by stressing that the hard, metallic weapon it sonically conjures stands at the farthest material remove from the trembling liquidity it overwrites. The formal frame of antithetical possibilities held in equipoise ("O that _____ / Or that _____") will return in the central antithesis of "to be or not to be," which shifts the terms but retains this self-divided formal structure. Stranded in the breach between motivation and volition, Hamlet longs for a death he experiences as profoundly off-limits. As delicate as a hypothetical drop of dew, "joy of the worm" mists the surface of Hamlet's mind with transitory ideation, but goes no further.

If we are looking for other examples of this liquid form of "joy of the worm" in *Hamlet*, its faint, trickling presence also surfaces in Gertrude's imagination of Ophelia's fatal, flowery drift downstream. Though it is ascriptively projected by Gertrude and thus cannot reliably transmit Ophelia's own experience, as an index of Gertrude's anxious desire to stage-manage loss it reveals with peculiar force the imaginary hold of pleasurable fantasies of self-annihilation. Diffusing political crisis through an eerie burst of pictorialism, Gertrude turns Ophelia's pathetic drowning into a sensorial pageant of pleasurable aesthetic effects:

> There is a willow grows aslant a brook
> That shows his hoar leaves in the glassy stream.
> There with fantastic garlands did she come
> Of crowflowers, nettles, daisies, and long purples,
> That liberal shepherds give a grosser name,
> But our cold maids do "dead men's fingers" call them.
> There, on the pendant boughs her coronet weeds
> Clambering to hang, an envious sliver broke,
> When down her weedy trophies and herself
> Fell in the weeping brook. Her clothes spread wide,
> And mermaid-like a while they bore her up,

Which time she chanted snatches of old lauds
As one incapable of her own distress,
Or like a creature native and indued
Unto that element. But long it could not be
Till that her garments, heavy with their drink,
Pulled the poor wretch from her melodious lay
To muddy death. (4.7.162–79)

Gertrude's speech reworks the floral language of Ophelia's mad displays, offering in this polychromatic set piece a compensatory "document in madness" to memorialize a sudden and wrenching loss. In Gertrude's representation of Ophelia floating gently toward her doom as the "melodious" turns "muddy," she becomes elemental as she exits corporeal life. With the flip of a mermaid tail, Ophelia goes from being "incapable of her own distress" to being a woman/fish assemblage already accustomed to the water and therefore unthreatened by her immersion within it as she glides into pleasure's currents.[62] Activating both its watery imagery and its "Or..." syntax from Hamlet's suicidal soliloquy in 1.2.129–59, Ophelia moves from air to water. It is in this casual slithering into view of the "element" of water that the Empedoclean poetics of materialist merger, with its ontologically consolatory softening of the threat of death, laps briefly again at the surface of the text.

Submerged within the "weeping" waters of Gertrude's speech before she is buried in the earth, Ophelia enjoys the curious fate of being simultaneously hypervisible and yet exorbitant to the play in which she suffers and dies, a fate reduplicated in critical characterizations of her, where she mostly serves as foil, mirror, or pawn. Mourning the gap left by Ophelia's death seems to upstage substantive engagement with her living actions, choices, and statements. Samuel Johnson offers a case in point when he arrests his catalog of the play's formal infelicities to dilate upon her hapless goodness: "The gratification which would arise from the destruction of an usurper and a murderer, is abated by the untimely death of Ophelia, the young, the beautiful, the harmless, and the pious."[63] As if throwing an emergency blanket over a shivering body, Johnson piles on this epideictic surplus in order to cover up the scant but suggestive indications of something far wilder that lived within "pretty" Ophelia. If Ophelia's distraction jars, perhaps it is not just because of the direct bawdy of "by Cock, they are to blame" (4.5.62), but because of the frightening way that her own fate confirms that "Lord, we know what we are, but know not what we may be" (4.5.43–44). Lacan's throwaway reference to her as "that piece of bait" is simply more crass about the critical habits that preceded the interventions of more sympathetic readers such as Elaine Showalter and

Carol Thomas Neely.[64] Wedged somewhere between the lowest of Hamlet's suspicions and the high but impersonal-sounding praise of others, Ophelia stays slippery.

Such slipperiness is, in a sense, a consequence of Shakespeare's decision not to grant her significant moments of extended soliloquizing interiority. She shows up as a "document in madness" for others within the play and for readers and onlookers beyond it, and risks being shrunk to the signifying level of "pictures or mere beasts" (4.5.87), prompting a diagnostic scrutiny that depersonalizes her plight.[65] This paucity of first-person perspective becomes acute given her offstage death, a circumstance that puts an enormous contextual pressure onto Gertrude's speech. That speech stands in for and significantly overwrites the act it redescribes, and in the process leaves permanently open the question of how much agency Ophelia did or did not express through that death (aligning her with other exorbitant female suicides such as Portia in *Julius Caesar*). As the gravediggers' innuendo demonstrates, this occultation troubles the issue of how to locate her death along the border between non compos mentis and felo-de-se readings. If Gertrude's language of envious waters works to liquefy the standing charge of self-murder within the play, its defensive distortion of muddy death into pleasurable drift has worked all too well, as its lengthy aesthetic afterlife attests.

The acute "prettification" of Ophelia's demise achieves its objective correlative in Sir John Everett Millais's triumphant 1851 Pre-Raphaelite masterpiece *Ophelia*. Picking up Gertrude's speculation that Ophelia is singing catches of old songs as she dies, in his preparatory sketches for the painting Millais shows us his model Elizabeth Siddal with her head tilted back, her eyes heavily lidded, and her mouth gaping open.[66] One is tempted to ascribe to this open mouth and reclining posture something of the orgasmic pressure of Bernini's St. Teresa, the quintessential artistic expression of ecstatic annihilation through divine *jouissance*, were it not for the obstreperous fact that Millais's earthbound model was shivering in a cold bathtub throughout her extended posing sessions for the work.[67] But whatever the truth of the model's experience might have been, the image transmits a seductive and highly mobile form of "joy of the worm." It teaches its viewers to imagine that death looks like pleasure.

Weaving back and forth between *Hamlet* and *Timon of Athens*, this chapter has argued that "joy of the worm" aligns within those texts the seemingly opposed polarities of trolling's cruelty and the liquid poetics of ideational reverie. On the one hand, the pronounced sadism of Hamlet's and Timon's pleasure in trolling others on the subject of self-killing shows us "joy of the worm" in one of its darker forms, transvaluing loss and death into an occasion for dark humor and amoral playfulness. In their

Figure 2. John Everett Millais, *Ophelia* (head study of Elizabeth Siddal) (1851) (acc. no. 1906P664). Photograph © Birmingham Museum and Art Gallery.

most obnoxious moments, Hamlet and Timon are essentially saying, "I don't care that Ophelia killed herself; I care that you sound like a bad actor when you mourn her," and "Are you frightened? I have a handy place where you can kill yourself," respectively, to their horrified auditors. These moments are, in a sense, of a piece with the "merry tale" from More's *Dialogue of Comfort against Tribulation*: like that story, they model a curious surge of humor and pleasure in the midst of imagined or enacted cruelty and death.

But these moments of outwardly directed cruelty are dialectically conjoined with moments of affective contrast that also constitute "joy of the worm": the material imaginary of suicide as a liquid dissolution of the self through a material merger with the elements that make up the world, and the fantasy of death as safe passage. What is the relationship of these seemingly opposed polarities to each other? Trolling others and grasping toward the "oceanic feeling" offer distinct relational inflections of "joy of the worm," different valences and alloys of what remains, at its bedrock, the same formation: pleasure at the prospect or act of self-destruction.

Though it is not verifiable but intuitive, a psychological framework situates this binary in the case of both these plays, I think. The troll channels a standing emotional reserve of hostility and anger. If, to use an Aristotelian shorthand, the basis of anger is the feeling that one has suffered and the longing to reroute or redirect that suffering, then the consolatory obverse of anger is the fantasy of a state of being in which one would be immune to injury. This is the positive poetics of lyrical elemental materialism: the fantasy of dissolving into dew or joining the "salt flood" is ultimately not a fantasy of violently punishing the self or other people, but instead a means through which to imagine an escape hatch from constraint into a primordial plenum. Whether it is articulated in the first person by Timon and Hamlet or ascriptively projected onto someone else, as when Gertrude imagines Ophelia's last moments in terms of liquid surrender rather than suffering, "joy of the worm" in its positive form as self-destructive reverie offers a calming and compensatory vision of a peace that lies beyond both decorum and the need to break decorum. After the rude noise of their "wagging tongues" and the turbulent surge of their theatrical assaults have died down, the melancholy trolls and misanthropes within these two plays ultimately submerge their rage within a self-soothing poetics of liquid dissolution. We are left to imagine in the place of their harangues only a long silence, or the quiet hiss of foam.

Coda: Toward a Good Enough Presentism

How do you walk away from tragedy? How might we let ourselves stop caring about Hamlet and *Hamlet*? However much he may have fantasized about his own dissolution into a drop of dew, Hamlet's "too too sallied" flesh remains stubbornly unsinkable. After all, the play and its titular character support a cottage industry of commentary devoted to demonstrating the universal applicability of this "poem unlimited" to any and all occasions. As a case in point, an opinion piece by Gary Taylor titled by the *Tampa Bay Times* editorial staff "What Hamlet Can Teach Us about Black Lives Matter" prompted immediate pushback against the bardolatrous presumption of such reaches for relevance: Who belongs to this "us," exactly?[68] If that headline is any indication, the need to keep *Hamlet* timely and relevant—the refusal, that is, to allow Shakespearean tragedy to abide within the past—now generates increasingly ugly and distorted forms. Accordingly, for some time now, there has been a broad and ongoing field-wide reconsideration of both the identificatory exemplarity of Hamlet as character and the canonical centrality of *Hamlet* as a play.[69] The increasingly frequent calls to downgrade Hamlet and *Hamlet* coming from within Shakespeare studies should be heard not simply as signs of field-wide exhaustion with a white male misogynist aristocratic troll but reflect a kind of nauseated response to "something rotten" within a masterpiece that has now calcified into an impacted, endless blockade against the expansion of our field's array of objects and interests.[70] Quite simply, there are other plays and other people worth thinking about.

For obvious reasons, Hamlet is not an RIP troll. But he is not not an RIP troll, either. Still, the analogy I have pressed in this chapter courts misunderstanding. In particular, it risks replicating what I see as the bad presentist dynamic presumed by the headline "What Hamlet Can Teach Us about Black Lives Matter." Namely, the direction of force presumed by that headline (not, necessarily, one presumed by Gary Taylor personally, but by the newsroom that greenlit that title) might be parsed as follows: *Hamlet* the play, William Shakespeare the author, or, worst and least likely of all, Hamlet the person, stand in some position of exemplarity above us and before us. These exemplary predecessors are in a position to instruct us in the present upon our own predicaments. In effect, this text, author, or character "already knows" what we are only now learning, and we must work to catch up with them as they await us within our own cultural past. Such a framing imagines an old play as a kind of timeless moral battery of rhetorical energeia that we must draw strength from as we do battle against injustice.

To invoke my own sense of decorum: faced with a relentless pattern of police killing black people with impunity, it is my hope that the urge to return to Elsinore would strike anyone as optional at best. In an acute moment of political crisis, it is surely time for those leading the Black Lives Matter movement to do the teaching, and for people, and for now "people" includes Shakespeareans, to learn something about how to respond to and act upon the present from that movement; it is not the time to halt activist proceedings so that the deus ex machina of the Shakespearean author function can descend from the rafters and rewrite pressingly specific structural issues of power and inequality (issues that call for remedy through police abolition and prison abolition) as vague examples of some timeless processual horizon on which people in general have always sought justice.[71]

That the present and the past of early modernity are joined in a specific material and historical relation of implicature is undeniable. As Saidiya Hartman puts it: "If slavery persists as an issue... it is not because of an antiquarian obsession with bygone days or the burden of a too-long memory, but because black lives are still imperiled and devaluated by a racial calculus and a political arithmetic that were entrenched centuries ago. This is the afterlife of slavery."[72] If it is therefore critically inadequate to cordon off the past because that past is not done with us yet, the question of *how* to activate the relationship between those "centuries ago" and the present moment remains acute, and is driving a new generation of scholars associated with the #ShakeRace movement and RaceB4Race conference series to press the field of early modern studies for change.[73] The teaching of Shakespeare constitutes a space in which that vexed relation between past and present can become mystified on behalf of an array of discourses: white supremacy, the English heritage industry, a comforting Anglo-American alliance rooted in the Cold War, nineteenth-century doctrines of "genius," nostalgia about a specific postwar moment in higher education, and so on. But it can also function as a means by which to identify and contest those discourses, up to and including discourses in which Shakespeare himself participated and from which he profited. The present can give us new analytics through which to think the causal links and structural persistence of past actions within present predicaments.

I am not, I hope, writing "What Hamlet Can Teach Us about RIP Trolling" but, rather, hoping to flip the direction of flow in the opposite direction: "What RIP Trolling Can Teach Us about Hamlet." It is my sincerest hope that this difference inflects my argument's rhetorical outcome. I am not encouraging those in the present, traumatized by trolls as their grief is subjected to a degrading and entirely gratuitous and unprecedented form of harm and insult, to search in the faces of their oppressors for a tiny glint of Hamlet's antic behavior or Timon's dark wit, so that they can extend some heretofore withheld and hidden surplus of sympathy, respect, or understanding drawn from some spurious Shakespearean (or, less likely, Middletonian) precedent.[74] Rather, I am hoping that the cruel pleasure that RIP trolls take in harassing and harming their victims might assist us in locating the antecedent, distinct, but overlapping array of cruel pleasures with which Hamlet's and Timon's own dark "joys of the worm" occasionally manifest themselves as they belittle and abuse those around them.

This prompts a distinction, not between "good" and "bad" presentism, but, perhaps, between "bad presentism" and what, with apologies to Winnicott, I term "good enough presentism." Bad presentism is bad insofar as it colonizes the present on behalf of extending the imperial reach of the past; there is nowhere that Shakespeare's "poem unlimited" cannot claim for itself as its impromptu stage platform, no movement, cause, occasion, or dynamic that the extended pseudopod of Shakespeare cannot stretch toward as it finds and absorbs new territory that it will have predicted. With a leading description like that, how could it not be bad?

"Good enough presentism" would, I hope, reflect the way that, as we move forward in time and thus farther and farther away from early modernity, the total set of resonances of resemblance, analogy, possible comparison, and thus possible activation of early modern textual meaning *at present and in the present* is going to shift, necessarily altering our experience of which passages and scenes and characters and moments matter to us and why.

Timon and Hamlet look like trolls from the angle afforded by certain scenes and passages, but they are not only trolls, and in time their troll-hood, too, will yield to new constructions and new forms. If we let them, these texts can assist us not only in thinking through their own historically particular poetics of dissolution but also in managing the experience in the present of our own equally inevitable if distinct passages into obsolescence. If Timon warns us that "graves only be men's works, and death their gain" (5.2.107), Hamlet "considers too curiously" (5.1.190) upon the thought of Alexander's dust plugging a beer barrel. The bad news *is* the good news: processes of flux, change, and reformation are both irreversible and inevitable. As contemporary readers, we "consider too curiously" upon the copia of increasingly brittle fragments of the early modern past that historical scholarship has preserved for us, and we subject that past to perverse new uses as we build our own presentist assemblages, some bad, some, I hope, good enough. As we do so, we realize the dark predictions and mad scenarios of decay, transformation, and uncanny survival once forecasted by these texts. But with every passing moment, we also build, change, and grow farther beyond them, too. For now, in the moment, we are the worms that have inherited their earth. Let us chew carefully.

The Open Window in *Biathanatos*

[CHAPTER FOUR]

What I hate I love. Ask the crucified hand that holds
The nail that now is driven into itself, why.

FRANK BIDART, "Catullus: Id Faciam"

Bidart's compact reworking of Catullus forces us to see the encounter between nail and hand as a scene of rapprochement, even love, between inanimate objects and suffering, dying flesh: active and passive, subject and object, body and thing are here pinned into a tense, temporary assemblage under the sign of an overarching transaction between the poem's classical and Christian resonances and the insistent contemporaneity of the word "now" at its center. Short-circuiting libidinal and death-bound energies, Bidart's revision hotwires a classical poem of amorous complaint and affective ambivalence into a Christian transvaluation of pain and pleasure. Which makes it an apt emblem for the crossroads at which this book now stands, for we pass in this chapter from works of romance and drama set in pagan and pre-Christian contexts to the cooler element of a work in prose written in private seclusion amid the heretic bonfires and relentless pamphlet wars of Reformation Christianity: John Donne's *Biathanatos*.

Christ's crucifixion and death fix at the heart of things a momentary submission to decreation and destruction, replenished by the Resurrection and the promise of the Second Coming, to be sure, but present all the same as a kind of absolute eclipse in the ontology of creation, a Dei-Suicide. This has consequences for how we think the intersection of ontology and political theology, reframing who is included within the gallery of self-murderers. If Christ as the head of the Body of the Church mirrors the sovereign as the head of the state, then imagining Christ as a suicide doubles down upon how we might think theological incarnation within political incorporation, death within life, and, more tendentiously still, the foundational role that self-killing might play for the communities that spring up in its wake. I want to do that in this chapter by bearing down upon a singular moment within a single early modern text in which the possibility of a divine submission toward death becomes anxiously thinkable: the presentation of Christ as a "self killer" within Donne's text *Biathanatos*. Considering how the hand might embrace the nail that delivers it from life, "joy of the worm" modulates to accommodate a Christ who loves his own death.

The "Misinterpretable Subject" of *Biathanatos*

John Donne's *Biathanatos* is more often referred to than read. Donne's text is notorious for its supposedly open consideration of the possibility of self-killing as something other than sin or madness, though his stifled presentation of such alleged openness remained unpublished by its author during his lifetime, and the circulation of the text was subject to symptomatic commandments from its author to the intimate circle of its first readers, who were granted access to the manuscript on the condition that they "publish it not, but yet burn it not."[1] Even in such an ambivalent twilight, Donne's prose style twitches and writhes noticeably. A self-cancelling artifact about self-cancellation, the text was written during the era of his shamed postmarital retirement to Pyrford and Mitcham (1604-8) but was kept private and only finally published by his son in 1647, long after Donne's death.[2]

Donne flags his typical acute self-consciousness in the snaking negativities of his title page:

BIATHANATOS
A Declaration of that Paradoxe
Or Thesis, that
Self-homicide is not so naturally Sinne,
That it may never be otherwise.[3]

Thesis or Paradox? At the level of genre and its concomitant affects, the very divergence of these twinned possibilities primes the reader with stroboscopically alternating expectations of a sober theological treatise and a witty scholarly trifle.[4] It is perhaps no accident that these generic modes lend themselves to critical alignment with the central antinomy at the heart of Donne's peculiarly bifurcated author function: the split between the Jack Donne of the erotic poetry and the holy concerns of the Dean of St. Paul's. Taking sides, Donne himself took pains to allege in a letter to Sir Robert Ker that the text was "written by Jack Donne, and not by D. Donne," a declaration whose forthrightness amplifies rather than resolves the authorial overdetermination at work within the text it introduces.[5] Such acts of disavowal only beg the question of how the sarcastic tone and paradoxical conclusions can be reconciled with the serious investment of casuistical labor on display: clearly the fashioning of this paradox-cum-thesis was a job that called for the energies of both Jack and D. Donne in tandem. While they often fuse, cracks appear. Donne's twinned personae and *Biathanatos*'s simultaneous quodlibet of witty paradox and sober treatise tends to make critics see double; Rosalie Colie, though she opts ultimately for paradox, offers a case in point when she notes that "*Biathanatos* is a book of casuistry in both neutral and pejorative senses"[6]; Camille Wells Slights builds upon this as she clocks Donne's "simultaneous use and mockery of the tools of casuistry."[7] In a manner akin to Pyrocles's witty self-digressions in the midst of sober argument in the *Old Arcadia*, the resulting generic space of *Biathanatos* seems contorted by affective shifts toward and away from the decorum of seriousness that the subject of self-killing primes readers to expect.

In the pages that follow this Janus-faced frontispiece, one finds a clash of exegetical armies upon its grim subject, with scholastic divisions, points, and responses swinging back and forth like a pendulum across the absent center: the open endorsement of self-killing. Such endorsement never quite arrives, as Donne instead hovers in its vicinity, hinting at the implicit "sometime" nonsinfulness, if not acceptability, of self-killing as an act whose open celebration languishes in a blind spot beneath, before, or beyond open articulation. After an initial account of his intentions, his method, and his desired reader, Donne embarks on a tripartite scholastic ascent of increasingly forbidding rhetorical obstacles to his thesis, first considering whether or not self-killing contradicts the Law of Nature, then considering whether self-killing contradicts the Law of Reason, and finally arriving at the question of whether self-killing contradicts the Law of God. In pursuit of a "relativist agenda," observes Eric Langley, Donne plays "one commentator against another, view against view, so as to effectively flatten the terms and efface the universalist objectivity of Scripture."[8] Citational copia becomes a form of leverage against authority, disguised as a respectful submission toward it.

Within this already queasily equivocal document, in his third section Donne cuts a particularly torturous course through the heretical thicket surrounding the disturbing possibility at the book's core: the claim that Jesus Christ committed suicide. Donne's presentation of this particular paradox is a masterpiece of indirection whose gnarled, knotty syntax and citational feints and dodges seem to purposefully solicit the very misinterpretation they protest too much against. Donne had warned his readers that his text was to be kept close because it was written "upon a misinterpretable subject," and the camouflage grows increasingly thick as Donne approaches what he might well have regarded as the most potentially inflammatory and damaging component within an already dangerous text.[9] In part 3, distinction 4, section 5, we finally arrive at the most relatively explicit discussion of Christ's willingness to suffer and die on the cross, an infinitely capacious act of charity whose praise almost upstages the impudence of its sheer presence within a gallery of accounts of "selfe-killing" in the first place.

Donne cannot, of course, literally state that "Christ committed suicide," even if he wanted to (and it is never clear that he did wish to simply and straightforwardly say this). There are some very basic reasons why such a statement would be unspeakable: nominal, historical, and doctrinal. First, Donne cannot say, "Christ committed suicide," for the very basic reason that, as stated in this book's introduction, the word "suicide" had not yet been coined. The term, now redolent with its Durkheimian sociological resonance as *"le suicide"* was simply not available when Donne wrote his text. Just as obviously, the statement "Christ committed suicide" cannot be put forward for basic narrative reasons. As related in the Gospels, Christ is not the actively violent agent or author of his own death, but a passive victim of the violent actions of others, and since Christ dies as a consequence of his crucifixion at the hands of the Roman state, he did not directly cause his own death in any straightforward causal sense.

No less obviously, this statement cannot be made for doctrinal reasons: though it was not always so, by the seventeenth century it would savor of blasphemy. Although scripture itself is equivocal about voluntary death, according to the tenets of Church Fathers, set into canon law by the Council of Orléans in 533, self-killing is a monstrous error.[10] Since Augustine, "Thou shalt not kill" has been taken to implicitly include oneself. In his careful consideration and ultimate rejection of suicidal logics in book 1 of the *City of God*, Augustine bypasses Lucretia and Cato, grants yet evades the trickier borderline cases of St. Pelagia and Samson, and reaches a decisive resting place in his response to the question "Should one commit suicide to avoid sin?" Having imagined a case in which one could circumvent all future sin with a single suicidal act, Augustine seems to decisively close the lid: "If there could be a valid reason for suicide one could not find one more valid than this, and since this is not valid, a valid reason does not exist."[11] In his response to the question "Whether one is permitted to kill himself?" in the *Summa Theologiae* (2A 2Æ Q.64, A.5), Aquinas is no less emphatic: "One who exercises public authority may lawfully put to death an evildoer, since he can pass judgment upon him. But no man is judge of himself."[12] Thus it would seem that, by definition, such ascription is ruled out. Given the premise that committing suicide is wrong, and that the Savior would not and could not do wrong, it follows that the Savior would not and could not commit suicide.[13] So, nominally, narratively, and doctrinally speaking, there is no straightforwardly declarative sense in which Donne could have openly said that "Christ committed suicide."

Yet we need not affirm this strong theory of Christ-as-suicide in order to be able to imply the weaker variant that Donne's text is scandalously eager to insinuate to the reader: a claim that we might phrase in many ways. "Christ let himself be killed," or "chose to be killed," or "embraced his own death," "permitted his own death," or that Christ simply "let his death happen."[14] This soup of suggestively amorphous, ambivalent, and indirect allegations—some of them sourced in precisely the same Church Fathers that seemed in other passages to forbid self-killing—defines the overdetermined causality that Donne complicates and explores.

Talking about indirection indirectly, Donne's text is a cento of quotations from authorities whose claims are edited into suggestive proximity in order to solicit this interpretation. Here is his cautious approach to the issue:

> His Soule sayth St. Aug: did not leave his body constrained, but because he would, and when he would, and how he would Of which St. Thomas produces this Symptome, That he had yet his bodyes Nature in her full strength; because at the last Moment he was able to cry with a lowd voyce. And Marlorate gathers it upon this, That whereas our heads decline after our Death, by the slacknesse of the sinews and Muscles, Christ did first of himselfe bow downe his head, and then give up the Ghost.[15]

In this blow-by-blow account of the final gestures of the crucified Christ, what we find is a kind of referendum upon the status of the divine power retained and expressed within the fact of the incarnation. Christ is and has a body, but remains free of the restrictive consequences that embodiment occasions for others. Christ is unconstrained, and thus free to leave his body when he wills to do so, and no sooner. He is not compelled by the fact of incarnation to be subject to the body's organic failures, hunger, thirst, or, as Donne puts it, "Inanition." This tone of forceful insistence upon an epideictic celebration of Christ's superhuman capacity is countered by a subtle but insistent undertone that suggests the opposite: that beneath the seamless surface of this divine power, Christ's Passion darkly pulses. Behind the language of "full strength," there is a downward pull into despair, misery, and doubt. This threatens to stain the being of Christ with the taint of melancholy; considered in the light of modalist Trinitarian doctrines in which the incarnate Christ is an expression of God's own being, this weary slump downward further threatens to blacken God's very being with a passionate stain of black bile.

Reduplicating at the level of his prose the very gesture of "self-cancellation" that marks his subject, Donne's text blurs his own authorial agency. In a classic essay on "Donne and the Casuists," A. E. Malloch indicates this mode of self-destruction-via-citation as, in part, the rhetorical tendency of casuistry as such: "The doctrine of the probable opinion was, in tendency at least, *a banishing of the self from moral action*, and a substituting of extrinsic and non-personal modes of judgment."[16] A convert from Catholicism jockeying for position in the Anglican church as the smoke of the Gunpowder Plot lingered, Donne could not avoid the charged political atmosphere in which casuistry offered a generic technology for massaging cases of conscience into permissions to act that Protestant propaganda associated with Catholic villainy and equivocation. This makes the gusto of his participation in casuistry within *Biathanatos* all the more striking. Smearing manifold sources—listed extravagantly on his title page—into a nonstop pageant of bickering and mutually incongruous authority figures in a manner that anticipates Burton's *Anatomy*, Donne keeps dissolving his Church Fathers and commentators into one another without ever quite stabilizing or reinforcing a clear central point of authorial security about his own relationship to the sources he cites.

This tactic—rooted in the aggregations and surveys of probabilist casuistry—affords him both legitimacy and a kind of layer of deniability that suits the delicacy of the subject. W. Speed Hill situates this strategy as a means to ward off psychobiographical speculation about its author's state of mind:

> Donne's anxiety to offer irrefutable authority for a (then) heterodox view of what he delicately refers to as 'a misinterpretable subject' accounts for the multiplication of authorities and their marginal itemization in the Bodleian MS, a process continued in the holograph that underlies the later quarto. Are we meant to understand the references? Probably not, at least in any detail. But we are meant to be impressed with them, to sense that here is a man of serious purpose, who is not so emotionally involved with his subject (as he patently was) that his arguments do not carry objective and authoritative weight.[17]

Donne himself seems to sense that the very preponderance of citation requires some excuses of its own: "If, therefore, in multiplicity of not necessary citations there appear vanity, or ostentation, or digression, my honesty must make my excuse and compensation, who acknowledge as Pliny doth, that to choose rather to be taken in a theft than to give every man his due is obnoxii animi et infelcis ingenii."[18] It is difficult to dispel these charges of vanity and ostentation once they have been acknowledged, insofar as the boilerplate of the modesty topos risks sounding insincere.

But the problem goes deeper than that, for Hill has raised the specter of intentionality. If the pileup of sources is meant to announce that "here is a man of serious purpose," guarantees of good intentions are harder to secure. From a safe distance, Donne's sheer accumulation summons a familiar early modern aesthetic of superabundance: copia. But the surplus that copia displays sits oddly with the discriminatory power we expect from scholarship; in a dynamic that contemporary literary scholars might not like to acknowledge, it makes citation practices look less like an ethical display of gratitude to precursors and more like filler, or worse. In a recent bravura reading of Erasmian textuality, Christine Hoffman has flagged the uncomfortable proximity between copia and contemporary internet spam:

> Copia asks us to make contact: to touch, to take in, to digest the absurdities we encounter as much as we do the profundities; humanists must develop a taste for both, a taste for ALL. Imagine the least sophisticated palate encountering a menu overstuffed with uncalled for signature dishes, moving from gourmet entrees to table scraps with equal gusto and no gag reflex. Jessica Wolfe refers to copia as "a generic form that distorts through overstuffing" ... and it is useful to imagine the distortion that occurs as a kind of distenstion; "a bellyful is a bellyful," the copious writer Francois Rabelais is said to have said, "whether it be meat or drink." ... [Spam] is a useful metaphor for copia as overacting, overdoing, overselling, overstuffing.[19]

If humanist scholarship as such is premised upon the capacity to judge and discriminate, to distinguish reliable from unreliable texts, sound doctrine from damnable heresy, logical argument from whimsy, copia tacks in the opposite direction, tending toward an indiscriminate pile-on of textual "primitive accumulation" for its own sake. Far from stabilizing his authorial person as "a man of serious purpose," Donne's overstuffing of exemplary matter risks turning *Biathanatos* from a temple of reason to a hoarder house, burying the lede in a chaotic compost heap of decaying textual matter.

Arising from within a dense thicket of citations lies a decisive passage, a single quotation that seems to articulate the tantalizing possibility that Christ's death might itself have been an example of voluntary death. Snapping to attention, Donne's amiable paddling through sources suddenly becomes arrested, stunned:

> And therefore St. Thomas, a man neither of unholy thoughts, nor of bold, or irreligious, or scandalous phrase, or Elocution (yet I adventure not so far in his behalfe as Silvester doth That it is impossible that he should have spoken anything against faith or good manners,) forebeares not to say That

Christ was so much the cause of his own death, as he is of the wetting, which might and would not shut the Window when the rayne beates in.[20]

Deploying citational folds as a means of self-protection, Donne here fashions a kind of scholarly "bulletproof vest" composed of tightly wound layers of Augustine, Aquinas, Marlorate, and Silvester in order to hedge against censure.[21] It is especially significant that Aquinas, whose already cited passage in *Summa Theologiae* (2A 2Æ Q.64, A.5) was regarded as a definitive repudiation of self-killing under any circumstances, should *also* be the source of this striking possibility.[22] As Lucio Biasiori notes, this passage was not exactly a buried heretical secret, but the title of "the first article of the forty-seventh question of the third part of the *Summa Theologiae*…, whose title was 'quod Christus non fuerit ab alio occisus, sed a seipso' (that Christ was not killed by someone else, but by himself)."[23] Aquinas more than entertains the possibility, and for Biasiori this means, *pace* Borges's famous pronouncement that "this baroque idea glimmers behind *Biathanatos*," that the idea is not subtext but text. But, to put it bluntly, Donne is not Aquinas, and in citing him, Donne is not just protecting himself from anticipated readerly resistance by wrapping himself in authority. What looks like caution and distance is in fact a way of focusing the power of what he deploys, amplifying and magnifying its impact. His showy, overstated negations of the unthinkable idea that St. Thomas Aquinas might have entertained an unholy, scandalous, and bold thought is designed not only to preempt misunderstanding but precisely to trigger a certain frisson of readerly anticipation of an utterance that *will* pleasurably and perversely demonstrate those very qualities. The premise that citational practice must denote the presence of a "man of serious purpose" yields to an alternate persona that reimagines the scholar as a purveyor of "joy of the worm": Donne on a tightrope over a suicidal abyss, wielding pious citations as if they were blasphemous jokes.

Once posed, Aquinas's assertion is all the more shocking for the homely and familiar register it deploys: "Christ was so much the cause of his own death, as he is of the wetting, which might and would not shut the Window when the rayne beates in." What fullness or emptiness abides within the ontology of this "so much"? What did Christ do in the negative space opened out by this "willing not" to do something preventative? Was this an action? Was this a cause? What forces rain down upon the reader through this open window within the text? What has Donne "let in" through this citational hole within the body of his own writing?

The focus upon the negative, already signaled upon the title page, repeats itself here, with Christ's charitable acceptance of his own situation, his refusal to refuse it, functioning here as a sine qua non of the crucifixion and death he suffered. Had he not "opened the window," the rain would not have been able to wet him down. Christ's death becomes a death by exposure, a death caused by an opening or openness to the surrounding fallen world. Having cleared his throat with the catalog of Church Fathers, Donne goes on to affirm this basic ur-responsibility in something more like his own voice: "And that it is a Heroique act of fortitude, if a Man when an urgent occasion is presented, expose himself to a certayne and assured Death, as he did."[24] Christ is thus imagined not as actively killing himself, but he is, I think, here pictured as committing a kind of premodern variant of "suicide by cop."[25]

I don't say this to be trivial. If we telescope backward through the Gospels and consider the provocations and refusals that ramp upward toward the arrest and across the Stations of the Cross, we can see a slow form of passive-aggressive presentation of the self before the authorities that borders upon what the Black Panther activist Huey P. Newton described in his memoir of the same name as "revolutionary suicide": "Revolutionary suicide does not mean that I and my comrades have a death wish; it means just the opposite. We have such a strong desire to live with hope and human dignity that existence without them is impossible. When reactionary forces crush us, we must move against these forces, even at the risk of death."[26] The certainty and assurance that Donne invokes is mirrored in Newton's full recognition, and acceptance, of death. But Christ goes beyond the Black Panthers in an absolute certainty about the necessity of a fatal outcome that eclipses the calculated potentiality for survival still implicit in a word like "risk." This has already been recognized by readers of the Gospels, as when, in *A Noble Death: Suicide and Martyrdom among Christians and Jews in Antiquity*, Arthur Droge and James Tabor cite Jesus's reprimand to those of his followers who attempt to prevent his arrest by violence: "Either thinkest thou that I can not now pray to my Father, and he wil giue me moe then twelue legions of Angels? Howe then shoulde the Scriptures bee fulfilled, which say, that it must be so?" (Matthew 26:52–53).[27] Christ's rejoinder betrays not just passive acceptance but a willingness to be persecuted, captured, and executed; implicitly, those events are treated as the desired completion of a preordained plan, rather than as an occupational hazard of political resistance. The supposition surfaces most directly in the Gospel of John 8:22: "Then said the Jews, will he kill himself? Because he saith, Whither I go, ye cannot come."

Opening the Window to "Communitas"

Setting aside this presentist juxtaposition of Christ and the Black Panthers, here I wish to leave the window open and run a further calculated risk of my own, in offering the tendentious claim that Donne's selection of Aquinas's metaphor of the open window, reinforced as it is by Donne's own use of the phrase "exposure" to imagine Christ's openness to his own death, constitutes an early modern theological mirror of a more modern theory: specifically, Roberto Esposito's theory of the constitutively subtractive force of community itself as an "opening" toward a radical exteriority, a crease or twist that Esposito identifies as the crossing point of nihilism and community, in his book *Communitas: The Origin and Destiny of Community* and in particular in the compressed but suggestive appendix to that volume, titled "Nihilism and Community." In this text, Esposito rejects theories of community as a shared property or as a collectively aggregated substantial assemblage in favor of a darker vision of the "no-thing-in-common" that underwrites the social. Beating in from outside, Esposito's examination of nihilism and community opens unexpectedly onto the theological ontology of negativity and death in play within Donne's text:

> According to the originary valence of the concept of community, what the members of a community share, based upon the complex and profound meaning of *munus*, is rather an expropriation of their own essence, which isn't limited to their "having" but one that involves and affects their own "being subjects." Here the discourse follows a crease that moves from the more traditional domain of anthropology or of political philosophy to that more radical terrain of ontology: that the community isn't joined to an addition but to a subtraction of subjectivity, by which I mean that its members are no longer identical with themselves but are constitutively exposed to a propensity that forces them to open their own individual boundaries in order to appear as what is "outside" themselves.[28]

To be joined to a community is not to possess some positive characteristic but to be cut open, exposed to an "outside." In this participatory relation to a negativity, subjects are joined—together—toward an exteriority. For Esposito, the "no-thing-in-common" that ontologically grounds community is a sort of syntax, a relational spacing that produces this breaching experience of an openness, a facing toward... what? Not a facing toward an Althusserian hailing or interpellating authority figure or some other sovereign emissary of power, but instead an "outside" that has no content, no "thing" to ground it. Paradoxically, this subtractive opening onto the outside is the "no-thing-in-common" characteristic of community as such.

It is my further speculation—going beyond Esposito—that for this reason the act of self-killing, an act that both cancels the subject and confirms its irreducibility, also constitutes the point at which the communal propensity to open individual boundaries toward that very "outside" achieves its most thorough and complete expression. Self-killing dissolves the subject into a total, radical exteriority without reserve. In this sense, voluntary death—far from simply delimiting the social or attacking it—constitutes the purest possible conclusion to the project of opening already in play at the heart of community itself.

Lest this rather abstract assertion of the negative political affordances of self-killing's potential for the creation or reinforcement of social bonds seem unclear, let me cite a single contemporary name by way of recent example: Mohamed Bouazizi, the Tunisian street vendor whose self-immolation on December 17, 2010, in a public square in front of a government building in Sidi Bouzid in protest against his humiliation and harassment at the hands of police precipitated a massive public uprising in solidarity. Less than a month after his death, the regime of Tunisia's president Zine el-Abidine Ben Ali was brought to an end, and the success of this political transformation is widely held to have provided a blueprint for subsequent uprisings and demonstrations in Egypt, Yemen, Saudi Arabia, Algeria, Libya, and beyond. Explaining and extending the lionization of Bouazizi within the region, Western media was seemingly unanimous in its posthumous recirculation of his causal efficacy: the *New York Times* offered a think piece titled "How a Single Match Can Ignite a Revolution," Reuters favored the declarative that "Peddler's Martyrdom Launched Tunisia's Revolution," while CNN referred to "the Tunisian Fruit Seller Who Kickstarted Arab Uprising," treating as a fait accompli his status as prime mover.[29] Without detaining myself in the analysis of Western media's representations of Arab experience, this desire to shrink complex and wide-ranging social movements down to heroic human-interest stories should not come as a surprise, nor can a Western representation of suicide within the world of Islam emerge innocently.[30]

That said, the celebration of Bouazizi across the global mediasphere also triggered anxious reflections from Arab news sources, Arab intellectuals, and Islamic clerics about where to locate Bouazizi within the complex politico-theological nest of distinctions and overlaps between self-killing, suicide, martyrdom, and sacrifice.[31] Copycat incidents proliferated, as did warnings against them. The troubling exemplarity of Bouazizi's act unleashed collective experiences of identification, mourning, and political action whose consequences are still reverberating, and a different scholar could pursue this act on its own terms in all their local complexity.

What I find portable is the undeniable demonstration of the reciprocal and generative feedback loop between self-killing and collective political feeling, no less in the present moment than in the fierce polemical debates that Donne prototyped in *Biathanatos* and went public with in *Pseudo-Martyr*, his partisan critique of Catholic martyrologies on behalf of a militant Protestant stance. In *Unknowing Fanaticism: Reformation Literatures of Self-Annihilation* (2019), Ross Lerner argues that Donne's rhetorical aim is to isolate what he terms "'inimitable' or 'unexemplary' martyrdrom from its contemporary recirculations—a redefinition of sacred self-immolation as utterly singular, free from labor, and impervious to the kind of mimetic transmission that can lead to individual or collective political antagonism."[32] Lerner's concept gets at the vexed rhetorical problem that drives Donne's agenda in *Pseudo-Martyr*: How to prevent Catholics in the present from claiming sanction in the sacred self-destructions attested in scripture? With reference to both lyric subjectivity in the *Holy Sonnets* and the prose works, Lerner limns Donne's theorization of martyrdom as an approximation to divine will that necessarily entails "self-annihilation," but that turns out to advocate a self-destruction of personal will within the life that God bestows, rather than a rashly overconfident arrogation of the right to destroy life itself.[33] Thus, the subject can annihilate itself without contesting the standing injunctions of church and state that forbid self-destruction. This reading suggests that Donne wanted to put a cap on the subversive forces potentially set loose by the "interminable consideration" that the text initiates as a substitute for punctual action or mimetic imitation.[34] Not all consideration is interminable. Sometimes, consideration leads to a decision, and the flames leap up.

Voluntary death cuts to the relationship between sovereign and subject, severing that bond in a gesture of absolute refusal and total resistance. But from this singular act a branching path of consequences radiate outward, reconnecting the dead political subject to the group. The collective posthumous memorialization of such acts ratifies the meaning of the relationship between the isolated death of the subject and the social surround as a whole, either closing it over through forgetting, disavowal, and pathologizing strategies that fix a pejorative meaning upon it as "suicide," or insisting upon heroically reifying that death as an index of a shareable commitment to a broader cause that defines an ethos of participation and obligation toward its recuperated meaning as "martyrdom" or "sacrifice." In the process, such reification purges the act of its suicidal associations with sin, weakness, despair, and insanity. Self-killing is not a unity, but a manifold susceptible to political reuse, revision, and appropriation, in which "suicide" and "martyrdom" struggle over explanatory territory while deforming and resembling each other. The anxious circuits of resemblance between these honorific and pejorative constructions of the "same" act remain heavily guarded and rhetorically invested because of the symbolic capital potentially afforded by such powerfully inspiring scenarios, a capital presumably lost to pathologies of shame by the accusation, or fact, of suicide.

Insofar as community is inherently committed to survival and persistence, community remains in its very essence determined through a definitive relation to death as its organizing threat. In *The Inoperative Community*—a text to which Esposito asserts that *Communitas* owes "an unpayable debt"—Jean-Luc Nancy influentially argued for their constitutive linkage. In order to clarify the extent to which Esposito's nihilistic account of community builds upon Nancy's articulation of the essential link between community and death, I have assembled the following catena of sequential excerpts from Nancy:

> Death is indissociable from community, for it is through death that the community reveals itself—and reciprocally.... Community does not weave a superior, immortal, or transmortal life between subjects (no more than it is itself woven of the inferior bonds of a consubstantiality of blood or of an association of needs), but it is constitutively, to the extent that it is a matter of a "constitution" here, calibrated on the death of those whom we call, perhaps wrongly, its "members" (inasmuch as it is not a question of an organism). Community is revealed in the death of others; hence it is always revealed to others. Community is what takes place always through others and for others.... The genuine community of mortal beings, or death as community, establishes their impossible communion. Community therefore occupies a singular place: it assumes the impossibility of its own immanence, the impossibility of a communitarian being in the form of a subject. In a certain sense community acknowledges and inscribes—this is its peculiar gesture—the impossibility of community.... A community is the presentation to its members of their mortal truth.[35]

However distinct from Donne's claims and language, Nancy's crypto-liturgical cascade of deconstructive pronouncements is strategically useful insofar as it offers a means to at once assert and re-estrange the foundational importance of death as the bonding agent of the Christian mystery (or rhetoric) of participation. Let's grant the obvious counterpoint: the "revelation of a mortal truth," so crucial to both Jack Donne's poetry and D. Donne's sermons, is always bundled with the compensatory fact of Christ's resurrection and the symmetrical possibilities of salvation or damnation for the Christian soul. The other side of the subject's "mortal truth" is surely *Holy Sonnet* 10's hopeful declaration that "Death, thou shalt die."

But Donne's imagination often becomes the site for an anxiously downward pull in which the claims of the body threaten to upstage, even compromise, the consolatory force of these outcomes on this side of mortality. This is a tendency that started early in his career, as the example of his "Paradoxes" and "Problems"—early prose works from his student days—

demonstrate. Preemptively cancelling vibrant materialism in favor of a morbid materialism, Donne's fifth paradox is titled "That all things kill themselves," and it begins thus: "To affect, yea to effect their owne death all living things are importuned, not by Nature only which perfects them, but by Art and Education, which perfects her. Plants quickened and inhabited by the most unworthy soule, which therefore neither will nor worke, affect an end, a perfection, a death; this they spend their spirits to attaine, this attained, they languish and wither."[36] Donne then works his way up the chain of being, finding in each link another witty demonstration of his paradoxical thesis, beating to the punch Freud's later declaration, in *Beyond the Pleasure Principle*, that "the aim of all life is death."[37] Such judo throws need speed to work. In both Freud and Donne, when the hot subject of death anxiety meets the cold form of paradox, "joy of the worm" leaps out. But paradoxes have a predilection for reversibility, and when this resolute and constitutional morbidity returns most showstoppingly in Donne's final sermon, "Death's Duell," the passage out of life becomes a noisomely productive process of material ruin-as-rebirth: "Though this be exitus a morte, it is introitus in mortem: though it bee an Issue from the manifold deaths of this world, yet is an entrance into the death of corruption and putrefaction and vermiculation and incineration, and dispersion in and from the grave, in which every dead man dyes over againe."[38] Donne cannot, it seems, refrain from "considering too curiously" upon the materiality of the process of death, and, insofar as he finds there a vividly populated scene of "vermiculation," in which activity and emergence burst forth within the corpse, this would seem to make him a potentially likely host author for Jane Bennett's project of "vibrant materialism" as advocated in *Vibrant Matter: A Political Ecology of Things*.[39] Surely Donne's corpse, writhing with maggots, is a case in point of a dead matter that refuses to lie still and play dead, and could be made to function as an early modern resonating chamber for rethinking corpses as vibrant agents of their own. Here "joy of the worm" becomes literally vermicular.

But in fact the valence goes the other way; as Ramie Targoff has noted, in "Death's Duell" Donne is engaged in a rhetorical process in which the entirety of life is itself shown to be already consumed and saturated by death, absorbed into an extended process of dying.[40] If Bennett wants us to see even a dead rat on the streets of Baltimore as suffused with a vibrancy, Donne wants us to see even a live rat as already preparing for its certain material annihilation even while still embryonically "buried" in its mother's womb.[41]

As Donne understood and practiced it, Christianity is itself "much possessed by death."[42] The community of Christendom that bears witness in the present to the meaning of Christ's suffering and death is founded upon an originary act of leaving the self open to the world and subject to a material death, and it memorializes that sacrifice through the yearly observance of Easter services, private meditations upon the Passion, and countless representations of the suffering of Christ, arresting the progression of a narrative arc in a frozen stance of affective stasis provocatively proximate to melancholy, epitomized by Christ's cry in Matthew 36:38 that "my soul is exceeding sorrowful, even unto death." We can see this sorrowful suffering and entry into death not only across Donne's poetry and sermons but also refracted across early modern culture more broadly, from Dürer's engraving of the Man of Sorrows to Milton's unfinished poem on Christ's Passion. In her comparative analysis of multiple religious traditions in *Ethical Issues in Suicide*, bioethicist Margaret Pabst Battin notes that "it is Christian theology that yields the paradox of both prohibition and invitation," flagging "the remarkable way in which Christian theology lends itself to arguments in favor of suicide."[43] Listening for such invitations, let us cock our ear to hear within the Gospels the intermittent, occasional, but manifest *hatred of life* that pulses within it: "If anie man come to me and hate not his father, his mother, and wife, and children, and brethren, and sisters: *yea, and his owne life also*, he can not be my disciple" (Luke 14:26; emphasis mine). In placing Christ within the suicidal archive of *Biathanatos*, Donne explicitly articulated this paradoxical intersection between voluntary death and Christian community, in the process anticipating the categorical interpenetration of death and community asserted by Nancy and redoubled by Esposito.

Donne understands the catalog of martyrdoms he marshals as a sequence of citations of this original act that resemble and replay its dynamic, stitching each self-killer back to the Savior, but also binding together Christendom itself into a web of connections and linkages constituted by these cuttings open and cuttings away. Yet each act, both those before Christ and those after, recapitulates his central and, in this sense, "originary" moment of surrender to death, a moment that collapses the distinction between martyrdom and suicide by relocating the adjudication of these conflicting descriptions within an unreachably abyssal privacy:

> And it is there sayd that Christ did so, as Saul did, who thought it foule and dishonorable to dy by the hand of an Enemy: And that Apollonia and others, who prevented the fury of Executioners; and cast themselves into the fire, did therein imitate this act of our Savyor, of giving up his Soule, before he was constrayned to do it. So that if the act of our B. Savyor, in whome there was no more required for Death, but that he should will that his Soule should go out, was the same as Sauls and these Martyrs actuall further-

ance, which could not dy without that, then we are taught that all those places, of Giuing up our body to death, and of Laying downe the Soule, Signify more then a yielding to death when it comes.[44]

The key word here is "will," a faculty that was both the motor driving action and the object of intensive moral scrutiny in the early modern period. As Andrew Escobedo argues in *Volition's Face: Personification and the Will in Renaissance Literature* (2017), "This dual quality of volition— the instrument of our self-control, but an instrument we must keep in our control—meant that the will's independence imposed liabilities as much as benefits."[45] For Donne, it is a shared *willingness* toward death that joins together Christ and Saul and the martyrs, and the ostensive indication of that will constitutes the end of the line of what posthumous interpretation and speculation can assess. While we might expect the comparison of martyrs with Jesus (however subject to bitter partisan debate), Donne's alignment of Jesus Christ with Saul grinds the gears of typological resemblance altogether.

In order to assess what is truly striking, and potentially disturbing, about Donne's passing comparison between Jesus Christ and Saul, some comparative scriptural reading may be called for. As narrated in 1 and 2 Samuel, Saul is selected by the prophet Samuel and becomes the first King of the Kingdom of Israel and Judah, then commits a massacre for which crime he is said to have lost God's favor. Saul suffers fits of madness and paranoia that are seemingly calmed by the harping of David, and David and Saul's son Jonathan become close. Having lost a decisive battle with the Philistines at Mount Gilboa, Saul kills himself. Or does he? There are conflicts between the two books, and these conflicts turn upon the need for assistance in the midst of self-killing as a messy and extended process along the lines that we have seen staged so laboriously in *Julius Caesar* and *Antony and Cleopatra* in this book. In the version in 1 Samuel 33:4-6, here quoted as it appears in the Bishops' Bible, Saul is rendered directly responsible for his own death:

> 4. Then said Saul unto his armour bearer, Draw out thy sword, and thrust me thorow therewith, least the uncircumcised come and thrust me thorew and mocke mee; But his armour bearer would not, for hee was sore afraid. Therefore Saul tooke a sword, and fell upon it.
>
> 5. And when his armour bearer sawe that Saul was dead, he fell likewise upon his sword, and died with him.
>
> 6. So Saul died, and his three sonnes, and his armour bearer, and all his men that same day together.[46]

The body is subjected to further indignities by the victorious Philistines, who cut off the head and strip the body of its armor. The armor is displayed on the wall of the temple of Ashtaroth, and the body is exhibited on the wall of Bethshan.

Notoriously, in 2 Samuel there is an alternate version of Saul's death that is narrated by an Amalekite who claims to have found Saul leaning on his own spear but not yet dead; the Amalekite disastrously boasts of having killed him.

> 6. Then the yong man that told him, answereth As I came to Mount Gilboa, behold, Saul leaned upon his speare, and loe, the charets and horsemen followed hard after him.
>
> 7. And when I looked backe, he sae me, and called me, and I answered, here am I.
>
> 8. And he said unto mee, Who are thou? And I answered him, I am an Amalekite.
>
> 9. Then said he unto me, I pray thee come upon me, and slay me: for anguish is come upon me, because my life is yet whole in me.
>
> 10. So I came upon him, and slew him, and because I was sure that he could not live, after that hee had fallen, I tooke the crowne that was upon his head, and the bracelet that was on his arme, and brought them hither unto my lord. (2 Samuel 1.6–10, in the Bishops' Bible)

The 1616 Bishop's Bible's gloss in the margins for the ninth verse says, "I am sorie because I am yet alive." When David learns of the death of Saul he rends his garment, and the Amalekite is killed in retribution. The rending of the garment repeats a gesture that already figures in the story of Saul; when Saul learns that he has lost the favor of the Lord, he rends Samuel's garment in passion, and so there is a curious sense of symptomatic return in this parallel transference of grief. Though scholars and critics disagree about the extent of a Jewish interdiction against suicide, later Christian commentators upon these passages show in their marginal glosses an attempt to intuitively connect the circumstances of his death to the emotional disturbances within the life that precedes it; because of Saul's transgressions, his end involves shame and cruelty. The 1616 Bishop's Bible gloss in the margins connects these circumstances to Saul's conflict with David: "So we see that his cruel life hath a desperate end, as is commonly seene in them that persecute the children of God."

I have tarried in this account of Saul in order to draw out what is truly bold in Donne's willful decision to compare the immediate circumstances of Saul's anguished and dubious death(s) on the battlefield with those of Jesus Christ as comparable cases that go beyond "yielding," and open onto the volitional terrain of willed self-destruction. Beyond the obvious, categorical objections that one might raise given the dissimilarity of their respective situations (Christ dies on the cross, executed by the Roman state; Saul dies in the aftermath of the disastrous battle at Gilboa) and the murky question of how Saul actually died lies the still-murkier question of what emotional state underlies such "yielding." Saul seems a particularly risky object of comparison: having been cast into shadow by the withdrawal of the spirit of the Lord, a shift that precipitates both an antisocial withdrawal and a murderous envy toward David, Saul is marked out by his curious despondency as an antagonistic figure, occasionally at cross purposes with the divine, and this lends the stench of a cover-up to David's posthumous praise of him as "the Lord's anointed."[47] Conjoining these deaths as voluntary interventions, Donne locates a shared agency within the matrix of military defeat in the case of Saul and apparent political defeat in the case of Christ without daring to fully articulate how that agency operates. Having said that this "laying downe of the Soule [signifies] more then a yielding to Deathe when it comes," without quite cashing out what precisely this "more" positively consists in, Donne coyly points toward something on the other side of mere yielding. The comparison flickers into view and Donne moves on.

Such attendance upon the moment of death suffuses the entirety of Donne's work. As Donald Friedman put it, "In the instant of parting Donne found, again and again, the stress, the pain, the terror, that could be chafed into illumination."[48] Expanding this assertion into an entire monograph that tracks the poetics of both the union and the valedictory separation of Jack Donne and D. Donne within the author's work, Targoff's *John Donne: Body and Soul* considerably amplifies the extent to which both identities remain enmeshed in an anxious consideration of the *ars moriendi* as the conclusion of a partnership fraught with finitude. As Targoff puts it, with disarming simplicity, "For Donne, the relationship between the body and the soul—a relationship he regarded as one of mutual necessity—was the defining bond of his life."[49]

But against the backdrop of that career-long obsession, the particular parting of this soul from this body has a definitive, absolute singularity. Donne's reference to "Laying downe the Soule" upon the cross recalls Christ's proleptic announcement in John 10:17–18, quoted as it appears in the Bishops' Bible: "Therefore doeth my Father love me, because I laye down my life, yet I might take it againe. No man taketh it from me, but I laye it downe of my self: I have power to lay it downe, and have power to take it againe: this commandment have I received of my father." Not desire, not choice, but not not those things, either. Donne and the Gospel both register in their own ways an eclipsed and yet indicated decisionist moment in which the Savior preempts pure passivity through a granting or giving, a *donum*. This term has become central to the "radical orthodoxy" of recent work at the intersection of critical theory and theology. Here I have in mind John Milbank's *Being Reconciled: Ontology and Pardon*, and in particular, a passage in which Milbank notes that "Creation and grace are gifts; Incarnation is the supreme gift; the Fall, evil, and violence are the refusal of gift; atonement is the renewed and hyperbolic gift that is for-giveness; the supreme name of the Holy Spirit is *donum* (according to Augustine); the Church is the community that is given to humanity and is constituted through the harmonious blending of diverse gifts (according to St. Paul)."[50] The problem is then the relationship between the gift of incarnation and the gift of the community. Is the accession to death a completion of the gift of incarnation, or its refusal? We cannot know, and pass here into either a mysticism or an epistemological abyss of access toward the Savior's unknown interior: the answer lies in how we evaluate the will within the mind within the head that slumps as a body that is the being of God gives up its ghost. If, in *Biathanatos*, the possibility that this was an act of self-killing is implied only to be muted and qualified and hedged, that hesitation does not in fact conclude the issue. In time, unspeakable things have a tendency to be spoken. What had been the "misinterpretable" and dangerously blasphemous suspicion buried within anxious casuistry became, at the end of Donne's life, in his final sermon in 1631, a ringing final affirmation of the Savior's positive affect in the midst of death: "There was nothing more free, more voluntary, more spontaneous than the death of Christ."[51]

Was this voluntary will toward death an example of "exposure" to the exteriority that Esposito, and Nancy before him, have alleged is foundational to community as such? We seem to be at a point where Esposito's insistence upon nihilism might seem to render his account minimally congruent with Donne's, for obvious intellectual historical reasons. The Christian tradition of thinking inclusion and belonging in a spiritual incorporation stands as a kind of vanished preliminary to the modern philosophical arc that Esposito traces in *Communitas* as its gradual displacement, an intellectual-historical process that effectively starts with the fearful contracts of Hobbes and proceeds through the general will of Rousseau, the categorical ubiquity of law in Kant, and the *Mitsein* of Heidegger before coming to rest in a contemporary moment that Espositio theorizes via Bataille on sovereignty and Nancy on community. But before his working-through of that extended sequence, Esposito offers a preliminary account of how we are to understand Christian brotherhood taking place under the shadow of a constitutively prior divine gift, and it is this moment in which Esposito usefully intersects with both Milbank and Donne:

And it is precisely this "given"—what is given to us, we ourselves as "given," "donated," born from a gift—that stands in the way of any hasty translation of *koinonia* into a simple *philia*—"friendship," "fellowship," "camaraderie," or "*Freundschaft.*" Yes, we are brothers, *koinonoi*, but brothers *in Christ*, in an otherness that withdraws us from our subjectivity.... What one participates in isn't the glory of the Resurrection but the suffering and the blood of the Cross (I. Cor. 10:16; Phil 3:10). Any possibility of appropriation is diminished; "taking part in" means everything except "to take"; on the contrary, it means losing something, to be weakened, to share the fate of the servant, not of the master (Phil. 3:10–11). His death.[52]

Death is precisely that which links the Christian *donum* with Esposito's nihilistic conclusion. The voluntary accession to death is foundational to Christian community and yet stands forever outside it as that which precedes it and founds it but which cannot be experienced firsthand: we cannot fix the meaning of Christ's accession unto death within the spectrum afforded by the rival terms of "martyrdom" and "suicide" because we are the bystanders and inheritors of that accession, located in a time and space apart. We are called to constantly bear witness to and remember this flicker of volition, but forbidden from actively seeking our own deaths; that intimate proxemics—a continual closeness that must never touch what it never stops approaching—defines Christian community as a shared participation in a death that we live through and beyond.

What was nearly unsayable in Donne's lifetime has become, in time, eminently sayable. Talal Asad's *On Suicide Bombing* (2007) asserts in its opening pages that "the crucifixion is the most famous suicide in history, whose horror is transmuted into the project of redeeming universal humanity."[53] What does it mean to live in the space of vicarious habituation to self-injury opened up by proximity to Christ's death? What might it mean to open the window, and let the rain beat in? "Joy of the worm" is here resignified. It does not simply indicate spectatorial pleasure in the death of a fictional character, whether they are heroically central or ancillary and subservient. Tangling casuistry and paradox, Donne's "joy of the worm" names the pleasure we are all invited to take in the voluntary death of God.

Inventing Suicide in
Religio Medici

As long as there is death, there is hope.

BROTHER THEODORE[1]

The invention of suicide was literally an afterthought. The word appears for the first time in the 1643 edition of *Religio Medici*, when Sir Thomas Browne adjusts "the end of Cato" to read "the end and Suicide of Cato."[2] The word "suicide" is not present in manuscripts or earlier pirated editions; its belated entry into *A true and full coppy of that which was most imperfectly and surreptitiously printed before vnder the name of Religio medici* (published by the aptly named Andrew Crook) constitutes a minor flick of the wrist of authorial revision, an additional flourish of a restless mind.[3] Browne's revisions to the text of *Religio Medici* were first cataloged by early editors of the author such as W. A. Greenhill, and have been sensitively analyzed by Jonathan Post, who notes the careful and self-conscious ideological adjustments Browne made to his original in order to better moderate his rhetorical flights to suit the increasingly polarized climate of the 1640s.[4] Against the backdrop of reformist agitation, Browne's bold declaration that "I can be a King without a Crowne" (2.11.2672) and similarly risky sounding sentiments had to go. The major revisions—four extended new passages—occur at other points within the text, and register the magnetizing force of a newly embattled Anglican via media upon Browne's loose and libertine prose wanderings.[5] In the context of the revision process as a whole, the addition of the word "suicide" is simply one of the "small dots on the rather large canvas of the *Religio Medici*."[6]

How significant was this dot? Did Browne invent "suicide" at all? What would it mean to say that? As Brian Barraclough and Daphne Shepherd note cautiously in an essay on the neologism and its uptake, "Browne appears to have used the word once only, which is surprising if he did invent it."[7] For many years, on the strength of a claim put forward by linguist David Daube, scholars granted credit for the coinage of "suicide" to Walter Charleton, a royal physician and key disseminator of Epicurean philosophy, whose 1659 *The Ephesian Matron* (a sly translation of a tale of graveyard seduction by Petronius) features a stormy speech from a repentant solider who cries out "to vindicate one's self from inevitable Calamity by Sui-Cide is not... a Crime but an act of Heroique Fortitude."[8] In *The Savage God: A Study of Suicide* (1971), A. Alvarez identified Sir Thomas Browne as the inventor of the word.[9] Writing before the dawn of comprehensive digital archives such as the keyword-searchable EEBO (Early English Books Online), Barraclough and Shepherd's cautious endorsement of Browne's credit for the coinage marks the verificationist problems that plague scholarly attempts to grant any individual an overly strong paternity claim upon innovations in language. We here straddle the formerly much fetishized and now rather shabby-looking structuralist binary of langue/parole. Communities use language and print fixes credit, but print lags notoriously behind the shape space of speech. The probable source of the word "literary," as well as "electricity," "hallucination," and "precarious," Browne's prodigious gift for construction tends to produce, understandably, more admiration and awe than analysis, as we analyze through the very lenses he provided. Bolting the prefix "sui-" and the suffix "-cide" together along the lines of other preexisting terms ("regicide," "infanticide," "patricide," "matricide"), the resulting word looks inevitable, as if it had always been there.

Moving from "the end of Cato" to "the end and Suicide of Cato," Browne's jolting addition displays his facility with a linguistic resource held in common: the diachronic density of English frequently generates effects at the level of both rhythm and significance through the tight juxtaposition of Anglo-Saxon monosyllables and Latinate multisyllabic words. Macbeth's self-glossing suggestion that "this my hand will rather / the multitudinous seas incarnadine / Making the green one red" (2.2.59–61) is a famous case in point of such effects of Latinate shock and Anglo-Saxon recoil as an expansive innovation gets read back in a short sharp phrase. There is a pleasing combination of overlap and antithesis in the pairing: "end," a brief and deeply familiar word seems somehow shorter and homelier when paired with "Suicide," a capitalized Latinate creation, at once fire-new and vaguely redolent of antiquity. "End and Suicide" telegraphs that we are looking not at synonymy but subsidiary containment: a suicide is a kind of end, a more precise way of telling us which kind. The pairing is not redundant padding but clarifying, exacting. Because Cato is the case in question, the Latinate register seems apt.

Browne's coinage, then, is both striking and yet fitting, and so from a certain perspective it seems to offer a case in point of what critics have long taken to be Browne's broader rhetorical strategy in *Religio Medici*: shocking and paradoxical declarations leap upward into the speculative heavens only to waft downward toward soft landings well within the established guidelines of orthodoxy. Unsettling effects at the level of the phrase and the sentence yield to stabilizing effects at the level of the paragraph and the broader drift of argument. Having absorbed Lancelot Andrewes's sermons on the Gunpowder Plot and the Oath of Allegiance while at Winchester, Browne had had orthodox piety drilled into him from a young age; as one might expect given his (arguable) reputation as a Laudian conformist and "sworn subject," Browne regarded the word "innovation" itself as pejorative.[10] In the context of the 1640s, the word had connotations of Puritanism and controversy that perhaps did not sit well with Browne's sensibility, which sought the "soft and flexible" center of community over the reformist edge wherever possible.[11]

What would it mean to credit Browne with "the invention of suicide"? Would Browne himself have regarded it as an "invention" in the first place? As Roland Greene has shown in his chapter on "invention" as early modern keyword in *Five Words: Critical Semantics in the Age of Shakespeare and Cervantes* (2013), the term is sundered in the period by a fundamental ambivalence between invention as *discovery* and invention as *conception*, in which the latter overtakes the former, revealing "invention" as "one of the key terms in which early modern relations of authority—the movement of power across divisions of society and culture—are enclosed in a seemingly neutral, classical marker."[12] As it went about its work designating and categorizing actions and persons across discursive fields, from literature to legal cases to sermons, the longer trajectory of "suicide" over the subsequent centuries, from Browne's clunky-looking novelty to its customary diagnostic utility at present, demonstrates this conjunction of apparent neutrality with authoritative force.

In the distinction between "invention" and "innovation" lies a key index of the period's habits of mind. Importations from Latin into English were not "novel," because they were rooted in precedent. But such imports could still threaten and jar, and that response can be detected in the reception of the word "suicide" in period dictionaries, which affect irritation at the impertinent novelty of the very words that grant the occasion for the existence of their books, which did not attempt to catalog a lexis but simply to offer usage guides for "hard" words. In *Glossographia* (1656), Thomas Blount's introduction blusters at innovation in general ("since our English Tongue daily changes habit, every fantastical Traveller, and home-bred Sciolist being at liberty, as, to antiquate and decry the old, so to coyn and innovate new Words"), but when it is time to gloss "suicide" the entry is coolly businesslike: "Suicide (from sui) the slaying or murdering of himself; self-murder."[13] In his *The new world of English words, or, A*

general dictionary containing the interpretations of such hard words as are de-
rived from other languages (1657), Edward Phillips, a nephew of Milton accused of plagiarizing Blount, offers a particularly colorful case in point of
objection on principle to Latinate inventions in general and "Suicide" in
particular:

> I have also met with some forged, as I shrewdly suspect, by such as un-
> dertook to explain them; so monstrously barbarous, and insufferable, that
> they are not worthy to be mentioned, nor once thought on, yet that ye may
> guesse at Hercules by his foot, one of them I shall produce, which is Sui-
> cide, a word which I had rather should be derived from Sus, a Sow, then
> from the Pronown Sui, unlesse there be some mystery in it; as if it were a
> Swinish part for a man to kill himself.[14]

While this fanciful mode of argument recalls the speculative flights of
Isidore of Seville's *Etymologiae*, Phillips is technically correct about "sus";
but this fussy scholarly pushback reveals more than simply a position pro
or contra. Here, resistance to the word "suicide" and disgust for the act
it names conjoin into a reflex of dehumanization at something rendered
both animalistic and "barbarous." On the whole, this contentious reception climate suggests that the survival of "suicide" as a word was far from a
given. Rather than entering the lexicon alongside "electricity" and "hallucination," Browne's invention might well have wound up on the scrapheap
alongside his other less popular coinages, such as "alliciency" and "zodi-
ographer," stillborn curate's eggs.[15] Such an outcome would have seemed
the likelier option, as the first inheritors of Browne's coinage didn't want
the word "suicide," much as they didn't care to think of the act it named.

Slanting discussion away from the accusatory language of "self-murther," with its implicit reminders of violence and criminality, Browne's
word offered later readers and writers in the period a semantic tool through
which to further the advance of tolerance for suicide as a rational decision
and away from the satanic and supernatural taint that Michael MacDonald and Terence Murphy have argued was characteristic of "the era of severity."[16] But the mere circulation of the term didn't guarantee a new attitude; indeed, if we consider Samuel Johnson's entry in the first edition
of his 1755 dictionary, "SUICIDE, n. s. [Latin, *suicidium*], Self-murder: the
horrid crime of destroying one's self," we can see that the English invention has now birthed a modern Latin neologism unattested in classical or
medieval Latin, and that Browne's coinage is relayed with a decided note
of abhorrence.[17]

Describing the gradual uptake of "suicide" into print circulation, Barraclough and Shepherd read its currency as a sign of precisely such a cultural shift: "*Suicide* appears to have been used first by those arguing for the right to commit suicide, placed in some dictionaries and word lists, and used in minor literary work, but probably not by the preeminent writers of the seventeenth and early eighteenth centuries."[18] For their part, in *Sleepless Souls* MacDonald and Murphy, though they touch very briefly upon Browne, Charleton, and Blount, focus their own chapter titled "The Invention of Suicide" on the philosophes and freethinkers and Deists of the eighteenth century, and track a gradual shift in educated opinion away from religious abhorrence that happens decades after Browne's early coinage.[19] Regardless of his own complex and critical relationship to the act his word newly designated, on the strength of that word's later career Browne has been conscripted into service as part of a broader cultural shift from the era of severity to something more like Enlightenment tolerance and lenience.

Such a broad-strokes change is arguably demonstrable over the arc of a century, but remains question-begging. Specifically, to suggest that suicide is a rational action does not mitigate its definitive status as sin. As I have already pointed out, the prevailing legal categories in play during the period distinguished acts of self-killing into distinct categories of intentionality and competence: for the comparatively small percentage of cases in which a deceased is ruled non compos mentis, self-killing is regarded as an accidental consequence of madness, and hence excused from posthumous legal penalty and the confiscation of the deceased's estate.[20] These rare exceptions were contrasted with the vast majority of cases in which agents were regarded as having made conscious decisions to kill themselves (felo-de-se). Since felo-de-se was by definition a rational decision while remaining, as an admixture of theft and murder, both a crime and a sin, Browne's semantic innovation does not resolve the salience of the act/identity assemblage that it newly compounds. How could it? If he was the first to come up with the term, does he commence a conceptually novel way of understanding self-killing?

The context of Browne's navigation of these murky waters matters more than the glittering lexical invention that bobs to its surface. To reconstruct that context we must run the necessary risk of fatal submersion in Browne's circuitous roundelay of self-doubts, objections, digressions, and counterpoints. For the rest of this interlude, I will focus directly upon the section of *Religio Medici* in which "suicide" first appears, which reads in its entirety as follows:

> I am much taken with two Verses of Lucan, since I have been able not as we do at School, to construe, but to understand:

Victurosque Dei celant ut vivere durent,
Felix esse mori

We're all deluded, vainly searching ways
To make us happy by the length of days;
For cunningly to make's protract this breath,
The Gods conceal the happiness of death.

There be many excellent strains in that Poet, wherewith his Stoical genius hath liberally supplied him: and truly there are singular pieces in the
Philosophy of Zeno, and doctrine of the Stoicks, which I perceive delivered
in a Pulpit pass for current Divinity; yet herein are they in extreams, that
can allow a man to be his own Assassine, and so highly extoll the end and
Suicide of Cato; this is indeed not to fear death, but yet to be afraid of life.
It is a brave act of valour to condemn death; but where life is more terrible
than death, it is then the truest valour to dare to live; and herein Religion
hath taught us a noble example: For all the valiant acts of Curtius, Scavola,
or Codrus, do not parallel, or match that one of Job; and sure there is no
torture to the rack of a disease, nor any Poynards in death itself, like those
in the way or prologue to it.

Emori nolo, sed me esse mortuum nihil curo. I would not die, but care
not to be dead. Were I of Caesar's religion, I should be of his desires, and
wish rather to go off at one blow, than to be sawed in pieces by the grating
torture of a disease. Men that look no farther than their outsides, think
health an appurtenance unto life, and quarrel with their constitutions for
being sick; but I that have examined the parts of man, and know upon what
tender Filaments that Fabrick hangs, do wonder that we are not always so;
and considering the thousand doors that lead to death, do thank my God
that we can die but once. 'Tis not only the mischief of diseases, and the
villainy of Poisons, that make an end of us; we vainly accuse the fury of
Guns, and the new inventions of death; it is in the power of every hand to
destroy us, and we are beholden unto everyone we meet, he doth not kill
us. There is therefore but one comfort left, that though it be in the power of
the weakest arm to take away life, it is not in the strongest to deprive us of
death; God would not exempt himself from that; the misery of immortality in the Flesh he undertook not, that was in it immortal. Certainly there
is no happiness within this circle of flesh, nor is it in the Opticks of these
eyes to behold felicity; the first day of our Jubilee is death; the Devil hath
therefore failed of his desires; we are happier with death than we should
have been without it; there is no misery but in himself, where there is no
end of misery; and so indeed in his own sense, the Stoick is in the right. He

forgets that he can die who complains of misery; we are in the power of no calamity while death is our own.[21]

Browne's thoughts nest points and counterpoints into tightly coiled jack-in-the-boxes of rhetorical display for which he was both celebrated and critiqued. Browne stands accused by Stanley Fish of being a "bad physician," for whom the conspicuous ostentation of ingenuity becomes an end in itself, and the result is a glib indifference to any outcome other than self-conscious admiration for the author's wit.[22] Browne's thought is fractal: the pattern of gradually mounting pressure finding striking release in an unexpected contrast at closure takes place at the level of these long-limbed sentences, but that architecture of coyly managed expectation is also replicated at the level of entire paragraphs and subsections. Browne's digressive wanderings across a sequence of paradoxical observations build their own readerly suspense as the cumulative interconnections of a given topos take on the semblance of a pattern and a tendency, only to have that pattern itself complicated and completed by a final *volta* of surprise. In the case of section 44, the motor of Browne's prose draws its energy by spinning rapidly back and forth across two contrary polarities of potentially incompatible yet powerfully exemplary archives of virtue: classical Stoicism and scripture.

We begin with an admission of the intoxicating power of classical poetry celebrating death with honor. The stirring lines come from Lucan's *Bellum civile*, which Browne would have studied at Winchester in the 1618 Farnaby edition; they relay a moment of high drama in which the commander Vulteius persuades his troops to die for Caesar rather than endure capture by the enemy.[23] But this throb of investment in voluntary death, already slightly distanced by the temporal lag between schoolboy encounter and adult understanding, is no sooner acknowledged than Browne, however "much taken," reverses direction. Seen at a historical distance and in personal retrospect after the initial rush of first reading, the seemingly brave doctrines of Stoicism and the stirring examples of Cato actually express a fear of life.

Christianized Stoicism "passes for Divinity," but that very verb cattily betrays that it is false coin. In a familiar antithesis of activity and passivity, the violent extremity of Stoic suicides is upstaged by Job's patient suffering. No sooner has this been stated than Browne begins to reflect upon the pain of disease, and admits that he would rather die quickly than slowly waste away, sapping his prior critique of some of its force. This observation carries with it a faint recognition of the arguments for euthanasia that Montaigne (Browne's pervasive precursor) had raised in "A Custom of the Island of Cea."[24] The fear of life, mocked as the secret truth of

Stoic doctrine, turns out to have a material basis in the close-up reality of what death from a painful illness really looks like. It is here that the *Medici* component of Browne's text surfaces as the material fact of corporeality is gloomily faced; his very familiarity with "the Filaments [from which] that tender Fabrick hangs" makes him wonder why we are not always sick, a startlingly honest admission of the limits of medical intervention, and of the certainty of mortal outcomes regardless. Browne expresses gratitude that we die only once, but the comfort of that truth gear-shifts into a proto-Hobbesian recognition that humanity is united by its members' shared, reciprocal capacity to kill one another.

In the wake of that fearful knowledge, the tension between playful tone and morbid content becomes flagrant, as Browne turns increasingly agile and spirited pirouettes upon the subject of inescapable limits and mortal absolutes. Browne's observation that the weakest can kill us, but even the strongest cannot save us from death looks paradoxical, but it is in fact more preparation, a launchpad for a further paradox, in which the strongest possible agent—God—is shown to have demurred from undertaking a logical possibility that remained open: immortality in the flesh. This momentary thought experiment of the divine Struldbrug, wasting and rotting into an endless eternity, courts blasphemy through its implication that the death of the incarnated Christ was, itself, an easy way out. We would do well to remember that "black humor" was born in the French surrealist appreciation of Swift as the founding creator of "humour noir"; the Struldbrug is a case in point of that anarchic pleasure in morbidity, but Browne precedes Swift's thought experiment, as here he already generates a disturbing sort of comedy from the prospect of incarnate immortality. Suddenly we have turned back to the very beginning, and the very Stoics who were wrong at the start of the section are now, astonishingly, declared to be "right."[25]

Browne's faintly facetious playfulness persists to the end. The Stoics are right to assert that "Felix esse mori," but wrong to derive from that a license to become the engines of their own annihilation. Rather, the contemplation that death is happy constitutes a means from within life through which to bear the pain that material, mortal life inevitably brings with it. We can be certain that the present form of our sufferings has a decisive end point, and that end point thereby becomes something to celebrate: "The first day of our Jubilee is death."

This advice is not an innovation. Indeed, Browne's stance can look, in its broad outlines, like a gesture toward an already crowded waiting area framed by a familiar homiletic distinction between (permissible, even admirable) self-destructive affects and (forbidden) self-destructive actions. Indeed, as Margaret Pabst Battin has pointed out, there is a long doctrinal history in Christian theological tradition in which "the line between the desire to die and suicide is... finely drawn; this is true for writers from St. Paul to the thirteenth-century mystic Angela of Foligno" and beyond.[26] Longing for the divine presence expresses itself in a desire to exit life experienced as painful separation from it, an emotional stance of yearning that achieves maximum compression in St. John of the Cross's poignant "Vivo sin vivir in mi / y de tal manera espero / que muero porque no muero" (I live yet do not live in me, / Am waiting as my life goes by / and die because I do not die.)[27] What distinguishes Browne is not his shared sense of the permissibility of this feeling, but his particular slant downward in modulating its force and postponing its outcome. Where the saints and mystics throb with a passionate desire for death that occasions a painful battle as they submit to the onerous obligation to survive, Browne's language of genial hope is cooler, lower in intensity, suggestive of someone casually playing a long game. True to the professional calling announced in *Religio Medici*'s title, this ramping down in amplitude is perhaps of a piece with the "medical dispassion" required of physicians in the period when confronted firsthand by cries of suffering in an age without anesthesia.[28] Finding "joy of the worm" in the cool certainty of a safe bet, Browne's bedside manner is morbidly ironic: death is coming, so there's nothing to worry about.

In the midst of mortal difficulty at present, we are accustomed to offering comfort to others, and to ourselves, via a ready-to-hand palliative slogan: "Where there's life, there's hope." Across its long arc from the Ciceronian motto *dum spiro, spero* to Snoop Dogg's "If you're breathing, you're achieving," the sentiment keeps us afloat amid precarity, and often surfaces as an affective life preserver amid the humiliatingly bureaucratic and inhospitable surroundings of the administered world in which terminal medical crises transpire.[29] The phrase draws succor from skepticism, hedging against impasse by invoking the limit of what we know, and finding optimism in our supposedly infinite capacity to be surprised. The slogan seems to assert that "as long as you are alive, you can always hope for more life, because, well, one never knows."

Cautioned by Browne to accept the certainties that mortal existence necessarily implies as he separates the mortal grain from the suicidal chaff of classical doctrine, we might observe that "Where's there's life, there's hope" can be immediately parsed into its implied inversion: "Where there's death, there's hope."[30] As long as we are alive, there's one thing we can still hope for, one last object of desire: death. Suicidal ideation is and is not quite the same as the vibrant hope for death with which Browne, somewhat cruelly, consoles us. In "hoping for death," we look forward to an event that we also posit as yet to come, not quite here, and thus forestall. Is this Browne as "bad physician" (Fish), "Laudian Idiot" (Shuger), or cruel tempter to the very act he would also judge and condemn?[31] The performance of irony on the page within *Religio Medici* presents the switchbacks of Stoically inspired suicidal ideation and its Christian reproof as the continuously oscillating pattern of mortal life for the educated early modern person, and suggests that such quotidian movements of the affections toward and away from self-destruction are the permanent warp and weft of embodiment even for those who have not read Lucan and Seneca. For Browne and his entranced and enervated readers over the centuries beyond, suicide turns out to be repudiated only by way of an irony strong enough to acknowledge that death really is the best we can hope for. Neither violent catharsis nor malingering despair, the birth cry of suicide's invention was a shrug.

CHAPTER FIVE

A Cartoon about Suicide Prevention in *Paradise Lost*

I know who the hangman is
So life's a joke.

SMOG, "Hangman Blues"

A few years ago, a student who had been missing class and behaving oddly when she did show up began to visibly fall apart in my office hours, going on crying jags that would leave her shaking and incapable of speech. On a particularly fraught Friday afternoon I found a note she left under my door containing a drawing that was ostensibly about her struggles to write a paper that was due. A gifted cartoonist, she had sketched a monotonous grid of panels in which she sat at her desk in panel after panel, staring ahead at her computer, immobile, waiting, with nothing to say, as she often did in class lately. In the last panel at the corner of the frame, she had drawn herself, hanging from a noose, dead.

I did what I hope anyone in my position would do: I contacted the student immediately to talk about how she was feeling, what she felt the cartoon did and did not mean, determined whether she had a plan or a weapon or intent to self-harm, spoke with counseling services, determined that she had a therapist, made sure that the therapist was aware of the seriousness of her crisis, and tried to determine that she was reasonably safe from herself. What does that mean? For me it meant that she would continue, come Monday, to be my student, because she would continue to be alive. Was this an act of kindness or the off-loading of responsibility? Was this about protecting a body from harm, or an institution from liability?

I relay this story because it is about the capacity of art to induce an affective experience that is also a critical searching of the affect that art manifests. I say "critical" not simply to suggest urgency but also to denote an interpretive double gesture of inhabitation and resistance, including skepticism (was this just an inflated way to ask for an extension?). My student's cartoon took me into the lockstep grid of a calendar in which every day is the same blank space, where inspiration never comes, and the mounting pressure of expectation suffocates the will to strive and try, upon which both education and academic writing rely. Caught in the feedback loop of pressure and failure and shame and self-hatred that is the inability to write (a loop that some of us inhabit for years as we try to write dissertations and books such as this one, a process Anne Boyer has termed a positive state called "not writing"),[1] her drawing expressed the will to die as a fantasy that art could contain and frame but also unleash, writing herself out of existence, breaking the cycle and "solving the problem" with a final, decisive cut in which life became a joke with death as the punchline.

The emotional transmission of that fantasy prompted sympathy—I felt, albeit at a spectatorial remove, some dimension of her own suffering—but also pressed me to respond to that fantasy in order to preempt its execution, and in the process to struggle to determine the valence of the work and the status of the person behind the work: Was she "serious"? What is a joke, and what is a threat? Answering these questions requires that we set aside our fear of gullibility and misreading, our fear of being wrong. Her drawing is a particular example of a general capacity that artworks have: to render affective experiences, even and especially suicidal ideation and fantasies of self-harm and self-killing, portable. But artworks also open these fantasies out to criticism, rethinking, and intervention, by showing agents thinking them through before they become irreversibly past actions. In the orderly making of art no less than in its disorderly reception, feeling cascades through thought to action.

Paradise Lost revolves around an irreversible action. In working through the causes and consequences of that irreversibility, Milton's great poem stages an exemplary reflection upon both the power of fantasies of self-killing and the means through which to sorrowfully think one's way through and beyond them. A. E. Housman pointed out long ago that "malt does more than Milton can / to justify God's ways to man"; heeding those words, I hesitate to admit a credulous investment in the salvific capacities of this or any poem to redeem humanity, one reader at a time, from their own despair.[2] Mileage may vary, and causality is tough to prove. Instead, inspired by the example of my student cartoonist, I would like to take a calculated risk of the ludicrous by straining the early modern fantasies of self-killing within that great poem through the conceptual sieve provided by a contemporary tool used in clinical suicide-risk assessment: the predictive acronym IS PATH WARM?

Created by the American Association of Suicidology, the mnemonic IS PATH WARM? is used by psychologists examining patients that are clinically depressed, borderline, or otherwise considered at risk for self-harm and self-killing.[3] The mnemonic stands for the following risk factors and component parts:

I is for Ideation
S is for Substance Abuse
P is for Purposelessness
A is for Anxiety
T is for Trapped
H is for Hopelessness
W is for Withdrawal
A is for Anger
R is for Recklessness
M is for Mood Changes

Seen as a list, the crushing triteness of this resulting catalog suggests alphabetical whimsy more than psychological insight. It looks like an intake-
interview variant on *The Gashlycrumb Tinies*.[4] At the risk of constructing
a Miltonic Hallmark card in which "M is for Mortal Taste," I'm going to
use the diagnostic frame provided by this acronym to conduct a kind of
symptomatic-assessment rundown of Adam and Eve as Milton depicts
them in the wake of the Fall. Seen from this perspective, I hope to consider
what *Paradise Lost* and suicide prevention might have to say to each other.
I do so not in order to claim a canonical masterpiece as a poetic ratification of contemporary biopolitical mandates toward obligatory survival;
the difference and distance between Milton's understanding of Adam and
Eve's despair and contemporary clinical understandings of patients at risk
of self-harm are so glaring as to go without saying. Inhabiting this willfully
ugly clash between method and moment might help us track the conflicted
space of Milton's poem as it mobilizes against the very feelings that it also
transmits and amplifies, while keeping the present in view. Written in response to the urgent prompt of my student's suicidal cartoon, what follows
is a suicidal cartoon of my own, divided accordingly into ten subsidiary
panels: not one chapter, but ten small chapters, each alphabetically keyed
to a symptom upon the warming path toward and cooling path away from
its central point of concern.

"I" Is for Ideation

"Ideation" is a clinical term for the play and pressure of suicidal scenarios
upon the mind of a person at risk: thinking about death, thinking about the
impossible yet certain state of "being dead," thinking about why one ought
to die, thinking about a world without you in it, and thinking about taking
conscious, purposeful steps toward the execution of self-harm all count
as forms of ideation.[5] By this definition, there is a patently obvious sense
in which both Adam and Eve, by their own admission "incapable of death

or pain" before the Fall, are plunged by this disaster and the subsequent divine judgment into states of suicidal ideation and intrusive thoughts of death (9.283).[6] Indeed, the argument to book 9 frames Adam's coparticipation in the Fall as itself already a matter of a suicidal desire: "Adam at first amazed, but perceiving her lost, resolves through vehemence of love to perish with her" (p. 517); his reaction upon learning of Eve's consumption of the forbidden fruit is clear: "Certain my resolution is to die" (9.907).

The sentence of judgment in the wake of the Fall plunges each of them deeper into a "troubled sea of passion" (10.718), albeit one worn with a gendered difference: Adam reflects at great length upon death, puzzling with himself about its meaning and trying to imagine it as a positive state, while Eve speculates about what free choices remain within the space defined by the divine sentence and selects self-killing as a possibly advantageous practical choice. Adam thinks about death and Eve thinks about suicide, and in their partial overlap and partial disjunction we see a gendered union-in-division of affective labor already announced by the terms of the judgment in Genesis: sorrow is the universal sentence, sorrow in the bed of childbirth for Eve, sorrow in the fields of labor for Adam. As they separately and then together weigh the condition of mortality, suicidal ideation permeates human consciousness for the first time.

Adam comes to long for judgment, and to revolt against life as a death row of sadistically protracted duration:

> I submit, His doom is fair,
> That dust I am, and shall to dust return:
> O welcome hour whenever! Why delays
> His hand to execute what his decree
> Fixed on this day? Why do I overlive,
> Why am I mocked with death, and lengthened out
> To deathless pain? (10.769–75)

The message is clear: get on with it. Troubled by passion in the wake of the Fall, Adam is divided from himself by the tension between his spurious acceptance of "whenever" and his urgent desire to experience the inevitable now rather than to "overlive." The phrase has given the title and the climactic example to Emily Wilson's monograph *Mocked with Death: Tragedies of Overliving from Sophocles to Milton* (2004); in her final chapter, Wilson argues that the recognition of this temporal lag constitutes a powerful challenge to the reparative vision of human history, including the coming of Christ, which is ostensibly meant to redress and undo its hold.[7] For its pained readers, the poem's passage from suspenseful awareness of counterfactual possibility to an awful dawn of irrevocable certainty brings with it a kind of corresponding slump in energy and investment. Testifying to the pervasive effects of this wearisome sensation of "overliving," Wilson's diagnosis is decisive: "Human despair dominates the last books of the poem."[8]

But that despair is subject to modulation, ripples, and contours in its valence. For it is here in tension with a kind of curiosity about the form that death—still unknown—might take; as Annabel Patterson notes, "Adam and Eve have to learn, in stages, what *Death* as an abstract noun can and cannot mean, to them."[9] This task prompts a curiously impertinent maternal counterfactual:

> How gladly would I meet
> Mortality my sentence, and be earth
> Insensible, how glad would lay me down
> As in my mothers lap! There should I rest
> And sleep secure; his dreadful voice no more
> Would thunder in my ears, no fear of worse
> To me and to my offspring would torment me
> With cruel expectation. (10.775–82)

Laps are dangerous places in *Paradise Lost*. Offering a floral couch for transgression, the sinful postlapsarian orgy of Adam and Eve is consummated on a bank of flowers that forms "earth's freshest softest lap" (9.1041), from which, dazed and confused, Adam rises like "Herculean Samson, from the harlot-lap / Of Philistean Dalilah" (9.1060–61).[10] As if replacing these bad images of feminine softness and receptivity and murderous treachery, Adam's image of death as a process of falling into his mother's lap can cause outraged responses in the undergraduate classroom from students understandably wrong-footed by the line: How would Adam know what a mother's lap was? Adam has no mother.

One could soften this problem. Adam is figuring the Earth itself as a kind of mother, drawing sustenance from its ready-to-hand metaphorical mythopoetic familiarity and literal support from the Hebrew pun of "Adam" and "אדמה" ("adamah").[11] In being ontologically reunited with his source element, Adam imagines creation in reverse. The Earth's maternal body provides soundproofing against the awful sound of paternal thunder, replacing a bad father with a good mother; this is the "fantasy of fusion with the idealized mother," which psychoanalyst Mervin Glasser describes as "the ultimate narcissistic fulfilment."[12] Returning to the womb in death is a comforting scenario of setting back the clock, undoing the fall into temporality as responsibility. In fantasy, Earth's dusty lap settles over the agitation that is the price of fallen life.

Adam's fantasy of dropping into the maternal lap will be repeated to him by Michael in book 11: "So may'st thou live, till like ripe fruit thou drop / Into thy mother's lap, or be with ease / Gathered, not harshly plucked, for death mature:" (11.535–37) To drop or to be gathered? These alternatives imagine the point of contact between fruit and tree as the infra-thin membrane of a connection sundered by the categorical difference between the human being that must patiently abide in ripeness and the divine gardener whose timely hand will, eventually, come to claim it (a botanical variant on the hopeful waiting room that Browne in *Religio Medici* offered to his readers). Michael's reply to Adam grants the very scenario that in the depths of his speculations in book 10 he had imagined: a maternal, receptive lap in which to fall and rest. Here passionate longing downshifts to a passive acceptance of death as due. *Paradise Lost* prevents suicide by modulating our fantasies of death to an ambient longing that simmers within the ongoing project of patience.

"S" Is for Substance Abuse

In the wake of her catastrophic ingestion of the forbidden entheogen in the garden, Eve is suffering the harshest of comedowns. The term "entheogen" comes from psychedelic chemistry and ethnopharmacology, and is used to describe the folkloric representation of shamanic and ceremonial uses of intoxicating or hallucinogenic plants, indexing the supposed capacity of certain plants to induce contact with divine entities via an involution toward "the god within."[13] Such access is (perhaps) implied by the divine admission that "ye shall be as gods," a proviso cynically exploited by Satan in disguise as the "spirited sly snake," who promises an extraordinary advancement in capacities and aptitudes (9.613, 9.708). In this sense, the fruit is less like LSD or DMT and more like modafinil, the amphetamine-like performance-enhancement chemical of choice for sleepy, overcommitted shift workers and tech executives and literature professors who long to be better, harder, faster, stronger.

No sooner has she tasted the fruit than she begins babbling about returning first thing each morning to tend to the sacred plant. As its juices spread across her system she entertains a manic rush of euphoria, delusions of superiority as she imagines keeping the odds in her favor and living "without copartner," and paranoid anxiety that Adam may replace her with another mate as punishment for her transgression (9.820–21). Following from the symptoms described by Kay Redfield Jamison in *Night Falls Fast: Understanding Suicide*, the effect of eating the fruit resembles mania: "There is a vast, restless energy and little desire or need for sleep. Behavior is erratic, impetuous, and frequently violent."[14] That said, Jamison also notes that "Paranoia, explosive rage, and despair not uncommonly lie beneath the expansive manic exterior."[15]

Is this a matter of the fruit's effects, Eve's own persona, or the catalytic interaction of both? Milton's grammar remains agnostic with respect to the powers afforded by the fruit; Eve's departure from the tree comes with a gesture of "low reverence done, as to the power / That dwelt within, whose presence had infused / In the plant sciential sap, derived / From nectar, drink of gods" (9.835–38). That pagan plural clangs shut upon the entire fantasy as an illusory comparison, yet Eve animatedly attests to the side effects of "dilated spirits, ampler heart, / and growing up to Godhead" induced by its taste, and Adam can read in her face the glowing flush of "distemper" (9.876–77). Once Adam too has tasted, Milton keeps it up, describing "that now / As with new wine intoxicated both / They swim in mirth, and fancy that they feel / Divinity within them breeding wings / With which to scorn the Earth" (9.1007–11). In this lurid description of the intoxicating and self-aggrandizing psychological impact of this wine-like fruit upon his pair, Milton depicts the quasi-satanic outcome of substance abuse; this pleasure is both born out of, and reinforces, the aspiration to transgress limits and ascend beyond. Adam and Eve binge upon this new delight and fantasize about the supremacy it grants them; the nature of their bond shifts as, in the words of Diane McColley, "Love becomes a greedy engorging."[16]

The despair, regret, shame, and self-hatred that the fruit brings in its wake connect substance abuse as cause with self-killing as a possible cure, erasing the sinful body and forestalling or evading the transmission of sin onto future generations. Eve as mother will be compromised by her substance-abuse history, leaving it as a stigmatizing legacy for her children.

The conflation of substance abuse with sin produces monsters. Consider, as a case in point, the disastrous federal sentencing policies of the so-called "War on Drugs," in which US legislators leveraged moral panic about "crack babies," a purely rhetorical social category invented upon a minimal and preliminary clinical basis, as a means to further stigmatize drug use by turning addiction during pregnancy into a civil matter of child abuse rather than a medical problem requiring treatment.[17] To state the obvious, this particularly racist formation was not yet available in early modernity; that said, as Dennis Kezar shows in "Shakespeare's Addictions" in a reading of *Othello* and tobacco, the idea and terminology of addiction as such was already beginning to circulate by the early seventeenth century.[18] It is hardly the case that Eve is "addicted" to the fruit, but it is certainly the case that in consuming it she has abused a substance that, in its consequence, has transformed her body and her mind, and altered the biological fate of her children accordingly. Eve's sin has wrought a so-matic stain, a marker we might understand as theologico-genetic, which her children are doomed to inherit unless she circumvents that transmission with a radical act. As the fulcrum of human history, Eve's momentary "substance abuse" occupies an overdetermined chasm between contrary understandings, at once a tragic act of self-destruction and a *felix culpa* that ironically engenders the possibility of Christ's sacrificial supersession.

"P" Is for Purposelessness

Suicidal people do not see a future worth surviving into. There is no task worth accomplishing, no pleasure worth the endurance of what medieval-ist Nicola Masciandaro has termed "the sorrow of being."[19] The ground that would legitimate or valorize the self has slipped. The weight of the future hangs like a stone around the neck, suffocating the present with the pressure of a futurity that has already arrived in the form of an existential obligation to continue to survive, and thus to continue to suffer. Purpose as such becomes vexed for Eve. The disastrous consequences of her most dramatic and purposeful action are only now becoming clear to her, in the gradually unfolding terms of an inescapable sentence that hedges in the space in which she might purposefully act.

It is then a notable irony, of a piece with the gusts of comedy that occasionally sweep across the weather system of the poem, that Eve becomes inspiring, powerful, even sublime and excellent, in the eyes of Adam as she rises from depressive torpor toward the upright, imaginative posture of her suicidal proposal.

> If care of our descent perplex us most,
> Which must be born to certain woe, devoured
> By Death at last, and miserable it is
> To be to others cause of misery
> Our own begotten, and of our loins to bring
> Into this cursed world a woful race
> That after wretched life must be at last
> Food for so foul a monster, in thy power
> It lies, yet ere conception to prevent
> The race unblest, to being yet unbegot. (10.979–88)

It is here that the conjunction of *Paradise Lost* and suicide prevention becomes a matter not of how to prevent suicide, but of how suicide itself might be a means of prevention: a way to ward off the future, puncturing the present to prevent a state of affairs yet to come. Eve imagines that another world is possible: one without humanity. Parsing this passage for its practical implications, wicked modern readers might well imagine that she could simply be describing contraceptive forbearance in a roundabout manner.

Addison's remark about Milton's Adam and Eve that they are "more new than any characters either in Vergil or Homer, or indeed in the whole circle of nature," describes their power to fascinate readers, but it also names their predicament and its power to estrange us from the givenness of our own condition.[20] What is troubling about the suicidal suggestion is the way that it tarnishes their newness; of a piece with her snide description of God as "Our great Forbidder, safe with all His spies / about him" (9.815–16), Eve's plot to circumvent divine decree has a secretive, canny, and deliberate manner that mottles her innocence. Since no one alive can have any direct experience of death, this shared condition brings us as readers closer to them in this respect, though we lack their absolute ignorance.

Eve goes on the offensive:

> Childless thou art, childless remain; so Death
> Shall be deceived his glut, and with us two
> Be forced to satisfy his rav'nous maw.
> But if thou judge it hard and difficult
> Conversing, looking, loving, to abstain
> From love's due rites, nuptial embraces sweet,
> And with desire to languish without hope,
> Before the present object languishing
> With like desire, which would be misery
> And torment less than none of what we dread,
> Then both ourselves and seed at once to free
> From what we fear for both, let us make short,
> Let us seek Death, or he not found, supply
> With our own hands his office on ourselves;
> Why stand we longer shivering under fears,
> That show no end but death, and have the power
> Of many ways to die the shortest choosing,
> Destruction with destruction to destroy. (10.989–1006)

In a manner that would have been familiar to Milton's readers in its citation of Senecan and Stoic commonplaces about the conscious fixation of "the proper time to slip the cable" and death as a "sensible removal," Eve offers a sneaky move on the chessboard. They must die, but if there is no further humanity, then that sentence can be both satisfied and evaded.

Far from purposeless, Eve has a proactive momentum here in her consideration of the possibilities that remain open. She hopes to swing through a loophole in that judgment's terms, thus "making short" the death sentence of protracted expectation that we already know Adam suffers.

There is a dimension of witty paradox here, modeled formally in the triple pirouette of the last line's folding of destruction upon itself. Beneath the display of rhetorical control, Eve hopes to jimmy an unforeseen dimension of choice out of the tight corner imposed by an irrevocably decreed outcome. Slinking past blasphemy, Eve presents herself not as the enemy of God but of Death, whose "rav'nous maw" she will cram with herself, leaving her unseen antagonist both fed and starved in the same gesture.[21] In a hypothetical case that recalls Donne's telling adjacency of casuistry and paradox, in doing Death's "office" for him, Death is technically satisfied while being effectively upstaged, even preempted. Eve's imaginative curiosity and her habit of circumventing restraint are made simultaneous.

In keeping with Milton's allegorical framing of Sin and Death as an antithetical yet incestuously entangled pairing, Eve's fatal plan is also a means of processing the aftermath of fallen sexuality: by openly choosing death as a consequence of the recognition of their own sin, they will realize the "mortal taste" the poem promises from its opening lines.[22] Flushed with the shared crime of tasting the fruit, Eve and Adam have experienced for the first time a different kind of intimacy; Adam now casts "lascivious looks" at his partner, and Eve responds "wantonly" (9.1014). These discordant energies transform the valence of paradisal unions, moving the pair beyond, or perhaps below, love into the realm of passionate lust. Eve's plan is pressurized not only by self-disgust and shame, in a moral register, but by an all-too-keen sense memory of the disorderly new powers granted to fallen desire and an alternately eager and horrified sense that repetitions of such scenes are likely to generate cursed offspring.

"A" Is for Anxiety

In the seminar on anxiety from 1962–63, Lacan declares that the object of anxiety cannot be stated.[23] The nature of anxiety is that it be nonspecific, that it not surface into presentation or naming, which would reduce and localize it into fear or terror.[24] Eve's death anxiety suits this mingled space of known unknowns: the death sentence has been laid down but the significance of such a sentence is partially lost upon Adam and Eve, whose responses speculate in a uniquely ignorant manner about the answer to the question: What is Death? The crypto-Spenserian parody of Milton's allegorical representation of Death as a crowned abstraction signifies this representational block across the poem, but for Eve it has a particular salience. Suicide promises a definitive end to anxiety and suffering by negating the life that entails that condition.

This position has recently been articulated forcefully by the foremost philosophical proponent of the "anti-natalist" position, David Benatar. His book *Better Never to Have Been: The Harm of Coming into Existence* (2008) makes this case with an admirable relentlessness: since existence always contains some suffering, while nonexistence contains no suffering, the morally optimal number of human beings is zero.[25] Keen to manage the misunderstanding that his argument proceeds from a misanthropic agenda or basic hostility to human beings as such, Benatar clarifies his views in ways that dovetail with Milton's Eve:

> Bringing a sentient life into existence is a harm to the being whose life it is. My arguments suggest that it is wrong to inflict this harm. To argue against the infliction of harm arises from concern for, not dislike of, those who would be harmed. It may seem like an odd kind of philanthropy—one that, if acted upon, would lead to the end of *anthropos*. It is, however, the most effective way of preventing suffering. Not creating a person absolutely guarantees that that potential person will not suffer—because that person will not exist.[26]

Moving from theory to practice, the activist group known as the Voluntary Human Extinction Movement (VHEMT) argues along similar lines, encouraging human beings en masse to stop reproducing so that wildlife can flourish as the human species peacefully and voluntarily proceeds toward extinction.[27] Their platform blends Gaia environmentalism with a chilly sort of cheerfulness that borders upon parody: "Phasing out the human race by voluntarily ceasing to breed will allow Earth's biosphere to return to good health. Crowded conditions and resource shortages will improve as we become less dense."[28] To note the obvious, the reformist language of resource management sits oddly with the long-term goal of a willed extinction of humanity. Yet the VHEMT insists that they are not a suicide cult, as they want to survive long enough to spread their gospel: "Shortening an existing person's life by a few decades doesn't avoid as many years of human impact as not creating a whole new life—one with the potential for producing more of us. We have a responsibility to help the world as much as we're able before we die. Leaving the work for others would be irresponsible. VHEMT is a cause to live for not to die for."[29] From the vantage points of both David Benatar's anti-natalist argument and the VHEMT, Milton's Adam and Eve stand in a uniquely responsible position while escaping the need to live in order to evangelize extinction. Having convinced only each other, they can maximize the consequences of a single abstention, stopping the flood of humanity before it starts, and making the dream of a morally optimal human population of zero into a global reality.[30]

In response to the angelic slide show of human history to come, Adam will in time come to feel a horror at the proliferation of life and, with it, the proliferation of suffering:

> O miserable mankind, to what fall
> Degraded, to what wretched state reserved!
> Better end here unborn. Why is life given
> To be thus wrested from us? Rather why
> Obtruded on thus? Who if we knew
> What we receive, would either not accept
> Life offered, or soon beg to lay it down,
> Glad to be so dismissed in peace. (11.500–7)

Adam's perspective here anticipates Benatar's anti-natalist position regarding extinction as the only guaranteed harm-reduction protocol. The "glad" affect that Adam imagines himself enjoying resembles the cheerfulness that VHEMT aspires to cultivate in its still-living adherents; here "joy of the worm" begins to approximate Walter Benjamin's remark that "the destructive character" is "cheerful".[31] Sensing it as both obtrusive and damaging, Adam imagines the refusal of life, and comes to adopt what Benatar terms, with reference to abortion, the "pro-death view." Tartly rephrasing the same Sophoclean nostrum—that never to be born is best—that gives Benatar's book its title, Adam blurts, "Better end here unborn," and we sense the lingering appeal of Eve's scenario within the mortal mind. Imagining reproductive potential as an ethical referendum upon the function and limits of life, Milton saw the possibilities of the last human beings within the first human beings.

"T" Is for Trapped

How much room for interpretation, for breathing space, does this author afford? According to some of his most influential readers, none at all. In *How Milton Works* (2001), Stanley Fish gleefully dismisses all apparent irony or ambiguity in the Miltonic text as the index of the fallen, sinful perversity of human readers: "Everything that many readers find interesting in Milton's work—crises, conflicts, competing values, once-and-for-all dramatic moments—proceeds from error and is finally unreal."[32] Where we think we see such spaces of difference within Milton, we are encountering only our own erroneous instincts. Hoping that this methodological sleight of hand will lead to hermeneutic closure if it is proclaimed with sufficient energy, Fish views the doctrinal commitments expressed in Milton's theological writings as inescapably contouring all possible interpretations of his poetry, steering them toward orthodoxy and away from heretical misprision, and preempting rival interpretive possibilities and pseudotensions within the art.

Happily, others working in the field of Milton criticism have widened the array of imaginable relations between author and work beyond such narrow framing. Offering as a counterpoint to Fish the supposition that "Milton's contradictions and uncertainties are central to the meaning of *Paradise Lost*," Neil D. Graves has recently argued that "the current critical vogue is to refrain from ironing out the uncomfortable creases in the poet's writing, and this is particularly the case with Milton's theology."[33] This intuition seems to me to be borne out by the diversity of positions within the work of, for example, John Rumrich, Gordon Teskey, Feisal Mohamed, Sharon Achinstein, Ryan Netzley, Joanna Picciotto, Daniel Shore, Timothy Harrison, or Russ Leo (to simply list an array of diverse Milton scholars at present).

And yet, however ruffled and unruly such "creases" and folds may be as something like "casual Friday" arrives within Milton studies, Fish's monomaniacal insistence upon the explanatory force of Milton's core theological convictions might help us explain the trapped feeling that the contemplation of God's nature can generate in the reader. It is the trapped feeling that I wish to consider in this subsection. (That sense of entrapment might be the opposite of the "delirious Milton" produced by more poetically open-ended considerations of Milton as artist, such as that proposed in the Gordon Teskey monograph of the same name.)[34] If we acknowledge that all that happens within the world of the poem takes place by the express permission of God, then the reach of that permissive omnipotence suffuses each action, each movement, each choice, even and especially when those choices run counter to his warnings and commandments but cannot, by definition, frustrate his plans. By this light, who wouldn't feel trapped within Milton's universe, trapped by the very definitive explanatory power of Milton's omnipotent, omniscient God?

In the 1755 essay "Of Suicide," unpublished in its author's lifetime, David Hume will come, in the midst of a thoroughgoing rationalism, to advance as witty paradox something like this same guiding position that humans cannot violate Providence.[35] Hume's larger goal is to demolish arguments regarding both the sanctity of life and the alleged unnaturalness of self-killing through an expansive reconsideration of the implications of human action. If you can do something, then the very fact that you can do it demonstrates that it is within the shape space of possible actions, and thus cannot be regarded as unnatural or contrary to divine permission: "All events, in one sense, may be pronounced the action of the Almighty; they all proceed from those powers with which he has endowed his creatures."[36] A great deal hangs upon that "one sense," and it is here that Milton's understanding of divine power and Hume's later position hover into proximity before their ultimate divergence. Into this seamless space of unchecked Providential powers, Milton has inserted the crux of his theodicy, a "freedom to fall" that can, in the open expression of its freedom, choose to ignore divine caution. Even in such catastrophic failures of obedience, humanity can never outflank the space defined by the divine permission to disobey that primordially precedes them.

The profound sense of divine inescapability that this produces in both Adam and Eve and, by extension, in the poem's readers can lead to a trapped, claustrophobic feeling at odds with the reassurance that such a doctrine hopes to relay. In the wake of the constitutive ruin of the Fall, the thought of such pervasive power—a thought that might otherwise convey feelings of wonder, security, and consolation, of the standing nearness of God's presence—instead segues into dread of punishment, shame at exposure, and desperation, as Adam and Eve attempt to comprehend the practical entailments of mortality. The terms of their punishment have now introduced an unforeseen possibility that mortal life in the wake of the Fall now necessarily brings with it: the possibility of murder.

If Adam and Eve kill themselves, they will be guilty of "self-murder." But having fallen, if they give life they will, paradoxically, give death in that very act. Milton is direct about this in his celebrated gloss "On the fall of the first parents and on Sin," in *De Doctrina Christiana* (suitably, it is chapter 11), in which, mincing no words, he damns humanity as "faithless, ungrateful, disobedient, gluttonous; he uxorious, she all too heedless of her husband, each of them a killer of their own progeny (the whole human race), a thief, and preyer on what was not theirs; sacrilegious, deceitful, a crafty and unworthy pretender to divinity, haughty and arrogant."[37] Adam and Eve are killers, the preemptive executioners of humanity, yet they are barred from killing themselves by their instrumental role in rescuing the very progeny they have also killed. There is a deep comic irony here: the son will rise from the primal guilt of Adam and Eve to redeem and transform their victims, just as, in Dante's *Epistola a Cangrande*, the shift from the dark of *Inferno* to the light of *Paradiso* reveals the essentially comedic template of Christian eschatology.[38] This makes the decision to let death into the world both necessary and, in the deepest sense, just. Where entrapment in murder is concerned, the only way out is through.

The sensation of being trapped can, itself, precipitate self-killing as a last resort. In an influential 1991 article in *Psychological Review*, "Suicide as Escape from Self," Roy Baumeister proposed "escape theory": suicide is precipitated by a sequence of events from which the subject feels that there is no escape.[39] The sense that something will never improve and cannot be escaped prompts suicide as a kind of trapdoor through which to evade the seemingly inescapable circumstances pressing in upon the sufferer. Subsequent experiments in clinical psychology and sociology have provided some empirical confirmation of key components of Baumeister's theory.[40] Building upon this theory but exceeding it, in "The Integrated Motivational-Volitional Model of Suicidal Behaviour," Rory O'Connor and Olivia Kirtley articulate the crucial role that the feeling of "entrapment" plays in precipitating suicidal ideation, specifying that "entrapment is the bridge between defeat and suicidal ideation."[41] Trapped within the smooth theological shape space of divine permission, the possibility of accelerating an inevitability (Adam and Eve are already doomed, and already doomed to an inevitable death) thus constitutes a baroque fold, a speculative dream of "escape from self" seemingly opened out within the unseen operations of God's implacable commandment.

"H" Is for Hopelessness

Hopelessness is a specific, and mysterious, object of scholarly study within suicide research. Is it an index of the lack of a positive emotion—the blank space where hope might be—or is it, itself, an emotion all its own? The question has been downsized from metaphysical abstraction to measurability through the construction of the Beck Hopelessness Scale (BHS), a checklist of statements that test subjects are asked to agree or disagree with, indicating the strength of their affirmation or distance from the terse, Beckettian utterances of the test: "I might as well give up because there's nothing I can do about making things better for myself," "The future seems dark to me," "All I can see ahead of me is unpleasantness rather than pleasantness," and so on.[42] Presented as literally twenty-one questions, the BHS tracks the subject's attitude toward the future. Seen in this stark light, suicide risk is thus not a matter of regret about the past, but about the presence or absence of hope for the future. As suicidologist Thomas Joiner describes it: "Beck and colleagues extended their work to a group of 1,958 psychotherapy outpatients, seventeen of whom eventually died by suicide. High scores on the hopelessness scale... predicted later death by suicide, correctly identifying sixteen of the seventeen."[43] Colleagues found that other clinicians using the BHS have found a strong correlation between a negative outlook on the future and suicide risk.[44]

    Hope gutters and trembles, a tiny flame threatened to be doused by the troubled sea of Adam's passions. In his reflection upon his sinfulness

Adam longs to be the only victim, and to protect future humanity from the aftershocks of the Fall, even as he senses that that is impossible and would be itself unbearable:

> Fond wish! Couldst thou support
> That burden heavier than the Earth to bear,
> Than all the world much heavier, though divided
> With that bad woman? Thus what thou desir'st
> And what thou fear'st, alike destroys all hope
> Of refuge, and concludes thee miserable
> Beyond all past example and future,
> To Satan only like both crime and doom.
> O conscience! Into what abyss of fears
> And horrors thou hast driv'n me: out of which
> I find no way, from deep to deeper plunged! (10.834–44)

Adam says that all hope is destroyed. But his pain is rooted in hope, in a manner akin to that defined by Lauren Berlant as "cruel optimism": hopes hurt by prolonging our sense that improvement is just around the corner, thereby prolonging our attachment to the very source of our suffering.[45] The irony of Adam's complaint is that hope is not here transcended into a flatline of static, catatonic hopelessness: rather, desires and fears endlessly roil the space of conscience with fond proposals that are then destroyed as the ramifications of fallenness frustrate each thought experiment. Adam finds that Sin has become a "burden heavier than the Earth," spoiling the prospect of material merger with the Earth by polluting the planet with a sinfulness that future generations can only compound and intensify.

Commonly used in the early modern period to indicate pregnancy, "burden" is a Miltonic keyword, rebounding across contexts throughout his public and poetic careers. In the introduction to the second book of *The Reason of Church Government*, the knowledge that God expects us to improve our own faculties so that we can know and worship him correctly constitutes "a sorer burden of mind, and more pressing, than any supportable toil or weight which the body can labor under."[46] Burdensomeness lightens up in *Areopagitica*, when Milton archly notes that "Many a man lives a burden to the earth."[47] Some people are "burdens" to the earth, the sheer weight of their embodiment a kind of insult to its own terrestrial support (an intuition that survives in the now-passé insult that someone one dislikes is "a waste of space"). This catena of burdensome passages indexes the weight of this figure in Milton's rhetoric, even in "the cooler element of prose." It carries over into the poetry and takes on a fatal, mortal weight: existence shows up to fallen humans as always already inherently burdensome, and this makes a kind of basic, intuitive sense against the ontotheological backdrops of Milton's monist materialist poetics, in which spirit is a lighter, purer, more refined mode of substance, suitable to angelic bodies unstained by transgression.

How widely distributed is this burden? How does self-killing function as an ideational fantasy of lightness and rest from the weight of being? In *Why People Die by Suicide* (2005), Joiner argues that three criteria must be present in order for someone at risk of suicide to actually commit suicide: perceived burdensomeness, a withering away of social connections, and the acquisition of the capacity to enact lethal self-harm.[48] It's a model that has traveled widely:

> "Patient stated that she felt like a burden to loved ones"—much later, when I read the notes from the emergency room, I did not have any recollection of the conversation. *A burden to loved ones*: this language must have been provided to me. I would never use the phrase in my thinking or writing. But my resistance has little to do with avoiding a platitude. To say a burden is to grant oneself weight in other people's lives; to call them loved ones is to fake one's ability to love. One does not always want to subject oneself to self-interrogation imposed by a cliché."[49]

This passage, from novelist Yiyun Li's memoir, *Dear Friend, from My Life I Write to You in Your Life* (2017), registers the clinical uptake of Joiner's theory of "burdensomeness" as a diagnostic tool, and the flattening effects of its deployment in the midst of acute psychological crisis. Here the heresy of paraphrase blurs the finely wrought specificities of Li's psychic life, clicking the patient onto the shaming generality of a template, and earning a tart rebuke.

Before "burden" was a cliché or a biopolitical weapon, it was a word in a poem, carefully chosen and precisely placed. Milton's burden is a downward pull, a weight that pushes the self to imagine descent and rest. By contrast, in Joiner's framing the self perceives itself as burdensome to others, and this imaginary sense of the self-as-burden facilitates suicidal ideation, limning death as a gift to the other, a setting free. Life has, in this imaginary framework, an ideal tempo, a sprightly openness that is held back and cramped by the burden of one's own particular being. It is as if the body has sagged and hardened into an obstacle in the imagined path of another, better life, both for a virtual self (my life would be better if I did not "overlive" past a quality threshold) and for imagined others (their lives would be improved by my absence). Up to a certain threshold, Stoicism measures one's capacity for endurance as an index of virtue; as David

Carroll Simon puts it, Milton's Adam and Eve, under the spell of doctrinal pressures at once Protestant and Stoic, are enjoined to "understand rectitude as the capacity to ignore the feeling of being burdened or even beaten down. The desire for moral standing functions as an anesthetic."[50] But sometimes the anesthetic wears off, one crosses a threshold, and the burden becomes too much.

In the worlds to come in the wake of Adam and Eve, the constitution of mortal life as burden will crystallize into an emergent utilitarian calculus and a corresponding ableist discourse that assesses the demands upon a social system by a variable array of forms of life, ranking and grading lives as viable or nonviable. Revisiting the specter cast originally by Diogenes's paradox of the *abiotos bios* (the life not worth living), there are ongoing and sharply polarizing debates among moral philosophers, bioethicists, and disability activists about precisely who determines the threshold at which a life can be called burdensome.[51] Immune to ethically calibrated arguments, insurers and health-care providers calculate and rank "disease burden scores" with grim biopolitical efficiency as they appraise which individual people with which kinds of ailments are exactly how "costly" with respect to their drain upon care-management resources; modern health care presumes and makes all too financially apparent the assertion that some conditions are more "burdensome" than others.[52]

Adam and Eve feel a special burden, one that is "heavier than the Earth" because it is singularly focalized: they bear a total responsibility for the ocean of deaths to come. In time, the inverse of that burden will resound in Christ's promise in the Gospels: "Come to me, all you that labor and are burdened, and I will refresh you. Take up my yoke upon you. For my yoke is sweet and the burden light" (Matthew 11:28–30). Not yet refreshed, not yet accustomed to the remediation of that yoke as a just and shareable condition, Adam and Eve stagger with the weight of their guilt for our suffering.

"W" Is for Withdrawal

As with other terms from our acronym, the word is at once off and all too apt. Eve has hardly had the chance for a notable "withdrawal" from her surrounding social community because it's only two people anyway. Yet withdrawal is an apt description of the project Eve proposes: a withdrawal from participation in the genetic obligation to be fruitful and multiply. This obligation locates Adam and Eve as the natal ground for the coming human community. In the *Nuremberg Chronicle*, we see Adam depicted as the root-stem of a network of filiation that radiates downward from his body and forward into human history, spreading its branches into the patronymic flowerings of genealogy.

Figure 3. Adam as the root-stem. From Michael Wolgemut and Hartmann Schedel, *Nuremberg Chronicle* (Nuremberg: [Anthonius Koberger], 1493) (Inc.0.A.7.2[888], f.9v). Photograph reproduced by kind permission of the Syndics of Cambridge University Library.

Cutting off at the root the human plantation to come, Eve's proposal is literally radical: no children. This would be, if you'll forgive me, the "withdrawal method" at work in her imagination. The plan is clear: "Childless thou art, Childless remaine: / So Death shall be deceav'd his glut, and with us two / Be forc'd to satisfie his Rav'nous Maw" (10.989–91). This plan places Eve in a curiously partial position of overlap with and distinction from the critiques of reproductive futurity mounted by Lee Edelman in his epochal contribution to queer theory's anti-relational turn, *No Future: Queer Theory and the Death Drive* (2004). A generation on from Edelman's shot heard 'round the world, we have witnessed both the substantive pushback of José Esteban Muñoz's critique of Edelman in *Cruising Utopia: The Then and There of Queer Futurity* (2011), and a broader uptake in which the Edelman position has proven to be proleptic, despite its sour title, of a subsequent flowering of affectively simpatico work on extinction, annihilation, and various apocalyptic and catastrophic scenarios both ecological and eschatological.[53] Yet in point of fact, Eve's very cutting off of the human bloodline and imagined withdrawal from reproductive labor does not constitute an embrace of the queerness of the death drive, but rather a confirmation of the implicit logic of Edelman's argument, which is that the rhetoric of the child to come, and of the need to politically protect the life of that child to come, constitute a key ideological contour against which queer childlessness and the work of the death drive are identified. In instituting a "no-child policy" Eve is herself acting "for the children," protecting their health by protecting them from the terror of their consumption by Death. As Eve imagines it, to live in proximity to Adam would doubtless lead to the surrender of both to their desire for each other, and it is that surrender, and the children to which it would inevitably lead, that she refuses. Ironically, her embrace of the scenario of self-killing is thus not an embrace of the machinelike, "empty, excessive, and irreducible" imperative of the drive that Edelman hails in "The Future Is Kid Stuff," but rather a terrified withdrawal in the face of the imagined tractor beam of *jouissance*.[54]

If "joy of the worm" names a situational tone of pleasure-in-destruction, such a dynamic suits some scenes in the poem quite directly. Satan as serpentine "worm" feels considerable joy in his imagined capacity to ruin God's creation: flush from the Fall, "With joy / And tidings fraught, to Hell he now returned" (10.345–46). Rippling outward, Satan's joy prompts Sin and Death's familial exultation in their imagined capacity to "Reign in bliss" (10.399) over a fallen Earth. But it must be said that Milton's high tone of moral seriousness renders *Paradise Lost* a seemingly inhospitable environment for human expressions of "joy of the worm," and seems particularly allergic to the comedic variants that have prevailed so far in this

book. Indeed, camp and slapstick are notably absent from Milton's repertoire, though the "dismal universal hiss" (10.508) that greets Satan's return
to Pandemonium does register as "failed seriousness" of a sort. But this
does not mean that "joy of the worm" itself is entirely absent from the text,
and it arguably surfaces in Eve's tremor of recognition of the fatal threat
posed by her sexual enjoyment of "nuptial embraces sweet" (10.994) on
the other side of divine judgment. Seen through tears of repentance, "joy
of the worm" as pleasure in the midst of self-destruction looks altogether
repellent, given the new consequences that attend reproduction as a compounding of Sin and Death's claim upon human beings yet unborn. This
relation to pleasure as a disturbing pathway toward death modulates "joy
of the worm" into a Miltonic register as the object of an imagined suicidal
askesis: Eve fears her own mortal susceptibility to pleasure and tries to
imagine a workaround so as to circumvent pleasure's hold upon her.

For his part, Adam imagines a withdrawal from the sight of others, both
divine and human, proposing a hermetic isolation that would evade Eve,
angel, and God together:

> O might I here
> In solitude live savage, in some glade
> Obscured, where highest woods impenetrable
> To star or sunlight, spread their umbrage broad
> And brown as evening: cover me ye pines,
> Ye cedars, with innumerable boughs
> Hide me, where I may never see them more. (9.1084–90)

The urge to protect the self from the unbearable brightness of God is thus
driven by a sense of shameful exposure before an imagined Other whose
sight burns, and the solitude of the "me" offers a passing repudiation of his
erstwhile helpmeet as one more burdensome intruder. One hears in these
lines Milton looking backward, rifling through the genial wooded melancholy of "Il Penseroso"'s cypress lawn, but now rendered insubstantial, a
frustrated wish to conceal the self from judgment. Looking forward, Adam's wounded dream of solitude is also perhaps momentarily anticipatory of the modern misogynist splinter group Men Going Their Own Way,
or MGTOW, a loosely affiliated cluster of online communities of "men's
rights advocates" whose hostility to feminism and contemporary sexual
mores has led them to become voluntarily celibate recusants from hetero-
sexual dating. Though much of their perspective and language is comparable to so-called incels (involuntary celibates), the key difference is the
posture of voluntary renunciation.

Adam thus reimagines himself, at least momentarily, as an "endling."

The word denotes the last surviving member of a species, the final spark before a species goes extinct, when a biological trail turns cold and dead forever. Sundered from the conversation and cohabitation that would make sex and procreative possibility available, Adam in isolation would be ignorant of Eve's fate and vice versa, a kind of absolute inversion of the *synapothanumenon* ideal. Adam imagines each as cut off from the other, unsure at which point they had attained their definitive status as "endling." Were they to separate and die apart, in the midst of their very estrangement they might come to occupy the space imagined by a literally impossible word: "endlings," in the plural.

"A" Is for Anger

It is perhaps arguable when, exactly, the world's first couple fight took place. In the poem, the crack appears in a dispute about solitary gardening, when Adam lets Eve go without having been convinced that she is correct in wanting to do so. But hot anger does not arise between Adam and Eve until after the Fall, when they awake and find their minds changed and darkened:

> Then sat them down to weep, nor only tears
> Rained at their eyes, but high winds worse within
> Began to rise, high passions, anger, hate
> Mistrust, suspicion, discord, and shook sore
> Their inward state of mind, calm region once
> And full of peace, now tossed and turbulent (9.1121–26)

The Fall registers as the coming of a new affective weather system; the loose correlation of resemblance between outward symptoms and inward passions (raining tears outside, winds within) is belied by a curious sense of tangled temporality. One expects tears, if they are tears of contrition, to purge or purify, and ultimately to calm. But the state of sinful embodiment after the Fall disorders such sequences; now, tears are the prelude of hostile intensities to come. The inward experience of fallenness is a persistent, malingering turbulence, a stew of bad feeling: "Love was not in their looks, either to God / Or to each other, but apparent guilt, / And shame, and perturbation, and despair / Anger, and obstinacy, and hate, and guile" (10.111–14). Anger is a component, but it's also an index of a broader volatility beyond anger in which states keep rapidly melting and reforming: anger hardens into obstinacy, a willful joy in frustrating the other, which then focalizes and ramps upward in intensity into hatred, a targeting of hostility onto another, perhaps in so doing offering a false relief from the pressure of "apparent guilt and shame" that started this rosary of destructive passions. Milton's circuit of fallen affects segues from "anger" through "obstinacy" and "hatred" and ends in "guile"; this precise sequence flags the effect of anger as the driving force that precipitates a mutual withdrawal of Adam and Eve from trust in each other toward ongoing separation and antagonism.[55] The Fall is complex, and it must be said that Adam and Eve have not fallen into anger alone, but into a constitutive variability between a range of negative affects in which these vexed yet contiguous states broil and blend and reinforce one another. But if "A is for Anger," then here we see evidence of anger's place in the affective repertoire of fallenness. Anger motivates action, producing plots and schemes of redress, revenge, and judgment; in its other-directedness, anger looks like a means of padding the self or warding off an interior process of self-reckoning.

That said, Eve does not seem angry when she proposes self-killing specifically. If anything, she is adopting what seems, at first, to be the posture of a certain experimental tendency already commenced in the "exorbitant desires" that drive her famous inquiry about the stars: speculation, wondering, imagining, asking.[56] There as here, Eve works by "sad experiment" (10.967), a phrase that she casually uses to refer to the wounding new forms of knowledge-gathering through conflict and failed persuasion that are required for postlapsarian conversation. Eve is considering the space of free possibility within the newly framed bounds of an altogether-unprecedented era, and that free space includes the possibility of self-killing even as she lacks firsthand experience of what Death would be or how it would be achieved. Eve's proposal can thus be explicated in the broad and general terms proposed by Joiner and, before him, Durkheim: suicide as a net gain for an imagined community of others. But there is a categorical difference, too. That community is a virtual future community being rescued from suffering by not being allowed to come into being, thus relocating the anti-natalist perspective within the matrix of suicidal motivation.

It is a commonplace of classroom reactions to *Paradise Lost* that the poem, with its interstellar travel and multiple "worlds," constitutes a work of science fiction, but here it becomes in a stricter sense a "speculative fiction": Milton is attempting to speculatively project himself backward to a moment in which Eve is attempting to speculatively project herself forward, seeing a world teeming with a human multitude endlessly reduplicating the evidence of error, and amplifying the ontological proof of her guilt. This transvalues suicide in striking ways: if secular philosophers sometimes defend the right to commit suicide as a matter of personal choice (as if our lives were not enmeshed with others), Eve is the one person whose decision to kill herself cannot be personal. Without her, there will be no human species at all. But can we say that Eve's choice "matters" for people who will not exist?

Eve's scenario uncomfortably resembles the thought experiments of antichoice advocates within contemporary abortion debates, in which rhetorically far-fetched but undeniably vivid scenarios of the "what if Einstein's mother had had an abortion?" variety find their cheap ripostes in the counterpoint that Hitler's mother didn't have one either. Pressed upon by the unseen horde of a humanity yet to come that they still have the power to short-circuit in advance, Adam and Eve inhabit a kind of logical antechamber before the launchpad of such dubious bioethical "arguments from fetal potential."[57] Suicide-prevention discourse and "prolife" discourse share a strategically narrow insistence upon the interdiction of a singular action that they disconnect from its causal surround; in both cases, the presumption that life is inherently and always positive is emptied out by this very narrowness, which from a distance looks like a structural disinterest in the wider social and institutional questions of how a life, having been "saved," is to be supported or at least endured.

To pan wide for a moment, this book was written in Microsoft Word on an Apple MacBook Pro laptop. Some of the Apple corporation's source parts are created in Shenzhen, China, by the Foxconn company in buildings ringed by suicide nets placed around the perimeter of their high-rise factory complexes so that factory workers won't succeed in taking their own lives and will continue to live and thus work, creating more Apple computers so that academics like myself have a stable platform on which to write, in this case, about suicide and pleasure in early modern literature. In such a world, the protection of something called "life" from something called "suicide" is largely a rhetorical screen for lived, ongoing processes of inequality and exploitation that make many of us want to end our lives rather than survive into the continuity of ongoing harm. Reflecting upon this dynamic, poet Cameron Awkward-Rich notes that "there is something deeply unsettling… to the insistence that someone ought to be alive in a world that did little to support that life."[58] The isolation of the suicidal act from its contextual and causal nexus is a work of ideological mystification, in which "suicide" is the enemy and "life" is re-enchanted on the other side of suicide's refusal. Life must be a glittering prize, the reward that awaits your capacity to reject self-killing, and this obligatory framing productively skips the humiliating details of life as a nonnegotiable scene of power's enactment.

Preceding the coming of these systems of coercion and enclosure while searching for an escape route from her own life, Eve becomes a casuist. The trickery through which Eve here plots to frustrate a divine decree suggests a malingering, Satanic stance of the adversary, and one that will be therapeutically undone by the softening, temperate force of book 11's angelic slideshow. But before she even knows of the specifics of the Son's heroic agenda (those circumstances are about to be relayed to Adam as she sleeps in a divinely ordained trance), there is a muffled typological resonance here, as Eve proposes her own sacrificial death.[59] Offering herself first to the prospect of suffering so that a vast human population can be redeemed and saved from sin through a brave action that is also a sin, typology wobbles across gendered lines as Eve's heroism inverts and approximates Christ's heroism.

"R" Is for Recklessness

Milton assigns self-killing its own page in his commonplace book, under the heading "Mors spontanea," a Latin phrase that means "voluntary death."[60] Are voluntary deaths thereby "reckless" deaths, hasty decisions that index passion's overmastering of reason? Early modern persons had a capacious archive of self-killing with which to consider the topic. The exemplary figures within that archive range in the timing of their execution from blindingly fast to achingly slow. The Lacedaemonian boy in Seneca's story and Montaigne's retelling, who bashes himself against a wall rather than countenance servitude and enslavement, constitutes perhaps the fastest death, while Eratosthenes's deliberate death from starvation would appear to be the most drawn out. But the speed or slowness of execution is not, quite, the same as the question of whether or not the decision to kill the self can ever truly be justified, however "reckless" it may appear from without. When Eve puts forward her proposal, is it a thought experiment, a passing impulse, or a deliberate plot?

If we grant that Eve's plan is not fully thought out, and borders upon the rashly precipitous, Milton's contrary ideal of patient suffering is the time of waiting: "They also serve who only stand and wait."[61] This capacity to suffer and endure is basic to the models of Christian heroism that populate his works, and its implicit opponent force is the urge to evade that suffering through death. Wracked with despair and doubt and himself subject to the trials of blindness and political defeat, Milton gives voice through textual proxies (most notoriously, Samson in *Samson Agonistes*) to the very passions that he then refutes. His poetry constitutes a site in which the problem of survival is continually in question; the absolute sway of doctrinal commandments ("Thou shalt not kill"; "Be fruitful and multiply") are subjected to hermeneutic working-through in order to render these categorical declarations as personal acts of judgment and lived subscription.

The goal of divine reeducation is the production of becalmed subjects who can decathect from attachment to their own life in both its affirmative and negative directions. As Michael puts it: "Nor love thy life, nor hate; but what thou liv'st / Live well, how long or short permit to Heav'n" (11.553–54). As Emily Wilson indicates, this is a gloss on Seneca's *Epistles* 24.25: "in utrumque enim monendi ac fimandi sumus, et ne nimis amemus vitam et ne nimis oderimus" (We need to be warned and strengthened in both directions: both not too love life too much, and not to hate it too much).[62] This double gong of negation sounds also in Surrey's rendering of Martial: "Ne wish for death, ne fear his might."[63] Both wishes and fears are to be dialed down. Milton's goal is not simply to cure us of despair, but to liberate us from affective excess, from entrapment in the illusion of our own affects as incorrigible. Comportment requires the just consideration that we must wait our turn, neither clinging to the world nor leaping from it. Life is to be worn lightly, but not discarded.

"M" Is for Mood Changes

This brings us to the end of the acronym, but also to the end of Eve's speculation, when Milton draws our attention from the message to the physical state of the messenger: "She ended here, or vehement despair / Broke off the rest, so much of death her thoughts / Had entertained, as dyed her cheeks with pale" (10.1007–9). Eve's passionate delivery shows her thinking through the implications of population control, species being, and extinction from the standpoint of a passionate body whose attitude and complexion reveal the disturbance within.

This passage has occasioned much critical commentary, primarily because of its obvious and deliberate proximity to Virgil's Dido in *Aeneid* book 4, who is said to be "pallida morte futura" (pale at the imminence of death).[64] In *Inside "Paradise Lost": Reading the Designs of Milton's Epic* (2014), David Quint argues that Milton courts this resemblance so that, in the broader pattern, Adam's ultimate rescue of Eve from self-killing can reconsider or critically transvalue the Virgilian epic tradition and, with it, the devaluation of Dido within that tradition.[65] In a recent critical intervention that pushes back against the idea that the "misogynist" tradition of allegorical readings of Dido was always dominant, David Adkins emphasizes a contrary tendency in more proximate humanist commentary on the *Aeneid*, and in particular the commentary of Nascimbene Nascimbeni, from which Milton draws as he "aligns Eve with Dido to stress her metaphysical freedom."[66]

Taking it as a given that "pale" and "pallida" are the means by which Milton cites Virgil, and acknowledging the complexity of the contrary forces of difference and resemblance, advocacy and critique, in which such a citation took place, I do not think that it is sufficient to emphasize only the backward-facing direction of force through which Milton, however critically, recirculates a tag from within Virgil's text when he revises "pallida morte future" as "so much of death her thoughts / Had entertained, as dyed her cheeks with pale" (10.1007-9). The image also produced meaning in its moment, and resonated against its more immediate circumstances and political and cultural surround. What would it mean to re-inscribe the pallor of Dido's suicidal ideation in the seventeenth century?

Here metaphor itself seems to blush, for Milton's evocation of pallor as "dye" courts oxymoron even as sonically its resemblance to both "die" and "Dido" summons its antecedent source. How could the draining of blood and corresponding weakening of vital animal spirits feel like the staining plunge of fabric into dye? In asserting that the thought of death "dyed her cheeks with pale," Milton's poem aligns the affective legibility of morbid passion with a somatic basis in whiteness that it presumes as ongoing background, even as the temporary state of noticeable pallor modulates a shift within that white ground. If the metaphor is unusual, the presumption of whiteness is not. Early modern writings about the passions—what one might term "affect theory avant la lettre"—pervasively presume, and, in presuming, recirculate, tacit racialized assumptions regarding how we gain access to affect's scripts in the faces and bodies of others.

As a case in point, consider a chapter in Thomas Rogers's *A Philosophicall Discourse Entituled the Anatomie of the Minde*, from 1576, titled: "Of Anger, Wrath, Palenes, Hatred and Discorde."[67] In the midst of describing these "perturbations" in the terms we expect from Seneca's *De ira*, the odd intrusion of "palenes"—whose very oddity requires a "Paleness, what" gloss in the margins—presumes a translucent subject without explicitly naming that assumption under the organizing rubric of race: "The next and thirde in order is Palenes, which is called an anger newly begon, or but newly beginning, and after a little whyle is quickly gone. A man so afflicted is soone hote, and soone cold, because reasons overcommeth the ourageousnesse of the passion. For if it shoulde persist and continue long, it should easily come to hatred."[68] Cataloguing what we might term without undue presentism a momentary flicker of aversion at the scale of the microaggression, the dead epidermal metaphor of "paleness" invokes standing medical assumptions that skin color registers affective change at a distinctly low intensity, beneath the threshold of hatred proper. Rogers does not state that the "pale" subject is a white subject, but he does not need to do so; the early modern discourse of signifying pallor presumes the default of a visually legible emotional body whose quasi-whiteness goes without saying. Ian Smith has usefully flagged "the normative invisibility of whiteness [as] a sign of its hegemony" that produces a corresponding "failure among critics to remark whiteness as a fully realized racial category" when assessing literary works in which that whiteness surfaces—literally—at the level of character.[69] Parsing Eve's "pallor" and Rogers's "paleness" as conceptual kinfolk, even with the founding Virgilian example of Dido in mind, we ought to avoid a false choice between affect and race; pallor sutures these overlapping discourses of embodiment.[70] Whether or not he had read Rogers, Milton, in his evocation of Eve's cheeks "dyed with pale," both cites a Virgilian past and perpetuates the ongoing quasi-racialization of the affective subject.[71] At this point in the poem's tracking of the physiological effects of the plan to die, to be "dyed with pale" is to be at once drained of vitality and dangerously subject to change. Thus, the tacit presumption of whiteness opens up Adam's capacity—and, by extension, the reader's capacity—to diagnose Eve's passions as they shift and pass.

That volatility, the speed at which one state can rise and change and replace another, is Milton's real interest, for it will be leveraged into a means of therapeutically traversing Eve's fantasy of voluntary death. While Adam grants that "thy contempt of life and pleasure seems / To argue in thee something more sublime / And excellent that what thy mind contemns" (10.1013-15), he ultimately rejects her proposal as savoring of "Rancor and pride, impatience and despite, / Reluctance against God and his just yoke" (10.1044-45). Scanning her subject for evidence of "mood changes," an intake interviewer could be alarmed by Eve's vehemence—but, paradoxically, they might also be reassured by it. The copresence of thinking and feeling cues a mixed response from Adam, a mingled recognition of her plight and disagreement at her proposed solution.

What does it mean that Adam perceives Eve as "sublime" precisely in the moment at which she proposes self-destruction? After its critical long march from Longinus to Burke to Kant and into the Romantic reception of Milton and his poem, the word is now shopworn with associations. That Milton is "sublime" seems to go without saying: his tone of high moral seriousness and the cosmic effects of scale within his text prompted Samuel Johnson's remark that "the characteristic quality of his poem is sublimity."[72] Yet critical inventories of sublimity in *Paradise Lost* rarely consider Eve's plan as a case in point. Perhaps the assumption is that we are immediately meant to grasp the proposal as devious in its intent and likely to be squalid in its outcome; and because it will be rejected as a bad idea and hovers at the level of the counterfactual, it jars against the transalpine scalar grandeur we associate with sublimity properly understood.

What makes Adam's application of the term troubling is not that suicide doesn't belong within the archive of the sublime, but the fearful possibility that it does. After all, part of the etymological root of "sublimity" is the suggestion of something crossing a limit, being carried over a threshold, and, typically, being carried upward; as Teskey notes, for Longinus "the purpose of reading is 'to turn the soul upward' (*anatrephein*) toward what is grand."[73] Within the materialist imaginary of Milton's poem, suicide can't be sublime in this sense of imaginary material ascent, because, per Mortalism, the passage into death is a passage downward along the vertical hierarchy of orders of being. If soul and body perish at once, then death is not an ascent upward to a pure spirit realm or a material refinement of the body-soul assemblage into pure spirit, but instead a passage decidedly downward to dust. Accordingly, death can't be ennobling or an apotheosis. And yet: there is a "sublimity" in the contemplation of willfully ending life, as an absolute refusal of a divinely bestowed gift, insofar as it confronts the subject with the vertiginous prospect of their own freedom to transgress a sacred boundary. It's the moral equivalent of *l'appel du vide*, the "call of the void," in which heights seem to solicit voluntary death as a response to scalar effects of distance.

In seeing Eve as sublime, Adam teeters upon the cutting edge of the love/subjection dyad that disastrously redoubled the Fall: Adam's stupefaction in the face of Eve's beauty might itself be better glossed as an example of Sianne Ngai's category of "stuplimity," that admixture of sublimity and stupidity that Adam relays as Eve's effect upon him, as her seemingly absolute self-sufficiency silences the force of his ostensibly superior reason.[74] Though it might feel perverse to even call this "pleasure," Adam feels a kind of infra-thin "joy of the worm" in his admiration for the "contempt of life and pleasure" that Eve's proposal manifests: this is pleasure at contempt for pleasure, a kind of askesis that thrills. But Adam's compliment to the sublimity within Eve is only half a gesture, and its counterweight is the repudiation of that sublimity in favor of a humble acceptance of their present state. He does not long to join in her present state, but to lead her gently out of it.

The problem, for Adam and, I think, for Milton, is passion itself. Passions are disorderly. This is not to say that passions as such are always bad and to be resisted; I share Jessie Hock's view that "Adam's Christian moderation, anchored in deeply felt emotion, links him even more firmly to his creator."[75] The problem is the tempo with which Eve's passions shift and flow. Eve speaks, thinks, plans, imagines, and experiments from within a body subject to a particular, passionate mood in the moment of her suicidal speech, and by that very fact, she remains subject also to the possibility that that mood might, perhaps must, change. "Mood changes" are predictive of self-harm in that the swings and flows of affect can amplify the present into a seemingly inescapable state. In *Tropes of Transport*, Katrin Pahl works to displace the singularity of affect or the taxonomy of discreet emotions as separate natural kinds, instead emphasizing "emotionality" as a process of movement in which our selves become self-differential as we move across emotionality's inward terrain.[76] Trembling on the threshold of suicidal action, Eve here is in motion as she thinks across the boundary of life and into the speculative possibility of a total, species-wide death, and her thoughts index an emotional disturbance registered in her being as the tremble of vehemence—but that very passionate fluctuation is its own argument to endure and persist across the arc of feeling. Enduring and entering dialogue with Adam, Eve rides the wave of hatred of life to its conclusion in other states: sorrow, contrition, and humiliation can yield in time to patience, trust, and, on the other side of trembling, other ways of feeling and thinking.

At key points across the poem, Milton responds to passion with alarm. Satan, possessing the serpent, "new parts put up, and as to passion moved," begins his fatally seductive speech; to make sure we don't miss the point, having compared the serpent to an Athenian or Roman orator, Milton repeats himself, introducing the serpent's rhetorical high point with "the tempter all impassioned thus began" (9.678). Hoping to cool the warming path that leads to self-killing, suicide-prevention discourse leverages the temporary, transitory nature of emotional states as a means by which to dissuade suicidal people: you feel this way now, but you won't always feel this way, and you owe it to your future self not to kill your present self. This is the substantive message of historian of science Jennifer Hecht's *Stay: A History of Suicide and the Arguments Against It* (2013): "Bear witness to the night side of being human and the bravery it entails, and wait for the sun."[77] Such advice is of a piece with Adam's own mingling of a recognition of the sublime excellence of Eve's contempt for life with a willed de-escalation into the ambient sorrow of everyday persistence.

In straining the sublimity of *Paradise Lost* through the transplanted acronym IS PATH WARM? I have perhaps risked an overcorrection, a queer tone of flippancy in the face of a treasured cultural artifact, "ruining the sacred truths" of Milton's masterpiece through soiling contact with the harm-reduction protocols of the present. Even if those tools are entirely serious in the therapeutic and diagnostic utility of their original context, they can seem somewhat flimsy and glib-sounding, reductive and garish, when forced into service as tools of literary analysis and set to tasks they were never designed to perform. The acronym is a checklist designed to flag an array of symptomatic presentations, to assist in the intake of someone at risk of self-harm in order, precisely, to determine seriousness and chart a path toward treatment or therapeutic resolution. Eve's plight matters to readers even as they are encouraged to critically reject her proposed solution to that plight. Seeing Eve within the diagnostic gaze of suicide prevention—obviously at some level a "presentist" gesture—might not bring us closer to Milton's own mind at work, but here, in resonant sympathy with others at the expanding fringes of Milton studies, if not those within its predominantly theological and historicist citadel, I hope to work within a disputed but crucial breathing space opened up between the poem's possible present uses and its author's commitments.[78]

Paradise Lost matters in the history of suicide prevention not because Milton was unusual in his opposition to suicide; his consistent rejection of suicide as an acceptable human action is in keeping with his intellectual moment, and even a bit more sternly unilateral than the cultural surround, engaged as it was in a gradual progression from severity to increasing tolerance, a process that was uneven and less Whiggish than some of the dominant historical accounts imply.[79] Milton did not soften, but he also took care to inhabit the mind prone to fantasies of self-killing with a curious tenderness and depth.

As a result of that imaginative labor, *Paradise Lost* stands out against the backdrop of anti-suicide discourse for the powerful generality of Adam and Eve as cases through which to imagine the bonds and burdens that join humans to one another in reciprocal belonging. Adam and Eve offer a prototypical test case for the condition that Brian Cummings has limned in *Mortal Thoughts* (2013) as mortality itself: not simply the capacity to die, but the feeling while alive of the difference that the fact of being subject to death makes within the space of life.[80] This pair occupy an utterly singular situation of profound guilt, deep sorrow, and inescapable responsibility: to live within the ruined confines of one's own choices has become a "burden heavier than the Earth," and it warms the path toward self-killing. I stated at the beginning of this chapter that I was not going to be overly credulous about the power of Milton's poetry to rescue people from despair. Here is where I break that promise, for here is where my own mood changes. I think the deep human processes of suffering within Milton's poetry have a disorderly power to make us different from ourselves, and to make us, in the process, critical readers of emotion (our own, and others). Not in order to thereby scorn emotion, but to feel our way across and through it, with Adam and Eve, as they carry our burden for the first time. If they, beset as they are by such a case for self-hatred, can still stand and walk into the wider world, then the reader, too, may imagine herself differently, and hold on.

CHAPTER SIX

Smiling at Daggers in *Cato, a Tragedy*

Witness the younger Cato. When I see him dying and tearing out his entrails I cannot be content to believe simply that he then had his soul totally free from disturbance and fright; I cannot believe that he merely maintained himself in the attitude that the rules of the Stoic sect ordained for him, sedate, without emotion, and impassible; there was, it seems to me, in that man's virtue too much lustiness and verdancy to stop there. I believe without any doubt that he felt pleasure and bliss in so noble an action, and that he also enjoyed himself more in it than in any other action of his life.

MONTAIGNE, "Of Cruelty" (1578)

When did "joy of the worm" conclude, and what replaced it? In the last chapter of this book, I would like to suggest that the popularity of Joseph Addison's *Cato, a Tragedy* (1713) in and beyond England throughout the eighteenth century indexes not only the persistent allure of the titular Roman exemplar of stalwart refusal but also the occultation of "joy of the worm" as an aesthetic phenomenon "of pleasure and bliss" along the lines suggested by Montaigne centuries before.[1] Addison's play struggles with the distinct challenge that Cato's suicide poses to dramatic representation, yet manages to find in his death, despite its negativity, a curiously pliant resource for political feeling. While this work overlaps with a significant number of discursive elements in play across this book, Addison's deviations at the level of tone and representation also signal, to me, the end of the line that I have been tracing. Reasons of space prohibit me from a full-dress reading of the play as a whole, but I hope to show, and to show in some detail in this concluding chapter, how Addison's representation of Cato's progress toward his own death models a distinct sensibility of patriotic republican suicidal masculinity, how that ideal negotiates a contest between rival contexts of Stoic ethics, materialist metaphysics, and Christian theology to come, and why that adjacency between a gendered political ideal and its subtending philosophies might matter for us at the present time.

Invoked over millennia with a resonance so forceful and insistent as to become a four-letter word of its own, "Cato" names Marcus Porcius Cato (95–46 BCE), also known as Cato the Younger and Cato Uticensis; the great-grandson achieving through the renown of his life and death a distinct eclipse over the prior glory of his great-grandfather Cato the Elder (234–149 BCE).[2] As a cultural readymade, Cato's name denotes a stern republican mode of patriotic Stoicism unto death, and thanks to a productive blending of the Younger with his predecessor, who was the author of *The Distichs of Cato,* "a much-used pocket book full of lofty moral principles" in the early modern schoolroom, the sounding of that name has unyieldingly signified unyieldingness ever since.[3]

Cato's firmness of character barrels forward from the annals of contemporary Roman historical records to the hagiographies of late antiquity to his purgatorial ascent in the medieval period to a broad array of occasionally ambivalent but mostly admiring responses in early modernity and beyond.[4] As we have seen, the thought of Cato prompts Sir Thomas Browne to coin the very word "suicide."[5] A stock that seems to have never stopped rising, Cato survives now as the intellectual pet of libertarian right-wing political actors, although their admiration is often at a secondary remove, as they mimetically perform admiration for eighteenth-century admiration of Cato. A case in point is the right-wing policy-oriented think tank the Cato Institute. Funded originally by the Koch family, the Cato Institute is named after John Trenchard and Thomas Gordon's pseudonymous series of "Cato's Letters," written in the 1720s in tribute to the ancient ego ideal of republicanism.[6] This organization now feeds neoconservative sound bites and talking points about "liberty" to news networks and sponsors an array of cultural initiatives that supposedly recirculate Cato's intellectual legacy across the more genteel and high-minded right-leaning circles of Washington, DC. Tellingly, they are also the publishers of the most current scholarly edition of Addison's play.

That cultural cache is now overdetermined by the rising stock of Stoic thought itself. Consider the publication of Donald Robertson's *Stoicism and the Art of Happiness* (2013), Ryan Holiday's *The Obstacle Is the Way: The Timeless Art of Turning Trials into Triumph* (2014) (which has sold over 100,000 copies), Massimo Pigliucci's *How to Be a Stoic: Using Ancient Philosophy to Live a Modern Life* (2017), and William B. Irvine's *The Stoic Challenge: A Philosopher's Guide to Becoming Tougher, Calmer, and More Resilient* (2019).[7] Indeed, even Gwyneth Paltrow's "personal book curator" Thatcher Wine recently gushed to *Town and Country* that "the Stoic philosophers are having a moment now."[8] But as the marketing of a book titled *How to Think Like a Roman Emperor* (also by Donald Robertson) makes clear, this is not the Stoicism of Epictetus, examining precarity from within the crucible of enslavement, but very much a Stoicism from above, in the spirit of Marcus Aurelius.[9] Stoic philosophy has been heralded as the preferred technology of mood stabilization within Silicon Valley start-up culture. One is toughening up in case the IPO goes poorly or the angel investors fall through, not steeling oneself for disappointment at being worked to death in a quarry.

But in this sense, precisely insofar as Stoicism functions in these contexts as a form of emotional attunement for an implied elite confronting an unstable world, these recently resurgent modes of Stoicism chime eerily with Addison's own reconsideration of Cato's example. As Julie Ellison made clear in *Cato's Tears and the Making of Anglo-American Emotion* (1999), the literary development of Stoic thought made the perfect foil for the emergent cult of sensibility, as elite males recalibrated how to represent and understand political conflict.[10] What has changed between Ellison's moment in 1999 and our own is the rise (and fall?) of affect theory as intellectual trend, the emergence of a new interest in the dissemination of classical theories of materialism in early modernity, and, with those contexts in mind, a corresponding shift in emphasis in how and why we might return to Addison's text anew. A shift in time, and a shift in affect; while Ellison is interested in Cato's "tears," I hope to examine Cato's "smile," specifically the threat to understanding posed by the play's climactic image of the philosopher smiling at the prospect of his own death, the productive joy that eases his passage toward the completion of his last act.

Telescoping into the final actions that consolidated the sturdy myth, Addison's play takes place in the aftermath of the Battle of Pharsalus, when an assemblage of holdouts against Caesar who remain loyal to the values of the republic and the Senate coalesce around Cato in the North African city of Utica. Their work of coalition-building takes place under the tense overhang of Caesar's imminent triumph. The plot itself might well have a good deal to do with the play's surprising popularity, as the tragic centrality of Cato's death is offset and counterbalanced by an intricately symmetrical cat's cradle of romantic intrigue: Cato's two sons Portius and Marcus vie with each other for the love of Lucia, a Senator's daughter, while the heroic North African prince Juba and the scheming, corrupt Sempronius compete for Cato's own daughter, Marcia. As vice is punished and virtuous suitors triumph, the play's marital closure in a double wedding offers a notably tragicomic salve to the lonesome death of the philosophical Senator-hero at its center.[11]

Recent criticism of the play from Lisa Freeman, Laura Rosenthal, and others has brought these marriage plots and the nexus of race and empire into sharp focus, in the process de-emphasizing the centrality of Cato.[12] Much has been done to indicate remarks made by Addison in *The Spectator* that might be used to widen his distance from Cato, or to critique his example. By contrast, without walking back the rich insights that these recent readings have generated, I would suggest that instead we consider the points of interaction between Cato and the tragicomedy in which he is enmeshed. Accordingly, my reading works to close rather than widen the current critical gap between the text and its central character.

Much of the play's texture emerges from the counterpoint between its quintet of young lovers and the stern, relentless high-mindedness of Cato himself, who accordingly occupies the "blocking father" role familiar from Terentian comedy. A case in point from act 2 shows quite clearly the tension between Cato and his social surround. Buttonholed by a bashful Juba's stumbling expressions of marital interest in his daughter, Cato rises skyward to thunderous oratory:

> Adieu, young prince; I would not hear a word
> Should lessen thee in my esteem: remember
> The hand of fate is over us, and heaven
> Exacts severity from all our thoughts:
> It is not now a time to talk of aught,
> But chains or conquest, liberty or death. (2.4.75–80)[13]

In context, when Cato speaks this line as a rebuke to a would-be suitor, it flags him as sexless, thinglike, cut off from the world of other people's needs, already bound for his own passage out of life. Excised from its local context as it enters the bloodstream of transatlantic political rhetoric, Cato's resonant insistence upon "chains or conquest, liberty or death" will become Patrick Henry's probable source for "Give me liberty or give me death!" Shorn of its classical Stoic source, this death-bound mantra has become a touchstone for American patriotism, and in particular for the libertarian right-wing movement that fetishizes both "liberty" as elastic keyword and Cato as its alleged precursor. But in the matrix of generic movements afoot within Addison's play, at the immanent level of this scene, such rhetorical set pieces jut oddly off dramatic axis. While they might well have prompted admiration for the grandeur of Cato's lofty utterance, one feels more than a little sympathy for the hapless Juba, who must smother his amorous intentions and nod gallantly at the father of his intended. However stirring as a transplanted sound bite of steadfast commitment, "liberty or death" makes for a distinctly chilly epithalamium. It may well have landed as a laugh line.

The refusal of middle ground in the insistence upon "liberty or death" constitutes Cato as an exemplar of a particularly inflexible ideal, who, as the Senecan epigraph from *De providentia* at the frontis of the text puts it, remains "inter ruinas publicam erectum" (standing erect amid the ruins), an icon of stubborn intractability whose principles cost their follower his life.[14]

Such sternness strains credulity, and surely prompted Samuel Johnson's witheringly faint praise of the play as "a splendid exhibition of fictitious and artificial manners."[15] Can an entire community, an entire military alliance, or, for that matter, an entire family embrace such a code? Addison's admiration for Cato's rhetoric is countersigned by the reproductive mandates of his plot, which insistently counters showstopping gestures of refusal with the counterpoint of emergence, desire, and life. To be fair to the playwright, we sometimes hear critiques of Roman values, as when the skeptical African general Syphax, hearing Juba praise Cato's pious gratitude for the adversity thrown upon him by the gods, snaps that "Tis pride, rank pride, and haughtiness of soul, / I think the Romans call it stoicism" (1.4.83–84). One suspects that at least for some in the audience this line provided much-needed ventilation.[16] Such carping aligns Syphax with Sempronius, the chief Machiavel of the play, as they are both agile figures whose realpolitik maneuvers act as foils for Cato's monotonous rectitude.

Yet Syphax's ignorance about Stoicism—if it is that—might also flag an intractably othered and protoracialized "African-ness," which the play tilts against Juba's identificatory longing for inclusion in Romanness, as Addison works through the mesh of racial and cultural implications of the imminent imperial project to come. Cato's capacity to build alliances and to prompt allegiance from Numidians and North Africans models a vision of Romanness as a virtual body open to anyone with the right internal temperament and principles. This would have been a matter of familial concern; the playwright's father, Lancelot Addison, had been chaplain to Lord Teviot at the British garrison in Tangiers, and, as Julie Ellison and Laura Rosenthal have shown, the Mediterranean setting and the concern with cross identification that underwrites the contrast between Juba and Syphax reads differently if we understand Rome and Britain as cognates, with the Numidians and colonial subjects standing in for each other.[17] Addison is keen to flag and then obviate both race and gender: Juba's love for Cato's daughter becomes another way to indicate his underlying, deeper love for her father. As Juba puts it, "Cato's soul / Shines out in everything she acts or speaks" (1.4.151–52). Such rectitude is imagined as inspirational to imperial and colonial projects as an idealized (and gendered) vision of sternly conservative self-identity, or, in Rosenthal's reading, as an emergent form of Enlightenment cosmopolitanism. But the relentless self-similarity of Cato does not model accommodation or incorporation so much as a fixity that seems already more than half-funereal in its stiffness.

The result is a jarring blend of shock and predictability. When actual death ceases to be a rhetorical flourish and enters the plot in the form of his own son's battle-fresh corpse, Cato stays relentlessly on message and repeats his prior catechisms in celebration of virtuous death: "How beautiful is death, when earned by virtue! / Who would not be that youth? What pity is it / That we can die but once to serve our country!" (4.4.80–82). These lines, which inspired Nathan Hale's own "I regret that I have but one life to give to my country" crystallize the sententious portability of Cato's slogans. There is a kind of compression that takes on the economy of wit while preserving a gravity that opposes it, and in the remorse at the singularity of death we hear the thrum of a death drive that would keep repeating such sacrifices ad nauseam. Cato's very fixity, his very unperturbedness in the midst of distress has been taken to be an admirable index of self-control over the passions, recalling as it does the Stoic ethical admonitions of Epictetus in the *Discourses* to treat the loss of a child with the equanimity one would show at the breaking of a cup.[18]

But such fixity might also itself be a part of the death-bound subject rather than the patriotic citizen; for the Cato who senses that his forces cannot hope to prevail against Caesar, let alone stem the eclipse of the republic, each speech act becomes another station en route to the exit from a world that has lost its way. If he doubts the outcome, he doesn't seem to doubt the object cause of such losses. Cato works to depersonalize the very question of mourning and loss by stressing the superior cause of the nation: "Thy life is not thy own, when Rome demands it" (4.4.87).

Not every son induces this peculiar shade of envy; Portius suffers from a stubborn attachment to survival. Cato's paean to Marcus finds its obverse in his equivocal response to the question of whether, and if so, how, his surviving child ought to endure under the coming conditions of tyranny:

CATO: Content thyself to be obscurely good.
When vice prevails, and impious men bear sway,
The post of honour is a private station.

PORTIUS: I hope my father does not recommend
A life to Portius that he scorns himself.

CATO: Farewell, my friends! (4.4.140–45; italics mine)

Quoted with a purr of approval by no less than former national-security advisor John Bolton in his memoir of the Trump administration, where it is cited as "one of George Washington's favorite lines from his favorite play," this nonresponse is its own telling response, confirming the gap in status separating the nobly dead from the merely alive.[19] Survival is downgraded to a private matter for the Portiuses of the world, but the sting of judgment implicit in his pivot away from his son's personal question to the plural generality of "Farewell, my friends!" rings out. Cato's nonresponse exemplifies Ellison's remark that "*deviation from family* models... masculine sensibility" in the Stoic representations of the period; his admirably Stoic virtue is precisely what makes Cato such a catastrophic father.[20] To ask "how shall I live?" is to presume that life itself is desirable in the first place. But Cato is on his way beyond those feelings.

When it is Addison's turn to make good on the fatal promises and premonitions with which he has loaded the play's first four acts, the result is act 5, scene 1, a curiously open-ended suicidal-ideation scene at pains to reconcile its admiration for Cato's principles with an equally pressing awareness of its Christian counterpoints, which function as a kind of politico-theological unconscious to the scene as a whole, and the larger work that surrounds it. Before a word has been spoken, we are already primed by the stage directions with an allegorical tableau of Cato's imminent passage from theory to practice: "Cato, solus, sitting in a thoughtful posture: In his hand Plato's Book on the Immortality of the Soul. A drawn sword on the table by him." Addison seems to have preemptively anticipated Chekhov's remark about the pistol on the mantelpiece. The thoughtful posture marks Cato's reflection upon the Platonic doctrines in his hand, but we are prompted to imagine that he is already conscripting into potential future use the naked sword before us.

Like a shell game of intellectual history, the ensuing soliloquy supplements the play's ongoing presentation of Stoicism with a contraption of additional moving parts: Empedoclean and Lucretian ontologies sketch a "pagan" materialist worldview that trembles in the cross breeze exerted by Christian theological norms yet to arrive.[21] Occupying the center of a play already overdetermined by its re-creation of familiar early modern dramatic motifs, Cato's soliloquy on the appeals and limits of self-killing bears strong resemblances to a pantheon of dramatic precursors—in particular, to the lines of characters from Marlowe and Shakespeare. Cato's disquisition commences in a Hamletian speculative mode, where the tenor is epistemological, and the chief query concerns the known unknowns.

The terror of death as "unknown country" is cushioned by the presence of Plato's *Phaedo*, which Cato cites as providing the secure assurance of the soul's immortality. With faith in the eternity of the soul established, the fate of the body ceases to inspire fear, and delivers Cato from his own hesitation about being the agent of bodily destruction. As many scholars have pointed out, this is, to say the least, an odd conclusion to draw from this particular Platonic text; had Cato continued into the *Phaedo* he would have read the clear condemnation of suicide that follows the passages he cites.[22] Whether we think Addison intended for his hero to make a gaffe or not is itself a referendum upon both the agent and the act: Is Cato wise or precipitous? Hasty or deliberate? One is reminded uncomfortably of Marlowe's Faustus, selectively quoting from scripture while breaking off before the flagging of redemption.

Bracketing this question of Cato's last-ditch Platonic seminar, Plato's theological doctrines are not the only classical exemplum in play. The opening citation of the *Phaedo* is not followed by a Stoic metaphysics of a universe governed by a benevolent logos. Instead, Addison gives us a moment of material ontological speculation that seems Lucretian in tone: "Eternity! Thou pleasing, dreadful thought! Through what variety of untried being, / Through what new scenes and changes must we pass!" (5.1.10–12). Perhaps reflecting the influence of Lucan's representation of Cato in the *Bellum civile* (61 CE), here Cato hails the world of matter as a world of transformation and endless change, a space in which forms undergo relentless processes of assemblage and destruction and reassemblage. Hailing the "varieties of untried being," Cato thinks atomistic chaos as a continuous flux of creation.

This quasi-Empedoclean/quasi-Lucretian material plenum of reshuffling matter is acknowledged, but acknowledged only to be delimited by the exceptionalism of the soul, whose eternity stands outside the reach of such material recombinatory shifts. It's a telling solution to the ongoing threat that atomic schema and elemental materialisms posed to the preeminence of Christian theological discourse, holding a rickety scaffolding across a series of categorical, conceptual, and disciplinary divides, with the ostensive indication of book and sword holding each other in momentary equipoise:

> This in a moment brings me to an end,
> But this informs me I shall never die.
> The soul secured in her existence, smiles
> At the drawn dagger, and defies its point.
> The stars shall fade away, the sun himself
> Grow dim with age, and nature sink in years,
> But thou shalt flourish in immortal youth,
> Unhurt amidst the wars of elements,
> The wrecks of matter, and the crush of worlds. (5.1.23–31)

Violent images of material recombination and planetary scenarios of extinction and destruction are imagined here only to be redemptively upstaged by a Platonic fantasy of youthful invincibility, an endless summer of risk-free spectatorship that can gaze upon the ongoing turbulence of a self-destroying universe and smile. "Joy of the worm" becomes here the thrilling fantasy of posthumous invulnerability in the midst of the elemental absolute. Addison's Cato is thus the Platonized opposite of Gerard Passannante's anxious "Catastrophists," recounted in his recent excavation of the catastrophic intellectual underlining to the history of the materialist imagination.[23] Cato's smile of serenity cannot wait to spectate upon the crush of worlds to come.

The book and the sword looked like an antithetical contrast between the active and the contemplative life, but Cato will come to achieve the suicidal masculine ideal later hailed by Yukio Mishima as "harmony of pen and sword" in an action of self-killing that expresses a philosophy of indifference to bodily harm.[24] Having threaded the needle of materialist annihilation with immortal-soul stuff, Cato is able to say by the close of his speech, "Let guilt or fear / Disturb man's rest; Cato knows neither of 'em / Indifferent in his choice to sleep or die" (5.1.38–40). This momentary balancing of scales (sleep or death) seems to revise the alternatives of book or sword with which this set piece began. But what announces itself as an indifference to the choice of two alternatives is in fact an indifference on the other side of a decision: he's going to sleep in order to offer himself, refreshed after his brief rest, upon an altar of death. Thus "indifference" is made to paper over a choice that is anything but indifferent: a decisive path from the book as cause to the sword as consequence. Like Timon of Athen's self-cancelling misanthropy, Cato's self-understanding has been achieved through a kind of strategic subtraction of the self from the species. He is no longer like "man," because he, unlike them, has transcended the hold of guilt and fear. He's ready.

Or at least he wants to sound like that. Dropping back to earth among garden-variety "man," one might speculate that the root cause of this difference within indifference is precisely that diagnosed by Syphax: Cato acts upon the earthly pride of his attachment to a version of himself that will not submit. True to the framing of "war slavery doctrine," here virtue can only be proved by the refusal to live under shaming political circumstances, and so the virtuous Stoic must pass judgment on life itself on behalf of the soul's eternity, which, seen in an unflattering light, can look an awful lot like the earthly fame of reputation. If this sounds churlish, the play itself is cultish in its relentless admiration for Cato's virtue, and the party line of adulation for its titular hero can grow, cumulatively, rather wearying.

If Addison's *Cato, a Tragedy* looks back to Lucretius, it also looks forward to contemporary materialisms, and tightens into focus an enduring

question: What are the affective consequences of philosophical materialism? How does it feel to know that you are headed toward material recombination? At the memorial for a close friend who died of cancer, the rec-
itation of a posthumous message that we are made of star stuff and will
return to that condition sounded powerfully consoling, a revision of "dust
you are, and to dust you will return" by way of the more homiletic passages
of Carl Sagan. But not everyone can be so easily consoled. Consider Emil
Cioran's remarks in *The Trouble with Being Born*:

> Why fear the nothing in store for us when it is no different from the nothing
> which preceded us: this argument of the Ancients against the fear of death
> is unacceptable as consolation. Before, we had the luck not to exist; now
> we exist, and it is this particle of existence, hence of misfortune, which
> dreads death. Particle is not the word, since each of us prefers himself to
> the universe or at any rate considers himself equal to it.[25]

While few at present would be so blatantly honest about their ambient narcissism to confess a preference for the self over the universe (a false choice
if ever there was one), Cioran's Nietzschean bravado papers over the terror within at the prospect of merger with the universe. To be apart, to be a
being, is a temporary state, and our sense of this temporary arrangement
abrades and stings. Materialism enables a speaker to speculate about the
future as a virtual problem space in which ontological potentialities and
combinatorial possibilities attend. The threat of death as annihilation is
reconfigured as one of experimental openness: the "trial" of trying out
what forms being could take.

Yet this is the result not of an orientation toward futurity but in fact a
case of anachronistically "feeling backward" (to use the phrase of queer
theorist Heather Love): for Addison's readers and spectators, such a perspective required the cancellation or bracketing of culturally dominant
Christian eschatological frameworks.[26] Those hoping to evade a head-on
collision with theology could find comfort and plausible deniability within
the historical clearing provided by a pre-Christian classical setting. Addison can throw himself backward in time historically to an imagined space
of classical antiquity before Christianity in order to voice a Lucretian ontological materialism that pressurizes his own speaking present.

In doing so, the suicidal heroics of Cato become valorized. Lucretian
ontology charges the would-be suicide with the "courage" necessary to
fling the self across the threshold of life. Cutting apart the body, severing
the bonds and connections that make the somatic assemblage vital, the
suicide must bet everything on a vital materialist intuition that the swerv-

ing ballet of indestructible atoms can only continue, and will never cease. In some ways, the suicide of Addison's Cato thus rehearses a prior materialist suicide: Empedocles hurling himself into Mount Etna.[27] That is, what is Lucretian about this attitude borders upon and overlaps with what is Empedoclean about this suicide.

Addison might not seem at first blush like an author who would be particularly amenable to Lucretius, insofar as Lucretius had become the pet author of the very Restoration libertines and rakes that Addison, the son of a preacher and himself prone to quasi-sermonizing Saturday missives on public morality, hoped to scold and correct. But as Laura Baudot has shown in a bravura reading of "Addison's Lucretian Imagination," though *De rerum natura* only surfaces a few times in direct quotation, its ideas pulse throughout Addison's essays in *The Spectator* on Lucretius's theory of atomic "films" that fly off the natural world.[28] Though Baudot is not interested in Lucretius in relation to self-killing, her analysis of Addison's use of Lucretius in the *Spectator* concludes with an investigation of the subtle manner in which Lucretian frameworks posit alternatives to Christian eschatology; a case in point occurs when, in the midst of a discussion of ghost lore, Addison imagines a longing for Lucretian "annihilation" as a foil to the fear of hell.[29] This contrast between a triumphant Christianity and its possible Lucretian counterpoint is preserved in Addison's rendition of Cato's final crisis but inverted into its historical obverse: the Roman senator is largely in the grip of ancient philosophy but seems, improbably, to glancingly anticipate Christian moral rebukes of self-killing to come.

But this is not all. In excitedly imagining "through what new scenes and changes must we pass," Addison's Cato predicts the role that materialist ontology can play in the precipitation of patriotic feelings of corporate embodiment, or corporate assemblage. To die for Rome, to sacrifice the self for the sake of the maintenance of a virtual ideal of both what Rome was and what Rome might yet be in a future to come is to model a kind of combinatorial confidence in a determinate identity's capacity to keep reemerging. This is the opposite, in some senses, of an openness to "variety"—the flipside of variety, and the attendant terror of chaos, is a wish that something like a stable form might endure amid the crush of worlds. Patriotic suicide is the staking of the death of the individual on behalf of the valorized ideal of a stable nation whose form is summoned or sustained through acts of martyrdom. Quite simply, to die for an ideal is to valorize that ideal as a fit repository for sacrifice, to charge it with value, to violently assert that "Rome," "the nation," the United States of America, or the like is *worth dying for*.[30]

In this sense, far from being a surrender to the chaos of recombination, the staking of an act of self-killing on allegiance to a value is a conserva-tive gesture, a refusal of present conditions on behalf of an attachment to an essence that the present is imagined as having betrayed. Rome as re-public is such an ideal, but the play's power lies in its capacity to render the identity of being "Roman" transferable. As Alexander Pope put it in his prologue, "Here tears shall flow from a more generous cause, / Such tears as patriots shed for dying laws: / He bids your breast with ancient ardor rise, / And calls forth Roman drops from British eyes."[31] Thus the affec-tive transmission of the text replicates in its own register the protoimpe-rial ideological transmissions already underway within the Roman history it depicts: just as North Africans can, if they adhere to Roman principles, become "Roman" themselves, so too English audiences and readers can, through sentimental participation in affective community, cry Roman tears, tears that exemplify the martial valor that Portius hoped to instill in his own troops: "love of freedom and contempt of life" (1.2.41). Thus, Horatio's transnational and transhistorical gesture of cross identification in the final act of *Hamlet* ("I am more an antique Roman than a Dane" [5.2.325]) is perhaps sublated within Pope's reading of how and why Cato's Roman death prompts passionate accord upon a London stage (permitting a tacit sense that the republic never fully ended, that "dying laws" never really died).

The easy transferability of Cato's ideals onto the American context in which Addison's play was recirculated shows us that death with honor for a corporate assemblage was not simply a Roman intellectual exercise but a powerful affective technology for marshaling troops, instilling discipline, and lending Stoic glamour to experiences of hardship and long odds. As the example of George Washington staging the play for his troops at Val-ley Forge in 1778 demonstrates, Addison's Lucretian Cato proved weirdly compelling and inspiring to those fighting on behalf of American indepen-dence.[32] The circuitous passages of Lucretian and Empedoclean material-ist ontologies and feelings of transcorporeal or transpersonal connected-ness that bob along as Cato passes from Utica to London to Valley Forge offer a curious mixture of stasis and change as we witness the unexpected longevity of a relentlessly static suicidal corpse. Precisely as a watchword of fixity, Cato is rendered into a uniquely portable emblem of the gendered refusal of unwanted political change.

What had to be cut away in order to render Cato portable? Readers of Plutarch will recall that Cato's actual death was in fact a grim and labor-intensive affair, fraught with accidental missteps and crisscrossed by con-flicting imperatives of rescue and release. It begins with a bungled jab from a dagger, and an embarrassing clash with nearby furniture:

His thrust, however, was somewhat feeble, owing to the inflammation in his hand, and so he did not at once dispatch himself, but in his death struggle fell from the couch and made a loud noise by overturning a geometrical abacus that stood near. His servants heard the noise and cried out, and his son at once ran in, together with his friends. They saw that he was smeared with blood, and that most of his bowels were protruding, but that he still had his eyes open and was alive; and they were terribly shocked. But the physician went to him and tried to replace his bowels, which remained uninjured, and to sew up the wound. Accordingly, when Cato recovered and became aware of this, he pushed the physician away, tore his bowels with his hands, rent the wound still more, and so died. (70.5–6)[33]

Far from a cosmic crush of worlds, we find here only the clutter and clatter of the real, as grand gestures of political and philosophical commitment are upstaged by an inconveniently placed object. To put it mildly, one does not find here in Plutarch the "pleasure and bliss" that Montaigne summons from this incident in the passage from "Of Cruelty" used as the epigraph to this chapter. That very absence makes the French essayist's imaginative leap toward those feelings all the more startlingly perverse and powerful as a response to the historical record. While one can imagine how Plutarch's grim narrative might be staged by Jacobean playwrights such as Webster or Ford as an anatomically explicit pageant of "coagulate gore," by the era of Addison that sort of grotesque butchery will not do. Across the long distance from Plutarch to Montaigne to Addison we can track a shift in the representational decorum of self-killing as an exemplary scene, from the stark outlines of ancient historical record to a perverse early modern flowering of imaginative voluptuousness and then forward to its Augustan reconsideration, in which Addison must purge the scene of its messes and misfires in order for the agent to remain admirable. Accordingly, when it is finally time for Addison's Augustan hero to actually die, the painful and violent circumstances of Cato's suicide are seamlessly removed from view.

Adhering to dramaturgical codes of decorum that keep catastrophic violence offstage, Cato's final scene in Addison's play commences with the assembled loyalists and family members—Lucia, Marcia, Lucius, Juba, and Portius—worrying about his state of mind; they think he is sleeping peacefully until an ominous groan prompts reconnaissance, and then the source of the groans is wheeled into view. Ensuring that the dying patriarch will "stand erect amidst the ruins" even unto his last breath, he is given a succinct and scrupulously aestheticized send-off that flags personal death as a blow to the health of the dying republic:

LUCIUS: Now is Rome fall'n indeed!—

[*Cato brought forward in his chair.*]

CATO: Here set me down,
Portius—come near me—are my friends embarked?
Can anything be thought of for their service?
Whiles yet I live, let me not live in vain.
....
Whoe'er is brave and virtuous, is a Roman.—
—I'm sick to death—Oh when shall I get loose
From this vain world, the abode of guilt and sorrow!
—And yet methinks a beam of light breaks in
On my departing soul. Alas! I fear
I've been too hasty. O ye powers that search
The heart of man, and weigh his inmost thoughts,
If I have done amiss, impute it not!—
The best may err, but you are good, and—oh! [*Dies.*] (5.4.78–99)[34]

Addison's pious construction of Cato as an exemplary bearer of fatherly and republican virtue reveals the anxious stage management required to overlay the pattern of Christian heroism onto the rougher contours of historical fact. Ventriloquized into an anachronistic recognition of their virtual audience to come, the self-killing subject is shown as already expressing a doubt about their own precipitous "haste," and offering a seemingly unforced interior apprehension of the countering salve of divine goodness, in a manner that registers the force of an outside transcendental authority assumed to both critique and pardon their act.

To ask "exactly how Christian is it?" about a scene of Roman suicide written by an English playwright in the eighteenth century is as awkward to answer as it is inescapable to ask; Addison's relationship to the particular strain of Protestant Christianity professed by his father complicates matters further. Joseph Addison was the author of numerous hymns, with "The Spacious Firmament on High" entering numerous period collections, but direct articulations of faith are rare in *The Spectator*.[35] Without collapsing into overly Oedipalized speculation, one can say that Addison's attempt to nudge Cato toward a kind of anticipatory reflection on quasi-Christian objections to self-killing marks his recognition of an imagined resistance that is deeply rooted in a widely shared, if individually inflected, theology of election. But it won't do to just tag things as Calvinist, for, as David Diamond has pointed out regarding conversations about the rise of the secularization hypothesis across the seventeenth and eighteenth centuries, "the existing conversations elide the breadth of relations to Calvinism still possible" across this period.[36] Dramaturgical decisions might stand in for doctrinal emphasis: self-killing is a matter of the mind adhering to its principles rather than a body destroying itself, and thus the gore of a DIY Calvary is evaded. At the level of spectacle, we are shown a man who simply succumbs with a suitably tragic "oh" groan rather than a man ripping and tugging at his own entrails in order to render himself inoperable.

The longing to be useful to and for others is telling, and sounds the note of ethical exemplarity that has been the special focus and concern of Addison throughout the play. In keeping this emphasis, Addison hopes to wield Cato's death in order to make good on the promise issued by Portius in the play's opening scene: "How does the lustre of our father's actions / Through the dark cloud of ills that cover him, / Break out, and burn with more triumphant brightness! / His sufferings shine, and make a glory round him" (1.1.27–30). The Christological implication promised in these opening lines and redeemed in his climactic death is that Cato is the anti-Caesar, a figure of suffering whose pathos becomes its own kind of power. The suicide is the tyrant in reverse. Where the tyrant is a bestial figure whose arbitrary enforcements of power over others debases both himself and his subjects, the noble suicide ennobles himself and others through a display of power directed only inward upon the self. Their obvious kinship—they are bonded by shared gestures, the rash taking of life— occasions a continual rhetorical labor of overdetermined separation.[37] Addison must ensure that Cato's sufferings shine with sufficient glory to dazzle viewers out of their customary revulsion at suicide and instead to open them to its pathetic force.

The breakout success of the play—thirty performances, speedy translation and adaptation into other languages, multiple print editions—hinged upon its capacity to produce and inspire such sympathetic feeling. Pope's prologue, spoken in the initial performance run by Robert Wilks, the actor who played Juba, turns upon a couplet that asserts that Cato's effect upon his witnesses goes from admiration to imitation: "Who sees him act, but envies every deed? / Who hears him groan, and does not wish to bleed?"[38] Pope's prologue primes the audience to respond to Addison's drama with a vicarious habituation to suicidal urges. The groan of death and the sigh of sentimental feeling become versions of each other: Cato's groans inspire not only pity at the suffering of a virtuous person but desire, desire to suffer with him, desire to be the bleeding and crying body that we hear and see upon the stage. Pope's question is rhetorical, and, I think, sincere. He does not imagine that anyone could hear such a groan and not feel this sympathetic desire. Or, more to the point, the question is posed in advance, to preempt and silence a certain sort of humorous demurral from tragic seriousness. "Joy of the worm" as pleasurable investment in the fantasy of self-destruction here requires protection from "joy of the worm" as a specifically comedic apparatus.

Which is precisely why Addison's play, and the sensibility that surrounds it, marks the end of a certain historical trajectory that interests me in early modern literature that precedes the age of Addison, in which tragic scenes of self-killing are frequently spun off axis by the intrusion of genre-breaking gusts of comedy. To see what I mean, recall the death scene of Anne Frankford in Heywood's *A Woman Killed with Kindness* (1607), when, as Anne starves herself to death in front of an assembled crowd at her deathbed, her husband expresses a wish to join her and the surrounding group cries out in unison: "So do we all!" only to have this dubious mimetic urge pointedly skewered by the carping aside of a servant:

FRANKFORD: I pardon thee. I will shed tears for thee
Pray with thee, and in mere pity
Of thy weak state I'll wish to die with thee.

ALL: So do we all!

NICK: So will not I!
I'll sigh and sob, but, by my faith, not die. (17.94–99)[39]

In method if not in circumstance, Anne's death from self-imposed starvation aligns her with philosophical deaths such as that of Isocrates, who starved himself to death in order to curtail the painful effects of advanced old age. Self-abnegation as penance thus overlays Christian repentance onto Stoic ideals of self-control unto death, enforcing a tense transhistorical congruence that leads to a communal deathbed experience of mimetic desire to share her exemplary fate.[40] This delicate moment is short-circuited by the comedic burst of a servant's oath. If Nick's faith could encourage a will toward death under circumstances of martyrdom or divine inner directive, here it acts as a brake upon the transmission of suicidal affect. What is more important for my purposes is Heywood's willingness to break the univocity of affective communion in favor of discordant relationships of class, genre, and feeling, to deliberately splinter the shared response. Introducing humor at precisely the point of maximum pathos within his own play, Heywood lets us hear "laughter at the foot of the cross."[41] Conversely, Pope's rhetorical gesture, his secure belief that all who hear Cato's groan must wish to bleed with him, can help us mark the transition out of early modernity's looser generic system and into the eighteenth century, when new systems of decorum banish the Nicks of the world in advance, and set in place in their stead a new ethos of mannered refinement suitable to what Voltaire termed "rational tragedy."[42]

Everyone may have wished to bleed, but some actually did so. The play's popularity led to oddly fatal interfamilial consequences, as S. E. Sprott notes: "In 1737, Addison's cousin, Eustace Budgell, after a life of financial and other intrigue, in which he was spattered by the Bubble, committed suicide by leaping into the Thames with his pockets loaded with stones, leaving an unfinished couplet: 'What Cato did and Addison approved / Cannot be wrong.'"[43] If this shortest of suicide notes functions as an all-too-vivid index of the capacity of life to inspire imitations in art that in turn inspire fatal imitations in life, consider the defensiveness of a suicide note that symptomatically concludes with the very word it works to disavow: wrong. Budgell's note somberly indicates the shadow cast by the popularity of his cousin's text: Cato's deeds and Addison's approval of them become a posthumous sanction for an act that imagines its own survival as reading matter for a public conversant with both classical example and artistic homage. Indeed, when we consider the regularity with which Cato was invoked across the English-speaking world when the time came to justify, mourn, or even contemplate the topic of self-killing, one senses that Addison's play, insofar as it revived and packaged Cato's death as an object of affective investment, may well have precipitated just as much vicarious habituation and cluster suicides as the more notorious exempla of Goethe's *The Sorrows of Young Werther* (1774) and Sylvia Plath's *The Bell Jar* (1963) or, more recently, Jay Asher's young-adult novel *Thirteen Reasons Why* (2007), later adapted into a Netflix series (2017–20).

Body counts are indeterminate. What is more important for my purposes in evaluating the impact of Addison's text is not the isolated decisions, tragic though those may be, that have been made by a small number of viewers and readers, but the broader social surround in which admiration for Cato has become a politically significant phenomenon, conflating masculinity, Stoicism, and self-harm and undergoing a dubious and retroactive adhesion of anachronistic principles and doctrines. First and foremost, the rising tide of veteran suicides at present—approximately twenty per day—is about the collapse of health-care infrastructure and, with it, mental-health resources.[44] But at some level, that stark statistic also demonstrates the fatal cost of adherence to a cultural ethos of warrior codes that valorize solitary death as a noble refusal to seek help, and that correspondingly frame seeking help as an ignoble submission to the humiliations of contingency.

Cato's forthright declaration that "a day, an hour of virtuous liberty / Is worth a whole eternity in bondage" (2.1.99–100) casts a disparaging judgment on those who might actually choose to survive and live even within conditions of slavery and bondage. Cato's sententious maxims, followed through by his choice to kill himself rather than submit, were themselves instrumentalized into a demonstration of a Stoic commonplace that functioned to cast aspersions upon the captives enmeshed in racial capitalism's ongoing economies of chattel slavery. As Mary Nyquist has shown in *Arbitrary Rule: Slavery, Tyranny, and the Power of Life and Death*, the slave who chooses to survive rather than commit suicide is through this very action constructed as less noble, less heroic, and thus more "submissive" than those who refuse survival under those conditions.[45] Through this victim-blaming technology, the living body of the slave is reified into an index of their supposedly "slavish" inner nature, which brooks such treatment as the cost of survival. It's a deeply self-serving rhetorical structure, in which free citizens can regard the slave not as someone suffering their own potential fate, but precisely as the abjected person that they would never suffer themselves to become.

This dynamic, afoot within the text of *Cato*, became acute as Addison's play was staged and admired in dramatic productions across the slave states of the antebellum South in the eighteenth and nineteenth centuries.[46] In *The Power to Die: Slavery and Suicide in British North America*, Terri Snyder addresses the curious infolding of sympathy and scorn directed toward dramatic stagings of noble slaves such as *Oroonoko* (her chief interest, for obvious reasons) and registers the weird mixture of fitness and hypocrisy in the reception of Thomas Southerne's melodramatic adaptation of Aphra Behn's novel.[47] But Addison's play triggered many of the same odd dynamics, as the problem of its suicidal exemplarity jangled harshly against the injunctions issued by slaveholders who penalized suicide attempts. The very act that would have, posthumously, demonstrated such greatness of soul was itself cordoned off from access to slaves who, as valuable property, were to be protected from their own free capacity to imitate Cato's exemplary nobility. As Snyder demonstrates, abolitionist literature mobilized the same act to explicitly contrary political ends, celebrating the nobility of slave suicides, and memorializing resistance unto death as heroic responses to injustice. In the *North Star*, Frederick Douglass compared the suicide of the enslaved person Stephen Redden to Cato and said it was done "in the spirit of Roman chivalry."[48] But who determines who has access to the capacity to cite and reaffirm Cato as suicidal readymade? Casting a more skeptical eye at the way that race gatekeeps the sacred grove of self-destructive virtue, a century later James Baldwin would bitterly note that "If a white man says, 'Give me liberty or give me death,' the world applauds. If a black man says the same thing, he is treated as a criminal."[49]

Not everyone in the period admired Addison's titular hero, just as not everyone in the period invested in the glamour and pathos of self-killing: in print and in sermons, the urge to die was just as frequently censured and rebuked as it was indulged and mourned.[50] To be sure, it is not as if the dawning of the Augustan age meant that one could no longer laugh at suicide. Look no further than Henry Fielding's *The Tragedy of Tragedies: or, The Life and Death of Tom Thumb the Great* for plenty of satirical mockery of the urge to die: when Queen Dollalolla learns of Tom Thumb's love for her daughter Huncamunca, she cries out in high dudgeon "Odsbsbobs! I have a mind to hang myself" (1.5.18); moving from ideation to act, the play's dizzying pinball sequence of final-act deaths concludes with the King's own suicide as its very final line.[51] Written in 1713, the play cadges knowingly from, among many other plays by Dryden and Theobald, Addison's own *Cato*. It is not the case that circa 1713 one simply couldn't find ideation toward and completion of self-killing a fit subject for comedy. If the history of representational art up to the present is any indicator, that capacity is transhistorically available and is likely to remain so. But the inflection points of how genre operates have consequences for how we do that, and which sorts of works permit what sort of response. There was no longer space within Addison's own play for such sentiments; instead, self-killing as noble and exemplary tragic choice was, within the framework of a self-serious tragedy, seemingly established. Fielding, too, had to present *Tom Thumb* as itself an Elizabethan play, already brought out in a faux-scholarly edition complete with rapturous citations of its celebrated lines, with notes upon their resemblance to current London productions. The suicidal affects within *Tom Thumb* were laughable because the characters were presented as both ludicrous and inherently passé.

What has ended, decisively, by the time of Addison's tragedy is the playfulness characteristic of early modern encounters with self-killing. Though we can laugh at the pathetic struggles of Tom Thumb and company, by the time we reach Addison, we are no longer in a position to take "joy of the worm" from within the space of tragedy as a comedic response that pulls us back from the edge. Different values and aesthetic priorities and political pressures have arisen, and the artistic and communal coordinates have been relocated. Much remains in place: a classical inheritance is the site of an anxious conflict of values, an envious admiration for the contempt of life manifests a relationship between self and world that is both congruent with certain aspects of the Christian view (the world is fallen and hence tyrannical) and yet also slyly out of sync with it (it is love of country, not love of God, that sanctions the assault upon life). What is gone is humor, the snap and jostle of competing generic frameworks, and a self-consciously playful attitude toward the formal affordances of drama. In its place, we find an emergent set of discourses that will rethink philosophical acts of self-killing as the psychological profile of suicide. If Addison's play models a certain pathogenic and vicarious transmission of morbid affect from work to world, it also filters out much of the humor and mercurial openness of the early modern cultural frames from which it borrows. A horse of a different color, it constitutes the end point of my analysis.

At that end point, we witness a flickering spark of the same, shared affect that has bound together the variegated conscripts in my pantheon of self-killers, the unexpected feeling that might overtake us when we least expect to find it: joy. To look at the dagger and be unmoved is one thing: it is a Stoic indifference to outcomes. But to "smile" at the dagger is another—it registers a trace of desire, a longing, a sense, that is, of joy in death and joy at the prospect of death that exceeds mere endurance or passive acceptance and overspills into an affective surplus of pleasure. Addison's text is conflicted with itself insofar as, juggling book and sword, it wants Cato's action to index the homeostasis of patriotic Stoic masculinity as essentially a matter of rock-hard self-similarity, an imperturbable flatline of thinglike sameness. But the cracking of the smile registers something else, a swerve toward death within the political space given by the collapse of the republic. It is this smile, this little micromovement of affective display that prompts its compensatory "oh" groan, and the quasi-Christian grace notes of remorse that Addison introduces into the play as he overwrites Plutarch's text. Together, these gestures flag the gendered problem within Stoic Roman self-killing, and the unfinished business that materialism as a philosophy has with the affects of love and strife that surge and recombine its forms. Wandering across intellectual history from classical philosophy to early modern literature to libertarian appropriation into the murderous patriotic masculinities of the present, Cato gives birth to a suicidal ideal whose political consequences continue to trouble and catalyze present actions, pulling "joy of the worm" forward. Caught amid the crush of worlds, a philosopher looks at his dagger and smiles.

Epilogue

There's nothing serious in mortality.
All is but toys.

MACBETH

Tragedy is when I cut my finger.
Comedy is when you fall into an open sewer and die.

MEL BROOKS

We are in a graveyard with a couple of clowns, as usual. The scene is *The Earth Seen from the Moon*, an absurdist fable shot by Pier Paolo Pasolini as part of the multistory anthology film *The Witches* (1967).[1] In the opening shot a clownish father and son—played by iconic Italian comic actor Totò with chalk-white face and huge sad eyes and Ninetto Davoli, his hair dyed fire-engine red—energetically weep at the grave of their beloved departed mama. Tears still wet on their faces, the father stands up and immediately sets off in search of a new spouse. After a few false starts, they find Miss Absurdity, played by a nonspeaking and green-haired Silvana Mangano. Upon marrying him, she magically transforms the family's dank hovel into a Dr. Seuss–esque playhouse, but the father and son grow restless and want to relocate. To raise funds for a larger home, Miss Absurdity pretends to be driven to suicide, standing on a ledge at the Colosseum and miming a tear-jerking story of poverty and misery as her husband and son interpret her dumb show and fundraise from a concerned crowd that gathers. About to get rich with this bogus performance of suicidal crisis, at the last moment, just as the funds are really rolling in, Miss Absurdity slips on a banana peel and falls to her death. The crowd howls with laughter as Pasolini cuts to a close-up shot: "She's really dead!" says a man between gusts of laughter, his eyes wet with tears. We end as we began, with widowed father and son weeping at a freshly dug grave, only to find Miss Absurdity magically reanimated. The short film cuts immediately to a slate that reads, "The Moral: whether you are alive or dead, it's all the same."

Sound familiar? Macbeth's self-serving declaration that "there's nothing serious in mortality" predicts Pasolini's brisk clowning with death and suicide. There is something both ludicrous and numbing about the film's agenda, which is already intimated by the distancing gesture of Pasolini's title: once we take a sufficient backward step to reach "the Earth seen from the moon," the ethical demands that individual characters can exert upon us start to flatten out. Seen across a vast distance in generic space, seemingly categorical differences (true/false, alive/dead, serious/unserious, comedy/tragedy) start to blur. Offering hip Beckettian absurdity via location shots from a real Roman slum, served with a commedia dell'arte twist thanks to Totò's clowning, this cinematic cartoon about suicide and meaninglessness is very much of its moment, but I begin the valedictory section of my book here because this short trip around the graveyard helpfully indicates the transhistorical portability of "joy of the worm" as a structure of feeling beyond the crucible of early modernity.

Pasolini's curious vignette encapsulates many of the representational strategies that interest me in this book: suicide as lure, ruse, or cliché has a strange proximity to "real" death that seems to empty such losses of their force and significance, but the outcome of that emptying is pleasurable, even calming. Totò died shortly after filming concluded, and the fact of his imminent death seems to overdetermine the mournful playfulness within the film. As the Mel Brooks zinger about cut fingers and open sewers makes plain, the genre you are in is a matter of how close you are standing to the edge. In the case of Pasolini and Brooks, but also, I think, Lyly and Shakespeare and others, deliberately deflationary assaults on moralizing have an odd way of making cruelty and tenderness trade places. There are early modern literary analogues within easy reach: if Pasolini's clowns in a graveyard offer an unmistakable echo of *Hamlet*, one could also compare Miss Absurdity's ruse that becomes fatal with the actual deaths within the plays-within-plays featured in the catastrophes of Thomas Kyd's *The Spanish Tragedy* or Thomas Middleton's *Women Beware Women*. Taking us farther back to the story with which this book began, in giving us a woman who magically reanimates on the other side of a suicidal death she both solicited and mocked, Pasolini's suicidal Miss Absurdity and the shouting severed head of the shrewish wife in Thomas More's "merry tale" from *A Dialogue of Comfort against Tribulation* are more than kin and less than kind. From 1534 to 1967 to 2022 and beyond, "joy of the worm" wriggles forward and "joy of the worm" wriggles back.

This book has argued that self-killing does not have an essence, need not generate a requisite tone of emotional response, and does not entail as its corollary the necessary generic mode of tragedy. It is my hope that the forms of "joy of the worm" gathered together in the preceding chapters have offered a wide range of pleasurable responses and positive affects that manifest that argument, and in the process illuminate the affordances of genre, and the ambivalence of our affects and their objects, both in early modernity and in the present reception of early modern texts. Beyond a rising and falling index of scorn phase-shifting into tolerance, countless small adjustments and major seismic shifts in religion and politics and aesthetics marked the passage from More writing a merry jest about decapitation in the Tower in 1534 to Addison writing stern endorsements of Cato for the theater in 1713.

How close to the edge are we standing? Early modern criticism takes place in a hybrid space that we might term, taking a resonant phrase from Miles Davis, the "yesternow": claims must be searched and sourced and verified against the textual templates of early modern meaning, but they are fashioned in the present to engage with, even as they resist and counter, problems in the present tense.[2] To seek to de-pathologize self-killing within this "yesternow" is to speak both backward and forward, to look into the archives of early modernity and work to dislodge the hold of our own present intellectual-historical location, but also to acknowledge the impossibility of such dislocation, its vanishing horizon. From the comedic early examples to the increasingly sorrowful examples at this book's close, the historical arc of my objects here reveals the complex shape space of decorum as it altered the available generic forms and affective tones with which early modern English writers could strategically raid the classical and scriptural archives that preceded them in order to speak back to their own contemporary moments. The pulse of pleasure runs from one to the other, and on into the present in modulated forms.

At the risk of a certain schematic reduction, here is a series of descriptive propositions that I think bind my chosen examples together and articulate "joy of the worm," with additional commentary on methodological linkages or subsidiary implications:

"Joy of the worm" joins positive affect to self-destructive action through an expressive assemblage. "Joy of the worm" names a relation between an action—real or imagined—as a stimulus and affect as a response. Though I have not used the language of assemblage theory from Manuel DeLanda and, before him, Deleuze and Guattari, in this volume because my primary orientation has been the description of an aesthetic rather than the stabilization of an ontology, one could describe the bond between affect and action created by "joy of the worm" as an assemblage in the terms proposed by assemblage theory insofar as "joy of the worm" has an expressive consistency that persists over time and across territory. "Good enough presentism" names a scholarly recognition of the mixed "yesternow" in which the claims we make about early modern literature can be right or wrong with respect to early modern meanings, context, and history, but our sense of which claims are worth making necessarily reflects our present

moment. From that standpoint, there is something that we can identify as "joy of the worm" that manifests itself in some cases and not in others, even if this category has no "essence" and is not a natural kind.

"Joy of the worm" links recipients (readers and audience members) with agents (characters within fictional forms, narratorial voices within prose, and, implicitly, authors who are the source of those characters and voices). This is the relational work that "tone" accomplishes as subject meets object when we feel pleasure through an aesthetic experience of a form. Whether we are laughing at a character or encountering a phrase as beautiful or imagining an experience as positive, we are in each case joined to representations and acted upon by them: they affect us. When that character is killing themselves, when that phrase is describing self-harm, self-sacrifice, or voluntary death, when that experience is an experience of dying that is presented as positive or pleasurable, then we are the recipients of "joy of the worm."

"Joy of the worm" is neutral with respect to attraction toward and aversion away from the conscious decision to enact lethal self-injury. "Joy of the worm" can take place in the pleasure that we feel as we laugh at someone else's misfortune, pain, or distress: the tears of laughter that run down the face of the man in Pasolini's crowd, or the implied laughter that More hoped to trigger in the readers of his merry tale. "Joy of the worm" thus includes schadenfreude, gloating, mockery, and various versions of what Hazlitt termed "the pleasure of hating";[3] necessarily, this includes some reactions that we might regard as wicked, evil, or cruel. At their worst, the sadistic "trolling" that Hamlet and Timon enact upon those around them partakes of this dynamic.

We can always use "joy of the worm" to "other" the agent of self-destruction, and sometimes we are most eager to do so when enmeshed in our own self-destructive crises. In such cases, this phenomenon is not really a complication with regard to the prevalent historical narrative of "the age of severity," insofar as it relays a censorious relation to an action through pleasure in its mockery. But "joy of the worm" also comprises identification, fantasy, and imagined pleasures that attend the thought of our own death, and the pleasure that we take in daydreaming, reverie, or ideation about our own deaths. Finding that identificatory linkage as pleasurable constitutes, I think, a stronger challenge to the "age of severity" historical narrative, because it shows us early modern people imagining such deaths not as shameful or abhorrent but as beautiful, sublime, and admirable. That pleasure need not impact our conscious choices or actions, but it can function for some as a "volitional moderator" that leads people to enact lethal self-injury. Accordingly, "joy of the worm" can lead us to avoid self-killing by encouraging us to laugh at other people's sufferings and actions, or it can lead us toward that same action by encouraging us to see such deaths as beautiful, pleasurable, or ecstatic.

"Joy of the worm" is variable across a scale of affective intensity and across a scale of proximity to death. An affective change needs to pass a certain threshold in order to become recognizable at all as a change. But as soon as that threshold is crossed, it counts as either a positive affect or a negative affect. Whether it is very minor or shattering in its intensity, "joy of the worm" subsists across a spectrum from thought to action. This book has shown "joy of the worm" at the level of ideation about voluntary death (Adam listening to Eve and experiencing her plan as sublime, Browne hoping for death while resolving never to attempt it), at the level of representations of attempts (in the case of Pyrocles and Gloucester), and along a spectrum of proximity to actual or completed death (from Hebe's mistaken sense of the imminence of her death to Cleopatra's and Timon's completed suicides). The variability of intensity of an affect and the variability of proximity to death are distinct variabilities. Though one might expect these scales to align, the fact that they do not is a crucial part of the formal variety and pervasiveness of "joy of the worm." One can feel very strongly about a daydream, and one can be barely impacted at all by an actual death.

"Joy of the worm" abides on either side of the historical and conceptual distinction between "suicide" and "self-killing." Historical conditions inflect how "joy of the worm" shows up, and which kinds of agents are imagined to be its objects, but that response can occur on either side of the invention of the word "suicide." Accordingly, one can take "joy of the worm" in contemplating suicide and one can take "joy of the worm" in contemplating acts of self-killing; the variable relation of agents to actions implied by these distinct terms inflects the ethics of how such responses might show up for their recipients. In an obvious sense, because it is simply a possible reaction of a living system, "joy of the worm" is not specifically and necessarily tied to any particular period in history: as long as we can feel pleasure and also die and also know what death is, then it is going to be possible to feel pleasure at the thought of death.

"Joy of the worm" is neither inherently antisocial nor inherently prosocial. As Durkheim already made apparent, one can commit suicide because of an overly strong identification with the social surround, or because of a collapse in one's integration into that social surround. The altruistic suicide

of self-sacrifice so that others may live is an index of a prosocial mode of suicidality, which I hope that my Donne chapter has shown also lies at the center of at least some understandings of Christian teaching. The hateful and aggressive suicide that is designed to wound, harm, or punish others, often emphasized in psychoanalysis, is an example of an antisocial suicide; Timon's lonely act of "self-massacre" routes such feelings.

"Joy of the worm" can further the overall cohesion or integration of a social group: an audience sobs together as it contemplates the beauty of Cleopatra's touching farewell speech, or laughs together with Nick in *A Woman Killed with Kindness* as he says, "So will not I!," and rejects self-killing entirely. There is a minimum threshold of sociality to encountering "joy of the worm" at all: to read a book or watch a play is to receive something and to allow oneself to be acted upon by something. But the outcome of the sensation of pleasure that "joy of the worm" affords can act to affirm social bonds, leading us closer to others around us, or it can act as a solvent upon those bonds, encouraging us to slip away from them as we dissolve our being.

"Joy of the worm" surfaces within and across the socially stratifying work of genre. Insofar as Derrida's foundational "law of genre" holds force, "joy of the worm" necessarily appears within genre's endlessly subdividable territory.[4] But, to quote the Clown, 'tis "an odd worm." Because of its own scalar variability, "joy of the worm" can surface as a momentary tone in the midst of a disparate array of texts across generic norms. The mere appearance of a single passage or momentary scene in which "joy of the worm" manifests itself does not thereby reconfigure the entire genre of the work that surrounds it. In a broad sense, "tragedy" occasions sad passions and "comedy" prompts joyful, positive affects. What makes "joy of the worm" distinct is that it generates positive affects from an action historically associated with tragedy and with tragic closure in particular.

Genre works to reinforce ongoing social stratification because classical, medieval, and early modern generic systems are themselves not just relational systems of differences between kinds of artworks but also models for hierarchical and unequal relations between persons. Genre encourages us to adopt relations to others that tether registers of speech to standing norms of comportment. In the early modern period in particular, genre restricts and distributes access to "seriousness." In many but not all cases, "joy of the worm" interrupts or blocks tragic seriousness; in at least some cases, "joy of the worm" is subsumed within it or serves as an intensifier of tragedy's generic aims and ends. Decorum names the tacit systems of expectation, recognition, and enforcement that underwrite both the texture of everyday lived social reality and the standards that underpin aesthetic representations of that social reality within artworks, even within the free space in which literature seemingly distorts or departs from any expectation of correspondence or apparent verisimilitude. "Joy of the worm" erupts within and against decorum in some cases, and acts to enforce decorum in others.

Before closing this summary of my book's axioms and outcomes, I want to head off a potential misunderstanding relayed to me by early readers of this manuscript. Is "joy of the worm" simply another name for "tragicomedy"? Birthed in a thunderclap of divine caprice by Mercury at the start of Plautus's *Amphitryon* ("I'll make it into a comedy with some tragedy mixed in"), this potent generic workaround traveled from ancient drama onto early modern stages and beyond, hooking up with pastoral to produce its continental flowering in Giovanni Battista Guarini's *Il pastor fido* (1590), and eventually migrating to England in John Fletcher's *The Faithful Shepherdess* (1609), a flop whose much-quoted preface defined the genre suggestively: "A tragi-comedy is not so called in respect of mirth and killing, but in respect it wants deaths, which is enough to make it no tragedy, yet brings some near it, which is enough to make it no comedy, which must be a representation of familiar people, with such kind of trouble as no life be questioned."[5] In Fletcher's theory, the Aristotelian safeguards against harm and destruction keep tragicomedy within line, but only just; swerving toward tragedy, the genre takes cruel pleasure in near misses softened by the assurance that everyone will make it to act 5 more or less intact. As I hope my readings have shown, "joy of the worm" is more volatile and more variable than that. Breaking the promise that tragicomedy keeps with its audiences, the surge of positive affects announced by "joy of the worm" can surface precisely at and in the midst of scenes of death and killing, though they need not realize that outcome to count as such. Though "joy of the worm" can and does occur within drama, its movement across the variable ecosystems of early modern pastoral, romance, tragedy, comedy, prose meditation, theological treatise, paradox, and epic break even the relatively elastic bounds of "tragicomedy."

The View from a Record Store

Having outlined what I take to be the underlying axioms that my readings of "joy of the worm" imply, in the space remaining I want to briefly address some further social consequences regarding pleasure, art, and ethics that I think follow from my analysis, while also pulling us closer to the distinctly fraught present moment. I will start with an obvious remark: pleasure and approval are not the same thing. We can, and do, enjoy things that we might also think of as bad, harmful, or in some way negative. The basic disjunction of aesthetics and ethics is a starting place within which we each make individual choices against the backdrop of institutions and social surrounds. When we have aesthetic experiences of pleasure or displeasure in our encounters with texts, we negotiate personal responses to collective situations through our local decisions about what we affirm, what we permit, what we tolerate, and what we forbid. I believe that the archive within this book not only demonstrates that these works were intended to generate pleasure for their readers, but that they can and still do so for readers and audience members at present. "Joy of the worm" can speak to us, and give us pleasure, now. That may be good for us in some cases and bad for us in others.

How bad? To bridge the gap between readings of "joy of the worm" in early modern literature and the changed landscape of the present, consider the following anecdote: Flipping through the New Arrivals bin in my favorite used-record store, I was struck by the sudden appearance of an extensive trove of rare "depressive suicidal black metal" CDs. Since the store didn't typically carry such titles, I asked the store's owner where they came from.

"Oh, those? Sad story. Somebody brought their dead brother's record collection in and sold it. I guess he killed himself."

Feeling guilt at my own ghoulish and prurient attraction to these objects (were they just some old discarded junk, or the souvenirs of an unalterable crisis for their previous listener?), I bought the entire collection and took it home.

This hearsay story of melancholy provenance offers up a crude—almost comedic—oversimplification of the messy feedback loops between art and life. In the context of heavy metal as a lucrative market, the vexed question of how broadly circulating representations prompt irrevocably personal decisions in some listeners but not others became the occasion for high-profile lawsuits in the 1980s, when the grieving parents of teenage metal fans who had died by suicide sued prominent genre stars such as Ozzy Osbourne, alleging in one case that his song "Suicide Solution" had precipitated their child's fatal mimesis.[6] Protesting too much, Osbourne's legal defense insisted that the titular "solution" was a metaphoric reference to alcohol, and that the song was a moralistic warning about the dangers of overindulgence. Pressed to account for their art's effects, artists with incomes to lose beat a hasty retreat to the epistemically privileged stronghold of intention. In the case of "depressive suicidal black metal" as an underground variant, there is less wiggle room regarding intent. To be blunt, the genre is based in the celebration unto solicitation of self-harm. The high/low point of this tendency occurred in 1991, when Per "Dead" Ohlin, the lead singer of Norwegian black metal band Mayhem, shot himself; upon discovering the scene, the remaining band leader Øystein "Euronymous" Aarseth took gruesome close-up photographs of the corpse (later used as cover art for Mayhem's album *Dawn of the Black Hearts*) before calling police.[7] Doubling down upon this celebration of a fatal gesture, Aarseth later mailed fragments of Ohlin's skull to an inner circle of admirers.[8] In this case and in the subculture it continues to inspire into the present, "joy of the worm" valorizes self-harm as an index of both aesthetic commitment and personal integrity, creating a scene in which self-killing is celebrated as a sacred means through which to solder art, death, and community together.

All sorts of people listen to all sorts of music, with variable effects. And yet the silent pile of discarded suicidal-black-metal CDs once owned by the fan of suicidal black metal who, yes, committed suicide seems to indicate all too clearly that the intuitive connection between the art we choose to consume and the larger choices we make, including when to end our own lives, are necessarily related. Are the stakes of consuming art about suicide really this high? Can talk of "joy of the worm" withstand proximity to such absolute consequences?

Suicide scrambles the already complex conjunctive disjunction of art and life. When art channels the emotions that surround lethal actions, intensifying and stylizing the path from despair to self-killing and rendering harm pleasurable, does that mean that art is responsible for the actions of its consumers, readers, and respondents? It is surely too easy to let artworks or the artists who make them off the hook by simply insisting upon the sheer fact of "freedom." That people are free to harm themselves is not the issue (consider the ongoing COVID pandemic as a lesson in the power of "freedom" to rhetorically obfuscate dynamics of harm, damage, and responsibility). Granting freedom, the sticky and debatable question remains: What is the relationship between art and action?

People make art about killing themselves, and then they kill themselves, and then other people make art about people making art about killing themselves and then killing themselves. Patterns repeat. Art is not life but happens in life, and the art that happens in our lives can encourage us or discourage us from actions that include acting to end our lives and acting to extend them. One of the risky aspects of caring about art is that sometimes we decide to shape our own lives to fit the formally curtailed and idealized proportions of artworks. One way that we can choose to impose such forms is through determining consciously the moment of our real deaths on behalf of a desire to make our life resemble a work of art as we imagine that life being spectated upon and received by those who will survive us and examine what we have done. I don't know anything about the person who once owned those CDs, and I don't know whether the pleasure that those CDs gave was one of consolation that held their previous owner onto life, or whether they acted as "volitional motivators" that precipitated his final departure from life. Did he derive "joy of the worm" from them?

What has bound together most, though not all, of the moments and scenes in this book has been a desire to deny that voluntary death entails an aesthetic outcome, and to insist upon the self-differentiality of its representations. But I have been especially magnetized by moments when the representation of such deaths fails to achieve tragic seriousness and collapses into slapstick, into camp, into generic modes that refuse to emotionally invest in the auras of grandeur that a long sequence of cultural representations, from Greek tragedies to contemporary heavy metal subcultures, attach to the act of self-killing. I have sought to emphasize these moments in which grandeur fails and seriousness curdles because of a basic skepticism about the tragic allure of self-destruction, which I see as a dubious cultural readymade, ambivalent at best and actively harmful at worst. What looks like a path out of the world might itself reify the world's norms and conventions.

That is, to make a Durkheimian point regarding the social forces that underwrite solitary acts, the will to sacrifice the self is not a subversive exception to a prevalent capitalist lifeworld predicated upon self-interest; rather, self-sacrifice is one of the key mechanisms through which the structure of the family and the structure of the workplace ensure obedience, compliance, and loyalty unto death. Self-sacrifice and self-destruction and suicide stand on a spectrum of social forms that I am hoping through reading and rereading to constellate and sympathetically understand. It is pointless to deny the beauty and pleasure that the thought of self-destruction inspires in fantasy; but one can grant that while working to dislodge and contest the operational force exerted by those very thoughts, so that those who think them can live to dream again. If this book has something to contribute to an intellectual-historical project, it is to offer evidence of a thread of deflationary comedic resistance to the many bad forms of "seriousness" that obscure and valorize self-harm that the classical world bequeathed to early modernity and that early modern authors in turn have relayed, complicated, and creatively transformed.

Can we relay that resistance now? Because of the canonical centrality of Shakespeare's tragic works and the frequency with which they represent agents deciding to end their own lives, the literature classroom is at present one of the key locations in which the act of self-killing is subjected to extended analysis and the more or less enforced scrutiny, if not admiration, implicit in "close reading." Crossing a spectrum from boredom and alienation to feigned interest for the sake of a grade to passionately bardolatrous overidentification and dangerous "vicarious habituation," such

a classroom is an emotionally variable space, a maze of pitfalls and possibilities.[9] Leading our students through that maze, teachers of Shakespeare
are in the "joy of the worm" business, and I hope that this book might inspire some reflection upon the causal nexus that radiates outward from
our pedagogical scenes.

The risks of working with hazardous materials do not simply flow from
the texts we assign outward toward our students. This book was in some
sense precipitated by my lifelong admiration for a great scholar of early
modern genre theory, paradox, and casuistry, Rosalie Colie, who took her
own life immediately after she completed her last book, *Shakespeare's Living Art* (1974).[10] Marking the timing while discreetly concealing the means,
in a poignant note appended to Colie's own preface to that book, Colie's
posthumous editors Bridget Gellert Lyons and George Robinson note that
"Rosalie Colie completed her work on the manuscript of this book, and delivered it to her editor, one week before her tragic death."[11] This timing has
haunted me as I worked on the completion of this book, perhaps because
the spirit of my book is meant to contest the annexation of self-destruction
to "tragedy," and yet I cannot entirely escape its conceptual force.

Accordingly, in the spirit of Colie's own urge to let counterarguments
breathe within her scholarship, as a valediction I will briefly trace how such
a tragic framing impacts the reading of Colie's last work, coloring her writing with the false knowingness that the biographical fact of suicide confers upon the intimate strangers that are readers. Seen from the perspec-
tival vista of her last act, certain passing judgments within Colie's writing
take on the lineaments of prophecy as they register the distorting powers
of "joy of the worm."

We don't know what Colie's last sentences were, if she actually wrote
the epilogue last, or to what precise extent the entire manuscript was la-
bored over. It is dangerous and speculative to project her final thoughts
onto the epilogue of her last book. A lot can happen in a week.

And yet, primed by Lyons (herself a scholar of melancholy) to see "tragic
death" within Colie's actions, I cannot help but hear resonances from suicidal processes of thought in Colie's evocation of Lear's withdrawal from
and reimmersion in human contact: "Lear comes to his end having fully
experienced what it means to be detached—deracinated, rationally and ir-
rationally distanced—from life, and (far more painful) what it means to admit overwhelming connections and attachment to a living human being."[12]
That parenthetical moment, with its registration of variable intensities of
pain, marks a quilting point in which scholarly assessment pierces inward,
moving from alignment into something more than identification (I realize that this double gesture cannot take place without the specter of my
own grasping identification with Colie as she identifies with Lear). Some-

thing vital breaks in this moment, for Colie, and it may register something like the pressure of suicidal ideation as a spiraling from the specific to the general that cannot arrest its own destructive outward movement. Freud's remark upon the formal resemblance between amorous love and suicidal crisis—they both split the ego, allowing it to attack itself—overdetermines the amorous circumstances behind Colie's recognition that when Lear loses a person he loses the attachment to life itself.

True to its proximity to New Critical doxa regarding the harmony of opposites, Colie's prose falls into tics of emphasis as she works to stabilize a claim about Shakespeare's capacity to organize and resolve contrary forces and promiscuously various materials into a functional, purposive whole: "Here the most disparate techniques of craft are called upon to make sense—literally, to make sense—of the consequential casuistry of living."[13] If the reader startles at the need the text manifests to urge itself toward sense, we might well miss the deadly force enfolded in Colie's passing judgment upon the texture of living itself: "consequential casuistry."[14] Though it risks a facile knowingness to overread such remarks as signs of an inescapable crisis to come, to see the processes that keep us alive as casuistry is to imagine stepping beyond or outside them.

One can worry and speculate too far at points in reading Colie for the suicidal roman à clef, as when, in her evocation of the love affair of Antony and Cleopatra, she says: "They make each other feel that age is no bar to living fully; they make each other feel, not still alive, but more than usually alive, a feeling, however illusory, which can exercise curious power over a man and a woman more than commonly experienced."[15] Knowing that the unhappy conclusion of a middle-aged love affair may have precipitated Colie's own death by drowning, it is hard not to see that passing qualifying phrase, "however illusory" as a lightly veiled lament intruding upon the page in the form of generalized wisdom.

Literary criticism can sometimes become a means through which we ratify standpoints we already hold, up to and including the tragic—or perhaps merely "depressive realist"—position that we are doomed to unhappiness and our lives are nonviable. I am not suggesting that exposure to the harmful vicarious habituations of Shakespearean tragedy somehow precipitated Colie's own choices, as if this brilliant scholar of tragedy was herself engulfed by its beguiling but necessarily limited—and therefore deceptive—forms. But I am marking the way that scholarship can function as a proxy through which we imagine, test, and reconsider the bonds that hold us to life. The "joy of the worm" that we find within literature can be a crucially stabilizing handhold that keeps us from leaping. It has steadied me through storms and confusion, and I am not alone in finding an anchor in literature. But it can also be a diving board from which we plummet into the void below. The suggestion that Colie might have reconsidered the force of her attachment to the losses that drove her to lose her life registers my frustration at her decision, the low-level proprietary rage of her reader and admirer. But doubting that decision risks pomposity and arrogance: Who am I to say that she succumbed to a bad form of seriousness?

Panning wider, the critique of "bad seriousness" within this book courts misunderstanding for some of the same reasons that second-guessing Colie's decision might well rankle. Seriousness is underrated at present. Given the rise of authoritarianism, fascism, and white supremacy, the annihilating endgame of climate catastrophe, and the fundamental structural deadlocks at the level of political economy that grip our planet and threaten the survival of our species, there are plenty of good reasons to be serious. As I write this epilogue, we have had a deeply unserious troll for a president, and large swathes of my own country are at present proudly performing public acts of deliberate en masse exposure to a deadly virus as a way of displaying their ideological commitment to an ideology of personal freedom unto death. Against such an untimely backdrop, I cannot fail to be aware of the extent to which my argument's tendency looks like decadent perversity, a willful refusal to "read the room" or, worse, some winking endorsement of the social surround's ongoing death cult.

Suicide as negative outcome can be rescripted into a warning, a cautionary tale, the ultimate object lesson in the irreversible consequences of our choices. Memorial reconstructions often serve this function, loading the life narration with proleptic warning signs and foreshadowings, as I have perhaps done in my return to Rosalie Colie. But tragedy is not the only convention available. Seen in the light of "joy of the worm" afforded by literature, at a crucially liberatory remove from the pressure of lived consequence, a death from suicide can also be rendered in language as a heroic gift, sexual release, elemental return, amorous fusion, or political self-rescue. These are genre's gifts to those who choose to take them up. They are costly and fraught and subject to revaluation, even if the agents who select them place themselves beyond our reach. Gifts can also be poison.

Then and now, the forms of self-rescue offered up by "joy of the worm" aren't always easy to swallow. As a case in point, consider this moment: "I had learned from many years of watching my mother that one way to join the body and mind together was through suicide. After she died, I tried to kill myself. But I laughed so hard watching myself do this in the bathroom mirror that the pills in my mouth spilled out. How could a handful of pills compare with the years my mother spent dying?"[16] Here, in his memoir *The Women* (1996), Hilton Als shows us someone tunneling through "joy of the worm" and out the other side; his laughter in the midst of self-killing in the midst of an attempted mimetic relation to his lost mother registers the ludicrous overfamiliarity of an image that one thought one wanted to align with until it looks back from the mirror and spits out the pills. Here "joy of the worm" falls on both sides of laughing-at and laughing-with; summoned by a fantasy of merger with the mother's body, it breaks into laughter at the bitter fact of separation. This *hard laughter* is a form of joy but not, always, a comfort.

Then and now, the spectacle of voluntary death occasions a curiously pervasive and enduring possible array of pleasures that "joy of the worm" gathers together and makes possible for some at the expense of others. In its most disturbing articulations, it can bring us closer to the edge of survival than is safe for all of us to venture, and flags the heavy human costs of fantasies of freedom; such fantasies transcendentally lead us to another world rather than encouraging us to alter this one. It is my hope that in better understanding pleasure-in-destruction we might therapeutically traverse the fantasies of death and harm that "joy of the worm" makes available and return to life anew without thereby treating as inevitable the ongoing conditions that make us want to leave that world in the first place. To resituate this analysis of pleasure and joy in the stark polarity of affects articulated by Spinoza, in the classroom and on the street, alone or with others, it is worth remaining mindful of whether we will increase our capacity to act via positive affects or diminish our capacity to act through the sad passions we suffer.

Trying to put some distance between this book and the actions it has focused upon, the affirmative yet still damning words of Fred Moten in *The Undercommons: Fugitive Planning and Black Study* (2013) have haunted and disturbed me, and they resonate with me still as I arrive now at my own end: "I believe in the world and want to be in it. I want to be in it all the way to the end of it because I believe in another world in the world and I want to be in *that*."[17] "World" can be scaled outward to the planetary chokehold of global capitalist political economy, or it can be scaled down to the university as just one more exploitive and hierarchical workplace that runs on anxiety and precarious labor alongside all the others. The former creates and conditions the latter. Across those scales, Moten hears a "joyful noise of the scattered, scatted eschaton, the undercommon refusal of the academy of misery" emergent within the din of the present.[18] Training our ear to listen for that "joyful noise" takes time, but it might teach us something. *There is a difference between choosing to survive and accepting the world.*[19] If this book has shown how the pleasurable thought of merging with the world has at times assisted those in search of a passage out of life, the decision to remain alive also opens out a different array of possible relations to the world, and, with it, the recognition that other joys are possible.

Acknowledgments

To follow the dark paths of the mind and enter the
past, to visit books, to brush aside their branches
and break off some fruit.

VIRGINIA WOOLF, *The Waves*

The "dark paths of the mind" must be approached with caution, but they offer us joy. I am grateful to so many who lit paths across that darkness for me and helped me during the extended time it took to write this book. Here is an alphabetical list of people who are owed thanks for their suggestions, encouragement, invitations to think and rethink, chances to push this project further or try out its ideas, sheer intellectual example, or cautionary warnings: Amanda Bailey, Jane Bennett, Lauren Berlant, Paul Brown, Doug Bruster, Stephanie Burt, Shane Butler, Stephen Campbell, Jeffrey Jerome Cohen, Andrew Cole, Kim Coles, Christopher D'Addario, Mario DiGangi, Ari Friedlander, Colby Gordon, Stephen Guy-Bray, Richard Halpern, Matthew Harrison, Tim Harrison, Earle Havens, David Hershinow, S. Lochlann Jain, Mira Kafantaris, Emily Kawasaki, Andy Kesson, John Kuhn, Aaron Kunin, Russ Leo, Jonathan Lethem, Heather Love, Julia Lupton, Carla Mazzio, Carol Mejia-LaPerle, Steve Mentz, Feisal Mohamed, Anna Moschovakis, David Norbrook, Christopher Nygren, Tavia Nyong'o, Lena Orlin, Sarah Osment, Katrin Pahl, Ben Parris, Gerard Passannante, Gabrielle Ponce, Christopher Pye, Richard Rambuss, Eugenio Refini, Kenneth Reinhard, Melissa Sanchez, Seth Sanders, Elizabeth Scala, Joshua Scodel, David Carroll Simon, Joel Slotkin, Nigel Smith, Eric Song, Sarah Sprouse, Walter Stephens, Will Stockton, Richard Strier, Ayanna Thompson, Henry Turner, and Christine Varnado. Some assisted in small ways, some assisted in large ways, and none are responsible for the errors in my thinking and writing. A poem by Lara Durback that appears in a novel by Anna Moschovakis says, "the opposite of suicide / is learning and creating with friends," and I'm grateful to my friends for letting me create with and learn from them.[1]

I am grateful to the University of Chicago, Brown University, Columbia University, the University of Pennsylvania, the City University of New York, the University of Pittsburgh, Gettysburg College, Princeton University, George Washington University, the University of California, Los Angeles, Civitella Ranieri Foundation, and the University of Texas for hosting talks that allowed me to test some of the material in this book. A section of chapter 4 appeared in earlier form as "A Political Necrology of God," in the *Journal for Early Modern Cultural Studies* 13, no. 3 (2013): 105–25. I would like to thank the University of Pennsylvania Press for permission to reprint that material here.

I cannot thank the Department of English at Johns Hopkins University enough for the support it offered me during a challenging time. As colleagues and collaborators, Chris Nealon, Doug Mao, Jesse Rosenthal, Jeanne-Marie Jackson, Lawrence Jackson, Sharon Achinstein, Andrew Miller, Mary Favret, Jared Hickman, Christopher Cannon, Nadia Nurhussein, and Mark Thompson continue to inspire and challenge me. I am also grateful to the community of current and former graduate students and undergraduates from whom I have learned so much over the last decade of teaching and collaboration; this group includes Royce Best, Nathaniel Doherty, David Hershinow, Seola Lee, Alex Lewis, Sede Makonnen, Daniel McClurkin, Elvin Meng, Ben Parris, Kevin Roberts, Connie Scozzaro, Andrew Sisson, Will Theodorou, Robert Tinkle, and Maggie Vinter. They will hear the sound of our conversations in seminars within these pages. I am indebted to Sarah Sprouse for her paleographic assistance in transcribing the Sir John Harington MS.

This book would not have the form that it has without the warm encouragement and tough questions of Anahid Nersessian and Nan Da; any author would be lucky to have such interlocutors. I am also grateful to the two anonymous reviewers of my book manuscript, who steered me away from some sticky traps while sharing a generous sense of the book's scope and ultimate destination. Insisting upon clarity, Stephen Twilley was an astonishingly observant and painstaking copy editor. Throughout the process of completing this manuscript, Alan Thomas and Randolph Petilos have been sensitive stewards of the project.

The continuous support of my family has sustained me through difficult years, snapping me out of my scholarly trance with precisely timed reminders that there is more to life than the contemplation of its end. I am also grateful for the webs of care work and assistance that surround and sustain them. The loss of my stepfather, Marty Sussman, during the process of writing this book was bitter; what remains permanently before me is his legacy of humor, compassion, and clarity.

Finally, to Martin, whose steadfast affection lights each day, I owe an unpayable debt, and at the risk of only compounding my indebtedness, I will borrow words from Milton's "L'Allegro" and express my continued astonishment at our unexpected life of "linked sweetness long drawn out."

Notes

Introduction

1. Dorothy Parker, *Enough Rope* (New York: Boni and Liveright, 1926).

2. Consider Charles Taylor's framing contrast between the "impossibility" of doubting God's existence in 1500 versus the "inescapability" of at least entertaining such doubts in the present. *A Secular Age* (Cambridge, MA: Harvard University Press, 2007), 25. There are, of course, many "post-secular" critiques and complications of this overly broad and Eurocentric framing.

3. William Shakespeare, *Hamlet*, in *The Norton Shakespeare*, 3rd ed., ed. Stephen Greenblatt et al. (New York: W. W. Norton, 2015), 1772.

4. Thomas More, *A Dialogue of Comfort against Tribulation*, ed. Leland Miles (Bloomington: Indiana University Press, 1965).

5. More, 102.

6. See "Did Women Have a Renaissance?," chap. 2 in *Women, History, and Theory: The Essays of Joan Kelly* (Chicago: University of Chicago Press, 1984). For an account of contemporary violence against women and its relation to ongoing misogynist discourse, see Kate Manne, *Down Girl: The Logic of Misogyny* (Oxford: Oxford University Press, 2018).

7. "*A Merry Jest of a Shrewd and Curst Wife Lapped in Morel's Skin, for Her Good Behavior*," in "*The Taming of the Shrew*": *Texts and Contexts*, ed. Frances E. Dolan (Boston: Bedford Books, 1996).

8. Aristotle, *Poetics I, with the Tractatus Coislinianus*, trans. Richard Janko (Cambridge: Hackett, 1987), 6. All subsequent citations of *Poetics* are from this edition unless otherwise noted.

9. The concept of "emotional communities" comes from Barbara Rosenwein, "Worrying about Emotions in History," *American Historical Review* 107, no. 3 (2002): 842.

10. "Self-killing" was not in wide use across early modernity either; it is invented in 1618, and I do not wish to be taken to imply that this was somehow the more popular term. See David Daube, "The Linguistics of Suicide," *Suicide and Life-Threatening Behavior* 7, no. 3 (1977): 7, 3, 159.

11. Sir Thomas Browne, *Religio Medici, The Works of the Learned Sir Thomas Browne, Knight, Doctor of Physick, late of Norwich* (London: [Brome,] 1686), 23–24. See Brian

Barraclough and Daphne Shepherd, "A Necessary Neologism: The Origin and Uses of *Suicide,*" *Suicide and Life-Threatening Behavior* 24, no. 2 (1994): 113-26.

12. The designation of suicide as "a complex behavior" is continual across the critical literature in the field. For a case in point, see the coroner's textbook by Ronald Holmes and Stephen T. Holmes, *Suicide: Theory, Practice, and Investigation* (Thousand Oaks, CA: SAGE, 2005), 13.

13. E. David Klonsky, Alexis M. May, and Boaz Y. Saffer, "Suicide, Suicide Attempts, and Suicidal Ideation," *Annual Review of Clinical Psychology* 12 (2016): 312.

14. For an exposition of the interpersonal theory dominant in the field, see Thomas Joiner, *Why People Die by Suicide* (Cambridge, MA: Harvard University Press, 2005). For the most recent model that builds upon Joiner, see E. David Klonsky and Alexis M. May, "The Three Step Theory (3ST): A New Theory of Suicide Rooted in the 'Ideation to Action' Framework," *International Journal of Cognitive Therapy* 8, no. 2 (2015): 114-29.

15. Thomas Richardson, Peter Elliott, and Ronald Roberts, "The Relationship between Personal Unsecured Debt and Mental and Physical Health: A Systematic Review and Meta-Analysis," *Clinical Psychology Review* 33, no. 8 (2013): 1148-62.

16. For a report from Kansas City, see Katie Wedell, Lucille Sherman, and Sky Chadde's "Seeds of Despair: Hundreds of Farmers Are Dying by Suicide," *FlatlandKC*, March 16, 2020, https://www.flatlandkc.org/news-issues/seeds-of-despair-hundreds-of-farmers-are-dying-by-suicide.

17. Jennifer Steinhauser, "V.A. Officials, and the Nation, Battle an Unrelenting Tide of Veteran Suicides," *New York Times*, April 14, 2019, https://www.nytimes.com/2019/04/14/us/politics/veterans-suicide.html.

18. Joshua Gordon and Nora Volkow, "Suicide Deaths Are a Major Component of the Opioid Crisis That Must Be Addressed," National Institute of Mental Health, September 19, 2019, https://www.nimh.nih.gov/about/director/messages/2019/suicide-deaths-are-a-major-component-of-the-opioid-crisis-that-must-be-addressed.shtml.

19. T. A. Blakeley, S. C. D. Collings, and J. Atkinson, "Unemployment and Suicide: Evidence for a Causal Association?" *Journal of Epidemiology and Community Health* 57, no. 8 (2003): 594-600. See also, more recently, Wolfram Kawohl and Carlos Nordt, "COVID 19, Unemployment, and Suicide," *Lancet Psychiatry* 7, no. 5 (2020): 389-90.

20. See Vivek Shraya, *I Want to Kill Myself* (2017), digital film, 8:35; see also hannah baer, *trans girl suicide museum* (Los Angeles: Hesse Press, 2019).

21. The relevance of intersectional analysis to the complexity of identity-based categorizing is evidenced early on in the field of suicidology, in the chapter-by-chapter striations of Herbert Hendin's *Black Suicide*, which divides by gender, sexual orientation, and generational cohort as it examines the black suicide rate in the United States. Herbert Hendin, *Black Suicide* (New York: Basic Books, 1969).

22. Richard A. Friedman, "Why Are Young Americans Killing Themselves? Suicide Is Now Their Second-Leading Cause of Death," *New York Times*, January 6, 2020, https://www.nytimes.com/2020/01/06/opinion/suicide-young-people.html.

23. Émile Durkheim, *Suicide: A Study in Sociology* (1897), trans. John A. Spaulding and George Simpson, ed. George Simpson (New York: Free Press, 1951), 145.

24. "Raising the minimum wage and the earned-income tax credit (EITC) by 10 percent each could prevent about 1,230 suicides annually, according to a working paper circulated by the National Bureau of Economic Research this week." Andrew van Dam, "Researchers Say There's a Simple Way to Reduce Suicides: Increase the Minimum

Wage," *Washington Post*, April 30, 2019, https://www.washingtonpost.com/us-policy /2019/04/30/researchers-say-theres-simple-way-reduce-suicides-increase -minimum-wage.

25. Anne Case and Angus Deaton, *Deaths of Despair and the Future of Capitalism* (Princeton, NJ: Princeton University Press, 2020).

26. Ian Marsh, *Suicide: Foucault, History, and Truth* (Cambridge: Cambridge University Press, 2010), 30.

27. Daube, "Linguistics of Suicide," 136.

28. Marsh, *Suicide*, 29.

29. Marsh, 22.

30. Rosalie L. Colie, *The Resources of Kind: Genre-Theory in the Renaissance*, ed. Barbara K. Lewalski (Berkeley: California University Press, 1973), 115.

31. In invoking this faintly Deleuzian-sounding language of "repetition and difference" to describe genre's capacity to both satisfy and confound expectations, I am indebted to film theorist Stephen Neale, *Genre* (London: British Film Institute, 1980).

32. For a reconsideration of the generality of character typologies in early modernity, see Aaron Kunin, *Character as Form* (New York: Bloomsbury, 2019).

33. *Oxford English Dictionary*, 2nd ed. (1989), s.v. "genre," accessed June 18, 2021, https://www-oed-com.proxy1.library.jhu.edu/view/Entry/77629?redirectedFrom =genre#eid.

34. Colie, *Resources of Kind*, 114.

35. Influential translations of the *Poetics* into Latin in 1498, and into Italian by Bernardo Segni in 1549, sparked a rapid dissemination and a cottage industry of commentary from Francesco Robortello (1548), Julius Caesar Scaliger (1561) and Lodovico Castelvetro (1570). See Rebecca Bushnell, *Tragedy: A Short Introduction* (London: Blackwell, 2008), 38. See also Micha Lazarus, "Aristotelian Criticism in Sixteenth-Century England," in *Oxford Handbooks Online*, ed. Colin Burrow (Oxford: Oxford University Press, 2016), https://www.oxfordhandbooks.com/view/10.1093/oxfordhb /9780199935338.001.0001/oxfordhb-9780199935338-e-148.

36. I take the concept of "aesthetic categories" from Sianne Ngai, *Our Aesthetic Categories: Zany, Cute, Interesting* (Cambridge, MA: Harvard University Press, 2015).

37. For a contrary argument about the relative lack of socially normative force in the Virgilian *rota*, see Alastair Fowler, *Kinds of Literature: An Introduction to the Theory of Genres and Modes* (Oxford: Clarendon Press, 1982), 35.

38. Richard Halpern, *Eclipse of Action: Tragedy and Political Economy* (Chicago: University of Chicago Press, 2017), 157.

39. *Oxford English Dictionary*, 2nd ed. (1989), s.v. "sadness," which cites Hoccleve's *De regimine principum*, from 1412, "Hem hoghte to be mirours of sadnesse, And wayue iolitee and wantonnesse"; accessed July 16, 2021, https://www-oed-com.proxy1.library .jhu.edu/.

40. For a transhistorical anthology of genre theories on the subject, see Paul Lauter, ed., *Theories of Comedy* (New York: Anchor Books, 1964).

41. Udall quoted in Lauter, 112.

42. William Shakespeare, *A Midsummer Night's Dream*, in *The Norton Shakespeare*, 3rd ed., ed. Stephen Greenblatt et al. (New York: W. W. Norton, 2015), 1087.

43. For more on the phrase "comedia tragica," see *The Complete Works of John Milton*, vol. 11, *Manuscript Writings*, ed. William Poole (Oxford University Press, 2019), 303.

44. *The Diaries of John Dee*, ed. Edward Fenton (Oxfordshire: Day Books, 1998), 2.

45. As quoted in Alec Ryrie, "Despair and Salvation," in *Being Protestant in Reformation Britain* (Oxford: Oxford University Press, 2013), 27.

46. *The Bloudy Booke, or the Tragicall and desperate end of Sir John Fites [Fitz], a Narration of the Bloudy Mvrthers commytted by the handes of Sir Iohn Fites (alias) Fitz, a Deuonshire Knight, vpon two seuerall Men: and lastly, to make vp the Tragedy, vpon himselfe also, at Twicknam, nine Myles from London, vpon the seuenth day of August last, 1605* (London: [Roberts] 1605).

47. Alexander Murray, *Suicide in the Middle Ages*, vol. 1, *The Violent against Themselves* (Oxford: Oxford University Press, 2009); Alexander Murray, *Suicide in the Middle Ages*, vol. 2, *The Curse on Self-Murder* (Oxford: Oxford University Press, 2011); Georges Minois, *History of Suicide: Voluntary Death in Western Culture*, trans. Lydia G. Cochrane (Baltimore: Johns Hopkins University Press, 1995); Marzio Barbagli, *Farewell to the World: A History of Suicide*, trans. Lucinda Byatt (London: Polity, 2015); Margaret Pabst Battin, ed., *The Ethics of Suicide: Historical Sources* (Oxford: Oxford University Press, 2015).

48. Michael MacDonald and Terence R. Murphy, *Sleepless Souls: Suicide in Early Modern England* (Oxford: Clarendon Press, 1990).

49. MacDonald and Murphy, 2.

50. MacDonald and Murphy, 5.

51. MacDonald and Murphy, 15–41.

52. MacDonald and Murphy, 15–41.

53. Paul S. Seaver, "Suicide and the Vicar General in London: A Mystery Solved?," in *From Sin to Insanity: Suicide in Early Modern Europe*, ed. Jeffrey R. Watt (Ithaca, NY: Cornell University Press, 2004), 26.

54. Seaver, 27.

55. Seaver, 28.

56. Seaver, 32.

57. Seaver, 37.

58. In broad strokes, the picture holds firm because it corresponds to a great deal of evidence. I do not dispute the utility of this narrative as a general trend; it constitutes a backdrop against which the objects and scenes that interest me stand out. See Jeffrey R. Watt, "Introduction: Toward a History of Suicide in Early Modern Europe," in *From Sin to Insanity: Suicide in Early Modern Europe*, ed. Jeffrey R Watt (Ithaca, NY: Cornell University Press, 2004).

59. The coinage of André Breton, "humour noir" was founded upon a transhistorical reach from surrealism backward toward the past; its founding example was Jonathan Swift's *Modest Proposal*. André Breton, *Anthology of Black Humor*, trans. Mark Polizzotti (San Francisco: City Lights Books, 1997).

For an activation of the implicit possibility of "blackness" within this phrase in concert with the complex interpretive questions generated by premodern logics of racialization, see the analysis of Terence's African identity and biography of former enslavement in Misha Teramura, "Black Comedy: Shakespeare, Terence, and *Titus Andronicus*," *ELH* 85, no. 4 (2018).

60. S. E. Sprott, *Suicide: The English Debate from Donne to Hume* (La Salle, IL: Open Court, 1961); Roland Wymer, *Suicide and Despair in the Jacobean Drama* (New York: St. Martin's Press, 1986); Eric Langley, *Narcissism and Suicide in Shakespeare and His Con-*

temporaries (Oxford: Oxford University Press, 2009); Marlena Tronicke, *Shakespeare's Suicides: Dead Bodies That Matter* (New York: Routledge, 2018).

61. Marie Kondo, star of *Tidying Up with Marie Kondo*, is a popular proponent of a de-cluttering technique in which each object is examined for its capacity to spark joy. See also Marie Kondo, *The Life-Changing Magic of Tidying Up* (Berkeley: Ten Speed Press, 2014).

62. For a discussion of *spoudaios* and *phaulos* see Matthew Lu, "Getting Serious about Seriousness: On the Meaning of *Spoudaios* in Aristotle's Ethics," *Proceedings of the ACPA* 87 (2013); see also Walter Kaufmann, *Tragedy and Philosophy* (Princeton, NJ: Princeton University Press, 1968), 41. As Micha Lazarus points out, "σπουδαιότερον, the comparative of σπουδαῖος, has a wide semantic range, the local sense of which is debated to this day." "Sidney's Greek Poetics," *Studies in Philology* 112, no. 3 (2015): 523.

63. See Terri Snyder, *The Power to Die: Slavery and Suicide in British North America* (Chicago: University of Chicago Press, 2015). Some scholars have drawn links between exemplary *Romana mors* cases and the situation of enslaved people; see Margo Hendricks's comparison of Lucrece's situation to "African women slaves who took their own lives rather than allow themselves to be raped or made slaves." "'A Word, Sweet Lucrece': Confession, Feminism, and *The Rape of Lucrece*," in *A Feminist Companion to Shakespeare*, ed. Dympna Callaghan (Oxford: Blackwell, 2002), 115.

64. Mary Nyquist, "Ancient Greek and Roman Slaveries," chap. 1 in *Arbitrary Rule: Slavery, Tyranny, and the Power of Life and Death* (Chicago: University of Chicago Press, 2013), esp. 25.

65. Nyquist, chap. 1.

66. Nyquist, 21–31.

67. Seneca quoted in Margaret Pabst Battin, "The Social Arguments Concerning Suicide," in *Ethical Issues in Suicide* (Upper Saddle River, NJ: Prentice Hall, 1995), 79.

68. See K. R. Bradley, *Slaves and Masters in the Roman Empire: A Study in Social Control* (Oxford: Oxford University Press, 1987); M. I. Finley, *Ancient Slavery and Modern Ideology*, ed. B. D. Shaw (Princeton, NJ: Markus Wiener, 1998); P. Garnsey, *Ideas of Slavery from Aristotle to Augustine* (Cambridge: Cambridge University Press, 1996).

69. Saidiya V. Hartman, *Scenes of Subjection: Terror, Slavery, and Self-Making in Nineteenth-Century America* (Oxford: Oxford University Press, 1997). For a broad survey of the "spectrum of coercion" within the early modern period, see David Eltis and Stanley L. Engerman, "Dependence, Servility, and Coerced Labor in Time and Space," chap. 1 in *The Cambridge World History of Slavery*, vol. 3, *AD 1420–AD 1804*, ed. David Eltis and Stanley L. Engerman (Cambridge: Cambridge University Press, 2011).

70. Cicero, *"Philippics" 3–9*, ed. Gesine Manuwald (Berlin: Walter Gruyter, 2007), 1:184.

71. For a broader, transhistorical argument about the relationship of the concept of freedom to the institution of slavery, see Orlando Patterson, *Freedom in the Making of Western Culture* (New York: Basic Books, 1991).

72. See Donald Ross, "Aristotle's Ambivalence on Slavery," *Hermathena*, no. 184 (2008): 55; Aristotle, *Politics*, trans. Carnes Lord (Chicago: University of Chicago Press, 2013), 9–11.

73. Daube, "Linguistics of Suicide," 151.

74. Kathleen Stewart, *Ordinary Affects* (Durham, NC: Duke University Press, 2007), 86.

75. Plautus, *Aulularia, or The Pot of Gold*, in *Amphitryon. The Comedy of Asses. The Pot of Gold. The Two Bacchises. The Captives*, vol. 1, trans. Paul Nixon, Loeb Classical Library (Cambridge, MA: Harvard University Press, 1916), 240.

76. Brian Cummings, *Mortal Thoughts: Religion, Secularity, and Identity in Shakespeare and Early Modern Culture* (Oxford: Oxford University Press, 2013), 266.

77. Stewart, *Ordinary Affects*, 87.

78. Earlier textual scholarship on Empedocles divided the fragments along disciplinary lines, imagining that Empedocles had written a scientific text *On Nature* and a separate, explicitly religious text called *Purifications*. By contrast, recent textual scholarship, bolstered by the recovery, in 1999, of a relatively intact papyrus with syncretic passages, has shifted toward a "single-work hypothesis." For a summary of the textual-editing history of Empedocles and the consequences of the Strasbourg papyrus for the "two works or one?" question, see Simon Trépanier, "The Single-Work Hypothesis," chap. 1 in *Empedocles: An Interpretation* (New York: Routledge, 2004).

79. Empedocles, *The Poem of Empedocles: A Text and Translation*, ed. Brad Inwood (Toronto: University of Toronto Press, 2001), 217.

80. For subsequent attempts in antiquity and into the Renaissance to read Homeric poetry as an expression of *philia* and *neikos*, see Jessica Wolfe, *Homer and the Question of Strife from Erasmus to Hobbes* (Toronto: University of Toronto Press, 2015), 21–23 passim.

81. Diogenes Laertius, *Lives of Eminent Philosophers*, vol. 2, trans. R. D. Hicks (New York: G. P. Putnam's Sons, 1925), 383. See also Ava Chitwood, *Death by Philosophy: The Biographical Tradition in the Life and Death of the Archaic Philosophers Empedocles, Heraclitus, and Democritus* (Ann Arbor: University of Michigan Press, 2004), 23.

82. Diogenes Laertius, *Lives of Eminent Philosophers*, 383–85.

83. See Kristen Poole, "When Hell Freezes Over: Mount Hecla and Hamlet's Infernal Geography," *Shakespeare Studies* 39 (2011): 152–87; see also John Gillies, *Shakespeare and the Geography of Difference* (Cambridge: Cambridge University Press, 1994), 87–91.

84. In a chapter titled "The Pythagoreans and Stoics, While they Hold the Immortality of the Soul, Foolishly Persuade a Voluntary Death," Lactantius states: "Thus it was with Cleanthes and Chrysippus, with Zeno, and Empedocles, who in the dead of night cast himself into a cavity of the burning Ætna, that when he had suddenly disappeared it might be believed that he had departed to the gods; and thus also of the Romans Cato died, who through the whole of his life was an imitator of Socratic ostentation." *Divine Institutes*, trans. Anthony Bowen and Peter Garnsey (Liverpool: Liverpool University Press, 2004), 203.

85. John Masson, "An Italian Scholar on Jerome's Commentary on Lucretius," *Classical Review* 12, no. 5 (1898).

86. See Jason S. Nethercut, "Empedocles' 'Roots' in Lucretius' *De Rerum Natura*," *American Journal of Philology* 138, no. 1 (2017): 85–105.

87. Joiner, *Why People Die by Suicide*, 92.

88. There is a distinction to be drawn between the motivational phase and the volitional phase that is worth preserving; specifically, Empedoclean materialisms constitute an example of "mental imagery" as a "volitional moderator" that facilitates the passage toward action. Rory C. O'Connor and Olivia J. Kirtley, "The Integrated Motivational-Volitional Model of Suicidal Behaviour," *Philosophical Transactions B* 373, no. 1754 (2018), https://www.ncbi.nlm.nih.gov/pmc/articles/PMC6053985/.

89. Christopher Marlowe, *Doctor Faustus: Based on the A Text*, ed. Roma Gill (London: Methuen, 2008), 79.

90. This has been defined as "the core complex" within narcissism by psychoanalyst Mervin Glasser, and centers upon "the fantasy of fusion with the idealized mother as a means of meeting the person's (originally the infant's) deep-seated longing for satiety and security. In this context, we may describe as the fantasy of ultimate narcissistic fulfillment, or the fantasy of primary narcissism." "Problems in the Psychoanalysis of Certain Narcissistic Disorders," *Psychoanalytic Psychotherapy in South Africa* 5, no. 2 (1997): 39.

91. *The Standard Edition of the Complete Psychological Works of Sigmund Freud*, ed. James Strachey (London: Hogarth Press, 1953), 23:148–50.

92. See, e.g., Jean Laplanche, *Life and Death in Psychoanalysis*, trans. Jeffrey Mehlman (Baltimore: Johns Hopkins University Press, 1976); Phillippe Van Haute and Tomas Geyskens, *From Death Instinct to Attachment Theory: The Primacy of the Child in Freud, Klein, and Hermann* (New York: Other Press, 2007).

93. Adrian Johnston, *Time Driven: Metapsychology and the Splitting of the Drive* (Evanston, IL: Northwestern University Press, 2005), 176.

94. Freud, *Standard Edition*, 22:104–5, quoted in Johnston, *Time Driven*, 126.

95. Johnston, *Time Driven*, 183.

96. Anne Sexton quoted in Edwidge Danticat, *The Art of Death: Writing the Final Story* (Minneapolis: Graywolf Press, 2017), 95.

97. Freud, *Standard Edition*, 14:289. Compare this with Baruch Spinoza, *Ethics*, part 3, prop. X: "An idea which excludes [the existence of our body] cannot be present in our mind, but is contrary to it." *Spinoza's "Ethics,"* trans. George Eliot, ed. Clare Carlisle (Princeton, NJ: Princeton University Press, 2020), 171.

98. "Mourning and Melancholia" contains the most widely cited of Freud's remarks on suicide. Building from his account of melancholia as an introjection of a lost object of love within the ego, Freud suggests that a perverse fold within this logic is required in order for the ego to gain the strength to act against its own interests: "The analysis of melancholia now shows us that the ego can kill itself only if, owing to the return of the object-cathexis, it can treat itself as an object—if it is able to direct against itself the hostility which relates to an object and which represents the ego's original reaction to objects in the external world." "Mourning and Melancholia," *Standard Edition*, 14:252.

99. For a survey of the distinct theorizations of suicide across the Freudian corpus, see Robert E. Litman, "Sigmund Freud on Suicide" (1970), in *Essential Papers on Suicide*, ed. Johan T. Maltsberger and Mark J. Goldblatt (New York: New York University Press, 1996), 209.

100. Durkheim concurs with Freud with regards to the essential starting point that suicide is not the expression of a distinct form of insanity. Durkheim surveys four possible subtypes of insanity that can lead to suicide ("maniacal suicide," "melancholy suicide," "obsessive suicide," and "automatic/impulsive suicide") and distinguishes these as a group from the many other cases of self-killing that are not caused by mental illness at all. Durkheim's analysis starts from statistics and then divides along fault lines of socially situated motives: egoistic suicide, altruistic suicide, anomic suicide, etc. *Suicide*, 62.

101. To compare this with the similar dynamic afforded by the Epicurean schema in

Lucretius's *De rerum natura*, see Charles Segal, *Lucretius on Death and Anxiety: Poetry and Philosophy in de Rerum Natura* (Princeton, NJ: Princeton University Press, 1990).

102. O'Connor and Kirtley, "The Integrated Motivational-Volitional Model of Suicidal Behaviour."

103. Hartman, *Scenes of Subjection*, 3–7; Paul A. Kottman, *A Politics of the Scene* (Stanford, CA: Stanford University Press, 2008), 99–116.

104. Sianne Ngai, *Ugly Feelings* (Cambridge, MA: Harvard University Press, 2005), 46.

105. Ngai, 46.

106. Ngai, 30.

107. There are exceptions. See the "expanded empiricism" of Brian Massumi, *Parables for the Virtual: Movement, Affect, Sensation* (Durham, NC: Duke University Press, 2002).

108. Eugenie Brinkema, *The Forms of the Affects* (Durham, NC: Duke University Press, 2014), xv.

109. Heather Love, "Close but Not Deep: Literary Ethics and the Descriptive Turn," *New Literary History* 41, no. 2 (2010): 387.

110. There are similar protocols in many countries, but Google searches in the continental United States for "suicide" are directed to the Suicide Prevention Lifeline, https://suicidepreventionlifeline.org/.

111. Terry Williams, *Teenage Suicide Notes: An Ethnography of Self-Harm* (New York: Columbia University Press, 2017), xiv.

112. Whitney Phillips, "LOLing at Tragedy: Facebook Trolls, Memorial Pages, and the Business of Mass-Mediated Disaster Narratives," chap. 5 in *This Is Why We Can't Have Nice Things: Mapping the Relationship between Online Trolling and Mainstream Culture* (Cambridge, MA: MIT Press, 2016).

Chapter One

1. "Time after Time," track 4 on Cyndi Lauper, *She's So Unusual*, Portrait Records, 1983. I take "holding environment" from D. W. Winnicott, "The Theory of the Parent-Child Relationship," *International Journal of Psychoanalysis* 41 (1960): 585–95. I am indebted to Connie Scozzaro for this suggestion.

2. It matters to the generic reception of the story that the wrist is not described as the site of extensive prior "cutting." Analysis of suicide adjoins but is not the same as the clinical analysis of NSSI (non-suicidal self-injury), which is a parasuicidal behavior for some and not for others. See Steven Levenkron, *Cutting: Understanding and Overcoming Self-Mutilation* (New York: W. W. Norton, 1998); Fiona Gardner, *Self-Harm: A Psychotherapeutic Approach* (New York: Brunner-Routledge, 2001); Sarah Chaney, *Psyche on the Skin: A History of Self-Harm* (London: Reaktion, 2017).

3. "Beyond the Pleasure Principle," in *The Standard Edition of the Complete Psychological Works of Sigmund Freud*, ed. James Strachey (London: Hogarth Press, 1955), 18:35.

4. Sidney was anointed by C. S. Lewis as "the man in whom the 'Golden' poetics, as by right, has become most fully articulate." C. S. Lewis, *English Literature in the Sixteenth Century, Excluding Drama* (Oxford: Oxford University Press, 1954), 346.

5. Durkheim's schema amounts to a kind of Aristotelian mean between excessive social integration that leads to egoistic suicide and its opposite complement in altruistic

suicide. Durkheim distinguishes "obligatory altruistic suicide" (where custom obliges one to kill oneself, as in Hindu customs for female widows, or warrior cultures where old age requires self-killing for honor) from other forms; this custom-driven obligation is directly relevant to Hebe's situation. *Suicide: A Study in Sociology* (1897), trans. John A. Spaulding and George Simpson, ed. George Simpson (New York: Free Press, 1951), 221.

6. Elizabeth Freeman, "Deep Lez: Temporal Drag and the Specters of Feminism," chap. 2 in *Time Binds: Queer Temporalities, Queer Histories* (Durham, NC: Duke University Press, 2010), 65.

7. Ross Lerner, *Unknowing Fanaticism: Reformation Literatures of Self-Annihilation* (New York: Fordham University Press, 2019), 81. For a formal linguistic analysis of the long trajectory of *imitatio Christi* into its present form as the phrase "What would Jesus do?," see Daniel Shore, "*WWJD?* and the History of *Imitatio Christi*," chap. 5 in *Cyberformalism: Histories of Linguistic Forms in the Archive* (Baltimore: Johns Hopkins University Press, 2018).

8. Bruce LaBruce, "Notes on Camp/Anti-Camp," public lecture at the Camp/Anti-Camp Conference at HAU Berlin, March 2012, http://www.natbrutarchive.com/essay-notes-on-campanti-camp-by-bruce-labruce.html.

9. Framed as a citation of Sontag's famous (and divisive) essay, which moved the term from its subcultural gay and lesbian circulation into visibility for the *Partisan Review* readership, the event arrived with its own readymade media campaign of explanation; see Bonnie Wertheim "What Is Camp? The Met Gala 2019 Theme, Explained," *New York Times*, May 4, 2019, https://www.nytimes.com/2019/05/04/style/met-gala-what-is-camp.html.

10. Christopher Isherwood, *The World in the Evening* (1953; repr., St. Paul: University of Minnesota Press, 2012), 10.

11. Susan Sontag, "Notes on 'Camp,'" in *Camp: Queer Aesthetics and the Performing Subject*, ed. Fabio Cleto (Edinburgh: Edinburgh University Press, 1999), 53. Subsequent citations from the essay will indicate simply the "note" number.

12. Sontag, note 14.

13. Sontag, note 26.

14. Sontag, notes 36, 38.

15. For more on the interruptive tempo of Sidney's plot and its basis in the ancient Greek novel in general and Heliodorus in particular, see Joseph Mansky, "'Variety' and Republican Violence in Sidney's *Arcadia*," *ELH* 86, no. 3 (2019): 587–613.

16. Katherine Duncan Jones, *Sir Philip Sidney: Courtier Poet* (London: Hamish Hamilton, 1991), 77.

17. Spenser quoted in Alan Stewart, *Sir Philip Sidney: A Double Life* (New York: St. Martin's Press, 2000), 223; Stanley quoted in Natasha Simonova, "'A Book That All Have Heard of... but That Nobody Reads': Sidney's *Arcadia* in the Eighteenth Century," *Journal of Medieval and Early Modern Studies* 50, no. 1 (2020): 145.

18. Heylyn's "Cosmograph of Arcadia in Greece" appears in *The Countess of Pembroke's Arcadia, written by Sir Philip Sidney, Knight. The Thirteenth edition. With his Life and Death; a brief Table of the principal Heads, and some other new Additions* (London: [Calvert], 1674), xxxii.

19. There are moments in academic life when an advisor and graduate student overlap in their interests to such an extent that their thinking dovetails. This is one such

case, for the chapter "Rape and Equity in Sidney's *Old Arcadia*" that appears in Connie Scozzaro's dissertation, "Cruel Intentions: Rape and Deliberation in the Time of Shakespeare" (Johns Hopkins University, 2019), informs my own reading of the sexual acts in Sidney's text as rapes. I anticipate the eventual publication of Scozzaro's work on Sidney as part of what will no doubt be a brilliant scholarly book.

20. Andrew D. Weiner, *Sir Philip Sidney and the Poetics of Protestantism: A Study of Contexts* (Minneapolis: University of Minnesota Press, 1978), 173.

21. For a radically transhistorical reflection on the question of style and the particular cases of Frank O'Hara and Thomas Wyatt, see Jeff Dolven, *Senses of Style: Poetry before Interpretation* (Chicago: University of Chicago Press, 2018).

22. Sir Philip Sidney, *The Countess of Pembroke's Arcadia (The Old Arcadia)*, ed. Katherine Duncan-Jones (Oxford: Oxford University Press, 1994), 252.

23. To clarify, Langley is not writing in hostile opposition to psychoanalysis so much as punting from the opportunity to stage an implied but optional work of historical dialogue with its formations: "Much of what follows has a Lacanian resonance, anticipating and ultimately informing post-Freudian ipseic models, but I am reluctant to approach the early modern text merely as embryonic or anticipatory." Eric Langley, *Narcissism and Suicide in Shakespeare and His Contemporaries* (Oxford: Oxford University Press, 2009), 6.

24. Freud, "Mourning and Melancholia," *Standard Edition*, 14:252.

25. See Robert E. Litman, "Sigmund Freud on Suicide" (1970), in *Essential Papers on Suicide*, ed. Johan T. Maltsberger and Mark J. Goldblatt (New York: New York University Press, 1996), 209.

26. John M. Cooper, "Greek Philosophers on Euthanasia and Suicide," in *Reason and Emotion: Essays on Ancient Moral Psychology and Ethical Theory* (Princeton, NJ: Princeton University Press, 1999), 531. See also Anton J. L. van Hoof, *From Autothanasia to Suicide: Self-Killing in Classical Antiquity* (London: Routledge, 1990).

27. For an account of Sidney's access to Greek texts, see Micha Lazarus, "Sidney's Greek Poetics," *Studies in Philology* 112, no. 3 (2015): 504–36.

28. Sidney, *Old Arcadia*, 252.

29. Blair Hoxby, "Simple Pathetic Tragedy," *What Was Tragedy: Theory and the Early Modern Canon* (Oxford: Oxford University Press, 2015), 114.

30. Sidney, *Old Arcadia*, 253.

31. Lauren Berlant and Sianne Ngai, "Comedy Has Issues," *Critical Inquiry* 43, no. 2 (2017): 234.

32. Jane Bennett, *Vibrant Matter: A Political Ecology of Things* (Durham, NC: Duke University Press, 2010).

33. Thomas Joiner, *Why People Die by Suicide* (Cambridge, MA: Harvard University Press, 2005), 46.

34. For the designation of the *Old Arcadia* as such a structure, see Elizabeth Dipple, "Harmony and Pastoral in the *Old Arcadia*," *ELH* 35, no. 3 (1968): 309–28.

35. Stephen Neale, *Genre* (London: British Film Institute, 1980), 28.

36. *The Complete Works of John Milton*, vol. 11, *Manuscript Writings*, ed. William Poole (Oxford: Oxford University Press, 2019), 123; Langley, *Narcissism and Suicide*, 201.

37. Sidney, *Old Arcadia*, 259.

38. Leah Whittington, *Renaissance Suppliants: Poetry, Antiquity, Reconciliation* (Oxford: Oxford University Press, 2016), 17.

39. Katrin Pahl, *Tropes of Transport: Hegel and Emotion* (Evanston, IL: Northwestern University Press, 2012).

40. Roland Wymer, *Suicide and Despair in the Jacobean Drama* (New York: St. Martin's Press, 1986), 96–110.

41. Debora Shuger, "Castigating Livy: The Rape of Lucretia and the *Old Arcadia*," *Renaissance Quarterly* 51, no. 2 (1998): 526.

42. Kate Manne, *Down Girl: The Logic of Misogyny* (Oxford: Oxford University Press, 2017), 196–204.

43. Dipple, "Harmony and Pastoral in the *Old Arcadia*," 309–11.

44. Elder Olson, *The Theory of Comedy* (Bloomington: Indiana University Press, 1968), 25.

45. Sidney, *Old Arcadia*, 266–67.

46. Though it is unwise to speculate past a certain threshold, the downward pressure of Sidney's classist mockery might be the obverse of his own shame at his own family's somewhat rocky financial position; in *Sir Philip Sidney: A Double Life* (New York: St. Martin's Press, 2000), Alan Stewart cites a letter to Leicester in which Sidney bemoans the expense of participation at court, noting Elizabeth's ignorance of his straits by wryly protesting that "she sees a silk doublet upon me and Her Majesty will think me in good case" (225).

47. Sidney, *Old Arcadia*, 193.

48. Fulke Greville quoted in Blair Worden, *The Sound of Virtue: Philip Sidney's "Arcadia" and Elizabethan Politics* (New Haven: Yale University Press, 1997), 362.

49. Robert E. Stillman, *Philip Sidney and the Poetics of Renaissance Cosmopolitanism* (London: Ashgate, 2008), 5.

50. See, e.g., Laurie Shannon, "Nature's Bias: Renaissance Homonormativity and Elizabethan Comic Likeness," *Modern Philology* 98, no. 2 (2000): 183–210; Valerie Traub, "The Quest for Origins, Erotic Similitude, and the Melancholy of *Lesbian* Identification," chap. 8 in *The Renaissance of Lesbianism in Early Modern England* (Cambridge: Cambridge University Press, 2002); Phyllis Rackin, "Androgyny, Mimesis, and the Marriage of the Boy Heroine on the English Stage," *PMLA* 102, no. 1 (1987): 836–58.

51. See, e.g., Philippa Berry, *Of Chastity and Power: Elizabethan Literature and the Unmarried Queen* (New York: Routledge, 1989); Ellen M. Caldwell, "John Lyly's *Gallathea*: A New Rhetoric of Love for the Virgin Queen," *English Literary Renaissance* 17, no. 1 (1987): 22–40; Leah Scragg, "The Victim of Fashion? Rereading the Biography of John Lyly," *Medieval and Renaissance Drama in England* 19 (2006): 210–26.

52. Andy Kesson, *John Lyly and Early Modern Authorship* (Manchester: Manchester University Press, 2014), 4.

53. Judith Butler, "Promiscuous Obedience," chap. 3 in *Antigone's Claim: Kinship between Life and Death* (New York: Columbia University Press, 2000).

54. Alex Woloch, *The One vs. the Many: Minor Characters and the Space of the Protagonist in the Novel* (Princeton, NJ: Princeton University Press, 2003), 12–13.

55. Sontag, "Notes on 'Camp,'" note 23.

56. Andy Kesson has called into question the availability and integrity of "comedy" as a category in pre-Shakespearean drama. "Was Comedy a Genre in English Early Modern Drama?" *British Journal of Aesthetics* 54, no. 2 (2014): 213–25.

57. Jacqueline Vanhoutte, "A Strange Hatred of Marriage: Elizabeth I, John Lyly, and the Ends of Comedy," *The Single Woman in Medieval and Early Modern England: Her Life*

and Representation, ed. Dorothea Kehler and Laurel Amtower (Tempe: Arizona Center for Medieval and Renaissance Studies, 2003), 98.

58. See Kesson, *John Lyly and Early Modern Authorship*, chap. 5.

59. M. C. Bradbrook "Artificial Comedy and Popular Comedy: Shakespeare's Inheritance," chap. 5 in *The Growth and Structure of Elizabethan Comedy* (London: Chatto and Windus, 1956), 65.

60. Lauren Berlant, *The Queen of America Goes to Washington City: Essays on Sex and Citizenship* (Durham, NC: Duke University Press, 1997), 223.

61. Though "drag" and "camp" overlap, they are not equivalent, as "camp" denotes a wide array of objects beyond subcultural stage performance. The problem of men's simultaneous emotional investment in and mockery of female icons within drag performance has occasioned critiques of drag-as-misogyny from within the radical-feminist tradition that are potentially relevant to this discussion. Consider Mary Daly's remark that "the phenomenon of the drag queen dramatically demonstrates... boundary violation. Like whites playing 'black face,' he incorporates the oppressed role without being incorporated in it." *Gyn/Ecology: The Metaethics of Radical Feminism* (Boston: Beacon Press, 1978), 48. This analogy erases the complex historical role played by queer people of color in the emergence of drag itself. For a more nuanced and historically sourced analysis, see C. Riley Snorton, *Black on Both Sides: A Racial History of Trans Identity* (Minneapolis: University of Minnesota Press, 2017).

62. See Richard Janko's introduction to his translation of Aristotle, *Poetics I, with the Tractatus Coislinianus* (Cambridge: Hackett, 1987).

63. Aristotle, *Poetics*, 6.

64. Ovid, *Metamorphosis*, trans. Frank Justus Miller, Loeb Classical Library 43 (Cambridge, MA: Harvard University Press, 1916), 227.

65. Pierre Grimal, "Hebe," in *The Dictionary of Classical Mythology*, trans. A. R. Maxwell-Hyslop (Oxford: Blackwell, 1986), 181.

66. John Lyly, *Galatea and Midas*, ed. G. K. Hunter and David Bevington (Manchester: Manchester University Press, 2000), 29; Peter Saccio, *The Court-Comedies of John Lyly: A Study in Allegorical Dramaturgy* (Princeton, NJ: Princeton University Press, 1969), 124–29.

67. John Lyly, *Galatea and Midas*, ed. Anne Begor Lancashire (Lincoln: University of Nebraska Press, 1969), 3. See also *Chambers Murray Latin-English Dictionary*, ed. Sir William Smith and Sir John Lockwood (Edinburgh: Chambers, 1933), s.v. "Hebe, hebes."

68. G. K. Hunter, *John Lyly: The Humanist as Courtier* (Cambridge, MA: Harvard University Press, 1962), 203.

69. Hunter, 204.

70. Cicero as quoted in *The Institutio Oratoria of Quintilian*, vol. 2, trans. H. F. Butler, Loeb Classical Library (Cambridge, MA: Harvard University Press, 1921), 401.

71. Sophocles quoted in Butler, *Antigone's Claim*, 9.

72. Charles de Saint-Évremond, "My Opinion of a Play Where the Heroine Does Nothing but Lament Herself," in *Dramatic Theory and Criticism: Greeks to Grotowski*, ed. Bernard F. Dukore (New York: Holt, Rinehart and Winston, 1974), 277.

73. Arthur Little Jr., "Altars of Alterity," in *Shakespeare Jungle Fever: National-Imperial Re-Visions of Race, Rape, and Sacrifice* (Stanford, CA: Stanford University Press, 2000), 3.

74. Adrian Johnston, *Time Driven: Metapsychology and the Splitting of the Drive* (Evanston, IL: Northwestern University Press, 2005), 176.

75. Sontag, "Notes on 'Camp,'" note 20.

76. Sontag, note 21.

77. As Michael Pincombe notes, "What happens at the sacrifice is unclear; but it seems to figure a rape of some kind, whether a *raptus*, or 'carrying off,' as the Augur says, or a sexual attack, as critics tend to think, and as Hebe seems to guess in her fear of being physically consumed by the Agar." "Galatea: We May All Love," in *The Plays of John Lyly: Eros and Eliza* (Manchester: Manchester University Press, 1996), 138.

78. Jill Stauffer, *Ethical Loneliness: The Injustice of Not Being Heard* (New York: Columbia University Press, 2015).

79. Marvin Herrick, *Comic Theory in the Sixteenth Century* (Urbana: University of Illinois Press, 1964), 46.

80. See Maebh Long, "'The Powerful Marvel of Irony': Derrida and the Structures of Irony," *Parallax* 20, no. 1 (2014): 83.

81. For a critical consideration of a countertradition of "feminist camp," see Pamela Robertson, *Guilty Pleasures: Feminist Camp from Mae West to Madonna* (Durham, NC: Duke University Press, 1996).

82. That said, humorous presentation is hardly the only way in which the phenomenon appears within the literature of the period; as Kim Solga's reading of the "in/visible act" makes clear, the archive is frequently the site not for the relay of violence against women but its structural effacement. *Violence against Women in Early Modern Performance: Invisible Acts* (London: Palgrave, 2009), 17.

83. Alastair Brotchie "Marly, Montjoie, and the Oak Tree Struck by Lighting," in *The Sacred Conspiracy: The Internal Papers of the Secret Society of Acéphale and Lectures to the College of Sociology*, ed. Marina Galletti and Alastair Brotchie (London: Atlas Press, 2017), 51.

84. Bataille, "Note to the Members of Acéphale," in Galletti and Brotchie, 382.

85. Bataille, "In Search of Joy in the Face of Death," in Galletti and Brotchie, 378.

86. "Suicide Statistics," American Foundation for Suicide Prevention, accessed July 16, 2020, https://afsp.org/suicide-statistics.

87. Global figures are hard to calibrate, but E. David Klonsky, Alexis May, and Boaz Saffer summarize recent World Health Organization data from 2012 as follows: "Suicidal behavior is a global cause of death and disability. Worldwide, suicide is the fifteenth leading cause of death, accounting for 1.4% of all deaths… In total, more than 800,000 people die by suicide each year. The annual global age-standardized death rate for 2012 is estimated to be 11.4 per 100,000, and the World Health Organization (WHO) projects this rate to remain steady through 2030." "Suicide, Suicide Attempts, and Suicidal Ideation," *Annual Review of Clinical Psychology* 12 (2016): 308.

88. Klonsky, May, and Saffer, 308.

89. This is the ratio discussed in Michael Macdonald, "The Inner Side of Wisdom: Suicide in Early Modern England," *Psychological Medicine* 7, no. 4 (1977): 565–82. Their collaborative book expands the range of examples considerably: see Michael MacDonald and Terence R. Murphy, *Sleepless Souls: Suicide in Early Modern England* (Oxford: Clarendon Press, 1990).

90. Edwidge Danticat, *The Art of Death: Writing the Final Story* (Minneapolis: Graywolf Press, 2017), 124.

Chapter Two

1. *Thelma and Louise*, directed by Ridley Scott (Los Angeles: MGM-Pathé, 1991); see also Becky Aikman, *Off the Cliff: How the Making of "Thelma and Louise" Drove Hollywood to the Edge* (New York: Penguin, 2017).

2. Michael Cobb, "The Inevitable Fatality of the Couple," chap. 1 in *Single: Arguments for the Uncoupled* (Durham, NC: Duke University Press, 2012). If all couples are fated to conclude, the timing and circumstances of how they conclude matter. The dark twin to the mutual suicide pact is the sadly common scenario of murder-suicide, in which a partner, usually male, murders their partner before taking their own life, thus violently enforcing the symmetry of the couple form. See Thomas Joiner, *The Perversion of Virtue: Understanding Murder-Suicide*, Oxford: Oxford University Press, 2014, 3–53.

3. Plutarch, *The Lives of the Noble Grecians and Romans Compared Together by That Grave, Learned Philosopher and Historiographer Plutarch of Chaeronea, Translated out of Greek into French by James Amyot and out of French into English by Thomas North* (1579; New York: Heritage Press, 1941), 2:1750. For a recent account of the performance issues generated by this ideal, see Lois Potter, "Assisted Suicides: 'Antony and Cleopatra' and 'Coriolanus,'" *Shakespeare Quarterly* 58, no. 4 (2007): 509–29. Though Janet Adelman only touches on *synapothanumenon* in a passing reference, she is the earliest critic that I can find to have considered the relation of the phrase to the play's broader generic instability, in *The Common Liar: An Essay on "Antony and Cleopatra"* (New Haven: Yale University Press, 1973). For a compelling tracing of an Ovidian grammar of self-reflection as it expresses itself in the pressurized ideal of *Romana mors* in the Roman plays, see Eric Langley, "*Romana mors* in *Julius Caesar*" and "*Romana mors* in *Antony and Cleopatra*," chaps. 4 and 5, respectively, in *Narcissism and Suicide in Shakespeare and His Contemporaries* (Oxford: Oxford University Press, 2009). For a recent biography of the monarch in question, see Stacy Schiff, *Cleopatra: A Life* (New York: Back Bay Books, 2010). For a transhistorical account of Cleopatra's recirculation across media, see Francesca T. Royster, *Becoming Cleopatra: The Shifting Image of an Icon* (London: Palgrave Macmillan, 2003).

4. *Poetae Comici Graeci*, vol. 5, *Damoxenus-Magnes*, ed. Rudolf Kassel and Colin Austin (Berlin: Walter de Gruyter, 1986), 71–80.

5. For more on the surrounding context in the history of ancient drama, see *The Birth of Comedy: Texts, Documents, and Art from Athenian Comic Competitions, 486–280*, ed. Jeffrey Rusten (Baltimore: Johns Hopkins University Press, 2011).

6. Here one might point out, by way of comparative example, that one of the most famous speech acts of decisive Roman machismo, Julius Caesar's declarative shrug "Alea iacto esto," was itself a citation of Greek comedy, quoting Menander's "Ἀνερρίφθω κύβος." See Plutarch, *Moralia*, trans. Frank Cole Babbitt (Cambridge, MA: Harvard University Press, 1931), 3.

7. *Ovid's Metamorphoses: The Arthur Golding Translation of 1567*, ed. John Frederic Nims (Philadelphia: Paul Dry Books, 2000), 216.

8. Brian Cummings, *Mortal Thoughts: Religion, Secularity, and Identity in Shakespeare and Early Modern Culture* (Oxford: Oxford University Press, 2013), 272.

9. Timothy Hill, *Ambitiosa Mors: Suicide and Self in Roman Thought and Literature* (London: Routledge, 2004), 1.

10. The emblem-book representation of Brutus from Geffrey Whitney's *Choice of*

Emblemes (1586), itself derived from the prior work of Andrea Alciato, illustrates the motto "Fortuna virtutem superans" (Fortune triumphant over virtue) while suppressing any representation of assistance in favor of solitary suicidal heroics.

11. *The Complete Works of Shakespeare*, ed. David Bevington (New York: Pearson, 2013). All subsequent references to both *Julius Caesar* and *Antony and Cleopatra* are from this edition unless otherwise stated.

12. See Potter, "Assisted Suicides," 509-29.

13. Richard A. Cohen, ed. "Dialogue with Emmanuel Levinas," *Face to Face with Levinas* (New York: SUNY Press, 1986), 23-24.

14. The question of how to understand the relationship between Levinas's account of the face as ethical foundation and the phenomenological experience of encountering actual faces is fraught, and the object of much discussion and debate in Levinas scholarship. See Levinas's remark that "ethics is an optics" as quoted in Laura Wayrick, "Facing Up to the Other: Race and Ethics in Levinas and Behn," *The Eighteenth Century* 40, no. 3 (1999): 212; see also Jill Robbins, "*Visage, Figure*: Reading Levinas's *Totality and Infinity*," *Yale French Studies*, no. 79 (1991): 139.

15. For an account of the changing legal history of euthanasia legislation and the policy problem of assisted dying, see Penney Lewis, *Assisted Dying and Legal Change* (Oxford: Oxford University Press, 2007).

16. Terry Williams, *Teenage Suicide Notes: An Ethnography of Self-Harm* (New York: Columbia University Press, 2017), xiv.

17. See Michael MacDonald and Terence R. Murphy, *Sleepless Souls: Suicide in Early Modern England* (Oxford: Clarendon Press, 1990), 42-76.

18. See Mary Nyquist, "Ancient Greek and Roman Slaveries," chap. 1 in *Arbitrary Rule: Slavery, Tyranny, and the Power of Life and Death* (Chicago: University of Chicago Press, 2013). For the subsequent rearticulation of the slavery/suicide/captivity nexus across the Atlantic, see Terri Snyder, *The Power to Die: Slavery and Suicide in British North America* (Chicago: University of Chicago Press, 2015), chaps. 1 and 3.

19. Nyquist, *Arbitrary Rule*, chap. 1.

20. See K. R. Bradley, *Slaves and Masters in the Roman Empire: A Study in Social Control* (Oxford: Oxford University Press, 1987), 135; M. I. Finley, *Ancient Slavery and Modern Ideology*, ed. B. D. Shaw (Princeton, NJ: Markus Wiener, 1998); Peter Garnsey, *Ideas of Slavery from Aristotle to Augustine* (Cambridge: Cambridge University Press, 1996).

21. See Orlando Patterson, *Freedom in the Making of Western Culture* (New York: Basic Books, 1991), chap. 1.

22. Maurice Charney, *Shakespeare's Roman Plays: The Function of Imagery in the Drama* (Cambridge, MA: Harvard University Press, 1961), 209.

23. Gilles Deleuze, *Nietzsche and Philosophy*, trans. Hugh Tomlinson (New York: Columbia University Press, 2006), 129. See also Moritz Gansen, "'Everywhere There Are Sad Passions': Gilles Deleuze and the Unhappy Consciousness," chap. 1 in *Deleuze and the Passions*, ed. Ceciel Meiborg and Sjoerd Van Tuinen (Santa Barbara, CA: Punctum Books, 2016).

24. Schiff, *Cleopatra*, 371.

25. Emily R. Wilson, *Mocked with Death: Tragedies of Overliving from Sophocles to Milton* (Baltimore: Johns Hopkins University Press, 2004), 12.

26. *Castelvetro on the Art of Poetry*, trans. Andrew Bongiorno (Binghamton: Center

242 Notes to Pages 72-76

for Medieval and Early Renaissance Studies, State University of New York at Binghamton, 1984), 216.

27. See Wylie Sypher "The Guises of the Comic Hero," in *Comedy* (Baltimore: Johns
Hopkins University Press, 1956), 228.

28. Adelman, *The Common Liar*, 119. Having set up that comparison, Adelman later
grants that the age of the central lovers is an "implicit reversal of the Menandrian pattern" (139) of young lovers against an old, rigid world. Richard Strier goes further, aligning the charismatic force of Antony with Falstaff, and taking the age, wisdom, and experience of both to embody a countermoralizing Nietzschean argument for the aesthetics
of personality and against the chilly Aristotelian ethics of the mean. "Against Morality:
Richard III to *Antony and Cleopatra*," chap. 3 in *The Unrepentant Renaissance: From Pe-
trarch to Shakespeare to Milton* (Chicago: University of Chicago Press, 2012).

29. Ray L. Heffner Jr. "The Messengers in Shakespeare's 'Antony and Cleopatra,'"
ELH 43, no. 2 (1976): 154–62.

30. John Milton, "Lycidas," in *Complete Poems and Major Prose*, ed. Merritt Hughes
(New York: Odyssey Press, 1957), 122.

31. For a sociological account of data on the causal force of "vicarious habituation,"
see Thomas Joiner, *Why People Die by Suicide* (Cambridge, MA: Harvard University
Press, 2005), 68–78.

32. In some productions, the "not dead?" line itself is cut, but the audience still re-
acts with laughter purely due to Antony's vexed and surprising situation; see the London production of *Antony and Cleopatra*, directed by Jonathon Munby (London: Shakespeare's Globe, 2014), DVD.

33. Seneca, "On the Proper Time to Slip the Cable," in *Epistles 66–92*, trans. Richard M. Gummere, Loeb Classical Library 76 (Cambridge, MA: Harvard University
Press, 1920), 70.

34. See David Read, "Disappearing Act: The Role of Enobarbus in 'Antony and
Cleopatra,'" *Studies in Philology* 110, no. 33 (2013): 562–83.

35. See, for example, Peter Paul Rubens, *The Death of Seneca* (1612–15), in the Alte
Pinakothek, Munich; a reproduction from his studio can be found in the Prado. The
vogue for such representations carried on past the period, and is perhaps epitomized by
the competition between Jacques-Louis David and Jean-François-Pierre Peyron, each
of whom submitted a *Death of Seneca* for the Prix de Rome in 1773. Peyron's winning
entry is lost. See James Ker, "Tracing the Tradition," chap. 7 in *The Deaths of Seneca* (Oxford: Oxford University Press, 2009).

36. E. M. Cioran, *The Trouble with Being Born*, trans. Richard Howard (New York:
Seaver Books, 1977), 32.

37. Langley, *Narcissism and Suicide*, 23.

38. I am grateful to Maggie Vinter for encouraging me to address this after reading
an early draft.

39. "If seen as part of the action of the play, the contest of genres explains the conflict of interpretations which the play has generated." Barbara Vincent, "Shakespeare's
'Antony and Cleopatra' and the Rise of Comedy," *English Literary Renaissance* 12, no. 1
(1982): 60.

40. Kim F. Hall, *Things of Darkness: Economies of Race and Gender in Early Modern England* (Ithaca, NY: Cornell University Press, 1995), 153–54; for a consideration
of the apparent textual tension between the Queen's offer of her "blewest veins" and

her black skin, see the introduction to *Race in Early Modern England: A Documentary Companion*, ed. Ania Loomba and Jonathan Burton (London: Palgrave, 2007), 16. For a reading of ways that racialization was extended beyond the somatic and into the disciplinary regimes of conduct manuals and cultural codes of behavior, see Patricia Akhimie, *Shakespeare and the Cultivation of Difference: Race and Conduct in the Early Modern World* (London: Routledge, 2018). See also Melissa E. Sanchez, "Was Sexuality Racialized for Shakespeare? Antony and Cleopatra," chap. 9 in *The Cambridge Companion to Shakespeare and Race*, ed. Ayanna Thompson (Cambridge: Cambridge University Press, 2021).

41. Arthur Little Jr., "Re(posing) with Cleopatra," in *Shakespeare Jungle Fever: National-Imperial Re-Visions of Race, Rape, and Sacrifice* (Stanford: Stanford University Press, 2000), 165.

42. Geraldine Heng, "The Invention of Race in the European Middle Ages I: Race Studies, Modernity, and the Middle Ages," *Literature Compass* 8, no. 5 (2011): 262.

43. Connections between the comedic and the rural would have drawn suggestive support from Aristotle's disputed etymological claim in the *Poetics* regarding the derivation of the word for comedy from a Dorian word meaning "village." *Oxford English Dictionary*, 2nd ed. (1989), s.v. "comedy," accessed July 8, 2020, https://www-oed-com .proxy1.library.jhu.edu/.

44. *OED*, s.v. "slapstick," accessed July 10, 2020, https://www-oed-com.proxy1 .library.jhu.edu/.

45. See Hill, *Ambitiosa Mors*, chap. 8.

46. Isaiah Berlin, *Liberty: Incorporating Four Essays on Liberty*, ed. Henry Hardy (Oxford: Oxford University Press, 2002).

47. *Plutarch's Lives*, 2:1010.

48. Bevington, introduction to *Antony and Cleopatra*, 75. For more on the production history of the play, see Richard Madelaine, ed., *Antony and Cleopatra*, Shakespeare in Production (Cambridge University Press, 1998), 310–15. Sometimes played with a red nose, sometimes delivered in a sinister whisper, the scene remains a strong challenge to staging. As Madelaine puts it: "Some reviewers have been wary of the episode itself, as at odds with modern taste" (315).

49. North's Plutarch clarifies that Cleopatra stages an elaborate testing of possible means of death through a gruesome series of experiments on condemned men: "So when had daily made divers and sundry proofs, she found none of all them she had proved so fit as the biting of an aspic; the which only causeth a heaviness of the head, without swounding or complaining, and bringeth a great desire also to sleep, with a little sweat on the face, and so by little and little taketh away the sense and vital powers, no living creature perceiving that the patients feel any pain." *Plutarch's Lives*, 2:1750–51.

50. It also jogs our memory of her prophetic earlier remark: "Now I feed myself / With most delicious poison" (1.5.26–27).

51. *Plutarch's Lives*, 2:99–100.

52. Paul A. Kottman, "To Defy the Stars: Tragic Love as the Struggle for Freedom in *Romeo and Juliet*," *Shakespeare Quarterly* 63, no. 1 (2012): 1–38.

53. Walter Benjamin, "Fate and Character," in *Selected Writings*, ed. Marcus Bullock and Michael W. Jennings (Cambridge, MA: Belknap Press of Harvard University Press, 2004), 1:205.

54. For a less flippant consideration of the intersection of staging Cleopatra's death

at present with the archive of "sati" in India, see Dorothea Kehler, "Cleopatra's *Sati:* Old Ideologies and Modern Stagings," chap. 4 in *Antony and Cleopatra: New Critical Essays*, ed. Sara Munson Deats (New York: Routledge, 2005).

55. David Hershinow, "Diogenes the Cynic and Shakespeare's Bitter Fool: The Politics and Aesthetics of Free Speech," *Criticism* 56, no. 4 (2014): 807–35.

56. Joiner, *Why People Die by Suicide*, 46.

57. Emma Phipson, *The Animal-Lore of Shakespeare's Time* (1883; Glastonbury: The Lost Library, 2011), 317.

58. Ania Loomba, *Shakespeare, Race, and Colonialism* (Oxford: Oxford University Press, 2002), 50–51; for more on the contemporary concept of "misogynoir," see Moya Bailey, *Misogynoir Transformed: Black Women's Digital Resistance* (New York: New York University Press, 2021), chap. 1.

59. The contrast between a Christianity for which self-killing is sinful and an ancient world that occasionally celebrated this free act should not be reified and oversimplified, given the deep thread within the mystic traditions of Christianity that embraces the will to die, which will surface in later chapters of this book. See "Life No Life," in *The Poems of St. John of the Cross*, trans. John Frederick Nims (Chicago: University of Chicago Press, 1959), 21.

60. As quoted in Jacques Rolland's annotations to *On Escape*, by Emmanuel Levinas, trans. Bettina Bergo (Stanford: Stanford University Press), 91.

61. Drew Daniel, "The Empedoclean Renaissance," in *The Return of Theory in Early Modern English Studies*, vol. 2, ed. Paul Cefalu, Gary Kuchar, and Bryan Reynolds (London: Palgrave Macmillan, 2014), 277–300.

62. Mary Beth Rose, "Suicide as Profit or Loss," *Shakespeare in Our Time: A Shakespeare Association of America Collection*, ed. Dympna Callaghan and Suzanne Gossett (New York: Bloomsbury Arden Shakespeare, 2016), 80.

63. The image of the soul as joined to the body by a knot pervades vernacular literature. I distinguish the "nodo" of constraint (a falconry image) in *Purgatorio*, canto 24, from the image of death as "disnodi" in *Paradiso*, canto 31. *The Divine Comedy of Dante Alighieri*, vol. 3, *Paradiso*, trans. Robert M. Durling (Oxford: Oxford University Press, 2011), 625.

64. Roland Barthes, *Mythologies*, trans. Annette Laver (New York: Farrar, Straus and Giroux, 1972), 116.

65. The topic has attracted substantial critical attention of late, most decisively in David Schalkwyk's foundational declaration that "Shakespeare's mimetic art depends in the deepest sense of the word on the conjunctive play of love and service." *Shakespeare, Love, and Service* (Cambridge: Cambridge University Press, 2008), 1.

66. "Of Death," in *Francis Bacon: The Major Works*, ed. Brian Vickers (Oxford: Oxford University Press, 1996), 343.

67. Elder Olson, *The Theory of Comedy* (Bloomington: Indiana University Press, 1968), 25.

68. See, for example, Vincent, "Shakespeare's 'Antony and Cleopatra' and the Rise of Comedy"; see also Peter Erickson, "Identification with the Maternal in *Antony and Cleopatra*," in *Patriarchal Structures in Shakespeare's Drama* (Berkeley: University of California Press, 1985), 123. Gender is often used to sunder the generic difference; this is the core argument of Linda Bamber, *Comic Women, Tragic Men: A Study of Gender and Genre in Shakespeare* (Stanford, CA: Stanford University Press, 1981).

69. For a reading of the threat posed to Cleopatra's stage-managed death by that extemporizing comedic improvisation, see J. K. Barret, "Improvised Futures: Absent Art and Improvised Rhyme in *Cymbeline* and *Antony and Cleopatra*," chap. 5 in *Untold Futures: Time and Literary Culture in Renaissance England* (Ithaca, NY: Cornell University Press, 2016).

70. Dirk Wildgruber et al., "Different Types of Laughter Modulate Connectivity within Distinct Parts of the Laughter Perception Network," PLOS ONE 8, no. 5 (2013): e63441, https://doi.org/10.1371/journal.pone.0063441.

71. I am not the first critic to detect this comedic resonance within the tragedy; for an earlier example, see Susan Snyder, *The Comic Matrix of Shakespeare's Tragedies: "Romeo and Juliet," "Hamlet," "Othello," "King Lear"* (Princeton, NJ: Princeton University Press, 1979), 166–68.

72. *The History of King Lear*, in *The Norton Shakespeare*, 3rd ed., ed. Stephen Greenblatt et al. (New York: W. W. Norton, 2015), 2452. All quotations from *King Lear* are from the Quarto text unless otherwise indicated.

73. For a contrary view, see Harry Levin's claim that the bareness of the Shakespearean stage would mean that the audience would not realize that the cliff was not present until the landing. "The Heights and the Depths: A Scene from *King Lear*," in *More Talking of Shakespeare*, ed. John Garrett (London: Longmans, 1959), 97–99. Levin's reading seems to me to only hold up until Edgar's aside, which generates in my view a dynamic of complicity and distance.

74. Rosemarie Garland-Thomson, *Staring: How We Look* (Oxford: Oxford University Press, 2009).

75. Snyder, *Comic Matrix*, 166.

76. Susan Snyder, citing George C. Odell's *Shakespeare from Betterton to Irving* (1920), notes that "Nineteenth-century productions regularly omitted Gloucester's ineffectual leap, bringing Lear on early to forestall it." *Comic Matrix*, 166.

77. *From Hand to Mouth*, directed by Alf. Goulding (Los Angeles: Rolin, 1919).

78. The painful overdetermination of such a performance, coming as it does in the wake of the damage inflicted by blackface minstrelsy traditions, indexes Ayanna Thompson's insight that "performing blackness is still a white property that uneasily sits on black bodies." "What Is the Legacy of Blackface? The Impact on Black Actors," chap. 6 in *Blackface*, Object Lessons (New York: Bloomsbury, 2021), 94.

79. Peter Erickson and Kim Hall, "'A New Scholarly Song': Rereading Early Modern Race," *Shakespeare Quarterly* 67, no. 1 (2016): 2. See also the essays that follow in that special issue by Urvashi Chakravarty, Vanessa Corredera, Ruben Espinosa, Kyle Grady, Arthur L. Little Jr., Ian Smith, and Sandra Young.

80. I take the term "predatory inclusion" from Keeanga-Yamahtta Taylor, *Race for Profit: How Banks and the Real Estate Industry Undermined Black Homeownership* (Chapel Hill: University of North Carolina Press, 2019).

Chapter Three

1. Andy Kesson, "Galatea, BritGrad, and Diverse Alarums," Before Shakespeare, June 4, 2018, https://beforeshakespeare.com/2018/06/04/galatea-britgrad-and-diverse-alarums/.

2. "The sexual aversion which Hamlet expresses in conversation with Ophelia is

perfectly consistent with this deduction—the same sexual aversion which during the next few years was increasingly to take possession of the poet's soul, until it found its supreme utterance in *Timon of Athens.*" "The Interpretation of Dreams," in *The Standard Edition of the Complete Psychological Works of Sigmund Freud*, ed. James Strachey (London: Hogarth Press, 1953), 4:265.

3. In terms of sheer mayhem, the most dangerous subsidiary form of trolling is probably "swatting," the name for a hoax in which trolls determine someone's home address and then call police officers and describe a violent crime in process so that a SWAT team conducts a raid on the location. This practice has resulted in fatalities, as in the case in Wichita, Kansas, described by Matt Stevens and Andrew R. Chow, "Man Pleads Guilty to 'Swatting' Hoax That Resulted in Fatal Shooting," *New York Times*, November 13, 2018, https://www.nytimes.com/2018/11/13/us/barriss-swatting-wichita.html.

4. For an archived column from the first wave of its passage into mainstream cultural familiarity, see Ed Zotti, "What Is a Troll?," *Straight Dope*, April 14, 2000, http://www.straightdope.com/columns/read/1764/what-is-a-troll.

5. For a complex analysis of schadenfreude, see David Carroll Simon, "The Anatomy of Schadenfreude, or Montaigne's Laugher," *Critical Inquiry* 43, no. 2 (2017): 250–81.

6. I am grateful to former student Elvin Meng, whose suggestions about the cultural history of trolling helped me frame this chapter.

7. Cicero, *Orator*, 21.71, as cited in Marvin Herrick, *Comic Theory in the Sixteenth Century* (Urbana: University of Illinois Press, 1964), 140.

8. For more on decorum see Herrick, 140. See also Patricia Akhimie, *Shakespeare and the Cultivation of Difference: Race and Conduct in the Early Modern World* (London: Routledge, 2018), 55.

9. Rosemond Tuve, "The Criterion of Decorum," in *Elizabethan and Metaphysical Imagery: Renaissance Poetics and Twentieth-Century Critics* (Chicago: University of Chicago Press, 1947), 195.

10. Tuve, 196.

11. This is obvious enough and yet embarrassing to say, particularly for English professors who see themselves as tasked both with the expansion of the capacity for sympathetic identification across differences *and* with sharpening the writing skills of students for a job market that places a premium upon not-so-secretly raced and classed rigors of professionalization. Are we in the business of imaginatively translating across sociocultural and historical differences or in the business of transmitting the monocultural skill sets and reference points required to diminish difference as such? Who is included in this Shakespearean "we" in the first place?

12. For an account of the world of play in which we see "the eclipse of action by activity," see Richard Halpern, *Eclipse of Action: Tragedy and Political Economy* (Chicago: University of Chicago Press, 2017), 158. For the pervasive citation of conventions drawn from humanist education, and Hamlet's own "attachment to the letter of humanist convention," see Rhodri Lewis, *Hamlet and the Vision of Darkness* (Princeton, NJ: Princeton University Press, 2017), 174.

13. For a curious essay on the topic of the imbrication of theatricality into the everyday "life of Man," see Lowell L. Manfull, "The Histrionic Hamlet," *Educational Theater Journal* 16, no. 2 (1964): 103–14.

14. Kathy Eden, *Poetic and Legal Fiction in the Aristotelian Tradition* (Princeton, NJ: Princeton University Press, 1986), 180.

15. See Virgil Whitaker, *The Mirror up to Nature: The Technique of Shakespeare's Tragedies* (San Marino, CA: Huntington Library, 1965).

16. Russ Leo, "John Rainolds, *Hamlet*, and the Anti-Theatrical Aristotle," chap. 3 in *Tragedy as Philosophy in the Reformation World* (Princeton, NJ: Princeton University Press, 2019), 123, 144.

17. George Garnett, ed., *Vindiciae, contra Tyrannos: or, Concerning the Legitimate Power of a Prince over the People, and of the People over a Prince* (Cambridge: Cambridge University Press, 2003); J. G. A. Pocock, "The Concept of a Language and the *Métier d'Historien*: Some Considerations on Practice," chap. 1 in *The Languages of Political Theory in Early-Modern Europe*, ed. Anthony Pagden (Cambridge: Cambridge University Press, 1987).

18. Thomas Hobbes, *Leviathan, or, The Matter, Form, and Power of a Common-Wealth Ecclesiastical and Civil* (London: [Crooke], 1651), 95.

19. For more on tyranny and cruelty in Shakespeare, see Stephen Greenblatt, *Tyrant: Shakespeare on Politics* (New York: W. W. Norton, 2018), 45–46, 53–66.

20. Peter Mercer, "*Thyestes* and Revenge Structure," in *Hamlet and the Acting of Revenge* (Iowa City: University of Iowa Press, 1987), 28.

21. For the complex intersection of felo-de-se rulings with *Hamlet*, see Luke Wilson, "Hamlet, Hale v. Petit, and the Hysteresis of Action," *ELH* 60 (1993): 17–55.

22. Ernest Jones, *Hamlet and Oedipus* (New York: W. W. Norton, 1949).

23. See *Ovid's Metamorphoses: The Arthur Golding Translation of 1567*, ed. John Frederic Nims (Philadelphia: Paul Dry Books, 2000), 173–81.

24. For more on the circulation of this wedding as a source in early modern literature, see Jessica Wolfe, *Homer and the Question of Strife from Erasmus to Hobbes* (Toronto: University of Toronto Press, 2015), 233.

25. George MacDonald quoted in William Shakespeare, *Hamlet*, ed. Ann Taylor and Neil Thompson (London: Arden Shakespeare, 2006), 430.

26. *The Complete Works of Ben Jonson*, ed. C. H. Herford and Percy Simpson (Oxford: Oxford University Press, 1925), 8:587.

27. See Whitney Phillips, "LOLing at Tragedy: Facebook Trolls, Memorial Pages, and the Business of Mass-Mediated Disaster Narratives," chap. 5 in *This Is Why We Can't Have Nice Things: Mapping the Relationship between Online Trolling and Mainstream Culture* (Cambridge, MA: MIT Press, 2016). For a brief critique of Phillips's analysis that contests the idea that such behavior is a kind of social critique, see Rebecca Greenfield, "RIP Trolling as Social Critique," *The Atlantic*, December 15, 2011, https://www.theatlantic.com/technology/archive/2011/12/rip-trolling-social-critique/334207/.

28. Phillips, "LOLing at Tragedy."

29. Angela Nagle, *Kill All Normies: Online Culture Wars from 4Chan and Tumblr to Trump and the Alt-Right* (London: Zero Books, 2017), 33–34.

30. I take the term "group form" from Kris Cohen, *Never Alone, Except for Now: Art, Networks, Populations* (Durham, NC: Duke University Press, 2017).

31. Nagle, *Kill All Normies*, 33–34.

32. Phillips, "LOLing at Tragedy," 27–37.

33. For more on the ethnography of the white male incel persona (though it arguably occludes the relationship between this persona and white supremacy), see the independently released documentary *TFW No GF*, directed by Alex Lee Moyer (2020). The racialized re-vision of the Central Park Five case and the shooting by Bernhard Goetz—

incidents that are both cited and sublated in the Todd Phillips film *Joker* (2019)—was analyzed by Richard Brody in "'Joker' Is a Viewing Experience of Rare, Numbing Emptiness," *New Yorker*, October 3, 2019, https://www.newyorker.com/culture/the-front-row/joker-is-a-viewing-experience-of-rare-numbing-emptiness.

34. Phillips, "LOLing at Tragedy," 1.

35. Samuel Butler quoted in Wolfe, *Homer and the Question of Strife*, 113.

36. James J. Marino, "Ophelia's Desire," *ELH* 84, no. 4 (2017): 823.

37. For more on the shaky impact of *The Mousetrap* on its spectators, see a searching reading of the play by Ellen MacKay, "Tyrannical Drama," chap. 2 in *Persecution, Plague, and Fire: Fugitive Histories of the Stage in Early Modern England* (Chicago: University of Chicago Press, 2011), esp. 58.

38. Amanda Bailey, "*Timon of Athens*, Forms of Payback, and the Genre of Debt," chap. 1 in *Of Bondage: Debt, Property, and Personhood in Early Modern England* (Philadelphia: University of Pennsylvania Press, 2013); G. Wilson Knight, "The Pilgrimage of Hate: An Essay on *Timon of Athens*," chap. 10 in *The Wheel of Fire: Interpretations of Shakespearian Tragedy* (Oxford: Oxford University Press, 1930); William Empson, "Timon's Dog," chap. 8 in *The Structure of Complex Words* (1951; Cambridge, MA: Harvard University Press, 1989); Julia Reinhard Lupton, "Job of Athens, Timon of Uz," chap. 4 in *Thinking with Shakespeare: Essays on Politics and Life* (Chicago: University of Chicago Press, 2011); James Kuzner, "Looking Two Ways at Once in *Timon of Athens*," chap. 5 in *Shakespeare as a Way of Life* (New York: Fordham University Press, 2016); Eike Kronshage, "Conspicuous Consumption, Croyance, and the Problem of the Two Timons: Shakespeare and Middleton's *Timon of Athens*," *Critical Horizons* 18, no. 3 (2017): 262–74.

39. See J. G. A. Pocock, *The Machiavellian Moment: Florentine Political Thought and the Atlantic Republican Tradition* (Princeton, NJ: Princeton University Press, 1975), 451.

40. Phil A. Neel, *Hinterland: America's New Landscape of Class and Conflict* (London: Reaktion Books, 2018), 55.

41. Jonathan Lear, "Death," in *Happiness, Death, and the Remainder of Life* (Cambridge, MA: Harvard University Press, 2000), 65.

42. Lear, 66.

43. Henri Bergson, *Laughter: An Essay on the Meaning of the Comic*, trans. Cloudesley Brereton and Fred Rothwell (New York: Macmillan, 1911), 109–15.

44. John Dollard, "The Dozens: Dialectic of Insult," in *Mother Wit from the Laughing Barrel: Readings in the Interpretation of Afro-American Folklore*, ed. Alan Dundes (Jackson: University Press of Mississippi, 1973), 277–94.

45. For more on this dynamic, see David Hershinow, *Shakespeare and the Truth-Teller: Confronting the Cynic Ideal* (Edinburgh: Edinburgh University Press, 2019).

46. See Hans Robert Jauss, "The Paradox of the Misanthrope," *Comparative Literature* 35, no. 4 (1983): 309.

47. Karl A. Menninger, "Psychoanalytic Aspects of Suicide," chap. 2 in *Essential Papers on Suicide*, ed. Johan T. Maltsberger and Mark J. Goldblatt (New York: New York University Press, 1996).

48. Seneca, *De ira* (*Of Anger*), in *Moral Essays*, vol. 1, *De Providentia. De Constantia. De Ira. De Clementia*, trans. John W. Basore, Loeb Classical Library 214 (Cambridge, MA: Harvard University Press, 1928), 295.

49. Cicero, "On the Contempt of Life," in *Tusculan Disputations*, trans. J. E. King, Loeb Classical Library 141 (Cambridge, MA: Harvard University Press, 1927), 99.

50. Cicero, 99.

51. Philip Massinger, *The Bond-Man, an Antient Storie*, in *The Plays and Poems of Philip Massinger*, ed. Philip Edwards and Colin Gibson (Oxford: Clarendon Press, 1976), 1:359.

52. Paz quoted in Luis Buñuel, "The Cinema: An Instrument of Poetry," *New York Film Bulletin*, February 1961, 112.

53. A. E. Housman "I Counsel You Beware," in *The Poems of A. E. Housman*, ed. Archie Burnett (Oxford: Clarendon Press, 1997), 130.

54. Aaron Kunin, *Character as Form* (New York: Bloomsbury, 2019), 129.

55. Baruch Spinoza, *Ethics*, trans. Edwin Curley (New York: Penguin, 1994), E4p18s.

56. For more on assemblage theory, see Gilles Deleuze and Felix Guattari, *A Thousand Plateaus: Capitalism and Schizophrenia*, trans. Brian Massumi (Minneapolis: University of Minnesota Press, 1987); Manuel DeLanda, *A New Philosophy of Society: Assemblage Theory and Social Complexity* (London: Continuum, 2006); and Drew Daniel, introduction to *The Melancholy Assemblage: Affect and Epistemology in the English Renaissance* (New York: Fordham University Press, 2013), esp. 7-11.

57. Steve Mentz, *At the Bottom of Shakespeare's Ocean* (London: Continuum, 2009), xii.

58. Sigmund Freud, *Civilization and Its Discontents*, in *Standard Edition*, 21:59-145.

59. Romain Rolland, "La sensation océanique: Une lettre à Sigmund Freud," *Psychanalyse YETU*, no. 43 (2019): 22.

60. Freud, *Civilization and Its Discontents*, 65.

61. Taylor and Thompson, *Hamlet*, 176.

62. For a reading of this mermaid transformation in dialogue with Michael Drayton's *Poly-Olbion*, see Tara Pedersen's afterword to her monograph on early modern mermaids: "'Drown'd? O! Where?': The Mermaid and the Map in Shakespeare's *Hamlet*," in *Mermaids and the Production of Knowledge in Early Modern England* (London: Routledge, 2016), 123-38.

63. *Selections from Johnson on Shakespeare*, ed. Bertrand H. Bronson and Jean O'Meara (New Haven: Yale University Press, 1986), 345.

64. Jacques Lacan, "Desire and the Interpretation of Desire in Hamlet," ed. Jacques-Alain Miller and trans. James Hulbert, *Yale French Studies*, no. 55/56 (1977): 11.

65. Here again I must mark a point of intersection in thinking between myself and a graduate student. I am indebted to Royce Best for reflections upon the "access to rhetoricity" of Ophelia, a theme he develops in a chapter of his dissertation, "Crip Estrangement: Shakespeare, Disability, Metatheatre" (Johns Hopkins University, 2021); the eventual publication of this strikingly imaginative project will advance our understanding of Ophelia's agency.

66. Alison A. Chapman, "Ophelia's 'Old Lauds': Madness and Hagiography in *Hamlet*," *Medieval and Renaissance Drama in England* 20 (2007): 111-35.

67. The tub in which Siddal posed was warmed by candles set beneath, but one day "Millais was so absorbed by his work that during one session he allowed the candles to go out, and when some friends saved the model from the chilly water she was close to pneumonia." Elizabeth Bronfen, *Over Her Dead Body: Death, Femininity, and the Aesthetic* (New York: Routledge, 1992), 169.

68. Published in the midst of national protests against a wave of incidents in which police killed black people with impunity, this opinion piece should be situated in the

broader journalistic climate in which expertise in Shakespeare is solicited by editorial teams to do a universalizing work; the titling of such opinion pieces is not necessarily up to their authors, but, regardless, its circulation indicates the force of a standing expectation about the universalizability of Shakespeare as author and *Hamlet* as narrative structure. Gary Taylor, "What Hamlet Can Teach Us about Black Lives Matter," *Tampa Bay Times*, June 14, 2020, https://www.tampabay.com/opinion/2020/06/14/what-hamlet-can-teach-us-about-black-lives-matter-column/.

69. There are many places to see this process at work. Margreta de Grazia's polemical *"Hamlet" without Hamlet* (Philadelphia: University of Pennsylvania Press, 2007) was a crucial intervention in widening the gap between character and play; subtracting Hamlet from the critical discourses of nineteenth-century philosophical critique and psychological typology and their twentieth-century inheritors, de Grazia's text attempted to change how we read *Hamlet* and downgraded the titular character's importance relative to the play that surrounds and explains him. At a wider angle, a number of ongoing efforts to push back against the ambient bardolatry within early modern drama studies as a field have inevitably reconsidered both Shakespeare's preeminence and the hold of *Hamlet* within the study of Shakespeare. Notable attempts to widen the array of texts under consideration include the Before Shakespeare project of Andy Kesson and others, Jeremy Lopez's monograph *Constructing the Canon of Early Modern Drama* (Cambridge: Cambridge University Press, 2014), and, more recently, *The Routledge Anthology of Early Modern Drama* (London: Routledge, 2020). Both within the play and without it, when the topic of Hamlet arises there is, I think, a shared and understandable desire to change the subject.

70. For an account of the mediating role of Hamlet's whiteness in its status as preeminent object of critical identification for a still mostly white early modern studies professoriate, see Ian Smith, "We Are Othello: Speaking of Race in Early Modern Studies," *Shakespeare Quarterly* 67, no. 1 (2016): 107.

71. For more on the complex question of how a movement can crystallize around a phrase and connect an array of political, economic, and policy demands, see Keeanga-Yamahtta Taylor, "Black Lives Matter: A Movement, Not a Moment," chap. 6 in *From #BlackLivesMatter to Black Liberation* (Chicago: Haymarket Books, 2016).

72. Saidiya Hartman, *Lose Your Mother: A Journey along the Atlantic Slave Route* (New York: Farrar, Straus and Giroux, 2008), 6.

73. It has been salutary to witness the scholarly sea change on this issue across the eight years in which I have worked on this manuscript; across that span, a flood of publications has emerged, a flurry of conferences and events have taken place, and a newly energized and sharply critical dialogue has emerged to address the role that premodern studies might play in connecting past archives to present struggles for social justice. A single footnote cannot hope to contain the entirety of these welcome developments, and it is a telling index of the sheer proliferation of the field of premodern critical-race studies that it has been accompanied by collectively generated bibliographies, as in the crowdsourced gathering of work in "Early Modern Race/Ethnic/Indigenous Studies" archived at https://docs.google.com/document/d/1AaMp1al8y715FklUq1x5scqBHYS9QpzvMzgYU_ZyFow/edit (accessed June 18, 2021).

For a critical assemblage of comparable work in medieval studies on premodern race, see Jonathan Hsy and Julie Orlemanski, "Race and Medieval Studies: A Partial Bibliography," *postmedieval* 8, no. 4 (2017): 500–531. For more on RaceB4Race events, publications and public conversations, see the Arizona Center for Medieval and Renaissance Studies website, accessed June 18, 2021. URL: https://acmrs.asu.edu/RaceB4Race.

74. This is also why I have not, in citing the studies of this behavior, included the proper names of any of the original individual targets of RIP troll "raids" upon memorial pages; given the ease of connection and recirculation that is now customary due to keyword searches, I do not want to replicate and compound harm done.

Chapter Four

1. Donne quoted in Michael Rudick and M. Pabst Battin's introduction to John Donne, *Biathanatos: A Modern-Spelling Edition*, ed. Rudick and Battin (New York: Garland, 1982), xv.

2. See Ernest Sullivan's introduction to John Donne, *Biathanatos*, ed. Sullivan (1604; Newark: University of Delaware Press, 1984), ix–xxx (hereafter cited as *BT*). The textual-editing hurdles in assessing *Biathanatos* are acute, as the text is bifurcated into a Bodleian manuscript copied out for Herbert and a posthumous 1674 quarto edition. In an acerbic critique of Sullivan's edition, W. Speed Hill discusses the textual situation in his article "John Donne's *Biathanatos*: Authenticity, Authority, and Context in Three Editions," *John Donne Journal* 6, no. 1 (1987): 109–33. Speed alleges that Donne continued to work on the text after creating the copy for Edward Herbert, which renders the differences in 1647 at least provisionally authorial. I cite Sullivan because his edition retains original spellings, but have consulted both Sullivan's and Rudick and Battin's editions in this chapter and indicate when that edition is being cited.

3. Donne, *BT*, 1.

4. See Adam Kitzes, "Paradoxical Donne: *Biathanatos* and the Problems of Political Assimilation," *Prose Studies* 24, no. 3 (2001): 1–17.

5. For a consideration of the case for the text as a paradox, see Ernest Sullivan II, "The Paradox: *Biathanatos*," in *The Oxford Handbook of John Donne*, ed. Dennis Flynn, M. Thomas Hester, and Jeanne Shami (Oxford: Oxford University Press, 2011), 155. That said, genre criticism of Donne has largely avoided *Biathanatos*; despite Rosalie Colie's interest in the work, the text is absent from *Donne and the Resources of Kind*, ed. A. D. Cousins and Damian Grace (Madison, NJ: Fairleigh Dickinson Press, 2002).

6. Rosalie Colie, *Paradoxia Epidemica: The Renaissance Tradition of Paradox* (Princeton, NJ: Princeton University Press, 1966), 499.

7. Camille Wells Slights, "John Donne as Casuist," in *The Casuistical Tradition in Shakespeare, Donne, Herbert, and Milton* (Princeton, NJ: Princeton University Press, 1981), 139.

8. Eric Langley, *Narcissism and Suicide in Shakespeare and His Contemporaries* (Oxford: Oxford University Press, 2009), 218.

9. Sullivan, "The Paradox: *Biathanatos*," 155.

10. See Arthur J. Droge and James D. Tabor, *A Noble Death: Suicide and Martyrdom among Christians and Jews in Antiquity* (San Francisco: Harper, 1992), 5.

11. Augustine, *Concerning "The City of God," against the Pagans*, trans. John O'Meara (New York: Penguin Books, 1972), 39.

12. David Novak, *Suicide and Morality* (New York: Scholars Studies Press, 1975), 68.

13. For a contrary claim, based upon the very Aquinas quotation that Donne will himself come to cite, that Christ's suicide was more like an "open secret" of theology

than a hidden and heterodox view, see Lucio Biasiori, "The Exception as Norm: Casuistry of Suicide in John Donne's *Biathanatos*," chap. 8 in *A Historical Approach to Casuistry: Norms and Exceptions in a Comparative Perspective*, ed. Carlo Ginzburg, with Lucio Biasiori (London: Bloomsbury, 2019).

14. As Roland Wymer puts it, "It is an important aspect of Donne's thoroughgoing intentionalist position that there is no real moral difference between acts of omission and acts of commission, between allowing oneself to be killed and actually killing oneself." *Suicide and Despair in the Jacobean Drama* (New York: St. Martin's Press, 1986), 18.

15. Donne, *BT*, 129–30.

16. Archibald E. Malloch, "Donne and the Casuists," *Studies in English Literature, 1500–1900* 2, no. 1 (1962): 68 (my italics).

17. Hill, "John Donne's *Biathanatos*," 116.

18. Donne quoted in Hill, 117.

19. Christine Hoffman, *Stupid Humanism: Folly as Competence in Early Modern and Twenty-First-Century Culture* (London: Palgrave, 2017), 4–5.

20. Donne, *BT*, 129–30.

21. For a nuanced account of Donne's relationship to Augustine in particular, see Katrin Ettenhuber, *Donne's Augustine: Renaissance Cultures of Interpretation* (Oxford: Oxford University Press, 2011), esp. 137–63.

22. Thomas Aquinas, from "Summa Theologiae: Whether One Is Allowed to Kill Himself," in *The Ethics of Suicide: Historical Sources*, ed. Margaret Pabst Battin (Oxford: Oxford University Press, 2015), 228–30.

23. Biasiori, "The Exception as Norm," 161.

24. Donne, *BT*, 130.

25. For an overview of the typology of cases, "officer-involved shootings," and their relation to mental health from the (highly situated) perspective of law-enforcement officers, see Alejandra Jordan, Nancy R. Panza, and Charles Dempsey, "Suicide by Cop: A New Perspective on an Old Phenomenon," *Police Quarterly* 23, no. 1 (2020): 82–105.

26. Huey P. Newton, *Revolutionary Suicide* (New York: Penguin, 2009), 3. For an analysis of the concept's literary circulation, see Katy Ryan, "Revolutionary Suicide in Toni Morrison's Fiction," *African American Review* 34, no. 3 (2000): 389–412.

27. See Droge and Tabor, *A Noble Death*, 113–29.

28. Robert Esposito, *Communitas: The Origin and Destiny of Community*, trans. Timothy Campbell (Stanford, CA: Stanford University Press, 2009), 138.

29. Note the domino-like timing of these articles as a consensus is generated about his causal centrality: Robert F. Worth, "How a Single Match Can Ignite a Revolution," *New York Times*, January 21, 2011, https://www.nytimes.com/2011/01/23/weekinreview/23worth.html; Lin Noueihed, "Peddler's Martyrdom Launched Tunisia's Revolution," Reuters, January 19, 2011, https://www.reuters.com/article/us-tunisia-protests-bouazizi/peddlers-martyrdom-launched-tunisias-revolution-idUSTRE70J1DJ20110120; Ivan Watson and Jomana Karadsheh, "The Tunisian Fruit Seller Who Kickstarted Arab Uprising," CNN, March 22, 2011, http://edition.cnn.com/2011/WORLD/meast/03/22/tunisia.bouazizi.arab.unrest/.

30. Edward W. Said, *Covering Islam: How the Media and the Experts Determine How We See the Rest of the World* (New York: Vintage, 1997).

31. In this sense, the response to Bouazizi's self-immolation inherited the epistemological deadlock surrounding terrorist actions—are they cases of "suicide" or "mar-

tyrdom," and who decides which term fits? As Mohammed Hafez notes in his introduction to *Manufacturing Human Bombs: The Making of Palestinian Suicide Bombers* (Washington, DC: United States Institute for Peace, 2006), "How one describes acts of self-immolation committed in order to kill others is a task fraught with controversy. Those who support these acts of violence prefer to call them 'martyrdom operations,' and their perpetrators 'heroes' and 'freedom fighters.' Those who oppose them prefer to call them 'homicide bombers,' 'suicide terrorists' or 'suicidal murderers'" (4). Bouazizi only killed himself, and this makes his act altogether distinct, and yet the ambient contest over semantics particular to suicide-terrorism recurred within the debates surrounding his suicidal exemplarity.

32. Ross Lerner, *Unknowing Fanaticism: Reformation Literatures of Self-Annihilation* (New York: Fordham University Press, 2019), 60.

33. Lerner, 61.

34. Lerner, 80.

35. Jean-Luc Nancy, *The Inoperative Community*, trans. Peter Connor et al. (St. Paul: University of Minnesota Press, 1991), 14–15.

36. John Donne, *Selected Prose*, ed. Neil Rhodes (London: Penguin, 1987), 10–11.

37. "If we may accept as an observation without exception that every living being dies for internal reasons, returning to the inorganic, then we can only say that the goal of all life is death, and, looking backward, that the nonliving existed before the living." Sigmund Freud, *Beyond the Pleasure Principle*, ed. Todd Dufresne, trans. Gregory C. Richter (Buffalo, NY: Broadview Press, 2011), 77.

38. "Death's Duell," in *The Oxford Edition of the Sermons of John Donne*, vol. 3, *Sermons Preached at the Court of Charles I*, ed. David Colclough (Oxford; Oxford University Press, 2014), 235–36.

39. Jane Bennett, *Vibrant Matter: A Political Ecology of Things* (Durham, NC: Duke University Press, 2010).

40. Ramie Targoff, *John Donne: Body and Soul* (Chicago: University of Chicago Press, 2008), 217.

41. Targoff, 217.

42. T. S. Eliot, "Whispers of Immortality," in *Collected Poems, 1909–1962* (New York: Harcourt, Brace, 1963), 45.

43. Margaret Pabst Battin, "Religious Views of Suicide," in *Ethical Issues in Suicide* (Upper Saddle River, NJ: Prentice-Hall, 1995), 27.

44. Donne, *BT*, 130.

45. Andrew Escobedo, *Volition's Face: Personification and the Will in Renaissance Literature* (Notre Dame, IN: University of Notre Dame Press, 2017), 79.

46. *Bishop's Bible* (London: [Robert Barker], 1616).

47. I am grateful to Seth Sanders for pointing out this possible reading.

48. Donald Friedman, "Christ's Image and Likeness in Donne," *John Donne Journal* 15 (1996): 75.

49. Targoff, *John Donne*, 1.

50. John Milbank, *Being Reconciled: Ontology and Pardon* (London: Routledge, 2003), ix.

51. *Sermons of John Donne*, 3:244.

52. Esposito, *Communitas*, 11.

53. Talal Asad, *On Suicide Bombing* (New York: Columbia University Press, 2007), 3.

Interlude

1. The phrase "As long as there is death, there is hope" was in fact emblazoned upon the tombstone of the Holocaust survivor and outré nightclub performer Brother Theodore (Theodore Gottlieb), who described his act as "stand-up tragedy." Douglas Martin, "Theodore Gottlieb, Dark Comedian, Dies at 94," *New York Times*, April 6, 2001, http://www.nytimes.com/2001/04/06/obituaries/06THEO.html.

2. For more on Browne's lexis and its context in period dictionaries, see Daniela Havenstein "'Suicide' and Other Words in *Religio Medici* and its Imitations," in *Democratizing Sir Thomas Browne* (Oxford: Clarendon Press, 1999), 173–98.

3. Brian Barraclough and Daphne Shepherd, "A Necessary Neologism: The Origin and Uses of 'Suicide,'" *Suicide and Life-Threatening Behavior* 24, no. 2 (1994): 113–26.

4. Jonathan F. S. Post, "Browne's Revisions of *Religio Medici*," *Studies in English Literature, 1500–1900* 25, no. 1 (1985): 145–63.

5. Post, 145–48.

6. Post, 152.

7. Barraclough and Shepherd, "A Necessary Neologism," 114.

8. Charleton's text also uses "Self-murder" and the rare form "self-homicide"; though it is not clear to me whether his insertion of a hyphen ("Sui-Cide") is authorial or a printer's decision, this formal choice and the capitalization of the word's components suggest a kind of typographic desire to assist the reader with a novel word. With its canny retelling of "The Widow of Ephesus" story from Petronius, Charleton's work solicits a stance toward self-destruction that is, itself, libertine; self-destruction is what people say they will do before they think of a more pleasurable outcome. Walter Charleton, *The Ephesian Matron* (London: [Herringman], 1659). Daube influentially alleged that this appearance was the coinage of "suicide" in a public lecture in 1970, but this was disproven. Awkwardly, his own article crediting Charleton with the coinage was published in 1972, after A. Alvarez's book establishing an earlier date for Browne's usage had appeared in print. For more on Charleton, see Margaret J. Osler, "Descartes and Charleton on Nature and God," *Journal of the History of Ideas* 40 (1979): 445–56.

9. A. Alvarez, *The Savage God: A Study of Suicide* (London: Weidenfeld and Nicolson, 1971).

10. Post, "Browne's Revisions of *Religio Medici*," 145–49; Reid Barbour, *Sir Thomas Browne: A Life* (Oxford: Oxford University Press, 2013), 43. Suggesting the syncretic mixture of influences that Browne absorbed from his tutor Lushington, Barbour summarizes: "Browne was interweaving the same tendencies toward probing skepticism, Platonism, and doctrinal flexibility that Lushington and Jackson had modeled, but he never wholly abandoned the Calvinist doctrine that he had imbibed as a boy in London" (83).

11. Browne quoted in Post, "Browne's Revisions of *Religio Medici*," 149.

12. Roland Greene, "Invention," in *Five Words: Critical Semantics in the Age of Shakespeare and Cervantes* (Chicago: University of Chicago Press, 2013), 40.

13. Thomas Blount, *Glossographia, or, A dictionary interpreting all such hard words of whatsoever language now used in our refined English tongue with etymologies, definitions and historical observations on the same: also the terms of divinity, law, physick, mathematicks and other arts and sciences explicated by T. B.* (London: [Newcombe], 1656).

14. Edward Phillips, *The new world of English words, or, A general dictionary containing the interpretations of such hard words as are derived from other languages… together with all those terms that relate to the arts and sciences: To which are added the significations of proper names, mythology, and poetical fictions, historical relations, geographical descriptions of most countries and cities of the world* (London: [Tyler], 1658).

15. For an assessment of these coinages and contemporary appreciation of Browne, see Colin Burrow, review of *The Adventures of Sir Thomas Browne in the 21st Century*, by Hugh Aldersey-Williams, *The Guardian*, May 21, 2015, https://www.theguardian .com/books/2015/may/21/the-adventures-of-sir-thomas-browne-in-the-21st-century -hugh-aldersey-williams-review.

16. Michael MacDonald and Terence R. Murphy, *Sleepless Souls: Suicide in Early Modern England* (Oxford: Clarendon Press, 1990), 1–109.

17. Johnson quoted in Barraclough and Shepherd, "A Necessary Neologism," 119.

18. Barraclough and Shepherd, 123.

19. MacDonald and Murphy, *Sleepless Souls*, 144–76.

20. MacDonald and Murphy, 132–36; See also Georges Minois, *History of Suicide: Voluntary Death in Western Culture*, trans. Lydia G. Cochrane (Baltimore: Johns Hopkins University Press, 1995), 59–86.

21. *Religio Medici*, section 44, in *The Works of the Learned Sir Thomas Browne, Knight, Doctor of Physick, late of Norwich* (London: [Brome], 1686), 23–24.

22. Stanley E. Fish, "The Bad Physician: The Case of Sir Thomas Browne," chap. 7 in *Self-Consuming Artifacts: The Experience of Seventeenth-Century Literature* (Berkeley: University of California Press, 1972).

23. For more on Lucan, Stoicism, and the Vulteius story, see Francesca D'Alessandro Behr, *Feeling History: Lucan, Stoicism, and the Poetics of Passion* (Columbus: Ohio State University Press, 2007), 39. See also Barbour, *Sir Thomas Browne*, 45.

24. "A Custom of the Island of Cea" (1573), in *The Complete Essays of Montaigne*, trans. Donald R. Frame (Stanford, CA: Stanford University Press, 1958), 251–62.

25. Browne's engagement pro and contra Stoic arguments recapitulates an ambient tension within the approaches toward antiquity modeled within his education at Winchester College, tensions Reid Barbour aptly terms "two potentially competing approaches to the past, one skeptical and critical, the other commemorative and reverential." *Sir Thomas Browne*, 37.

26. Margaret Pabst Battin, *Ending Life: Ethics and the Way We Die* (Oxford: Oxford University Press, 2005), 169.

27. *The Poems of St. John of the Cross*, trans. Willis Barnstone (New York: New Directions, 1972), 62.

28. For more on the emotional restraint expected of surgeons and doctors in the period, see Linda Payne, *With Words and Knives: Learning Medical Dispassion in Early Modern England* (London: Routledge, 2016).

29. Snoop Dogg's phrase appears in his guest verse on Lil Duval's single "Smile (Living My Best Life)," also featuring Ball Greezy and Midnight Star (Rich Broke Entertainment, 2018).

30. Martin, "Theodore Gottlieb."

31. Debora Shuger, "The Laudian Idiot," chap. 2 in *Sir Thomas Browne: The World Proposed*, ed. Reid Barbour and Claire Preston (Oxford: Oxford University Press, 2008).

Chapter Five

1. Anne Boyer, "Not Writing," in *Garments against Women* (Boise, ID: Ahsahta Press, 2015), 7.

2. A. E. Housman, "Terence, this is stupid stuff," *A Shropshire Lad* (1896; New York: John Lane, 1906), 33.

3. Thomas Joiner, *Myths about Suicide* (Cambridge, MA: Harvard University Press 2010), 31. Perhaps because of its practical orientation toward treatment across all kinds of environments in which people might interact with at-risk individuals (hospitals, schools, workplaces, etc.), acronyms proliferate in suicidology; a case in point is ICARE, which is "a technique for restructuring negative thoughts," and denotes "I" (identification), "C" (connection of the thought to cognitive distortion), "A" (assessment of the basis of the thought), "R" (restructuring), and the perhaps infelicitously chosen "E" (execute, as in "act in ways that logically flow from the restructured thought"). Thomas Joiner, *Why People Die by Suicide* (Cambridge, MA: Harvard University Press, 2005), 214–15.

4. Edward Gorey's book is a principal exhibit of the poetic combination of comedy with violent death that can still generate a kind of subsidiary pathos in the midst of mockery; from the gloom of "N is for Neville who died of ennui" to the "Z is for Zillah who drank too much gin," the microscale and Edwardian stylization make this abecedary of mortality increasingly funny. *The Gashlycrumb Tinies* (New York: Harcourt, 1963).

5. See E. David Klonsky, Alexis M. May, and Boaz Y. Saffer, "Suicide, Suicide Attempts, and Suicidal Ideation," *Annual Review of Clinical Psychology* 12 (2016): 307–30.

6. *Paradise Lost*, in *The Complete Poetry and Essential Prose of John Milton*, ed. William Kerrigan, John Rumrich, and Stephen M. Fallon (New York: Modern Library, 2007), 517. All following citations of Milton are from this edition unless otherwise noted, and will consist of book and line number unless otherwise indicated.

7. Emily R. Wilson, "'Why Do I Overlive?': *Paradise Lost*," chap. 8 in *Mocked with Death: Tragic Overliving from Sophocles to Milton* (Baltimore: Johns Hopkins University Press, 2004).

8. Wilson, 170.

9. In "*Paradise Lost* and the D-Word," Annabel Patterson notes the striking frequency in the poem of the word "Death," which appears 120 times (in comparison with "Adam" at 88 times and "Eve" at 95). In *Milton's Words* (Oxford: Oxford University Press, 2009), 95–96.

10. For more on this curious crossing point of *Paradise Lost* and *Samson Agonistes*, see Mary Nyquist, "Textual Overlapping and Dalilah's Harlot-Lap," in *Renaissance Texts and Literary Theory*, ed. Patricia Parker and David Quint (Baltimore: Johns Hopkins University Press, 1986), 140–72.

11. This is the spirit in which the line is glossed by the editors of Dartmouth's *Milton Reading Room*: "Adam wishes for his substance to become earth once again; as a return to Mother Earth" (https://milton.host.dartmouth.edu/reading_room/pl/book_10/text.shtml). The line is not glossed by Gordon Teskey in the 2005 Norton edition, nor is it glossed by Merritt Y. Hughes in the 1957 Odyssey Press edition.

12. Glasser as summarized by Fiona Gardner in *Self-Harm: A Psychotherapeutic Approach* (New York: Brunner-Routledge, 2001), 10.

13. See Carl A. P. Ruck, "Poets, Philosophers, Priests: Entheogens in the Formation of the Classical Tradition," part 2 of *Persephone's Quest: Entheogens and the Origins of Religion*, by R. Gordon Wasson et al. (New Haven: Yale University Press, 1986).

14. Kay Redfield Jamison, *Night Falls Fast: Understanding Suicide* (New York: Vintage Books, 1999), 107.

15. Jamison, 107.

16. Diane McColley, *Milton's Eve* (Chicago: University of Chicago Press, 1983), 208.

17. The media picked up a story from physician Ira Chasnoff, distorting the significant overlap between prematurity and the supposed behavioral indexes of the effects of maternal cocaine use. "Crack Babies: A Tale from the Drug Wars," *New York Times*, May 20, 2013, https://www.nytimes.com/video/booming/100000002226828/crack-babies-a-tale-from-the-drug-wars.html.

18. Dennis Kezar, "Shakespeare's Addictions," *Critical Inquiry* 30, no. 1 (2003): 31–62.

19. Nicola Masciandaro, "The Sorrow of Being," *Qui Parle* 19, no. 1 (2010): 9–35.

20. Addison quoted in Stephanie Hershinow, *Born Yesterday: Inexperience and the Early Realist Novel* (Baltimore: Johns Hopkins University Press, 2019), 19.

21. The image of the belly as both womb and site of hunger has already appeared in the hellhound offspring bursting from Sin's body in 2.654.

22. Stephen Fallon, "Milton's Sin and Death: The Ontology of Allegory in *Paradise Lost*," *ELR* 17, no. 3 (1987): 329–50.

23. "Seminar 14: Wednesday, 13 March, 1963," in *The Seminar of Jacques Lacan: Anxiety, 1962–1963*, trans. Cormac Gallagher (Eastbourne, UK: Antony Rowe, 2012), 164–66.

24. Jonathan Lear notes, "Anxiety is a general preparedness for an unnamed threat; fear is that preparedness directed to a particular object or situation." *Happiness, Death, and the Remainder of Life* (Cambridge, MA: Harvard University Press, 2000), 72.

25. David Benatar, *Better Never to Have Been: The Harm of Coming into Existence* (Oxford: Oxford University Press, 2008).

26. Benatar, 223–24.

27. The Voluntary Human Extinction Movement (VHEMT) consists of a single website, which follows through upon its species-wide ambitions by offering translations of its core ideas in a bewildering array of global languages, including Volapük.

28. VHEMT (website), accessed May 3, 2021, http://www.vhemt.org/.

29. "Is This Another One of Those Suicide Cults?," VHEMT, accessed May 3, 2021, http://www.vhemt.org/death.htm#suicide.

30. While this book was in production, I learned of Urvashi Chakravarty's completion of a manuscript on slavery and servitude in early modern literature in which she also addresses the intersection of anti-natalist thinking and Milton's poem. See the chapter titled "Faithful Covenant Servants and Inbred Enemies: Indenture and Natality in *Paradise Lost*," in Chakravarty, *Fictions of Consent: Slavery, Servitude, and Free Service in Early Modern England* (Philadelphia: University of Pennsylvania Press, forthcoming).

31. "The destructive character is young and cheerful." Benjamin quoted in Irving Wohlfarth, "No Man's Land: On Walter Benjamin's 'Destructive Character,'" *Diacritics* 8, no. 2 (1978): 47.

32. Stanley Fish, *How Milton Works* (Cambridge, MA; Harvard University Press, 2001), 572.

33. Neil D. Graves, "Typological Aporias in *Paradise Lost*," *Modern Philology* 104, no. 2 (2006): 173.

34. Gordon Teskey, *Delirious Milton: The Fate of the Poet in Modernity* (Cambridge, MA: Harvard University Press, 2006).

35. David Hume, "On Suicide," in *On Suicide* (London: Penguin, 2005), 1–12.

36. Hume, 2.

37. *The Complete Works of John Milton*, vol. 8, *De Doctrina Christiana, Part 1*, ed. John K. Hale and J. Donald Cullington (Oxford: Oxford University Press, 2012), 413.

38. For an assessment of the attribution controversies concerning Dante's authorship of the epistle, see Robert Hollander, *Dante's Epistle to Cangrande* (Ann Arbor: University of Michigan Press, 1993), 1–7. For my purposes, what matters is that the epistle was taken to be authorial in the early modern period.

39. Roy Baumeister, "Suicide as Escape from Self," *Psychological Review* 97, no. 1 (1990): 90–113.

40. Jesse Bering, *Suicidal: Why We Kill Ourselves* (Chicago: University of Chicago Press, 2018), 89–90.

41. Rory C. O'Connor and Olivia J. Kirtley, "The Integrated Motivational-Volitional Model of Suicidal Behaviour," *Philosophical Transactions B* 373, no. 1754 (2018), https://www.ncbi.nlm.nih.gov/pmc/articles/PMC6053985/; see also Shuang Li et al., "Entrapment as a Mediator of Suicide Crises," *BMC Psychiatry* 18 (2018), https://bmcpsychiatry.biomedcentral.com/articles/10.1186/s12888-018-1587-0.

42. Aaron T. Beck et al., "An Inventory for Measuring Depression," *Archives of General Psychiatry* 4, no. 6 (1961): 561–71.

43. Joiner, *Why People Die by Suicide*, 39.

44. Dora Perczel Forintos, Judit Sallai, and Sandor Rósza, "Adaptation of the Beck Hopelessness Scale in Hungary," *Psychological Topics* 19, no. 2 (2010): 307–21.

45. Lauren Berlant, *Cruel Optimism* (Durham, NC: Duke University Press, 2011), 24.

46. Excerpted in John Milton, *Paradise Lost*, ed. Gorden Teskey (New York: W. W. Norton, 2005), 331.

47. Excerpted in Milton (Teskey ed.), 342.

48. Joiner, *Why People Die by Suicide*, 34.

49. Yiyun Li, *Dear Friend, from My Life I write to You in Your Life* (New York: Random House, 2017), 144. I am indebted to Nan Da for the suggestion to examine this text.

50. David Carroll Simon, "The Paradise Without: John Milton in the Garden," in *Light without Heat: The Observational Mood from Bacon to Milton* (Ithaca, NY: Cornell University Press, 2018), 169.

51. For an account of the conflict between philosopher Peter Singer and lawyer Harriet McBryde Johnson, see Harriet McBryde Johnson, "Unspeakable Conversations," *New York Times Magazine*, February 16, 2003, https://www.nytimes.com/2003/02/16/magazine/unspeakable-conversations.html.

52. Thomas E. Kottke et al., "Validating a Method to Assess Disease Burden from Insurance Claims," *Journal of Managed Care* 25, no. 2 (2019): 39–44.

53. For an account of the Muñoz/Edelman debate, see Drew Daniel, "Trading Futures: Queer Theory's Anti-Anti-Relational Turn," *Criticism* 52, no. 2 (2011): 325–30.

54. Lee Edelman, "The Future Is Kid Stuff," in *No Future: Queer Theory and the Death Drive* (Durham, NC: Duke University Press, 2004), 27.

55. For an account of anger's relation to the epic tradition as remobilized within the

poem generally, see Gordon Braden, "Epic Anger," *Milton Quarterly* 23, no. 1 (1989): 28–34.

56. I take the phrase "exorbitant desires" from Marshall Grossman's chapter of the same name, where it largely designates the nondialectical extremity of the fallen angels as forces of resistance to inclusion in divine order. "Exorbitant Desires," chap. 2 in *"Authors to Themselves": Milton and the Revelation of History* (Cambridge: Cambridge University Press, 1987).

57. There is, of course, a very extensive critical literature on these debates. See Bonnie Steinbock, *Life before Birth: The Moral and Legal Status of Embryos and Fetuses* (Oxford: Oxford University Press, 1992); David Boonin, *A Defense of Abortion* (Cambridge: Cambridge University Press, 2003); Jim Stone, "Why Potentiality Matters," *Canadian Journal of Philosophy* 17, no. 4 (1987): 815–29.

58. Cameron Awkward-Rich quoted in Hil Malatino, *Trans Care* (Minneapolis: University of Minnesota Press, 2020), 4.

59. For an account of "Milton's use of both orthodox and unconventional biblical typology in his portrayal of the Son" in the poem, see Graves, "Typological Aporias in *Paradise Lost*," 174.

60. Joseph Horrell, "Milton, Limbo, and Suicide," *Review of English Studies* 18, no. 72 (1942): 419.

61. John Milton, "Sonnet XIX: When I Consider…," in *Complete Poems and Major Prose*, ed. Merritt Y. Hughes (New York: Odyssey Press, 1957), 168.

62. Seneca quoted in Wilson, "Why Do I Overlive?," 199.

63. Henry Howard, Earl of Surrey, "The Means to Attain Happy Life," in *Poetical Works of Henry Howard, Earl of Surrey*, ed. Robert Bell (London: John W. Parker and Son, 1854), 86.

64. "at tredpida et coeptis immanibus effera Dido, / sanguineam volvens aciem, maculisque trementis / interfusa genas, et pallida morte futura, / interiora domus inrumpit limina, et altos / conscendit furibunda rogos, ensemque recludit / Dardanium, non hos quaesitum munus in usus." (But Dido, trembling and frantic with her dreadful design, rolling bloodshot eyes, her quivering cheeks flecked with burning spots, and pale at the imminence of death, bursts into the inner courts of the house, climbs the high pyre in a frenzy and unsheathes the Dardanian sword, a gift sought for no such purpose.) Virgil, *Aeneid*, book 4, in *Eclogues. Georgics. Aeneid, Books 1–6*, Loeb Classical Library 63, trans. H. Rushton Fairclough, rev. G. P. Goold (Cambridge, MA: Harvard University Press, 1916), 466–67. Pallor abounds in Milton's Latin poetry; as a case in point, consider the description of the Sibyls in "Ad Patrem": "tremulae pallentes ora Sibylae." Kerrigan, Rumrich, and Fallon, *Complete Poetry and Essential Prose of John Milton*, 220.

65. David Quint, *Inside "Paradise Lost": Reading the Designs of Milton's Epic* (Princeton, NJ: Princeton University Press, 2014), 200, 221.

66. David Adkins, "Weeping for Eve: Dido in *Paradise Lost* and Humanist Commentary," *Studies in Philology* 116, no. 1 (2019): 164.

67. Thomas Rogers, *A Philosophicall Discourse Entituled the Anatomie of the Minde Newlie made and set forth by T. R.* (London: [Mausell], 1576).

68. Rogers, 15.

69. Ian Smith, "We Are Othello: Speaking of Race in Early Modern Studies," *Shakespeare Quarterly* 67, no. 1 (2016): 107.

70. Eve's pallor in the midst of the contemplation of death also aligns her with Adam

standing "astonied... and blank" (9.890) at the moment of the Fall; I am indebted to Sharon Achinstein for pointing out this resemblance.

71. For an ambitious argument examining the way that, according to the article's abstract, "Milton remade white identity into the racially unmarked category of universal liberal personhood," via a reading of the Hamitic curse in *Paradise Lost*, see Daniel Shore, "Was Milton White?," *Milton Studies* 62, no. 2 (2020): 252–65.

72. "Milton," in *The Lives of the Poets*, vols. 21–23 of *The Yale Edition of the Works of Samuel Johnson*, ed. John H. Middendorf (New Haven: Yale University Press, 2010), 21:189.

73. Gordon Teskey, "On the Sublime in *Paradise Lost*," in *The Poetry of John Milton* (Cambridge, MA: Harvard University Press, 2015), 414.

74. Sianne Ngai, "Stuplimity," chap. 6 in *Ugly Feelings* (Cambridge, MA: Harvard University Press, 2005).

75. Jessie Hock, "The Mind Is Its Own Place: Lucretian Moral Philosophy in *Paradise Lost*," in *Milton's Modernities: Poetry, Philosophy, and History from the Seventeenth Century to the Present*, ed. Feisal G. Mohamed and Patrick Fadely (Evanston, IL: Northwestern University Press), 67.

76. Katrin Pahl, *Tropes of Transport: Hegel and Emotion* (Evanston, IL: Northwestern University Press, 2012), 152–81.

77. Jennifer Michael Hecht, *Stay: A History of Suicide and the Arguments Against It* (New Haven: Yale University Press, 2013), 234.

78. Writing in the afterword to the important new collection *Milton's Modernities* (2017), Sharon Achinstein notes that its contributors "move away from both poles of work dominating professional Milton studies today, namely theodicy and historical, materialist analysis." "Suddenly Emergent Milton," in Mohamed and Fadely, *Milton's Modernities*, 352. Such movements constitute what I am calling the "edge" rather than the "citadel" of Milton studies. Poems are complex documents of conflict and emotional change, fashioned by the regulative force of a given artist's own author function, faith, and intentions, but mobile across time as we return to them and read them in a changing world.

79. Michael MacDonald and Terence R. Murphy, *Sleepless Souls: Suicide in Early Modern England* (Oxford: Clarendon Press, 1990), 109–44.

80. Brian Cummings, *Mortal Thoughts: Religion, Secularity, and Identity in Shakespeare and Early Modern Culture* (Oxford: Oxford University Press, 2013), 318.

Chapter Six

1. As Robert Otten puts it: "After its first performance in April 1713, it ran for thirty nights, an unprecedented performance for the time. One contemporary caught the popular opinion when he hailed *Cato* as the first 'perfect piece' upon the English stage for many years." *Joseph Addison* (Boston: Twayne, 1982), 141. Otten notes that, despite Addison's Whig affiliation, both Tories and Whigs found components of the play that were imagined to be amenable to their politics, perhaps adding to its popularity.

2. Christopher Celenza, "Cato the Younger," in *The Classical Tradition*, ed. Anthony Grafton, Glenn W. Most, and Salvatore Settis (Cambridge, MA: Belknap Press of Harvard University Press, 2010), 179.

3. Alexander Murray, *Suicide in the Middle Ages*, vol. 2, *The Curse on Self-Murder* (Oxford: Oxford University Press, 2011), xiv.

4. Celenza, "Cato the Younger," 179.

5. Daniela Havenstein, "'Suicide' and Other Words in *Religio Medici* and its Imitations," in *Democratizing Sir Thomas Browne* (Oxford: Clarendon Press, 1999), 173–98. See also Brian Barraclough and Daphne Shepherd, "A Necessary Neologism: The Origin and Uses of 'Suicide,'" *Suicide and Life-Threatening Behavior* 24, no. 2 (1994): 113–26.

6. A libertarian press has published the most recent scholarly edition of "Cato's Letters" as well: John Trenchard and Thomas Gordon, *Cato's Letters: or, Essays on Liberty, Civil and Religious, and Other Important Subjects*, ed. Ronald Harnowy (Indianapolis: Liberty Fund, 1995).

7. Robertson's text includes a notable warning that "toughness training is not appropriate for children, teenagers, or anyone undergoing treatment for a physical or emotional condition." Donald Robertson, *Stoicism and the Art of Happiness: Practical Wisdom for Everyday Life* (London: Hodder and Stoughton, 2013); Ryan Holiday, *The Obstacle Is the Way: The Timeless Art of Turning Tragedy into Triumph* (New York: Portfolio, 2014); Massimo Pigliucci, *How to Be A Stoic: Using Ancient Philosophy to Live a Modern Life* (New York: Basic Books, 2017); William B. Irvine, *The Stoic Challenge: A Philosopher's Guide to Becoming Tougher, Calmer, and More Resilient* (New York: W. W. Norton, 2019).

8. Olivia Hosken, "Gwyneth Paltrow Hired a Personal Book Curator—Here's What He Chose for Her Shelves," *Town and Country*, August 20, 2019, https://www .townandcountrymag.com /style /home-decor/a28680227 /how-to-organize-books -thatcher-wine-gwyneth-paltrow/.

9. Donald Robertson, *How to Think Like a Roman Emperor: The Stoic Philosophy of Marcus Aurelius* (New York: St. Martin's Press, 2019).

10. Julie Ellison, *Cato's Tears and the Making of Anglo-American Emotion* (Chicago: University of Chicago Press, 1999), 10.

11. In openly calling the play a tragicomedy I am drawing out a potentiality that critics both acknowledge and seek to keep at bay: "The almost tragi-comic conclusion of Addison's *Cato* thus signals a turn away from the larger-than-life aspirations and dreams of empire toward the domestic and private as the grounds for developing the virtue and strength of the nation." Lisa A. Freeman, *Character's Theater: Genre and Identity on the Eighteenth-Century English Stage* (Pennsylvania: University of Pennsylvania Press, 2013), 99. For more on prior models for the genre, and for pushback after an overemphasis upon the definitive force of Fletcher's preface, see Marvin Herrick, *Tragicomedy: Its Origin and Development in Italy, France, and England* (Urbana: University of Illinois Press, 1955), and *The Politics of Tragicomedy: Shakespeare and After*, ed. Gordon McMullan and Jonathan Hope (London: Routledge, 1992).

12. Freeman's response to the play is particularly interested in Dennis's 1764 variant edition *Cato, A Tragedy, by Mr. Addison, without the Love Scenes*; in Freeman's reading, such subtraction on behalf of a more homosocial play thus addresses the threat that femininity poses to tragic values. *Character's Theater*, 102–3; Laura J. Rosenthal, "Juba's Roman Soul: Addison's *Cato* and Enlightenment Cosmopolitanism," *Studies in the Literary Imagination* 32, no. 2 (1999): 63–76.

13. Joseph Addison, *Cato, a Tragedy*, in *"Cato: A Tragedy," and Selected Essays*, ed.

Christine Dunn Henderson and Mark E. Yellin (Indianapolis: Liberty Fund, 2014). It is worth noting that the press that publishes this scholarly edition of the work is "a foundation established to encourage study of the ideal of a society of free and responsible individuals." The press's online archive announces itself as "a collection of scholarly works about individual liberty and free markets."

14. Addison, 3.

15. Johnson quoted in Robert Otten, *Joseph Addison* (Boston: Twayne, 1982), 153.

16. For a discussion of self-killing being seen as fundamentally a problem of pride in the popular press during the period, see the broadsides summarized in Eric Parisot, "Framing Suicidal Emotions in the English Popular Press, 1750–80," chap. 10 in *Passions, Sympathy and Print Culture: Public Opinion and Emotional Authenticity in Eighteenth-Century Britain*, ed. Heather Kerr, David Lemmings, and Robert Phiddian (London: Palgrave, 2016).

17. Julie Ellison, "Cato's Tears," *ELH* 63, no. 3 (1996): 571–601; Rosenthal, "Juba's Roman Soul."

18. "This is what you ought to practice from morning till evening. Begin with the most trifling things, the ones most exposed to injury, like a pot, or a cup, and then advance to a tunic, a paltry dog, a mere horse, a bit of land; thence to yourself, your body and its members, your children, wife, brothers. Look about on every side and cast these things away from you. Purify your judgments, for fear lest something of what is not your own may be fastened to them, or grown together with them, and may give you pain when it is torn loose" (1.109–15) Epictetus, *Discourses, Books 3–4. Fragments. The Encheiridion*, trans. W. A. Oldfather, Loeb Classical Library 218 (Cambridge, MA: Harvard University Press, 1928), 283.

19. The line is quoted during the courtship phase in which Trump clearly wishes to bring Bolton into the administration and the future national-security advisor plays both high-minded and hard to get, angling for a position as secretary of state. John Bolton, *The Room Where It Happened: A White House Memoir* (New York: Simon and Schuster, 2020), 22.

20. Ellison, "Cato's Tears," 25.

21. A Stoic metaphysics would see the world as governed by a benevolent logos, but here we approximate instead what R. Sklenář, with reference to Lucan's representation of Cato in the *Bellum civile* has flagged as a "nihilist cosmology." "Nihilist Cosmology and Catonian Ethics in Lucan's *Bellum Civile*," *American Journal of Philology* 120, no. 2 (1999): 281–96.

22. For more on the array of Platonic positions on voluntary death across the *Laws* and the Socratic dialogues, see John M. Cooper, "Greek Philosophers on Euthanasia and Suicide," chap. 23 in *Reason and Emotion: Essays on Ancient Moral Psychology and Ethical Theory* (Princeton, NJ: Princeton University Press, 1999).

23. Gerard Passannante, "Catastrophizing: A Beginner's Guide," introduction to *Catastrophizing: Materialism and the Making of Disaster* (Chicago: University of Chicago Press, 2019).

24. For more on Mishima's views on gender and tradition, see *Mishima on Hagakure: The Samurai Ethic and Modern Japan*, trans: Kathryn Sparling (New York: Charles Tuttle, 1981). The phrase "harmony of pen and sword" names one of the sections in Paul Schrader's biographical film on the author. *Mishima: A Life in Four Chapters*, directed by Paul Schrader (1985; New York: Criterion, 2008), DVD.

25. E. M. Cioran, *The Trouble with Being Born,* trans. Richard Howard (New York: Seaver Books, 1977), 95.

26. Heather Love, "Emotional Rescue: The Demands of Queer History," chap. 1 in *Feeling Backward: Loss and the Politics of Queer History* (Cambridge, MA: Harvard University Press, 2007).

27. This death is described in Diogenes Laertius, *Lives of Eminent Philosophers,* vol. 2, trans. R. D. Hicks (New York: G. P. Putnam's Sons, 1925), 383. For more on the relationship between Empedoclean thought and the circumstances of his death, see Drew Daniel, "The Empedoclean Renaissance," in *The Return of Theory in Early Modern English Studies,* vol. 2, ed. Paul Cefalu, Gary Kuchar, and Bryan Reynolds (London: Palgrave Macmillan, 2014), 277-300.

28. Laura Baudot, "Joseph Addison's Lucretian Imagination," *ELH* 84, no. 4 (2017): 891-919.

29. The primary support for Baudot's case for a Lucretian component within Addison's thought is *Spectator* 411, whose publication date in June of 1712 precedes *Cato, a Tragedy* by a year but remains comfortably within range.

30. In a sense, this is the inverse of the metonymic substitution whereby the death of Cato stands in for the death of the republic itself.

31. Alexander Pope, prologue to Addison, *Cato, a Tragedy,* 5.

32. Famously, the performance is described in a letter written in May of 1778 by Colonel William Bradford Jr. to his sister: "The Camp could now afford you some entertainment: the manouvering of the Army is in itself a sight that would charm.—Besides these, the Theatre is opened—Last Monday Cato was performed before a very numerous & splendid audience." Mark Evans Bryan, "'Slideing into Monarchical Extravagance': *Cato* at Valley Forge and the Testimony of William Bradford Jr.," *William and Mary Quarterly* 67, no. 1 (2010): 123-44. For more on Washington's own relation to Stoicism, see H. C. Montgomery, "Washington the Stoic," *Classical Journal* 31, no. 6 (1936): 371-73. See also Celenza, "Cato the Younger," 180.

33. Plutarch, "The Life of Cato the Younger," in *Lives,* vol. 8, *Sertorius and Eumenes. Phocion and Cato the Younger,* trans. Bernadotte Perrin, Loeb Classical Library 100 (Cambridge, MA: Harvard University Press, 1919), 407.

34. Addison, *Cato, a Tragedy,* 96.

35. Otten, *Joseph Addison,* 106-9.

36. David Diamond, "Secular Fielding," *ELH* 85, no. 3 (2018): 692.

37. Consider, in this light, Xenophon's curious counterexample of the suicidal tyrant, a kind of alternative predecessor to the stock depictions of miserable tyrants who cannot enjoy their power in the *de casibus* tradition. Xenophon, "Hiero or Tyrannicus," in *On Tyranny,* trans. Marvin Kendrick (Chicago: University of Chicago Press, 1961), 3-21.

38. Addison, *Cato, a Tragedy,* 6.

39. Thomas Heywood, *A Woman Killed with Kindness,* ed. Brian Scobie (1607; London: Methuen, 2012), 273.

40. For an account of the complex generic possibilities of the theatrical space of the deathbed in early modernity, see Maggie Vinter, *Last Acts: The Art of Dying on the Early Modern Stage* (New York: Fordham University Press, 2019).

41. Michael A. Screech, *Laughter at the Foot of the Cross* (Chicago: University of Chicago Press, 1997).

42. Otten, *Joseph Addison*, 141.

43. S. E. Sprott, *Suicide: The English Debate from Donne to Hume* (La Salle, IL: Open Court, 1961), 114–15.

44. See Jennifer Steinhauser, "V.A. Officials, and the Nation, Battle an Unrelenting Tide of Veteran Suicides," *New York Times*, April 14, 2019, https://www.nytimes.com/2019/04/14/us/politics/veterans-suicide.html.

45. Mary Nyquist, "Ancient Greek and Roman Slaveries," chap. 1 in *Arbitrary Rule: Slavery, Tyranny, and the Power of Life and Death* (Chicago: University of Chicago Press, 2013), 55.

46. One can imagine the resonance with lynching and torture that such audiences might hear in Sempronius's lines: "There let 'em hang, and taint the southern wind / The partners of their crime will learn obedience / When they look up and see their fellow-traitors / Stuck on a fork, and blackening in the sun" (3.5.53–56).

47. Terri L. Snyder, "The Paradoxes of Suicide and Slavery in Print," in *The Power to Die: Slavery and Suicide in British North America* (Chicago: University of Chicago Press, 2015), 101–121, esp. 101–102. See also Frederic M. Litto, "Addison's *Cato* in the Colonies," *William and Mary Quarterly* 23, no. 3 (1966): 431–49. Though reasons of space prohibit a full-dress reading of Behn's text, it must be said that the language of *Oroonoko* notably writhes with "joy of the worm" in its representation of Imoinda's affect at the prospect of death: "He found the heroick wife faster pleading for death, than he was to propose it, when she found his fix'd resolution: and, on her knees, besought him not to leave her a prey to his enemies. He (grieved to death) yet pleased at her noble resolution, took her up, and embracing her with all passion and languishment of a dying lover, drew his knife to kill this treasure of his soul, this pleasure of his eyes; while tears trickled down her cheeks, *hers were smiling with joy* she should die by so noble a hand." Aphra Behn, "Oroonoko, or the Royal Slave," in *Oroonoko and Other Stories*, ed. Maureen Duffy (London: Methuen, 1986), 93; italics mine.

48. See Richard Bell, "The Problem of Slave Resistance," in *We Shall Be No More: Suicide and Self-Government in the Newly United States* (Cambridge, MA: Harvard University Press, 2012), 237.

49. James Baldwin made this remark during a taping of the *Dick Cavett Show* in 1968; see *I Am Not Your Negro*, directed by Raoul Peck (New York: Velvet Film, 2016).

50. For more on the sermons and debates in print regarding how to evaluate this act, see Parisot, "Framing Suicidal Emotions."

51. Henry Fielding, *The Tragedy of Tragedies: or, The Life and Death of Tom Thumb the Great*, ed. Darryl P. Domingo (Toronto: Broadview, 2013).

Epilogue

1. *The Earth Seen from the Moon*, directed by Pier Paolo Pasolini, in *The Witches* (Rome: Dino De Laurentiis Cinematografica, 1967).

2. Miles Davis, "Yesternow," track 2 on *A Tribute to Jack Johnson*, Columbia Records, 1971.

3. William Hazlitt, "On the Pleasure of Hating," in *On the Pleasure of Hating* (London: Penguin, 2005), 111–28.

4. Jacques Derrida, "The Law of Genre," trans. Avital Ronell, *Critical Inquiry* 7, no. 1 (1980): 55–81.

5. Plautus, *"Amphitryon" and Two Other Plays*, trans. Lionel Casson (New York: W. W. Norton, 1971), 3; Fletcher quoted in Marvin Herrick, *Tragicomedy: Its Origin and Development in Italy, France, and England* (Urbana: University of Illinois Press, 1955), 161.

6. "Father Sues Ozzy, CBS over His Son's Suicide," *Variety*, November 6, 1985, 2.

7. Michael Moynihan and Didrik Sonderland, *Lords of Chaos: The Bloody Rise of the Satanic Metal Underground* (Port Townsend, WA: Feral House, 2003), 49.

8. Moynihan and Sonderland, 49.

9. I am not alone in my concerns in this regard; see Jeffrey Wilson's both alarming and moving reflection on this same pedagogical dynamic: "*Hamlet* Is a Suicide Text— It's Time to Teach It Like One," *Zócalo Public Square*, September 28, 2020, https://www.zocalopublicsquare.org/2020/09/28/hamlet-suicide-contagion-teaching-shakespeare/ideas/essay/.

10. Rosalie Littell Colie, *Shakespeare's Living Art* (Princeton, NJ: Princeton University Press, 1974). See also Kathleen B. Jones, "Hannah Arendt's Female Friends," *Los Angeles Review of Books*, November 12, 2013, http://lareviewofbooks.org/article/hannah-arendts-female-friends.

11. Colie, viii.

12. Colie, 358.

13. Colie, 361.

14. Colie, 361.

15. Colie, 191.

16. Hilton Als, *The Women* (New York: Farrar, Straus and Giroux, 1996), 65.

17. Stefano Harney and Fred Moten, *The Undercommons: Fugitive Planning and Black Study* (New York: Autonomedia, 2013), 118.

18. Harney and Moten, 118.

19. Years ago, Lauren Berlant and I had a long exchange about suicide and suicidal ideation, and we continued to send each other our writing on the subject afterward. Revising this book in the wake of the news of Lauren's death, I see that my own sentence is in conversation with a work in progress titled "Being in Life without Wanting the World: Living in Ellipsis" that Lauren shared with me. I mark this entanglement as a way of acknowledging a debt that cannot now be repaid.

Acknowledgments

1. Lara Durback quoted in Anna Moschovakis, *Eleanor, or, The Rejection of the Progress of Love* (Minneapolis: Coffee House Press, 2018), 202.

Index

Page numbers in italics refer to figures.

Hock, Jessie, 188
Hoffman, Christine, 136
Holiday, Ryan, *The Obstacle Is the Way*, 192
hopelessness, and suicidal ideation, 174–77
Housman, A. E.: "I Counsel You Beware," 118–19; "Terence, this is stupid stuff," 161
Hoxby, Blair, 40
Hume, David, "Of Suicide," 172–73
humour noire, 157, 230n59
Hunter, G. K., 47, 52, 53
Hunter, Joseph, 122

imitatio Christi, 32, 235n7
incels (involuntary celibates), 180
"Integrated Motivational-Volitional Model of Suicidal Behaviour, The" (O'Connor and Kirtley), 174
Irvine, William B., *The Stoic Challenge*, 192
Isherwood, Christopher, *The World in the Evening*, 33, 34
Isidore of Seville, *Etymologiae*, 153

Jackson, Thomas, 254n10
Jamison, Kay Redfield, 165–66
Jephthah's daughter, 50
Jerome, Saint, 19
Jocasta, 8
John of the Cross, Saint, 158
Johnson, Samuel, 123, 153, 187, 195
Johnston, Adrian, *Time Driven*, 21–23, 55
Joiner, Thomas, *Why People Die by Suicide*, 19, 41, 82, 174, 176, 182
Joker (film), 108, 247n33
Jones, Ernest, *Hamlet and Oedipus*, 104
Jonson, Ben, 106
Joubert, Laurent, 52
"joy of the worm": and affect, 42–43; alternative to tragic outcome of suicide, 88, 223; and *Antony and Cleopatra*, 82–85, 90; as attraction and aversion to self-killing, 214–15, 222–24; and *Biathanatos*, 143, 149; and *Cato, a Tragedy*, 193, 199, 206; and Christian injunctions against self-killing, 23–24;

and fusion of libido and death drive, 20–23, 44, 55; and *Gallathea*, 54–55; and genre, 14, 216–17; and *Hamlet*, 94, 121–26; and hard laughter, 224; linking of readers with characters, 214; neither anti- nor prosocial, 215–16; and ontologies of materialist merger, 17–20, 23–24, 84, 121–26, 191, 198–201, 232n88; and *Paradise Lost*, 179–80, 188; and positive affective responses to self-killing, 10, 13–17, 23–24, 25; and relation of affect to action, 213–14; relevance beyond early modernity, 212; shift away from in eighteenth century, 209–10; spectrum of, 215; and *Timon of Athens*, 94, 116, 124; transhistorical relevance, 215

Kant, Immanuel, categorical imperative, 119, 148, 187
Ker, Sir Robert, 131
Kesson, Andy: Before Shakespeare project, 250n69; on "Euphuism," 47, 51; *John Lyly and Early Modern Authorship*, 47, 51, 53; and Shakespeare's "grumpy man aesthetic," 94; "Was Comedy a Genre in English Early Modern Drama?," 237n56
Kezar, Dennis, "Shakespeare's Addictions," 166
Kirtley, Olivia, 174
Klonsky, E. David, 239n87
Knight, G. Wilson, 111
Koch family, 192
Kondo, Marie, 231n61
Kottman, Paul: *A Politics of the Scene*, 24; "To Defy the Stars," 81
Kronshage, Eike, 111
Kunin, Aaron, 119
Kuzner, James, 111
Kyd, Thomas, *The Spanish Tragedy*, 212

LaBruce, Bruce, "Notes on Camp/Anti-Camp," 33–34
Lacan, Jacques, 123, 169
Lacedaemonian boy, story of the, 15, 68
Lactantius, *Divine Institutes*, 19, 232n84

Lancashire, Anne, 53

Langley, Eric, *Narcissism and Suicide in Shakespeare and His Contemporaries*, 13, 38–39, 41, 74, 132, 236n23

language, and race and class, 97, 246n11

Laplanche, Jean, 21

La Tour, Georges de, 34

laughter: ethics of, 90; "hard," 224; norms of objects of in early modern period, 56

Lear, Jonathan, 21, 113, 257n24

Ledger, Heath, 108

Leo, Russ, 172; *Tragedy as Philosophy in the Reformation World*, 100

Lerner, Ross, *Unknowing Fanaticism*, 141

Lessing, Gotthold Ephraim, 40

Levin, Harry, 245n73

Levinas, Emmanuel: account of the face, 67, 72, 241n14; drama of responsibility, 67, 83; *On Escape*, 84

Li, Yiyun, *Dear Friend, from My Life I Write to You in Your Life*, 176

Little, Arthur, Jr.: "Altars of Alterity," 30, 55; *Shakespeare Jungle Fever*, 76

Livy, 15

Lloyd, Harold, 92

Locke, John, 112

Longinus, 187, 188

Lopez, Jeremy, *Constructing the Canon of Early Modern Drama*, 250n69

Love, Heather, 26, 200

Lucan, *Bellum civile*, 154–55, 156, 198, 262n21

Lucretia, story of, 43, 133, 231n63

Lucretius: allegation of self-killing, 19; alternatives to Christian eschatology, 201; *De rerum natura*, 19, 201; ontological materialism, 23, 198, 200–201

Lupton, Julia, 111

Lushington, Thomas, 254n10

Lyly, John, *Gallathea*, 94; "Diva Citizenship," 51, 54; euphuism, 50–51; "failed seriousness," or camp, 27, 33, 46, 54–57, 212; flawed status of sacrificial victim, 51–53; "joy of the worm," 54–55; nature of sacrificial attack, 239n77; and obligatory altruistic suicide,

234n5; sacrificial longing, 32–33, 47–48, 53–55, 58, 94; suicidal altruism, 32, 42; undermining of justice of sacrificial gestures, 48–50

Lyons, Bridget Gellert, 221

MacDonald, George, 105

MacDonald, Michael, 10–11, 12, 59, 153, 154

Madius, Vincentius, *De ridiculis*, 52, 56

Malloch, A. E., "Donne and the Casuists," 135

Mangano, Silvana, 211

Manne, Kate, 43

Marcus Aurelius, 192

Marino, James, 110

Marlowe, Christopher: *Doctor Faustus*, 193; and fantasy of elemental reabsorption, 20; Jonson on, 106

Marsh, Ian, *Suicide*, 6–7, 26

Marullo, Michele, 19

Marx, Karl, 36

Masciandaro, Nicola, 167

Massinger, Philip, *The Bond-Man, an Antient Storie*, 117–18

materialism: and Christian eschatology, 200; ontologies of materialist merger, 17–20, 23–24, 84, 121–26, 191, 197, 198–201, 232n88

May, Alexis, 239n87

Mayhem, 218–19

McColley, Diane, 166

McGowan, Todd, 21

Men Going Their Own Way (MGTOW), 180

Menninger, Karl, *Man against Himself*, 114–15

Mentz, Steve, *At the Bottom of Shakespeare's Ocean*, 120

Met Gala, 2019, "Camp: Notes on Fashion," 33–34, 235n9

Middleton, Thomas: *Timon of Athens* (*see* Shakespeare, William, *Timon of Athens* [with Middleton]); *Women Beware Women*, 212

Milbank, John, *Being Reconciled*, 148

Millais, Sir John Everett, *Ophelia*, 124, *125*

Made in the USA
Columbia, SC
22 February 2024